Children of the Father King

Children of the

Father King

Youth, Authority, &
Legal Minority in Colonial Lima

Bianca Premo

THE UNIVERSITY OF
NORTH CAROLINA PRESS
CHAPEL HILL

© 2005
The University of North Carolina Press
All rights reserved

Designed by Kimberly Bryant
Set in Adobe Caslon by Keystone Typesetting, Inc.
Manufactured in the United States of America

The paper in this book meets the guidelines for permanence and durability
of the Committee on Production Guidelines for Book Longevity of the
Council on Library Resources.

Library of Congress Cataloging-in-Publication Data
Premo, Bianca.
Children of the Father King : youth, authority, and legal minority in colonial
Lima / by Bianca Premo.
p. cm.
Includes bibliographical references and index.
ISBN 0-8078-2954-4 (cloth : alk. paper)
ISBN 0-8078-5619-3 (pbk. : alk. paper)
1. Children—Peru—Lima—History. 2. Children—Peru—Lima—Social
conditions. 3. Youth—Peru—Lima—History. 4. Youth—Peru—Lima—Social
conditions. 5. Juvenile delinquency—Peru—Lima. 6. Minorities—Legal
status, laws, etc.—Peru—History. 7. Peru—History—1548–1820. I. Title.
HQ792.P4P74 2005
305.23′0985′09032—dc22
2005000607

A version of Chapter 4 appeared as "Pena y protección: Delincuencia
juvenil y minoridad legal en Lima, siglo XVIII," *Histórica* (Lima, Peru) 24,
no. 1 (July 2000): 85–120. Chapter 4 also appeared, in somewhat different
form, as "Minor Offenses: Youth, Crime, and Law in Eighteenth-Century
Lima," in *Minor Omissions: Children in Latin American History*, ed. Tobias
Hecht (Madison: University of Wisconsin Press, 2000), 114–38; it is
reprinted here with permission.

cloth   09 08 07 06 05   5 4 3 2 1
paper   09 08 07 06 05   5 4 3 2 1

for Barry and Maggie

Contents

Illustrations, Figures, and Tables

ILLUSTRATIONS

FIGURES

TABLES

Acknowledgments

First in my thanks are those friends and colleagues in Lima who have welcomed me into their homes and academic institutions, and sometimes even into the legendary *bóvedas* that hold the most coveted of old documents. I wish to acknowledge those associated with the Instituto de Estudios Peruanos in particular, and thank Carlos Contreras, Luis Miguel Glave, Jorge (Tito) Bracamonte, Vicky García, and Cecilia Gianella for their personal and intellectual generosity, especially for that which they offered over curling mounds of ceviche and glasses of Cuzqueña. Others who offered encouragement, suggestions, and space to present my work include historians María Emma Mannarelli, Susana Aldana, Margarita Zegarra, and Scarlett O'Phelan Godoy. Miguel Rabí went so far as to share a transcribed copy of a research find with me. Laura Gutiérrez, the director of the Archivo Arzobispal de Lima; Nora Gomero Sánchez, Silvia Montesinos Peña, and other staff members of the Archivo General de la Nación; and the staff and directors of the Archivo de Beneficencia Pública, the Archivo Municipal de Lima, the Biblioteca Nacional del Perú, the Archivo General de Indias, and other archives in Spain worked diligently and patiently on my behalf. *Gracias.*

I could not have been there to make my *pedidos*, of course, without financial support. My research in Peru and Spain and the time I spent writing were funded, respectively, by a J. William Fulbright Dissertation Grant, a Ford Foundation Dissertation Fellowship through the Consortium in Latin American Studies at the University of North Carolina and Duke University, a UNC Graduate School Off-Campus Dissertation Fellowship, and a UNC Graduate School Dissertation Completion Fellowship. The Lewis Hanke Prize from the Conference on Latin American History permitted me to return to Spain in the summer of 2002.

Some of this financial assistance in turn paid for the superb research assistance of Peruvian historians Claudia Valdivieso García and Ilana Aragón. Asmaa Bouhrass followed up on archival leads in Seville that I could not pursue during the AGI's restoration, and Agnieszka (Agnes) Czeblakow ably provided bibliographic help during the final phases of writing. Philip Misevich also deserves thanks for the thankless tasks he performed as a graduate research assistant.

Among the many people in the United States who have shared their research or offered critiques on parts of the manuscript, I would like to acknowledge Charles Walker, Ann Twinam, Donna Guy, Valentina Tikoff, and Kathryn Burns. Kenneth Mills kindly arranged for permission to use one of the paintings I present here. I would also like to thank the conference audiences and panelists who helped hone my arguments, as well as the anonymous readers who reviewed my work for other publications. I offer special appreciation to Christine Hünefeldt and Sonya Lipsett-Rivera, who served as reviewers for the University of North Carolina Press. At UNC Press, Pamela Upton and Stephanie Wenzel could not have been more pleasant or professional, and my editor, Elaine Maisner, showed this first-time book author extraordinary enthusiasm and trust.

I owe a heavy debt to colleagues and teachers and to my close friends, who also happen to be a remarkably smart group of scholars. On a daily basis, David Sartorius contributes immeasurably to my scholarship by pen and by phone. Mariola Espinosa, Michele Strong, Joann (Jody) Pavilack, Philippe Rosenberg, Adriana Brodsky, Marie Francois, and Jan Hoffman French also have been strong sounding boards and demanding editors. Jody even performed a bit of impromptu research for me in the Duke Special Collections Library in the middle of a move. Frederick Solt, for his part, performed a miracle in remedial education by helping me work through some of my statistics. It is especially appropriate that I mention now that all errors contained in this work are my own.

At the University of North Carolina at Chapel Hill, my dissertation director, Sarah Chambers; John French (Duke University); Louis A. Pérez; John Chasteen; and Irene Silverblatt (Duke University) were an attentive, sharp doctoral committee. Perhaps more importantly, they have become cherished friends who continue to pull up a chair for me at their kitchen tables and conference roundtables years after I completed the Ph.D. Really, I have been spoiled by an unusually fun, friendly, and challenging intellectual life not only as a graduate student in Chapel Hill but also in my work at Emory University. Jeffrey Lesser,

Susan Socolow, and James Melton have gone especially out of their way to make sure I am at home in Atlanta, for which I am very appreciative.

The academic and professional accomplishments of my mother and best friend, Blanche Premo-Hopkins, make her quite unlike most women of colonial Lima. But she will undoubtedly recognize the difficulties many of them had in raising children alone. For most of my youth, I lived in a small, loving family of laughing women. The strength and wisdom of my mom and my older sister, poet and scholar Cassie Premo Steele, undoubtedly influenced a key interpretation I advance in this book: even when the normative value is placed on households headed by men, women can exercise a great deal of authority over others, especially generationally! Crale Hopkins, my stepfather, influenced other arguments and ideas in this book. He taught me that biological kinship is not the only family relationship that matters. A scholar of American literature, his favorite character was a child, the indomitable Huck Finn, who concluded his own story by saying, "If I'd a knowed what a trouble it was to make a book I wouldn't a tackled it." I cannot say the same, since I believe it made Crale proud that I was writing this book. I wish he had lived to see it published.

If my personal experiences influenced my work on this project, the reverse is true as well. I have come to regard some of the ordinary people of colonial Lima whose stories are contained here almost as friends. But I suspect that, by now, young Simona Laredo, Agustín de Castro, and the illegitimate Melgarejo siblings have become even more familiar to my husband and intellectual hero, Barry Levitt. No matter how tired from conducting interviews with real, live people, no matter how preoccupied with his own scholarship on modern politics, he listened attentively as I recounted their dramas every night when I returned from the archives of Lima to our little apartment on Calle Teruel. He also read and critiqued multiple versions of their stories as they became first a dissertation and then a book manuscript. I am deeply grateful that he has allowed me to become part of his life and permitted them to become part, ultimately, of our family history. I hope I have conveyed in this book that they are an important part of Peru's history, as well.

Children of the Father King

Writing a History of
Father Kings and Colonial Minors

Introduction

On any given weekday afternoon, children fill the streets of Lima's historic downtown district. Many trot toward a midday meal with their families, their rumpled school uniforms emblazoned with the name of a Peruvian patriot or Inca ruler. Some pass sullied rags over the windshields of cars held hostage in endless traffic, requesting some coins in return for the dubious favor. Others run errands, plastic sandals clapping on the cement as they sprint in and out from dark, yawning doorways. They sell candies from boxes strung around their necks, or they beg in front of restaurants or churches. Fewer still, although a greater source of public anxiety, become *pirañitas* (little piranhas), robbing pedestrians and living in gangs.

The streets of the modern-day capital of Peru seem a long way from historians' descriptions of the city in centuries past, and they seem particularly distant from portraits of Lima when it was a capital in Spain's colonial American empire. In most of these historical accounts, children are almost completely absent. Although today a popular subject for anthropologists, sociologists, and journalists, children and youths seem to have emerged from behind the great walls of the city's mansions or from institutions such as convents, schools, and foundling homes at some unspecified point in the nineteenth or twentieth century, expelled from within by the force of poverty, the "breakdown" of the family, and the rise of capitalist forms of economic dependency. While the visibility of children in our times certainly has much to do with these historical phenomena, in fact children and youths have always been a vital feature of the city's profile. Even during the era of Spanish rule of the Americas, when the imposing institutions of the crown and the Catholic Church encircled and enclosed the city's colonial inhabitants, children overflowed into Lima's streets. Then, as now, children occupied a central position in the political imagination of the city's residents.

This book is a history of childhood, as it was both lived and imagined, in colonial Lima. It enters the social world children and youths inhabited, and it situates that world in the political universe of Spanish rule. Asking how children lived in colonial Lima necessarily entails asking how colonial *limeños*, or the residents of Peru's capital city, understood childhood. Children were considered legal minors and were represented by elders before crown and church authorities. As a result, documentation capturing their words or penned in their own hands is exceptional. Rather than view children's relative silence in the historical record as a methodological obstruction, I have taken up their legal status and the status of those who raised them as subjects of analysis. At the core of this history of colonial childhood in Lima, then, is a legal history of the changing relationships between children and colonial adults—parents, masters, judges, and officials.

The ideal relationship between adults and children in Lima enacted and refracted the broader political relationship between king and colony. Adult authority over children—and, in particular, the right of the father over his children—was conceptually related to the authority of the Spanish monarch over his colonial subjects. One of the most salient and commonly understood political philosophies of Spanish rule of the Americas cast the king in the role of father to a wide array of colonial "children," including adults. But there existed a disjuncture between the ideal functioning of patriarchal authority codified in Spanish law and actual child rearing practices in the city. This disjuncture lay like a fault line deep within colonial Lima until the late eighteenth century. It was then that Enlightenment philosophies of childhood, coupled with the trajectory of reforms implemented by the Spanish Bourbon monarchy, shifted the terrain of political authority, both domestic and imperial, in the city.

Since the 1960 publication of Philippe Ariès's vastly influential *Centuries of Childhood*, the number of historical studies of European and U.S. children, and of definitions of childhood and youth, has grown exponentially.[1] Yet the history of childhood remains in a nascent state for many regions and historical periods. For colonial Spanish America it is still so spare that Ann Twinam could comment relatively recently, "Historians know little about the childhood years of colonial Latin Americans."[2]

To be sure, historians have not completely overlooked children in Latin America's past. In the last decade, scholars investigating issues such as custody, early education, welfare, and child labor have begun to ask how the histories of Latin American children fit into, or depart from, a field staked out principally by historians of Western Europe and the United States.[3] If, from such an early vantage point, this new and quite diverse body of scholarship can be said to share any overarching thematic concern, it would have to be the interaction between nation-state and family, for most of these studies gravitate toward Latin America's modern history.[4]

In histories of the colonial period, children occasionally can be spotted, almost as if they were darting in and out of the field of vision of historians whose sights are trained on other subjects, such as the nature of the colonial family or the history of inheritance among propertied elites. Scholars have become particularly interested in illegitimacy in Latin America's past, and this, perhaps more than any other subject of research, has yielded what most approximates a "history of childhood" for colonial Spanish America.[5] Beginning in the 1980s, scores of studies probed the cultural meanings and mores associated with extraconjugal sexual relations and, in turn, natal status. These works link Latin America's historically high rates of illegitimacy and child abandonment to colonial codes of honor, demonstrating how the public shame associated with procreating outside church-sanctioned unions prompted many parents to abandon their illegitimate progeny.

The scholarship on illegitimacy points toward several salient themes in the history of Spanish colonial childhood. It highlights the social implications of the circulation of children through the homes of adults who were not their parents. It reveals the critical role that caste, social class, and gendered norms of sexual behavior took in turning out, generation after generation, a reliable population of abandoned colonial children, and it traces the lives of these children through foundling homes. As this book progresses, a narrative about Lima's own foundling home unfolds within it, and at various junctures issues surrounding illegitimacy and illegitimate children are considered. But the story of colonial Spanish American childhood, it will become obvious, implicates a plethora of historical phenomena—some related to legitimacy status, others not. The historiography of illegitimacy and abandonment, rich as it is, still leaves unexamined certain basic social historical questions about how colonial children lived, learned, and loved as they grew into adults.

As social history, this book in part takes a methodological approach "which embraces the officially powerless as well as the powerful and [stresses] a presentation of the past and of change in terms of shifts in patterns of behavior and outlook."[6] The type of historical records that are the mainstay of social historians, such as institutional reports, censuses, and notary contracts, shed light on common interactions between adults and children in the colonial capital city. These records permit us to reconstruct something of the stories of ordinary colonial lives: to tour the sites where children were raised; to map out children's interactions with parents and other elders with whom they formed intimate, familial bonds; to explore the nature of their education at home and their training in workshops; to diagram the social structure of the schools they attended. Thus, this book attempts to offer at least a baseline social history of children and youths in Lima during the period 1650–1820.

Social history has been described, albeit not without objection, as "history with the politics left out," and one might imagine that children, the most protected and historically "inarticulate" of social groups, had little to do with a master narrative of traditional political history or with the deeds of kings and popes. Yet child rearing in colonial Lima was an inherently political process regardless of how politics is defined. As the abundance of historical works on childhood in Europe and the United States has shown, the study of children and childhood can unite disparate methodological approaches to prove, from multiple disciplinary angles, that "children in the past were central to the reproduction of class and the transmission of culture, important elements in the maintenance of political stability, and a significant source of labor for their families and communities."[7]

Childhood and adolescence were critical stages in the lives of limeños because during these first years of life, the customs and ideologies of the larger political and social order were imparted to future generations. The concept of "social reproduction" is particularly useful for understanding the transmission of colonial culture and political ideologies to the young. In conventional feminist definitions, social reproduction primarily refers to a modern, industrial system in which women's labor and role in sexual reproduction were unremunerated and politically devalued by relegation to the "domestic sphere."[8] Used here, the concept is expanded to include preindustrial child rearing practices involving multiple members of society, from mothers to wet nurses, from priests to the masters of slave children. Each of these adult actors had a hand in raising Lima's youths. Each, in her or his own way, had an interest in passing on social norms that merged into what we might call "colonial culture," and each often transmitted a perspective on the proper ordering of society that reinforced, directly or indirectly, Spanish rule of the Americas.[9] Practices that, for example, instilled Spanish culture in Lima's children or imbued in youths the social mores of Catholicism rendered child rearing intrinsically political.

Yet the participation of adults in the political process of child rearing and the private control they exerted over children in the home did not necessarily translate into public, legal authority in colonial society. Color, social class, and gender hierarchies contoured the social topography of colonial Lima, powerfully conditioning the experiences of both youth and adulthood. These hierarchies had everything to do with the broader political and economic environment of Spanish colonial rule. As one example, we might consider how the officials of Lima's foundling home carefully inspected the skin color, the phenotypic features, and even the type of fabric used to swaddle infants who had been abandoned at its doors. These details, which priests dutifully recorded in baptismal records, designated the natal, color, and class statuses of these children. By assigning caste in the cradle, priests shaped the children's futures: whether they would be considered free or slave; whether boys would be school-educated or trained as artisans; whether girls could receive dowries that would facilitate their marriages to "Spaniards" and the reproduction of a colonial elite.

The quotidian practices and rites of passage associated with youth, such as birth, training, and education, as well as marriage or placement in a monastic institution, tell us a great deal about colonial Spanish American society. But the central characters in this history of childhood—namely, children, elders, and representatives of the church and the royal state—interact most dynamically at moments where adult authority was in dispute or children were in trouble. Much of what we know about the past in Spanish America, and much of what we can know about colonial childhood, was recorded in the ink flowing from quills in the hands of notaries, court scribes, and lawyers. This is because the creation and maintenance of Spanish hegemony in the New World was, in many respects, a legal endeavor.[10] Legalism permeated Spanish colonialism, from the litany of declarations conquistadors read as they claimed dominion over the native populations, to the community-level suits brought by Indians who streamed into the courts in the immediate wake of conquest, to divorce proceedings aired in the tribunals of the Catholic Church throughout the seventeenth and eighteenth centuries.[11]

Simply put, colonial Spanish Americans were notoriously litigious. While most never left behind letters, diaries, or autobiographical narratives, they frequently used the ecclesiastical and secular courts to settle all manner of disputes. As a result—especially for those seeking to write histories of subjects such as laywomen, slaves, or indigenous peoples—the "historical record" can sometimes appear to be synonymous with criminal cases and civil litigation.

In exploiting the rich historical materials associated with the law, however, I attempt to do more than simply follow the documents into the city's courts. Even while the legal system figured as a key arena for enforcing and negotiating royal and adult authority, it certainly did not encompass the whole of the lives of children and adults in colonial Spanish America. What is more, how colonials used the court system, particularly in matters concerning their children, changed over time. As a legal history, then, this book in part represents an exercise in pressing legal records into telling us what childhood and adult authority, as expressed in the courts, meant for the way childhood and adulthood were experienced in the homes, institutions, and streets of the colonial city.

Methodologically, this means contextualizing written laws and legal practices concerning children in three ways. First, I step back from the sources to reflect on what the presence of so much litigation indicates about colonial Lima as a place to grow up or raise children. I argue that the legalistic nature of Spanish colonialism directly influenced how limeños conceived of age and power. It meant that the very definition of childhood as a biological stage or state of life was, in many ways, predicated on legal grounds—a point to which the ubiquity of the category of "minor" (*menor*) to refer to children and youths in the historical record attests. While at first glance the assertion that children were considered legal minors appears tautological, it is in fact a historical phenomenon that warrants explanation and description.

Juridical categories both reflected and shaped the social identities of adults as well as children in colonial Lima. Indeed, for most colonial inhabitants, "minority of age" lasted twenty-five years, and Indians were considered perpetual legal minors. This is because "minority" was an ascribed legal identity and was tightly bound up with other categories that had little to do with actual biological age, such as "miserables," "orphans," and the "unprotected." Age thus combined with other social markers to form a complex of statuses and identities for colonial adults and children alike.[12]

In such a context, the ambit of autonomy the law provided to many royal subjects was highly circumscribed. With some exceptions, Spanish laws required married women, slaves, Indians, and minors of age—in short, just about everyone in colonial society—to be represented by powerful adult men in legal matters. Furthermore, the inhabitants of colonial Spanish America claimed relatively low rates of literacy, and official procedure stipulated that scribes and notaries turn litigants' experiences and words into formal statements for judges to read.

These factors heighten the methodological challenge for the historian of childhood and adult authority. Spanish colonial legal case dossiers contain long sections written by lawyers and court scribes who were not only versed in the law but also highly attuned to tectonic historical shifts in politics, ideology, and culture. Their arguments provide evidence about official understandings of childhood, domestic authority, and the power of the Spanish king. But they do not necessarily reveal shifts in how ordinary people reared children and thought about childhood and adult authority.

The fact that so few inhabitants of colonial Lima were full legal subjects may lead us to conclude that most adults and children were more objects than agents of the law and, ultimately, of their own histories. Yet a close analysis of the everyday operation of the colonial justice system makes it clear that it would be a mistake to dismiss legal records as wholly mediated artifacts or to draw too stark a distinction between the legal and the real. Laws that restricted individuals from bringing litigation and that limited who held rightful authority over children do reveal fundamental features of power in colonial society, and they served as real constraints on individuals. But laws were not always followed, and constraints on legal behavior proved far more flexible than we might think.

To assume that ordinary colonials participated in the processes of law solely as objects rather than as agents cannot, for example, account for the fact that the eloquent disquisitions of university-trained lawyers comprise only a portion of most legal dossiers. The rest of the pages are filled with witness interviews, statements taken during interrogations, and short petitions filed in the names of litigants and defendants, many of whom operated in the court system without authorization from husbands, masters, or fathers. Dismissing colonial legal practice as a wholly mediated realm of action also fails to explain the case of an impoverished free black mother who sued the owner of her twelve-year-old slave son in 1792. She successfully petitioned the court for pro bono legal representation in order to file the suit, but when her court-appointed attorney was slow to file his brief, this litigant took matters into her own hands. She seems to have contracted a scribe to draft an argument, which he registered alternately in the first person and in the voice of the attorney, referring to the litigant as "my client." The attorney subsequently signed his name over the top of the page.[13] Thus, reading court cases and legal contracts not only for their content but also for textual subjectivity is the second way that I have attempted to understand how the law functioned in the lives of children and adults in colonial Lima.

Of course, few cases provide such compelling evidence of legal autonomy among ordinary colonial subjects as does the petition mentioned above. For the most part, litigation in which children figure as protagonists was written in language derived from legal boilerplate. But the structure and form of petitions and contracts—the very boilerplate of legal documents—shifted in significant ways over time. The legal system is therefore an arena where transformations in culture, attitudes, and everyday behaviors can be detected even when the laws themselves do not change. Remaining attentive to the shifting formulas of legal cases and contracts involving children—analyzing the cultural "grammar" of legal practice, as historian Cynthia Herrup calls it—proves as illustrative of historical change in concepts of childhood and adult authority as does analyzing the content of cases or changes in written law.[14]

Beyond the cultural grammar of court proceedings, I have also engaged in a close analysis of the actual grammar of petitions and arguments. Scribes varied widely in how they recorded statements in civil and criminal suits and contracts, and I have tried to remain faithful to the language they used in court documents when describing cases. Some simply recorded the first-person statements of petitioners or criminal suspects, even to the point of including common colloquial expressions or vernacular grammatical constructions. Others used the third person and smoothed over statements with detached and erudite legal language. Sometimes the mediation fell somewhere between these two extremes, as it did in a 1791 suit between an eight-year-old slave's mother and her female master. In one petition in the case, a scribe meshed first and third person in such a way as to render a sentence nonsensical. The case, the petition reads, was filed "by the mother over her daughter, a minor of eight years of age, that I have in her custody."[15]

These kinds of grammatical curiosities remain in the historical record because legal documents are artifacts of the very process by which scribes fashioned oral statements and personal experiences according to formulaic legal dictates. Put another way, the cacophony of subjectivities in a single petition reveals that the process of transforming everyday practice into lawful, mediated practice was often incomplete.[16] Analyzing these narrative inconsistencies alongside other types of historical evidence exposes substantive information about age and authority as they were lived outside the courtroom. In particular, such inconsistencies reveal a gap between how colonials presented concepts of childhood and power before officials in the justice system and the manner in which they actually raised their children.

Comparing what was said in petitions and lawyers' arguments with demographic, statistical, and institutional evidence constitutes the third methodological approach of this book. During the period under study, and particularly from 1650 to 1750, most civil court cases concerning minors of age nominally involved legal contests between men over inheritance and the public role of guardianship. But as an analysis of the language of some of these suits demonstrates (see Chapter 2), women were also key actors in these suits. Although their role as caretakers and even litigants was rarely openly discussed in secular legal petitions, it is substantiated by comparing these cases with ecclesiastical disputes, city censuses, and institutional records. Juxtaposing social historical evidence, laws, and legal practices allows us to explore how child rearing and customary understandings of authority sometimes aligned with, but often diverged from, normative legal models of generational and gender power.

The ideal-typical form of authority in colonial Spanish America is, I argue, best described as "patriarchy." In its strict classical Roman definition, patriarchy entailed a father's rulership over his children, and thus one of its principal constituent elements is generational.[17] But in a broader theoretical sense, I use it to refer to colonial practices based on the belief that multiple individuals—male and female, young and old—were naturally subordinate to an authority figure, usually a male, who held superiority based on the hierarchical model of the Western family.[18]

Historians of Latin America often parse the concept of patriarchy in order to describe various relations of power and subordination in different periods and regions. When describing certain facets of social relations they might refer to "patriarchalism," "paternalism," or "patronage" or layer these terms with modifying adjectives, producing expressions such as "democratic" or "normative" patriarchy and "qualified paternalism."[19] The advantage of treating different social relations of dependency as discrete is obviously one of conceptual specificity. For example, it might seem absurd to categorize the authority a young female slaveholder possessed over an elder male slave as patriarchal. Indeed, historians have long considered "paternalism" to be the appropriate term for the emotional currency circulated within the moral economy of African bondage.[20] Occasionally I use "paternalism" in this work, along with other constructs such as "gender patriarchy" and "generational patriarchy," to refer explicitly to a particular feature of power relations in colonial society. But fracturing each of these relations into multiple, separate categories can prevent us from seeing them as colonial limeños did—as different aspects of an integrated whole.

That ideological whole is best described as "patriarchy," for the term evokes the complex of legal and social relations of power that joined normative models of household governance to the larger legitimacy of Spanish rule. To return to our example of slavery, placing the relationship between master and slave under the rubric of patriarchy rather than paternalism highlights the ideological affinity between the social and legal infantilization of slave adults and the subordination of children to elders, of wives to husbands, and of colonized to colonizer.[21] Each of these relationships was founded on laws and customs that naturalized relations between ruler and ruled according to a generational family model.

Patriarchy, then, was a political ideology that transcended even if it often implicated gender. And because authority in the colonial Spanish American household contained gendered, racial, and generational dimensions simultaneously, patriarchy could never be rigid or stable. Its encompassing nature—and this is perhaps the very source of its formidability in Latin America—meant that mothers as well as fathers, and female slave masters as well as priests, could exert control over others based on socially constructed notions of what natural familial authority entailed, even if only momentarily and conditionally.[22]

Just as the ideal model of domestic governance was erected on the framework of patriarchal right, so, too, was the political paradigm of the Spanish monarchy. If, as in Joan Scott's now famous formulation, political history has been enacted on the field of gender, it was also enacted on the field of age, and these historical terrains were more concentric than contiguous in colonial Lima.[23] This book argues that the ideal-typical model of household authority, fashioned on a patriarchal family, was replicated in political ideology at the level of the Spanish empire, with the king taking the role of father and colonial subjects conceived of as children.[24]

Historians of Latin America have long noted that the idea of king as father reserved a privileged place in the political imaginary alongside other foundational metaphors of rule, such as king as judge, king as divine agent, and king as unifier.[25] More than thirty years ago, Richard Graham stressed the potency of the patriarchal metaphor when he explained that the "Hapsburgs thought of themselves as patriarchs who occupied their position not because of the divine right of kings, but because of the divine right of fathers. . . . In a sense, the Hapsburgs ruled over a family, not a state."[26]

The symbiotic relationship between authority in the home and on the throne should not be construed to mean that either was absolute. As we shall see here, colonial women exerted a surprising amount of control over themselves, their property, and other human beings, both legally and extralegally. Furthermore, Spain's crown was a "limited" absolute monarchy, particularly under the Hapsburg dynasty, which ruled the vast Spanish empire from the sixteenth century until the turn of the eighteenth century.[27]

But the notion of king as father could stay above the fray of the intense corporatist competition that comprised Spanish governance at least in part because this ideology was an easily comprehensible metaphor on which the broader legitimacy of the Spanish monarchy rested.[28] To the question, "How should a king treat his people?" Spanish laws answered, "As a father who brings up his children with love and punishes them with mercy." What is the nature of the people's love for their king? The law responded that it was "the love which arises from the obligation of lineage."[29] Throughout much of colonial history, it mattered little whether the real king was distant or weak, since as William Taylor has commented, for colonial Spanish Americans, sovereignty was derived merely from holding "the position of authority." Possessing authority, especially legal authority, was "more important than its comprehensive exercise."[30] Colonial inhabitants actively reinforced this philosophy of sovereignty in their countless appeals to local judges to be "paternally benevolent" and their references to the Spanish monarch as Father of the Americas, or simply the Father King.

To distinguish the official authority of the king and his royal agents from the power male elders exerted in the household, the terms "public" and "private" patriarchy prove useful. But although boundaries between the public and the private existed in colonial Spanish America, both notions were ideologically and practically different from the public and the private we have become familiar with for other regions and times. What constituted the private realm in Lima derived not only from biology or kinship. It also derived from relations between unrelated individuals based on intimacy, confidences, and notions of authority—particularly, as this study argues, on the bonds created by rearing children.[31] The public realm, which includes the court system, was where those relationships were tested and where judges or church officials either sanctioned or denied their validity in the patriarchal order.

The political analogy between father and king in Spanish America shares elements with monarchical societies in Western Europe and in British North America, but Lima is not simply one more setting in which we can watch the ideological workings of early modern monarchies in action in the household or observe family metaphors enacted at the level of the state.[32] It is of critical comparative value to consider that, after the collapse of the Old Regime in Western Europe, paternal political metaphors were far from dissolved. They were sustained, though reconstituted, to bind the new European nation-states of the nineteenth century to colonies in Southeast Asia, South Asia, and Africa. Ann Laura Stoler extracts a "common thread" from these diverse colonial situations, "namely, that racialized Others invariably have been compared and equated with children, a representation that conveniently provided a moral justification for imperial policies of tutelage."[33]

Spanish colonial rule, for all of its uniqueness, bridged these two historical eras. It rested on political ideologies foundational to other early modern Western European monarchies while it also embodied characteristics of the "new imperial" tutelary colonialism of the nineteenth and twentieth centuries. Limeños' belief in the king as father would be recognizable to early modern Londoners or to eighteenth-century Parisians. But the notion of indigenous peoples as perpetual children also would be more than familiar to the inhabitants of Bombay or to the Zulus of Natal in the nineteenth and twentieth centuries. City dwellers in Havana under U.S. occupation in the early twentieth century, if they were to read American newspapers, might see themselves depicted as bratty subordinates disciplined by Uncle Sam.[34]

Although at the outset of colonial rule Spanish American viceroyalties were considered kingdoms but not colonies per se, Lima's legal traditions and culture were, in many respects, classically colonial. Spanish colonizers imagined the indigenous inhabitants of the Americas to be infantlike Others who possessed a protected, diminished status within political society. In addition, a great number of slaves of African descent inhabited Lima, and their condition as chattel redoubled categories of legal subjugation based on color and social class. As historian of U.S. slavery Eugene Genovese once remarked, anyone studying colonial societies of the late nineteenth and twentieth centuries would realize that racial subordination exists independent of the institution of slavery.[35] Yet in colonial Lima, both forms of racial subordination not only co-existed; they were tightly bound together in the Spanish colonial system of color and class ranking.

Lima was characteristically colonial in other respects as well. Its population, while not demographically typical of all Peru, represented the racial and cultural mélange Spanish colonialism produced. Because early contact with Spaniards all but decimated the indigenous population in the craggy coastal region where it is located, Lima was more a city of migrants and mixed-raced inhabitants than a conquered land. Shortly after Francisco Pizarro founded the city in 1535, Indians descended from the heights of the Andes to this new urban center, which was dubbed the City of Kings. In the neighboring port of Callao, Spanish settlers disembarked in clusters while slave marketers led enchained Africans from ships along a highway into the city. The city square where slaves were sold at auction rested on seismic ground, and the cathedral that sat within it had to be rebuilt three times after earthquakes in the coming years. Each time, the building was reconstructed at angles that made it face more directly toward Spain—an architectural symbolism that points to the markedly conservative character of Lima's aristocracy, whose united loyalty to colonial rule has been documented by Peruvian historian Alberto Flores Galindo.[36]

Just as Spain ideally would be in the direct line of vision of Lima's institutions, the bloodlines of its most distinguished inhabitants ideally would also directly trace back to the metropole. For the city's inhabitants, what most deeply marked Lima's social hierarchy as intrinsically colonial was a correlation between elevated social status and genealogical ties to Spanish Christendom (expressed as *limpieza de sangre*, or cleanliness of blood). Lima's socio-racial and social class categories were pierced by sharp distinctions between the elite and the mass of those of the "lower sphere" (*la baja esfera*), also called the *plebe*.[37] Although high rates of miscegenation and "passing" increasingly frustrated a strict correlation between color and social class status, local elites and officials attempted to thwart social ascendancy through the imposition of an ever more complex system of caste categories. As a result, throughout three centuries of colonial rule, caste distinctions remained fundamental if not completely stable legal and social markers, particularly from the perspective of officials.[38]

The terms "elite" or "elites," when used in this work, refer to the propertied classes, almost exclusively of Spanish ancestry (*españoles*), who used the honorific titles "don" and "doña." Aristocrats, owners of landed estates or mines, large-scale merchants, top-ranking members of the viceregal and municipal government, and the high clergy sat atop the hierarchy. Within this group, Spanish-born individuals (*peninsulares*) held a relative advantage in status over those who were American-born (*criollos*, or in English, creoles), since the links of peninsulares to the metropole were stronger both genealogically and culturally.

The urban elite was somewhat fluid at its fringes. Lima was comprised of some individuals—the great majority defined as españoles, whether creole or peninsular—who could claim social privileges based on color and genealogy even if they did not belong to the high elite in terms of wealth and political power. Lower-ranking clergy, soldiers, and artisans in exclusive trades, from silversmiths to scribes to shopkeepers, comprised a small middle sector. While still español in the majority, the middle sector was more racially diverse than the colonial elite. Some free mixed-race individuals (or, in the parlance of the eighteenth century, *castas*) occupied the middle ranks, as did Indians of noble descent who were exempt from tribute. These individuals sought and sometimes enjoyed alternate versions of the privileges and honors associated with the elite; some even assumed the title "don."

Most of the city's inhabitants were of non-European and, increasingly over time, mixed-race ancestry. The plebe was defined as comprising, and sometimes was synonymous with, the swelling ranks of castas—free nonwhites—and a small (by Andean standards) population of Indian tribute-payers, many residing in the Cercado district in the northeast corner of the city. If employed and not serving state-mandated labor duty, these individuals spent their days toiling as manual laborers, tailors, street peddlers, and domestic servants. Finally, Lima was comprised of a sizable number of slaves of varying degrees of African descent, who, by the middle of the seventeenth century, outnumbered both Indians and españoles.[39]

While both the internal social structure of the city and the larger external political and economic structure in which it was enmeshed obviously qualify as "colonial," not until the late eighteenth century was the term *colonia* (colony) commonly used to refer to territorial units in the Spanish American empire.[40] This linguistic transition occurred when the Bourbon dynasty, which had claimed the Spanish crown in the early eighteenth century, instituted absolutist policies designed to fortify the secular state and to tighten its grip on overseas dominions. These "Bourbon Reforms" amplified royal paternalism as a political philosophy. However, Bourbon social measures directed at children often paradoxically drew from the same Enlightenment philosophies that were giving rise to radical new ideas about the political sovereignty of kings—ideas that ultimately toppled several European monarchies during the Age of Revolution. When, in the late eighteenth century, elite limeños instituted new royal policies on youths and grappled with new philosophies concerning childhood, they began to reconsider their own relationship of colonial dependency on the Father King. Local Bourbon officials and the city's upper classes were not alone in rethinking foundational patriarchal ideologies at the end of the eighteenth century. Transformations in concepts of childhood and authority permeated and, in turn, were reconstituted at the household level in Lima—in the great houses of the elites as well as in the humble dwellings of castas, poor españoles, and slaves.

Far from history with the politics left out, the social history of children and of adult-child relations in colonial Lima cannot be separated from colonial politics, particularly from the overarching political ideology that bound colonial subjects to the Spanish Father King. Popes, kings, and viceroys make appearances as protagonists in this book. But so, too, do poor and powerless people such as vagrant youths, orphaned infants, and the mothers of slave children, whose stories and statements (particularly the rare elocutions of children and youths) receive close attention. In this way, this book takes up a challenge that social historians have repeatedly issued since the 1980s: to integrate more fully our inquiries about how people experienced the "everyday" with what have been taken to be the "major" events, powerful men, and grand institutions that once dominated historical narratives; to look to the intimate, the private, and the domestic to understand what historically specific forms of politics and colonialism meant to the people who lived them.[41]

OUTLINE OF CHAPTERS

The period of time considered in this study, while extensive, provides a historical perspective that includes Spanish concepts of legal minority, the social universe of childhood and adult authority from 1650 to 1750, and dramatic historical change during the Bourbon years.[42] Covering almost two centuries of Lima's history proved less daunting than it may seem, since the different types of historical sources I use often cluster around particular themes and particular decades or centuries. In many cases, I argue that this clustering is not simply a trick of the archive but instead signals actual historical transformations in concepts of minority and child rearing. The organization of chapters, therefore, is at once chronological and thematic, opening with a broad overview of medieval laws and the development of colonial legal practices concerning minority and the governance of children. The following two chapters consider the period from the middle of the seventeenth century until the middle of the eighteenth century, while the remaining chapters spotlight the late colonial period, the era of enlightened reform.

Chapter 1 provides detailed analysis of medieval Spanish laws on minority and adult authority to provide the legal context for later explorations of the interactions between adults, children, and the Father King in colonial Lima. But colonial authority and definitions of minority were derived only in part from medieval law. The establishment of legal categories to protect and control the conquered populations of the New World altered the very concept of minority, transforming it from a legal status exclusive to propertied orphans into a broader category that included an array of adults in colonial society. The expansion of minority paralleled a growth in secular supervision over matters between adults and children during the course of Spanish rule, and both, I argue, were inexorably colonial processes.

Chapter 2 asks how Spanish law was applied in a city where adult-child relations often operated outside the ideal patriarchal boundaries established in edicts and codes. A city census taken in 1700, which recorded rare information about the city's free children, invites us into Lima's households and demonstrates that colonial racial, gender, and class hierarchies often were reproduced in homes and neighborhoods where inhabitants crossed social barriers to form intimate bonds that joined generations together. Because many limeños raised children in situations that defied the normative notions of the family enshrined in law, they developed a set of legal practices—a "politics of the child"—that accommodated multiple, though often extralegal, types of adult authority while preserving the patriarchal foundations of the law.

Chapter 3 builds on the argument that patriarchal authority in colonial Lima was lived as a generational as well as a gendered system. It visits the institutions of the city—convents, a school for Indian noble boys, and the city's foundling home—and proposes that the "colonial family" could be based as much on the ties of dependency created by rearing and controlling children and benefiting from their labor as on consanguinity or law. Within colonial institutions, nuns, priests, and even ordinary city inhabitants replicated the model of the family as they took charge of youths who were not their own children and oriented them in the colonial order.

Because it was a capital city, Lima boasted strong bricks-and-mortar institutions in which adults reared subsequent generations according to colonial models of order and hierarchy. Yet many youths nevertheless found themselves facing punishment by Lima's courts for acts that were deemed threatening to the social order. Eighteenth-century criminal records involving minors of age, the focus of Chapter 4, allow us to explore the reach and limits of state paternalism and the courts' direct interactions with minors. It reveals how Lima's legal system functioned as a substitute father in a colonial setting, meting out discipline especially to those youths deemed to be unattached to private patriarchal control. This chapter also introduces us to the transformations taking place in the city during the late eighteenth century, when growing fears of crime and an emphasis on social control met with longer-standing normative institutions of honor and social precedence.

It was during this period that new policies and projects designed to reassert Spain's control of its vast empire converged around the issues of childhood, adult authority, and the judicial authority of the Spanish king. Chapter 5 follows these reforms in detail and explores how the Bourbon state's new philosophies of education, economic productivity, and rightful adult authority were related to the broader intellectual and cultural movements of the era. The dynamic interplay between Bourbon social reform policies, official projects, and Enlightenment philosophies merged into what I term the new politics of the child.

Chapters 6 and 7 examine lawsuits over the custody and care of Lima's ordinary children to demonstrate just how pervasive the new politics of the child was. In these cases, litigants and lawyers put forward arguments about the proper rearing of children that reflected Bourbon social policy and the Enlightenment philosophies analyzed in Chapter 5.[43] Because limeños had always relied on the labor and love of multiple individuals to raise children, many adults, including mothers, wet nurses, and the parents of slave children, now found that they could use new notions about child rearing to argue that they were entitled to "natural rights" over children. When ratified by judges, these rights could undercut the patriarchal legal premise on which colonial society had been founded by limiting the dominion of fathers and, most effectively, of slave masters.

The conclusion briefly describes how the concept of the Father King lost its power in Peru and how an independent nation could be constructed on other founding fictions.[44] Yet racialized paternalism, political patronage, and gender inequalities—in other words, fundamental sociolegal pillars of colonial Spanish patriarchy—have proven to be sturdier than the political arrangement they once supported. The children who fill downtown Lima's streets today walk to school under distinctively colonial filigreed wooden balconies that hang from the second story of historic mansions. They amble along crumbling walls enclosing old nunneries. They sell their wares in front of elaborate Catholic churches. And they gaze up at the regal edifices of Spanish administrative buildings, long since converted into the seats of national government. If they think of their nation's history, perhaps they call to mind Inca rulers of a glorious pre-Hispanic past or remember the heroes of their republic. But these buildings are reminders that it was the Spanish Father King who bequeathed the inhabitants of this city, and the country that it crowns, an enduring political and social legacy.

A Short History of
Minority in Colonial Lima

D uring his 1782 interrogation in Lima's high court, the Real Audiencia, José Bernabel de la Carta claimed that, because he had been so drunk, he could not remember whether he had committed the dreadful crime of raping a two-year-old boy. After the questioning, a lawyer set about writing a series of arguments in José's defense. Rather than specifically refuting the accusation, Francisco Espinoza de Monteros denied that his forty-year-old client was a *mestizo*, of mixed Indian and Spanish ancestry. "He is a poor immigrant from Trujillo, not a mestizo, but rather of the Indian caste," Espinoza argued, "and as an Indian, he should receive the privileges assigned to minors."[1] Forty years earlier, Agustín de Castro, a youth of Spanish origin, had appeared before the same tribunal for killing a man during an altercation over livestock. At sixteen years of age, Agustín was a minor according to Spanish law, yet he resisted seeking refuge from prosecution in his legal status. Indeed, during his interrogation he claimed that the homicide was the result of an argument between men and thus that he should be absolved for defending his honor, not because of his age.[2]

This chapter explains how José Bernabel, an adult, could cloak himself in the Spanish colonial state's special legal guardianship of minors and why Agustín, a youth, might attempt to shed the status of minority in his legal dealings with the court. It shows how minors' protected status in the colonial legal system was derived from medieval law but also grew out of the Spanish colonial experience in the Americas. Conquest and colonization transformed the status of minor into a multivalent legal category based only partially on age and, as a consequence, also transformed the state's role in protecting and restricting a broad range of colonial subjects through the legal system.

Written law is an ideal place to begin to explore the normative relationships between children, adults, and the colonial state because, despite often being written for contexts far from the colonies, it continued to be the touchstone of political philosophy with which the inhabitants of Lima, and all colonials, oriented their relationship to the monarchy. Spanish law formed the basis of colonial conceptions of what "minority" meant in the court system—the specific privileges to which José Bernabel's lawyer referred—but it was more than a blueprint for court proceedings. Law also served as the screen onto which the ideal functioning of the Spanish monarchy as a political entity had been projected in remarkably vivid detail long before the conquest and colonization of the Americas.

In addition to serving as the basis for political ideologies of monarchy, Spanish law also guided the relationship between the legal system and household governance. Thus this chapter pays special attention to the reaches of public authority, or the authority of the king through his courts, into the home. Mapping out the overlapping legal spheres of judicial and domestic authority demonstrates that, as long as the ideal model of governance was intact in the household, the courts were relatively noninterventionist. However, the law was more protectionist, particularly in regard to the generational transmission and maintenance of property, in domestic situations that did not conform to the ideal. When patriarchal domestic ties slackened, the king took up the reins and lent his own patriarchal authority and defense to any of his subjects who were unprotected (and unrestrained) by private dominion.

Of course, a legal history of minority in colonial Lima based only on codified medieval laws would be incomplete, since Spanish colonial justice was what Tamar Herzog calls "the public's enterprise" rather than a "public enterprise."[3] Political improvisation and responsiveness to local needs—captured in officials' ability to refuse to comply with royal mandates without disobeying the king—are well-known features of Spanish colonial jurisprudence. In fact, no specific royal ruling or law allowed José Bernabel, even if he proved to be an Indian, to receive the benefits of a minor of age. Therefore, the second part of this chapter traces the development of Spanish American legal practice involving minority status through the colonial period. It focuses in particular on how the political justifications for Spanish domination in the New World broadened the definition of minority and expanded the number of legal agents who supervised domestic governance.

The history of the office of the Defensor de Menores, a legal representative-cum-judge who came to occupy a central position in overseeing court cases involving minors of age in Lima, reflects the crown's increasing interest in protecting and controlling children in the American colonies. Through this office, the royal state extended its reach beyond the oversight of propertied children's financial affairs, which was its principal role in the early colonial period. By the end of the eighteenth century, the Defensor had begun to adjudicate a broad array of matters involving children of all castes and classes.

The development of concepts of minority had a profound effect on the legal practices of ordinary individuals in colonial Lima. They were aware that they could use the courts to limit private patriarchal power and that there were agents of the law who specialized in representing those who were considered especially deserving of the king's protection. The provision of special attorneys and the existence of laws protecting and restricting different classes of subordinates figured centrally in how limeños viewed their relationship to royal authority. In fact, they produced a legal vocabulary that defendant, accuser, and lawyer alike employed in court, a language through which many of the city's inhabitants, of whatever age, sought special consideration by their Father King as minors and orphans.

FATHERS AND KINGS: PRIVATE AND PUBLIC AUTHORITY IN SPANISH LAW

Montesquieu's appeal to scholars to "illuminate history through laws and the laws through history" is especially fitting when we are trying to cast light on the meanings of minority in colonial Spanish America.[4] Rather than being tethered by the yoke of precedent that bound common law, Spanish American judges were obliged only to interpret the laws as they were written. This meant that Lima's lawyers and their clients could marshal even the most archaic and arcane statutes to their legal causes.[5] A detailed examination of the written laws is, therefore, an especially crucial starting point for understanding how the legal relationship between adults and children paralleled the monarch's political relationship to his subjects in colonial Spanish America.

When colonial Spanish Americans spoke of *derecho*, or law, they were referring to a long genealogy of codes compiled at different points in Castilian history, local practices (*derecho vulgo*) that had developed around these sources of written law, and the flurry of edicts and provisions the Spanish monarch issued for the American colonies during and after conquest.[6] In civil and criminal trials, agents of the courts drew from the three corpuses of Spanish law in a privileged order: the Castilian *Leyes de toro*, royal laws promulgated in 1505; regional medieval Spanish *fueros* such as the seventh-century *Fuero juzgo* and the *Fuero real*; and finally, *Los códigos de las siete partidas del Rey Alfonso el Sabio*, compiled in the thirteenth century.[7] The *Leyes de toro* was considered the key body of family legislation for the Americas. However, these royal laws primarily treated property arrangements between family members and focused intently on restricting inheritance rights based on natal status. They were far less comprehensive than the encyclopedic *Siete partidas* and detailed only a few of the specific issues that minors and their guardians faced in daily life in colonial Lima. As a result, the city's litigants, lawyers, and judges especially relied on the *Siete partidas*, the most detailed of the corpuses, in cases involving minors of age.[8]

Importing from Roman law, Spanish law established the age of legal majority at twenty-five, alternately phrased as having "completed twenty-five years" or as "having completed twenty-four years of age."[9] Any individual under the age of twenty-five, regardless of sex, natal status, or social class position, was considered a "minor of age." Over time, additional Castilian and canonical legislation concerning specific legal practices—such as betrothal, the ability to draft a testament, criminal responsibility, and the ability to enter monastic or professional careers—effectively subdivided the period of minority. Seven years of age was deemed an appropriate point for youths to become engaged to marry. At ten, children could leave wills, and at ten and a half, they could be tried for crimes. At eighteen, youths were sentenced as adults for criminal offenses. The Council of Trent (1545–63) fixed the age for marriage at twelve years for females and fourteen years for males, and the age for professing holy vows was sixteen. At eighteen, a male could become an attorney, and at twenty, a judge.[10]

Taken as a whole, then, laws pertaining to minors were scattered through secular and canon legislation on a variety of topics, from inheritance to marriage to trial processes. As a result, the laws as they were written did little to express a coherent rationale behind special legislation for children and youths. Nonetheless, civil laws do illuminate youths' ideal position within political society. Because individuals in Spanish Christian society derived status from their membership in groups, legal personae were derived relationally. Just like many other statuses defined in Spanish law, minors were categorized based on their relationships to the authority of others.[11] Each tier of authority, from the family to the royal state, overlapped to form a continuum that ranged from lesser to greater powers. Let us begin with the smallest (but by no means least important) unit of society, the family, and move up progressively through the hierarchy until we reach its pinnacle, the king, legally conceived to be divinely commissioned as sovereign. Along the way, we will see how the family was imagined to function ideally and what the role of the courts would be in the event that it did not conform to the ideal.

Household Authority

Two interlocking issues set the parameters of public and private authority over all individuals in Spanish civil law: class status and patriarchal authority. An articulated version of the Roman concept of *potestas*, or authority, provided a guiding political philosophy for laws governing the households of the Spanish territories.[12] In its codified form, paternal power was described with the Spanish equivalent to potestas, *potestad*, which expressly referred to a man's lordship over his subordinates, such as his children and slaves, although not specifically over his wife.[13] Potestad was expressed principally in terms of generational and economic right, and only secondarily in terms of gender.

Above all else, the status of minor of age implied that, from birth until age twenty-five, an individual ideally would fall under the potestad of a father or male head of household. Within the family, authority over children was vested first and foremost in a child's biological father through *patria potestad*. The primary legal persona of the minor of age was that of an *hijo de familia*, or a child whose property and person fell subject to the male head of household, who was referred to in Spanish as the *padre de familia*.[14] In fact, don Sebastián Covarrubias's 1611 dictionary of the Spanish language placed the term "minor" definitively on this axis, stating that it was "absolutely taken [to mean] an hijo de familia, a minor of age."[15] According to this definition, to be a minor was a relational as much as an age-based status, for it implied a situation of subordination to the padre de familia.

Although the relationship between hijo de familia and patriarch was said to derive from divine law, money matters seemed to lie at the heart of most Spanish civil statutes regulating the relationship between forebears and their progeny. In the *Siete partidas* we find the following crassly patrimonial statement tucked into a discussion of the divine order of paternal-filial love and responsibility: "Fathers have power over their children because they are born of them and because they leave inheritance to them."[16] As if to emphasize the inseparability of patrimony and paternal right, patria potestad passed along the same lines as forced inheritance in the Spanish tradition, which required parents to bequeath a third of their estates to be divided equally among their offspring.

Patria potestad was also conditioned by the circumstances of a child's birth, for it applied to those children who "through direct lineage, are born of legitimate marriage." Correspondingly, fathers did not possess the rights of paternal power over certain categories of illegitimate children. These offspring included those classified as *bastardos* or *sacrilegios*—children born of irredeemably sinful unions, such as incest or intercourse with a person who had made a vow of chastity. *Naturales*, or illegitimates whose parents were not impeded from marriage at the time of conception by canonical barrier, fell under the authority of fathers as long as their progenitors recognized them as their own offspring.[17] In turn, naturales possessed certain inheritance rights. Legal authority over children, therefore, was more than a simple matter of biology. Derived from a combination of economic relations and religiously sanctioned sexual behavior, it was also a matter of descent and bequest.

Since Spanish family law was anchored to economic moorings, the rights that fathers gained by virtue of patria potestad were expressed in distinctly financial terms. Fathers possessed the right to manage any assets a child had acquired and held usufruct over any property children gained while under their power (*peculio adventicio*), with some exceptions for certain types of earnings.[18] They also could sell their children as servants and control their labor. Ideally, the padre de familia also was to serve as the public representative of all members of the household. Like wives and slaves, minors possessed a juridical personality (*personería*) independent of the padre de familia or master, but it was limited, and in most circumstances, these household dependents were to appear in court proceedings or sign contracts only with the consent of a patriarch.[19]

Mothers' authority over children is an area of colonial legal history that has proved somewhat vexing for modern historians, apparently because Spanish laws failed to discuss maternal right except indirectly.[20] Injunctions in written Spanish law against women's full participation as public subjects have led some historians to claim that "women and children were always minors under the tutelage of a senior male," and "married women were legally minors."[21] It is indisputable that women were, in many legal arenas, stridently restricted in ways that men were not. Strictly speaking, however, women were not minors.

Although laws mandated that women be placed under the tutelage of male relatives or court-appointed attorneys in legal transactions, in certain instances they could manage their own assets, possess property if not always usufruct over it, and even represent themselves or others in court.[22]

Nevertheless, colonial Spanish Americans saw enough of a parallel between a husband's governance of his wife and the authority that men exercised over children and other household subordinates that they used the term "potestad" to refer to a man's right over his wife. Juan Machado de Chávez y Mendoza, an archbishop of Quito who wrote a treatise on canon and civil law in the seventeenth century, interpreted a husband's power as a kind of potestad. Yet he qualified his own usage of the term by claiming that "this potestad is not like that over a slave, and [a husband] should not treat [a wife] as such, but as a companion and sister in his cares and life."[23]

Despite the colonial practice of referring to all patriarchal authority, whether generational or gendered, as potestad, the legal distinction between different types of authority proved crucial. As wives, women occupied a position within the family hierarchy that was legally distinct from that of minors of age, and as mothers, they could wield authority over their children and control their property in the absence of a patriarch. Yet when they did so, it was not classified in written law as potestad.[24] As the *Siete partidas* defined it, patria potestad was "the power that fathers had over their children," and the *Partidas* specifically stated that "the mother [does not] claim children in her power, even if they are legitimate."[25] Women could not hold this authority because, again, it was more than simply a right endowed by biology; patria potestad was a gender right rooted in the management of family finances and patrimonial control. As we will see momentarily, a woman could perform the kind of economic functions for her children that patria potestad entailed, but the law required her to obtain the permission of a patriarchal authority in order to do so. In short, a mother's authority over her children was recognized in civil law, but it was contingent upon the approval of a patriarch, whether husband or judge.

Although the *Siete partidas* clearly restricted patria potestad to fathers in its statutes on parental authority, the laws became more "equal" when addressing parental responsibilities as opposed to rights. Both parents—fathers and mothers—were obligated to perform certain duties for children. These parental responsibilities were regulated under a statute concerning *crianza*, or the rearing of children.[26] Legally, crianza referred to satisfying a child's material needs such as food, drink, clothing, shoes, and shelter, "according to the means" of his or her parents. There existed a clear legal distinction between educating a child, as a teacher or journeyman might do, and raising a child, or "giv[ing] them of his own in all that is necessary." Parental responsibility was legally distinct from education or instruction because it expressly implied a material relationship based in the provision of property and goods.

Laws on parental custody (*guarda*) focused almost exclusively on the secular courts' regulation of instances in which married parents separated. The general law held that when parents no longer lived together, mothers were responsible for *alimentos* (support or nourishment) for children until age three, when children traditionally were weaned. Fathers received custody and the responsibility of providing for children after that age. But the *Siete partidas* also included caveats about custody based on constructs of morality and social class. If one parent was at fault in a separation, that parent assumed financial responsibility for children, and the other parent retained custody; the wealthier parent was responsible for rearing and received custody in the event that one parent was too poor to raise a child on his or her own wealth.[27] If parents had never married, it was not specified to whom custody should fall, only that a father who provided for the rearing of an illegitimate child was said to be extending support as a courtesy rather than a responsibility, since he might never know if the child was truly his.[28]

Thus, laws on minority of age, property, and parental rights cannot be said to have universally denied mothers authority over their children, but on balance, the reward of taking on the responsibilities for rearing children fell to fathers rather than mothers. While both parents were required to make economic investments in their children "according to their riches," under ordinary circumstances the father possessed most control not only over the physical being of his children but also over their property and labor.[29]

This authority was not without its limits. A father could suffer a "civil" death for committing certain grave crimes, including incest, heresy, and treason, and be deprived of control over his children.[30] But being found guilty of any other type of crime, even one resulting in banishment, did not nullify patria potestad. In general, a child remained under the father's authority unless the man seriously defied the only patriarchal authorities to which he himself was subject—God and king—or until a minor advanced to a stage of legally recognized maturity.

A father could also formally "emancipate" his child, a legal action regulated by detailed procedures, or a minor could request dispensation of age in order to perform certain acts (*venia de edad*). Another set of conditions that terminated a father's dominion over his children occurred when his offspring "took state" (*tomar estado*), literally assuming their position as adults in society. The *Leyes de toro* stipulated that emancipation would occur automatically upon marriage, smoothing the generational transference of property and reproduction of class status.[31] Sons and daughters who married became, in turn, padres de familia or wives themselves, forming a new household with its own relations of authority. If a child took holy vows or a son took certain ecclesiastical, military, or royal administrative offices, he or she was also considered emancipated. Thus, a father's right endured until his child advanced to an age or state in life that defined him or her as someone other than an hijo de familia, be it husband or wife, soldier or nun.

In sum, laws on minority were primarily concerned with retaining the economic order of things by firmly placing children, as conduits of property and wealth, under the authority of the father. Both parents had obligations to their offspring, and Spanish law indirectly recognized a mother's authority over her children. However, because the family was principally defined as a patrimonial economic unit comprised of propertied individuals, a mother's authority was relegated to a secondary position in favor of the economic rule of the father. Minority was a station in life in which a child's public persona and property fell under the father's power, a dominion checked by the state through its courts only in specific circumstances. Built into the model functioning of society was the reproduction of social class status and, ultimately, patriarchal authority. When male children advanced to adulthood and married, they garnered the rights of the padre de familia. Women, servants, and slaves ideally remained under the authority of a male head of household. They lost minority status as they grew older, but they were still subordinate in other ways to husbands and masters, as well as limited in their authority over their own children.

The King's Judges as Guardians

In situations where a clear succession of patriarchal authority did not exist, the Spanish royal state, through its courts and jurisprudence, exercised power in households, attempting to rebind to fictive families those who answered to no patriarchal authority by kinship or lordship. Either the state would appoint an individual to serve or the king himself would serve through his judges as the padre de familia for those who had somehow come loose from the natural order of generational or gender relations at the private level.[32]

The death of a patriarch was particularly problematic in a legal society built around his economic authority. A constellation of laws thus treated situations in which fathers had died leaving minor children. The overarching goal of these laws was the reestablishment of patriarchal authority through the appointment of a substitute father for the orphan—a man who could fill the role of the padre de familia until the minor of age could assume his or her position as an adult in society. The *Siete partidas* divided guardianship of orphans into two official roles. *Tutela* encompassed the guardianship of the person and property of children under the age of puberty, established at twelve years for females and fourteen for males. *Curaduría* entailed the guardianship of the property of those who were above the age of puberty but still younger than twenty-five.

Historians have long noted that a particularly patriarchal point of Spanish law prohibited women from being named as guardians of orphans. But an emphasis on this proscription should not cloud the fact that Spanish law favored mothers, if not women, to be named *tutoras* and *curadoras* of their children when fathers died without naming another male to care for their children.[33] Some laws, in fact, even attempted to eradicate the common habit of referring to children whose fathers had died as "orphans" by restricting the use of the term to children whose mothers were also dead. The seventh-century *Fuero juzgo* stated, "Although until now only small children who do not have fathers were called orphans, because the mother does not have less concern for the child than the father, it therefore is ruled that [only] children who are without father and without mother until the age of twenty-five be called orphans."[34]

Yet, even if Spanish lawgivers privileged mothers as guardians of their own children, they did not mandate that fathers leave guardianship to their wives and always bowed to the wishes of the deceased patriarch when he had appointed a man to fill his role. In fact, a father's or grandfather's choice of guardian was, one law implied, more binding than a woman's wish to assume the role for her children.[35] The same law insisted that mothers who wanted to act as guardians over their children should appear before a judge to be confirmed. These women were required, in a sense, to live under the public authority of the king by adhering to a set of gendered moral conditions. The widow was to be "of good reputation" and was required to "promise by the hand of the king or the judge of the district to renounce second nuptials." If she were to marry, the judge was instructed to "remove the children from her power and . . . pass them to the next closest relative."

This was a stringent limitation on women's authority over their children, but it was a logical equation within the calculus of patriarchal control. The law recognized a widow's authority over her children only as long as the courts deemed her appropriate according to gendered social mores, and only as long as she fell subject to no other man but the king. In the case of the mother's death or second marriage, she enjoyed the right to name the new guardians for her children, but, as if the king were her husband, she had to obtain official endorsement of her decision.[36] A similar restriction existed in adoption laws. Because women were thought to be vulnerable to deception, they were barred from legally adopting children in all cases but one. If a woman lost a "son in a battle service to the King," she could adopt a son "to take the place of the one she had lost," but she still had to seek the king's approval to do so.[37]

A series of laws dealing with nonparental guardians imposed strict requirements for appointing a man to the office, particularly for ensuring that he properly manage the wealth of a minor of age.[38] Tutors were required to submit an accounting of their dealings in the assets of minors annually and were beholden to spend, guard, or invest these assets with prudence.[39] The courts acted as a temporary patriarch to children in these cases, stepping in to offer guardians official consent and confirmation but then withdrawing from the daily interactions between adults and minors. In general, Spanish law cannot be said to have been as much interventionist in the naming of guardians for minors as palliative in reestablishing a substitute family order.

In other situations, however, the state could play a more active role in overseeing private matters between guardians and their wards. An entire section of the *Partidas* was dedicated to procedures for removing "suspicious" guardians from their offices. Guardians could lose their control over the property and persons of minors for "teaching the orphan bad customs," but the lawgivers predictably were most concerned that guardians not dissipate minors' property.[40] In fact, minors of age enjoyed the special right to request that any legal action or court ruling not benefiting them or their property be reversed. The right to *restitutio ad integrum*, a concept derived from Roman law, provided minors of age the ability to dissolve legally binding contracts undertaken on their own or by their guardians—quite literally to return legal situations to their prior state.[41] While in theory the right to restitution was conceded to all minors of age, the wording of the *Partidas* and the placement of laws within the corpus reveal that the privilege was imagined to be especially pertinent to orphans whose property was in the hands of an incompetent or greedy guardian. In these cases, the king assumed the role of padre de familia through the court system primarily to prohibit guardians from interrupting the chain of transference of wealth. But nowhere was the royal state at its most potent in the domestic realm than when removing children and slaves from the authority of real fathers and masters.

As we have seen, fathers could be deprived of their paternal authority for certain behavioral reasons, such as for committing incest, treason, or heresy. In addition, a father might lose authority over his children for "cruel punishment" (known as *sevicia*) or for "teaching or obligating his daughters to prostitute themselves."[42] Just as fathers might lose patria potestad over children for cruelty, slave masters also could be stripped of *potestad dominica* if they were proven to be excessively cruel, a charge also known as sevicia. The fourth *Partida* stated, "If one is so cruel toward his slaves that it is insufferable, slaves can complain to the judge, and from this office investigate the truth, and if it is so sell them, giving the owner a price in order that they never return to his power."[43]

In such situations, subordinates could count on judges to serve as ultimate patriarchal authority figures. A child could even bring suit against his or her father. Children could sue fathers to demonstrate paternity and argue for financial support or the right to inherit.[44] Although slaves were considered to be devoid of personería, or the juridical right to represent oneself in court, they, too, were permitted to bring suit for themselves or for family members against masters if they believed they were wrongly enslaved.[45] Therefore, subordinates could use the court system to ensure that padres de familia and masters did not wield power outside accepted boundaries.

The law attempted to correct the obvious power imbalance in these cases by providing legal agents to minors and slaves who went to court against padres de familia, masters, or guardians. If minors sued these men, or when a private patriarch could not represent them in another kind of suit, judges appointed advocates to their cases, including both legal experts without formal training (*procuradores*) and university-trained attorneys (*abogados*). This type of guardian was known as a *curador ad litem*, a court-appointed legal representative and guardian. Minors of age, prohibited from legally representing themselves, were either provided with a curador ad litem or could name their own with their guardians' consent for any suit, civil or criminal, in which they were involved.[46] Individuals who sued over unjust enslavement were granted a vicarious juridical personality in the form of a representative called a *personero*.[47]

Widows, orphans, and the destitute also enjoyed a protected status and easy access to legal representation in the court system. The *Siete partidas* stipulated that these three types of individuals held a special legal status known as the *caso de corte*. Their cases bypassed local courts to be heard directly by the king or by the highest court in the land, and litigants were provided the services of an attorney, who was to charge only a moderate price for his services or work pro bono.[48]

A common term for these individuals—the "unsheltered" (*desamparados*)— evoked the image of the patriarchal household as a place of protection. In many ways, Spanish civil laws on minors of age aimed to rebuild the scaffolding of the household when it had collapsed due to either a patriarch's death or misuse of authority. The other unhappy legal terms used to refer to these individuals, such as *miserables* or *desvalidos* (the helpless), underscore that those who lived outside normative, propertied Spanish households were regarded as weak and vulnerable. The role of the courts was to bring these unfortunates under the protection and control of a patriarchal authority figure, even if it must be the king himself. In this way, the king protected the unprotected in his dominion through the legal system. However, after the conquest and colonization of the New World, protecting the unprotected in the Spanish dominions took on a size, scale, and specialization beyond what could be embodied in medieval laws.

COLONIALISM'S PROGENY: THE EXPANSION OF MINORITY

As the Spanish fought their way through the Americas in the early sixteenth century, native inhabitants quickly recognized that, for their conquerors, power rested in legal institutions. They soon familiarized themselves with the rules of litigation and began to flood into the court system.[49] The "discovery" of peoples and civilizations of this unknown part of the world also produced a legal transformation for Iberians. Strident philosophical debates about the nature of the Indian and Spain's right to conquer America forced the Spanish to ask whether their basic assumptions about law, religion, and society could explain the peoples they beheld and sought to dominate. As men such as Bartolomé de las Casas, Francisco de Vitoria and Juan Ginés de Sepúlveda struggled to press the New World into legal and theological categories of the Old World, the categories themselves were in many ways irrevocably stretched into new shapes.

Minority was among the legal concepts that were transformed by Spain's creation of a New World empire. At the close of the sixteenth century, the category of minor was reconceptualized to include the native inhabitants of the Americas, and offices were established for the legal representation of Indians in

Spanish courts. The special legal status provided to Indians drew heavily from the medieval laws we have just examined concerning minors and the unprotected. Yet minority was implicated in Spanish colonialism, and Spanish colonialism affected minority, beyond restricting and protecting Indians based on preexisting laws and legal traditions.

The exigencies of colonization and, particularly, royal concern with turning the first generation of conquerors' offspring into an elite colonial class prompted the crown to establish legal offices such as the Defensor General de Menores, who was charged with specially supervising the wealth of minors of age. Eventually, the office of the Defensor de Menores became uprooted from its origins in legal traditions of guardianship and inheritance. By the end of the eighteenth century, this official acted as a key state agent who reached deeply into the affairs of colonial families and limited the authority of padres de familia and masters on a regular basis.

Although colonial Spanish Americans continued to distinguish between minority of age and the minority of Indians, the expansion of the concept of minority to include native inhabitants influenced how Lima's inhabitants viewed both the term and its legal implications. Over time, they developed a broad notion of minority, associating it with the weak, the poor, and the inferior of caste. By the end of the eighteenth century, the practical legal definition of "minor" could be applied to a far greater number of individuals than medieval codes implied. No longer a guardian only of propertied children, the Defensor protected all individuals under age twenty-five, propertied or poor, orphaned or not, slave or free. For colonial limeños, minority assumed multiple significations, some based on age and others on social position. Depending on one's status in society, it was linked with either legal advantages and protection or social limitations and degradation.

The Natural Child: Indians as Minors

Spanish theologians and intellectuals initially argued that the native inhabitants of the New World were ruled by passions rather than Christian rationality and were incapable of free will. Thus, the Spaniards maintained, Indians should be considered "natural slaves." By the middle of the sixteenth century, the image of Indian as natural slave was replaced by that of the Indian as child, naturally subordinate to a paternal, adult Spaniard.[50] The notion that Indians were in need of paternal tutelage worked its way into the writings of many Spanish intellectuals and jurists, regardless of the type of rule they believed they were entitled to in the American colonies.[51] For example, even Sepúlveda, considered the most extreme proponent of colonial rule by force, expressed his belief in the political superiority of Spaniards in familial terms when he offered his famous syllogism, "Indians are as inferior to Spaniards as children are to adults and women to men."[52]

Thomist theologian Francisco de Vitoria was perhaps the most prominent craftsman of a model of Spanish rule that positioned the king as protector and guardian of the childlike inhabitants of the New World. In an influential lecture, *Relectio de Indis*, which he delivered at the University of Salamanca in 1539, Vitoria promoted the Aristotelian argument that Indians were like slaves, children, and women: deliberatively defective and thus incapable of participating fully in civic life unless by relation to their masters, fathers, and husbands.[53] Other Spanish thinkers proposed models of colonial rule less saturated with patriarchal concepts of authority. Theologians such Vasco de Quiroga and Las Casas (who, ironically, would be remembered as the Father of the Indians and "tutelary genius of the Americas") maintained that Indians were civilized peoples who could self-govern without Spanish guidance except in the tenets of Christianity.[54] Yet even though the Spanish crown followed Las Casas's model of political administration by establishing a separate commonwealth of Indians, the legal status of indigenous peoples remained more analogous to that of children than that of full subjects—or padres de familia—in Spanish legal tradition.[55]

Far from the lecture halls in Salamanca and the royal court of Madrid, where these views on the nature of the Indians and of Spain's right to rule them were voiced, sixteenth-century Catholic missionaries created a functioning, rather than purely theoretical, system of colonial rule that also drew heavily from the notion of patriarchal right. Christianizing priests in the viceroyalties of New Spain and Peru, particularly the Franciscans, based their conversion efforts on the notion that Indians were children who should be instructed by Spanish priest-fathers, and they liberally employed paternal metaphors and imageries. They also organized educational campaigns aimed directly at the youngest generation of Indian noble children under the assumption that their efforts would be most efficacious among those untainted by the "barbaric" and "sinful" traditions of Indian society.[56]

The paradigm of Spanish fathers ruling infantile Indians was a "hegemonic ploy" that, as Richard Trexler phrases it, "cast nations as generations" in order to justify colonial rule.[57] Still, this discursive pretext went beyond metaphorical language and was enacted into law, transforming it into quotidian legal practice in the colonies. Early edicts concerning Indians were cast in the same protective and paternal terms as medieval Castilian laws on orphans, widows, and the poor. Secular authorities were charged with harshly punishing any Spaniard who aggrieved or wrongly dispossessed Indians, while priests were commissioned with "defending them as true spiritual Fathers."[58] In order to ensure that Indians were protected, courts were required to provide a salary to an attorney who would represent native clients at no charge.[59]

In legal practice, Indians were classified as miserables and taken to be, in many but not all respects, perpetual minors regardless of their age. Juan de Solórzano Pereira explained in *Política Indiana* (1647) that this meant that Indians were to be treated as minors in legal proceedings, particularly in sentencing and punishment. Judges, he stated, should punish Indians swiftly and with "paternal love," and he argued that the same infantile qualities of "fragility, gullibility (*facilidad*) and lack of constancy" that characterized Indians in terms of criminal guilt also meant that they were too immature for civil procedures. Thus, said Solórzano, Indians possessed the right to restitutio ad integrum. "Just like minors and women, to whom Indians compare," he reasoned, they should be protected from legal contracts that could cause harm to them or diminish their property.[60]

To shelter Indians from the treachery of ill-intentioned Spaniards, the crown established the post of the protector general of natives (*protector general de indios*), who was charged with defending natives and safeguarding their property in court, particularly from the abuses of the early colonial lords of land and labor, the *encomenderos*. In effect, the office of the protector general legally embodied the king's tutelage of Indians. Charles Cutter notes that jurists such as Solórzano even likened the role of the protector to that of a guardian of orphans.[61] The analogy was perhaps predictable, given Indians' customary status as perpetual legal children. Yet the functional role of the protector was quite different from the role of tutor. It soon evolved into a permanent office of advocacy for the defense of Indians in the court system.

Therefore, although the king had always extended special legal care and favor to minors and miserables, after conquest these aspects of Spanish law were retrofitted to afford protection to a far greater population of desamparados than ever before. The sheer scale of the legal machinery and the personnel needed to enforce Spanish treatment of Indians as minors also led to the creation of multiple official bureaucratic posts that could facilitate Spanish colonial hegemony, including over minors of age.[62]

The Defensor de Menores in Lima

One of the inaugural acts of Lima's Cabildo, or town council and court of first instance, was to establish posts to oversee vagrant youths and vagabonds. The Cabildo established the post of *amo de mozos*, a master of youths, who was to receive a salary for placing boys in apprenticeship positions with artisans.[63] Whether such an official ever existed is doubtful. Indigenous officials, and later a provincial magistrate with jurisdiction over Indians, the *corregidor de indios*, rounded up male youths in Lima's Indian district, the Cercado, and placed them in apprenticeship posts.[64] *Alcaldes ordinarios* (civil magistrates) normally found posts for youths of white or mixed-race ancestry, apparently subsuming the role of amo de mozos into their ordinary functions.[65] At times, the alcalde would claim he was acting as the "father of minors" (*padre de menores*) in overseeing the terms of the apprenticeship contract. For example, in 1645, alcalde ordinario Juan de Figueroa used this title when he turned a nine-year-old free *mulato* (of mixed African ancestry) orphan named Bernabé over to haberdasher Bartolomé Narbaes for five years, instructing the hat maker to "indoctrinate him and raise him as he would his own son."[66]

This kind of official institutionalization of poor children and orphans had been practiced in Spain since at least the twelfth century.[67] By the early modern period, indigent widows and orphans filled the streets of peninsular towns like Zaragoza, a city notable as a temporary home to rural transients. In 1474 its city council created the post of *padre de huérfanos*, conferred to a distinguished resident of the city who was charged with gathering up vagrant youths and putting them to work.[68] In 1598 several charitable projects were under way in various parishes of Madrid to house and employ impoverished vagrants, including youths.[69] And there was, in seventeenth-century Seville, an official who worked under the title of padre de menores.[70]

But if Lima's office of Defensor de Menores had precedents in Spain, its evolution was local in development. The responsibilities of colonial Defensores de Menores were not part of empire-wide law, and similar offices, each holding a different title, originated in a distinctly local manner at different times in various Spanish colonies.[71] Even decades after the office of Defensor de Menores had been established in Lima, its existence was news to the viceroy. Viceroy Conde de Monclova (1689–1705) scribbled in the margins of an order he received from the Council of the Indies to confirm a candidate to the office, "I cannot find a dispatch of confirmation for said office going back more than fifty years."[72] There is, however, evidence that the office was in use at least as early as 1643.[73] The confusion over the post appears to have stemmed from the fact that it conflated Spain's long tradition of judges' supervision of the financial affairs of orphans and their guardians with royal laws issued specifically for the colonies.

From its inception, the colonial office of Defensor de Menores reflected the crown's preoccupation with fixing in place a colonial elite by stabilizing the transfer of the dazzling wealth some conquerors had gained from their war exploits. In 1525 Emperor Charles V, concerned with the unregulated inheritance and management of property on the island of Hispañola, ruled that the Audiencia of Santo Domingo keep an account of minors' property, submitting any liquid assets to the depository of the Bienes de Difuntos.[74] Royal oversight of minors' property only increased after the conquests of Mexico and Peru, and in 1543 Philip III created a separate office for supervising the affairs of orphans in the American colonies.[75] This appears to have been the birth of the office of Defensor de Menores, although Philip III did not christen the post with a formal title. The office was to be filled by a "person of confidence," who was empowered to supervise minors' financial assets, compel guardians to repay minors if they had taken advantage of their wards' estates, and remove guardians if they were deemed unfit to continue to serve. As concern mounted about controlling the offspring of Spaniards who died in the wars of conquest, the crown began to direct regulations about guardianship specifically toward Spanish executors in the New World who took advantage of mestizo children.[76]

In short, the formally dispersed powers over minors of age that judges and other court officials once held were vested in a single agent of the state, not unlike the *protector de indios*. This official would direct his attention to the heirs of conquerors just as the *defensor de indios* protected the peoples they had conquered. In fact, in provinces outside Lima, such as in the northern coastal city of Piura, the same individual would fill the offices of protector de indios and Defensor de Menores simultaneously in the eighteenth century.[77] However, in Lima, a capital city that did not suffer the dearth of Spaniards of appropriate legal education and inclination to bureaucratic office that provincial areas experienced, the offices were held separately throughout the colonial period.

In the early seventeenth century, the office slowly became formalized, and eventually a set of procedures for civil cases involving minors of age coalesced. By the middle of the century, officials were using the impressive title *defensor y curador ad litem de menores* when they supervised the accounts of minor inheritors.[78] Domingo Gómez de Silva, perhaps better known for having founded with his wife, María, the Colegio del Carmen—a school for girls of the Spanish elite—even published a book about the powers of the office in order to systematize its use.[79] The members of the Cabildo who wrote an introduction to the book, though valuing Gómez's work as Defensor de Menores, nonetheless observed that "it is not imperative that those who hold this office must be *letrados* (university-trained) nor that there should be such an office in all places." Indeed, the Cabildo damned Gómez with faint praise by emphasizing his legal experience, which only underscored his lack of education in law, and portrayed the position of Defensor as more a philanthropic activity than a prestigious official post.

Even if the office was primarily a pastime for wealthy philanthropists, Gómez's *Instrucción general, y práctica para la buena adminstración de los bienes de los menores destos reynos del Pirú* described the office of the Defensor as a specialized post quite similar to the office of protector of indios, although it was not yet salaried. By the time of the book's publication, the Defensor had taken over many of the responsibilities that the law had conferred on judges, such as naming guardians to minors of age if their parents had failed to name guardians in their wills or if they had died without drafting a testament (*ab intestato*). But at this stage, the Defensor still removed himself from minors' legal affairs after a guardian had been appointed, unless he learned that property was being mishandled.[80]

Despite the consolidation of authority over cases involving orphans' property in the office during Gómez's tenure, few colonial elites viewed the post as an attractive position, perhaps because it lacked a salary and did not require formal educational training. In the 1660s, amidst the Hapsburg crown's drive to bring in increased royal revenue, the post of Defensor de Menores was put on the auction block as an office available for sale to the colonial elite (*oficio vendible y renunciable*).[81] A permanent salary now came with the position, but the city still faced a great deal of difficulty in finding willing candidates. Even though the town crier paraded through the streets more than thirty times, chanting auctioneer-style the availability of the office, the post remained officially vacant for more than twenty years during the 1660s and 1670s. In the meantime, minors of age involved in civil disputes were finding it hard to obtain legal representation, and procuradores from the courts only halfheartedly took on the office's cases.[82]

Finally, there was a taker: Alonso Durán Visente, an *abogado de número* of the Audiencia, or a university-trained lawyer who held an appointment in the high court.[83] Durán offered to purchase the post of Defensor at the price of 1,000 pesos. Because he was the sole interested candidate, Durán had confidence that, for the price he was willing to pay, he could convert the office of Defensor into a more prestigious and powerful position than it had been under Gómez. In his bid for the office, he changed the name of the post to the more impressive Abogado Defensor de Menores and enumerated thirteen conditions that would have to be met in exchange for his 1,000 pesos.

The role of the Defensor, as Durán laid it out, would be primarily to act as an advocate for minors in civil and criminal cases. This advocacy was to be exclusive (*privatibo*), meaning that none of the procuradores de número of the court could be named to civil cases over the division of property that minors inherited, and Durán asked for the privilege to sit on the bench reserved for abogados in the courtroom of the tribunal of the Real Audiencia during any hearing in which he took part.

These conditions effectively elevated the post of Defensor de Menores far above a mere charitable appointment and placed its occupant in a position superior to that held by the self-styled lawyers of the city. Logically, such conditions rankled Lima's procuradores de número, and they swiftly petitioned the Council of the Indies to prevent Durán from assuming office.[84] But Durán's conditions had enticed potential competitors for the post. Antonio de la Celda, another abogado from the Real Audiencia, made a counteroffer to pay 1,500 pesos for the office, and eventually the Council of the Indies ordered his confirmation as Defensor de Menores under the conditions that Durán had laid out.

De la Celda's ascension to the office at the end of the seventeenth century marked a turning point in state oversight of the affairs of Lima's propertied minors. During the next century, the office of Defensor de Menores continued to expand in both function and prestige. It was filled by a succession of university-trained lawyers who saw it as a rung on Lima's bureaucratic ladder. For example, don Domingo Larrión, a native of Santiago de Chile and an abogado de número in the Audiencia, occupied the office with particular zeal in the 1750s before moving on to higher-profile positions in the colonial bureaucracy.[85]

As the prestige of the office grew, the judicial influence Defensores possessed over cases reaching Lima's courts also expanded. In the seventeenth century the Defensor generally appeared in the civil case record engaged in activities such as confirming guardians of minors and overseeing the division of the property children inherited. Though Defensores continued to perform these roles throughout the eighteenth century, beginning with de la Celda's term in office, they increasingly brought cases involving inheritance themselves, serving as actual attorneys for the minors involved.[86] During Larrión's tenure in the 1750s, the Defensor had also begun to act as a *fiscal*, or judge of sorts. He heard arguments put forward by lawyers named to cases, assessed evidence, and made judicial recommendations to the magistrates of both Lima's first instance court and the high court of the Real Audiencia. By the late colonial period, judges were even calling on the Defensor to issue opinions on conflicts dealing with issues far removed from the management of orphans' property, including those involving slave children and child custody.[87]

The tenor of such cases, including some heard by the Defensor, is analyzed in Chapters 6 and 7. For now, two cases from late colonial Lima will illustrate how much the office of the Defensor had changed by the end of the eighteenth century. In 1775 Abogado Defensor Buenaventura de la Mar presided over the division of property a woman left to her five minor children. What was unusual about the case is that the executor of the estate was the children's own biological father, who reported to the Defensor on his punctual completion of an inventory and sought approval for his legal actions as executor and the children's guardian.[88] While Spanish laws specified that an executor must comply with the testator's requests within a certain amount of time, the fact that a child's father would answer to the Defensor de Menores for approval to serve as the guardian of his own children was remarkable.

More extraordinary still is the 1817 case in which a slave woman brought suit against the master of her five-year-old slave daughter, requesting compensation for the money she had spent in dressing, housing, and feeding her child. The mother, Teresa Altolaguirre, claimed that the child's master had shirked the responsibility of paying for the girl's upkeep by promising Teresa that her child would eventually be freed. In lieu of compensation for what she had invested in raising her daughter, Teresa suggested she would accept her daughter's freedom. The scribe wrote on behalf of this woman, "In this sea of confusion . . . my daughter appeals to the protection of Your Excellency as the protector of the helpless." The case was passed to the Defensor de Menores, who ruled that the slave owner should remunerate Teresa for the expenses she incurred in raising her own child.[89]

Here we are confronted with an official legal post in Lima that arbitrated the relations between adults and children, and masters and slaves, in matters that extended far beyond the state's role as it was prescribed in medieval law codes. At the end of the eighteenth century the court system did not simply restore patriarchal authority in domestic situations that departed from legal norms by naming and supervising propertied orphans' guardians; it exercised that authority itself.

Expanded definitions of minority and the existence of offices such as the Defensor de Menores turned the paternalism of the king and his judges into a living political and legal philosophy for colonial Spanish Americans. In Lima, the image of the judge as a patriarch of last resort for the unprotected left a deep imprint on understandings of justice and infused the legal vocabulary ordinary city dwellers used to articulate their relationship to court officials and, by extension, the king. As Teresa's words indicate, limeños could avail themselves of the protection of the courts, seeking favorable resolutions to their cases or legal representation by appealing to judges' long-standing protective, paternal mandate to hear cases in which the powerless confronted the powerful.

We need only recall the case of José Bernabel to be reminded that minority held distinct advantages for adults facing colonial judges. In fact, colonials of all ages could demand to be assigned lawyers to serve them pro bono as *protectores de pobres* by using terms that underscored the court's role as protective patriarch and their own positions as "miserables," the "helpless," and "minors."[90] Just as colonial minority did not apply only to orphaned inheritors under age twenty-five, neither did the state of being an orphan apply only to minors of age. When requesting lawyers to argue their cases, adult litigants referred to themselves as "poor orphans with no one to assist" them, regardless of their age or their family situation.[91] Even an eighty-year-old slave called himself an orphan when he requested legal counsel after he had been accused of attacking another man.[92] Ultimately, anyone in need of legal representation could, in fact, be considered a minor, an orphan, or a miserable. Colonial understandings of law and authority thus positioned many litigants as children standing before the Father King in the courtrooms of Lima, hoping that he would provide them with the paternal consideration they needed to ensure that justice would be done.

Yet, as the cases with which we began indicate, not everyone in colonial Lima saw emphasizing his or her powerlessness, *orfandad*, or even minority as a benefit or an effective legal strategy. Young Agustín, the español youth on the brink of adulthood whose story began this chapter, believed that he could gain more advantages—perhaps socially as opposed to strictly legally—by being considered a man rather than a child. He presented himself as an adult who stabbed another in defense of his honor rather than as a minor who could not understand the consequences of his actions. It seemed that to Agustín minority implied not only age but also weakness. As an español, Agustín wanted no part of the special protection extended to Indians, slaves, and widows. He wanted to stand trial as a budding español patriarch and was confident that the court would recognize his legal privileges as such.

CONCLUSION

In 1794 lawyer Pablo Ramírez defended a female minor in a suit against her father, the Marqués de Corpa, a former Audiencia judge. Arguing for the restitution of the daughter's dowry, he told ministers of the Audiencia that, although his client was suing a man whose power was derived both from patria potestad and from his standing in the judicial community of the city, there was a higher paternal power to which she could appeal. "The King," he asserted, "is her best Father and guardian."[93]

When this lawyer reminded Audiencia ministers that they could rule against the marqués, he referred to the areas of the law explored in this chapter where the courts could limit even the most powerful patriarch's right over his children. But to truly grasp what Ramírez's claim meant to colonial limeños, it must be understood in its moment as well as within the tradition of medieval Spanish law. Ramírez voiced his statement precisely during the last decades of a century that had witnessed increased court intervention into the domestic realm on behalf of all minors of age.

Increased court oversight of interactions between private patriarchs and their underlings was visible in the changing role of the Defensor de Menores. This office was created in a particularly colonial context where the definition of minority had been stretched to bring an entire hemisphere under the paternal auspices of the Spanish king. The increased specialization of the legal personnel who advocated for the indigenous population paralleled the increased specialization of legal officials charged with overseeing the property of minors—first mestizos, then all children of the propertied colonial class—and of securing and maintaining a wealthy ruling elite in the colonies. But these colonial adjustments held the potential to weaken the borders that medieval laws had erected between the private and public patriarchal authority. At the end of the eighteenth century, the Defensor could use his position to reach into the city's homes on behalf of young subordinates of all castes and classes.

Still, there was no guarantee that the Defensor de Menores would recommend judgments that were in the best interests of minors of age, that court-appointed attorneys would vigorously defend their clients, or that secular judges would rule against powerful men and in favor of those who called themselves miserables, minors, and orphans of all ages. But this was not pre-cisely the point for most of Lima's colonial inhabitants. It was the law's promise of protection that mattered for those who had no recourse to or against private patriarchal authority. It assured colonials that their king's justice was paternal and that his authority, like that of a father, was perfectly natural.

Between the Written and the Real

Child Rearing and Adult Authority,
1650–1750

In seventeenth-century Lima, lawyers and judges paged through oversized volumes of law and legal treatises, searching these texts to resolve pressing conflicts between city inhabitants. More than a few of the printed works that survive today in Peru's national library bear traces of their quests. Words are underlined or circled in browning ink, and occasionally the word *ojo* (literally "eye," or "look here") appears in the margins. At times, pupils were added to the *o*'s, transforming the letters into eyes forever fixed on sections of the texts deemed especially crucial.

If any seventeenth-century limeños had marked the definition of the word "law" in don Sebastián Covarrubias's 1611 dictionary, *Tesorero de la lengua castellana*, they would have had to draw one eye facing inward toward the printed word and another pointing outward to the world around them. Covarrubias placed Cicero, "Lex est quae scripto sancti," beside the jurist Papinian, "Lex est commune praeceptum."[1] Law is what is written; law is what is commonly practiced. Law in colonial Lima was, by definition, an interaction between the written and the real.

In order to reconstruct a history of adult authority and childhood in colonial Lima, then, we must look beyond volumes of codified law and royal edicts, into the city's streets, homes, and workshops. A census conducted in 1700 provides a statistical starting point, a city map of sorts. Together with an array of other social historical sources, it allows us to glance into Lima's homes, to glimpse colonial children being raised in domestic settings that often stood at odds with the model of family order enshrined in Spanish law.

Recently the "new imperial historians" have refined our image of colonial regimes as omnipotent by arguing that metropolitan impositions of power are only "partially realized" efforts to dominate the lives of colonial subjects. They tell us that colonial authority is not an abstract theory for those who live under it but a negotiation between metropolitan mandates and everyday practices.[2] In colonial Lima, the imposition of Spanish law indeed was only partially realized in terms of child rearing and adult authority. Despite the law's overarching emphasis on patriarchal authority over children, a wide array of adults other than ideal-typical Spanish patriarchs nurtured future generations. Social reproduction in Lima relied on multiple, though often extralegal, types of adult authority over children—particularly on a tacit, customary dependence on women, including nonwhite women, to raise the city's young.

Yet, in a sense, we can never get away from the law. Even the mundane records colonials left behind, such as censuses, notary contracts, and institutional records, were official—even legal—documents. These sources inevitably circle back into the realm of law, to the problematics of historical documentation and to the inescapable fact that colonial childhood and adult authority were legally mediated categories. By returning to Lima's courts after a tour of the homes and workshops of the city, this chapter explores how adults, children, and colonial officials defined and redefined adult authority in a society where the legal rights of fathers and masters were supreme but also where fathers and male masters were not the sole figures of authority in children's lives. In legal matters involving minors of age during the period 1650–1750, patriarchy emerges as a core feature of adult-child relations. But it was more than the actual authority male heads of household exerted in domestic governance. It was a legal practice of containing the contradictions between written law and the manner in which colonial limeños actually reared their children.[3]

MAPPING CHILDREN IN THE CITY, CIRCA 1700

During the last days of the seventeenth century, a group of census takers marched through the streets and alleyways that sliced Lima's eleven neighborhoods and its Indian district into dozens of square blocks. They marched on the orders of Peru's new viceroy. The Conde de Monclova had entered Lima in 1689 only to find his new headquarters in rubble. Two years earlier an earthquake had leveled churches, homes, and even the viceregal palace. Monclova ordered the census, known as the Numeración General de 1700, to bring administrative order to rebuilding projects and to assess the number of men capable of defending the city in case a foreign enemy attacked the port of Callao.[4]

Census takers knocked on door after door and asked for information about the living arrangements of limeños of all backgrounds and the number of fire-arms in their homes, but they would not compile a rigorously accurate statistical portrait of the urban population. They were more interested in counting all adult men "capable of bearing arms" than in recording details about women, certain individuals of the lower castes, and most important for our purposes, children.[5] Since a visit from curious agents of the colonial state was sure to arouse suspicion, census takers undoubtedly encountered a sizable number of reticent informants or dwellings that appeared to be empty. Nonetheless, they registered a significant number of Lima's inhabitants, including many of its smallest residents. The census recorded details about 6,110 of the city's free children out of a total population that hovered somewhere between 35,000 and 37,000.[6]

The enumerators organized their information by households, marked with a *c* for *casa*. A sample of 658 of 3,940 of the households listed in the Numeración places the average number of occupants of a single casa at 6.9.[7] (For an explanation of sampling procedures, see Appendix A.) Individual methods varied widely, but most enumerators recorded the name of only the head of the household and tabulated the aggregate numbers of remaining residents in columns that corresponded to twenty categories based on combinations of racial designation, age, sex, and free status.[8] It seems a variety of inhabitants occupied Lima's casas: slaves living alone, extended families, multiple families living in one unit, and individuals potentially unrelated by kinship residing together. But because census takers did not indicate what the relationships among household residents were, we cannot know how often individuals living in the same dwelling were related through biology or marriage.

Nonetheless, the sheer variety of arrangements in which colonial limeños lived and, indeed, the very difficulty involved in correlating Lima's casas to what we consider today to be families provide important pieces of historical evidence. To census takers, it seemed logical to record as single units households that contained tenants of multiple social classes and castes. Some casas were large elite residences that, according to French traveler Amedée François Frézier, typically consisted of a large hall that led to a receiving room and two or three smaller rooms.[9] These rooms opened to one another, and servants and

Map of Lima, 1685. This map is drawn upside-down and lightly slanted east, with the northern Río Rimac at the bottom. (AGI Maps y Planos, Perú y Chile, 13 bis, reproduced in Durán Montero, *Lima en el siglo XVII*, 244)

slaves slept on the floor in the sleeping chambers, limiting privacy and maximizing proximity between servant and master. More often, however, "casa" referred to modest common dwellings—the multiroom *aposentos* or small *corrales* that speckled the urban landscape, many of which contained residences for smaller household units.[10]

Even if casas commonly were types of apartments, individuals of diverse racial and social origins lived over, under, next to, and with one another. While certain parishes certainly were more "white," "black," or "Indian" than others in the aggregate, the racial profiles of individual blocks and individual households were highly heterogeneous. For example, on a block in the eastern quarter of the city—in an area close to the Indian district—a number of white children, Indian women, free people of mixed African ancestry, and slaves of all ages occupied a house headed by three españolas. Next door lived a priest with an Indian woman and man, and three black slaves. On the other side resided four Indian men and two Indian women.[11]

Spatial proximity did not preclude social differentiation among Lima's inhabitants. Census categories only vaguely mirrored the way that individuals self-identified or, more precisely, how they were officially identified and thus socially, if not physically, segregated.[12] Although Lima's population was not proportionally representative of the viceroyalty in terms of caste, the capital city was a showcase for the region's ethnic diversity. In 1700 the city was a destination for rural indigenous migrants, Spanish immigrants, and African slaves, as well as the birthplace of the descendants of earlier arrivals and an ever-growing population of mixed-race peoples. The census strained this rich ethnic brew into four highly concentrated categories: español (either Spanish or of Spanish descent), *indio* (which seems to have included both Indians and some mestizos),[13] mulato (of mixed African ancestry), and *negro* (of pure or predominantly African ancestry). Over half of the population—56.5 percent—was listed as español; 22 percent, as negro; 11.7 percent, as indio; and 9.7 percent, as mulato. More than two-thirds of those who claimed pure or partial African descent lived in bondage.[14]

Colonial caste hierarchies colored census data about children because enumerators' attention to details about the young population waned the lower a child figured in the social hierarchy of the city. In fact, no information about slave children can be gleaned from the Numeración, since they were not counted separately from adult male and female slaves. This likely occurred because legal prohibitions against slaves carrying weapons made determining the age of male slave adolescents immaterial.[15] Therefore, as a result of biases in both the census and the social world of Lima, statistical conclusions about children in the city must be limited only to the free population.

Gender, too, conditioned the manner in which census takers counted the city population. Español boys younger than sixteen years and girls younger than twelve were tallied separately from their adult counterparts. But the extreme disparity between español girls and boys in the census—the female segment of español children comprised only 4.6 percent of the total population, contrasting sharply with the 10.6 percent counted as español boys—suggests that census data was strongly biased in favor of recording male youths, who could take up arms in the city's defense. The remaining children counted in the census, comprising around 6 percent of the total population, consisted of indios and free mulatos and negros, whom enumerators listed separately from their adult counterparts but did not distinguish by sex, with boys and girls occupying the single category of *niños*.

Social hierarchies affected not only the reported but also the real numbers of children living in the city, since caste correlated with poverty, infant mortality, and low birthrates. The average number of free children per household (1.54) and the percentage of households containing children (52) indicate that Lima had relatively high child mortality and/or low birth rates. In fact, its population was in what demographers refer to as "negative growth."[16] Analyzing the percentage of children in each caste category can produce only indirect conclusions about the frequency of birth and death among children, but it does indicate that there were more children among españoles, the most economically and socially privileged census category, than among any other group.[17] Children comprised a solid 30 percent of españoles listed in the census. Those listed as free mulatos demonstrated the next highest proportion of children, at 26.2 percent. Indians and free blacks counted far fewer children among their ranks.

Poverty, epidemics, natural disasters, and common childhood diseases such as smallpox determined how many children survived their first years of life as well as how many women lived long enough to bear children at all. Individuals with weak immune systems, including infants and those who suffered from malnutrition, such as slaves and the poor, were especially vulnerable to disease. Epidemics also affected children indirectly by reducing the reproductive capacity of adult women, creating a generational hole whenever an outbreak occurred.[18] Natural disasters, such as the massive earthquakes that struck Lima in 1687 and 1746, in theory killed indiscriminately. Yet they seem to have been especially devastating for the many impoverished inhabitants who lived in ramshackle dwellings, which crumbled into graves whenever tremors and tidal waves crashed through the city and its neighboring port.[19]

Documents of many types, from wills to records of criminal trials, reveal just how ordinary death during infancy seemed, and how the loss of an infant during the first days or months of life was often met with a sense of resignation that has been misinterpreted by modern Westerners as indifference.[20] Yet, in colonial Lima, memories of dead children were indelible despite high rates of infant mortality, and limeños often listed in their testaments and testimonies all children conceived during their marriages and even in extraconjugal relations. The dead sometimes outnumbered the living. The reproductive history of the freed slave Paula Marchán provides a staggering example: only five children survived from her seventeen pregnancies.[21] High rates of infant mortality, while undoubtedly higher among the poor, also touched the lives of the elite. One gentleman who owned no fewer than four houses and a retail store was prolific in more than real estate. He reported in his will that eight of

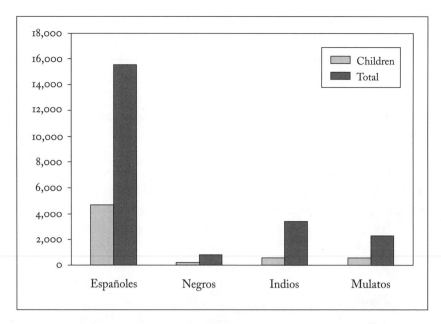

FIGURE 2.1   Total Free Population by Age and Caste, Lima, 1700.
Source: Peréz Cantó, *Lima en el siglo XVIII*, 59

the twenty-two children he sired during three marriages died "during their minor age."[22]

A baby's death carried enough of a shock that some families would conceal it from mothers while they were recovering from childbirth.[23] But once everyone in the family had received the sad news, limeños grieved in the streets and churches as well as in their homes. In fact, the frequency and scale of funeral processions and rites of mourning for dead children disturbed city officials. In 1753 the Cabildo attempted to regulate the type of clothing in which babies' corpses could be buried and to limit the number of candles that could be lit for the deceased's soul. Municipal officials were especially concerned with funerals for dead slave infants, who apparently were mourned with a suspect degree of ritual and pomp.[24] These funeral processions served as collective expressions of what individuals knew only too well: infancy was a precious stage of life precisely because it was so perilous.

If high rates of mortality did not prevent limeños from forming emotional attachments to children, residential patterns and child rearing practices in the city extended these attachments across biological lines and caste boundaries. Many of Lima's children grew up in households surrounded by individuals to whom they were not related by kinship and who were, at least in terms of census categories, different from them.

The caste diversity in living arrangements began within children's age cohorts. According to the sample of the 1700 census, most español children (81.5 percent) grew up in households where free nonwhite children also lived. Had slave children been identified separately in the census, that number surely would be higher, since according to the sample, almost 40 percent (235) of Lima's residences contained slaves, and españoles headed the vast majority (219) of these households. The close living arrangements between masters' children and slaves sometimes spawned an emotional intimacy. In a civil case brought forward in 1670, a witness testified that a female master and slave had such a "close friendship," derived from living and having grown up together, that they "ate from the same plate and slept in the same bed."[25] Scattered evidence also suggests that español adults might "give" their children slaves of approximately the same age to serve as companions.[26] In addition, youths of different castes who lived on the same block or in the same aposentos knew one another as neighbors and could become friends. The español youth don Tomás Loyasa played with a fourteen-year-old slave named Juan every day in the 1710s. The two youths even shared meals at a bakery belonging to Tomás's mother, although an español elder did admonish Tomás "not to go around with the said *negrito* (little black boy) because it looked bad."[27]

Just as Lima's children commonly grew up near other youths from different caste categories, they also grew up around adults from a variety of backgrounds. Because enumerators did not note the relationship between individuals living in the same household, it is difficult to refer unequivocally to "parents" and "sons and daughters" in the census. Even the assumption that adults and children of the same caste who lived together were biologically related can only be applied to some of the census categories, since the high incidence of miscegenation and the mutability of caste categories in colonial Spanish America make inferring parentage especially tricky. However, by examining households in which adults and children of the same caste category resided, it is possible to conjecture that many of the city's children were raised apart from their parents and relatives.

According to the sample, español men, including priests, were missing in 21.5 percent of residences containing español children. Only 5.5 percent of these households lacked an español woman. It appears free children of African descent were separated from their parents and relatives even more frequently, especially from male adults: 15.6 percent of homes in which they lived lacked a black female adult, slave or free, while 37.5 lacked a black male adult.[28] Indian children also were more likely to live in households where Indian males were absent (30 percent), and another full 30 percent of Indian children were listed as living in households where no indigenous adults were present at all. It should be recalled, however, that the category "indio" included mestizos, meaning that some of these children may have been living with español adults who were their biological fathers and mothers. Miscegenation creates an even greater problem in analyzing the living situations of mulato children in the census: since "mulato" is a mixed racial category, assumptions about parentage cannot be narrowed by race for mulato children as they can be for other groups.

Although it may not yield to a pointed interrogation about biological kinship, the census does divulge a highly gendered dimension to children's residence patterns. Indeed, colonial Lima was particularly reliant on its women to raise children. Only 2 percent of city homes counted in the sample contained children but no women, whereas 54 percent of households claimed children but no men. Women headed one-quarter, or 116, of the households in the sample. This figure is a bit smaller than the proportion of female-headed households historians have identified in late colonial Latin American cities such as Mexico City, Caracas, Santa Fé de Bogotá, and São Paulo, especially given that women held a statistical predominance in Lima in 1700.[29] Nevertheless, women were in dominant positions of authority in a significant percentage of Lima's homes. One census taker even thought doña María Farfán merited the distinction of being listed as the first resident in a home where several men, including a priest and a forty-seven-year-old white merchant, lived. Yet doña María is an exception; only three entries down, the same census taker listed fifteen-year-old don Martín de Mendoza as the head of a household that contained seven girls and one woman of Spanish descent, as well as two male and two female slaves.[30]

Gendered patterns of servile labor also conditioned children's living arrangements. The overwhelming majority of español children in the sample of the 1700 census lived in households with nonwhite adults, both slave and free. In fact, free children of all castes statistically clustered in residences that contained casta women, particularly free black women, likely because women of African descent often worked as midwives and nannies. The same labor practices also gave domestic slavery a highly gendered dimension. When don José de Torre "donated" a slave woman and her three-year-old son to his sister, he commented that, since he had no children of his own, "I will not miss them" (*no me hacen falta*).[31] Torre here alluded to an elite reliance on female slave labor for child care, a reliance that also extended to a general belief in slave women's expertise in fertility and birthing remedies.[32] And the most common form of work that drew elite children close to nonwhite women was wet nursing.

Breastfeeding held a certain mystical resonance as the spiritual source of motherhood during the early modern period. Most denizens of Lima would have been very familiar with the artistic image of the *Virgen de la Leche*, a maternal Mary holding an infant Jesus in one arm, her breast exposed, with a single drop of white milk dangling from her nipple. This popular theme for painting conveyed the sanctity of nursing, since as the priest Joseph Aguilar preached to the nuns in one of Lima's convents during a 1681 sermon, Mary was believed to divinely nourish all Christians, not only her anointed son.[33]

Because nursing was believed to generate spiritual intimacy between women and children, early modern Spanish moralists and physicians urged mothers to breastfeed their own offspring. Damián Carbón's 1541 instructional *Libro del arte de las comadres o madrinas*, although intended to provide guidelines for selecting women to nurse and raise infants, nonetheless extolled the benefits of mother's milk by declaring it to be "sweetest for the child."[34] He based this assertion, in part, on the conviction that mothers were "most like" their children in terms of "blood," "customs," and "quality"—racially and religiously coded language to be sure. In a similar fashion, the physician of the Cabildo of Jaen, don Juan Gutiérrez de Godoy wrote in 1629 that the milk from the woman biologically closest to the infant was the best form of nourishment.[35] He reminded his readers that, although many upper-class mothers felt nursing their own children was too onerous or demeaning a chore, mothers no less revered than the Virgin Mary and the queens of Spain had undertaken this "ennobling" task.

This romance with the maternal breast remained more prescriptive rhetoric than practice for elite colonial limeños, who were heavy consumers in the wet nursing business. In fact, they might pay a higher price for a pregnant slave woman because she could nurse their children, as did one man who discovered in 1583 that he had been duped in a sale. The female slave he purchased to nurse his infant daughter, it turned out, was not pregnant after all.[36] Masters also loaned or hired out their slave women to nurse the children of their relatives or upper-class neighbors, but it was nursing their owners' children that some slave women regarded as a task of special significance. In 1690 Ysabel Congo, an *esclava ladina*, or Spanish-speaking slave originally from Africa, testified on behalf of the seven-year-old girl who claimed to be the illegitimate child of her dead owner. Ysabel stated that her relationship with the girl derived from the

Virgen de Leche, Lima, early eighteenth century. This image of the Virgen de la Leche, typical of those produced in Lima during the period, is from the workshop of Escuela Limeña painter Mateo Pérez de Alesio (1725–50). (Used by kind permission of Paul Bayly, Lima, Peru.)

fact that she had "nursed [the infant] at her breast as the daughter of her master" rather than as a hired wet nurse.[37]

Because breast milk was a valuable commodity and wet nursing fetched an income of 15 to 18 pesos a month at the turn of the century, any woman who recently had been pregnant could ply the trade to support herself.[38] She might offer her services as wet nurse to poor or enslaved children as well as the city's elite. When slave children had been separated from their own mothers by death or sale away from Lima, or when elite men sought to hide scandalous sexual relationships with slave women, women like Rosa Fajardo came to the rescue.[39] In 1718 a man hired Rosa to nurse Juan Pablo, an eleven-month-old *mulatillo* he claimed to have just purchased. Rosa never received any wages from the man but continued to care for Juan Pablo "as if he were my son" until he was six years old.[40] Still, because of the informal nature of most arrangements with wet nurses—and because some women were contracted clandestinely to raise illegitimate children—little direct evidence of the wet nursing business appeared until the late eighteenth century, when the press began to run advertisements announcing the availability of these "mistresses of milk" (*amas de leche*).[41]

Colonial labor practices also meant that a sizable proportion of nonwhite children grew up in households with español adults, as Figure 2.2 shows. Often, members of the same biological family lived in bondage or service to another family, and this surely accounted for a good deal of the caste mixing among the generations in colonial Lima. Yet many nonwhite children also entered español homes alone. A 1613 census of the Indian population of Lima identified a number of indigenous girls and boys as young as eight years old living as domestic servants in español households, many "stolen away" from rural communities.[42] Because notaries would collect a fee for drafting binding agreements between adult patrons and youths, colonial Spaniards did not normally trouble themselves with formal domestic service contracts (*conciertos de trabajo*) for indigenous children such as these, whom officials blithely classified as orphans whether or not their parents were living. However, a review of 359 apprenticeship contracts—the most formal of tutelary labor arrangements— reveals that child labor contributed to the cross-caste, cross-generational nature of living patterns in the city. (See Appendix B for a description of the *asiento de aprendiz* sample.)

To date, historical scholarship has addressed apprenticeship in Lima by focusing on particular ethnic or racial groups.[43] Perhaps this is because complete censuses of the city are rare and it is impossible to perform a direct

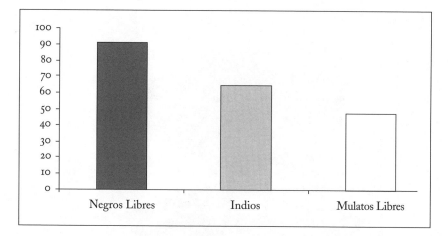

FIGURE 2.2 Percentage of Free Nonwhite Children in Households with Español Adults, Lima, 1700. Source: Sample of Numeración General de 1700

comparison between apprenticeship contracts and the population as a whole. Yet the broad impression the sample yields is that this kind of labor arrangement was not exclusively associated with any one racial sector. While free youths of African descent entered apprenticeships in greater numbers than they appeared in the city's population, and while the proportion of español apprentices is underrepresented in terms of overall population, apprenticeship was a common life path for male youths of all racial backgrounds except the very elite.

Inside the workshops of the city's artisans, among the wooden shells of future carriages, the leather to be worked into shoes, and the reams of cloth to be stitched into garments, male youths and adults from all backgrounds crossed caste divisions for the sake of their trades. As historian Frederick Bowser observed, "In no other area of endeavor did Spaniard, African and Indian work together so closely, on so wide a scale and under such relatively equal terms."[44] But even if a certain degree of caste equality was evident in work routines, the overall character of apprenticeship was one of generational hierarchy.

For male plebeian and slave youths in the colonial period, formal apprenticeship served as a counterpart to the formal education of español youths.[45] The ages of apprentices, when recorded, extended from eight to more than twenty-five years, but most boys entered artisans' workshops between the ages of fourteen and sixteen. Only in the rare case when an apprentice, usually a young man in his early twenties, had previous work experience in the trade

Child Rearing and Adult Authority   55

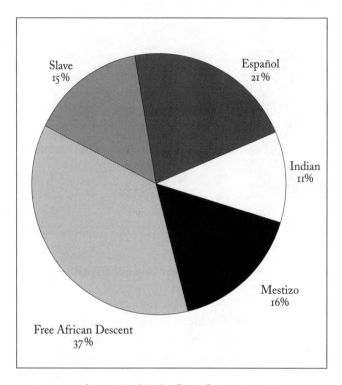

FIGURE 2.3   Apprenticeships by Caste, Lima, 1645–1800.
Source: AGN, PN, Sample of Asientos de Aprendiz

would the artisan agree to pay an apprentice a salary.[46] For most apprentices, remuneration came in the form of care and instruction. While some notaries left their personal imprints on the structure of the contracts, a uniform element in most required the apprentice to live in the artisan's *casa y compañía* (house and company) and held the artisan responsible for "punishing and correcting" the youth.[47] If an unhappy apprentice fled the workshop, the artisan could use force to bring him back and "imprison" him. One notary even went so far as to require parents to return their sons to the artisan if the lads found their way back home.[48] Artisans thus assumed the primary adult role in the lives of these youths, promising to provide food, clothing, shelter, limited health care, and a comprehensive education in the trade, "without withholding a single thing" (*sin ocultar cosa alguna*).

By being named in the contract, minor apprentices surrendered their right to use the privilege of *restitutio ad integrum*, which otherwise might have allowed them to dissolve the contract.[49] In a legal culture that vigilantly

TABLE 2.1   Custodians Present at Apprenticeship Signing,
             Lima, 1645–1800 (n=191)

Mother	72	Uncle	7
Father	39	Godfather	5
Grandmother	3	Stepfather	4
Aunt	6	Orphanage director	10
Master (amo)	10	Priest	4
Mistress (ama)	12	Curador/defensor/albacea	5
Patron (male)	6	Brother	4
Patron (female)	2	Sister	2

Source: AGN, PN, Sample of Asientos de Aprendiz

protected minors of age from entering contracts that might disadvantage them, it is surprising to see such an unbalanced surrendering of minority's privileges in colonial apprenticeships. Yet, to colonial limeños, signing an asiento de aprendiz was more an exchange of authority between adults than a legal action undertaken by the youth.

An adult custodian appeared alongside the apprentice during the contract signing in over half of all sampled cases (191 of 359). Within this subset, parents placed their sons into apprenticeships in just less than half of the entries, with mothers turning their children over to artisans for training with almost twice the incidence of fathers. In the remaining entries, a wide spectrum of adults—legal guardians, slave owners, patrons, or other relatives—gave the youths to artisans. Among these, women appeared with slightly more frequency than men (51.7 percent compared with 49.3 percent). In short, fathers were the primary figures of authority in few of these contracts, while an array of other adults—many of whom were women—possessed enough control over the labor of a youth to be able to transfer that control to an artisan.

In 38 percent of the sampled contracts, alcaldes ordinarios and Indian corregidores also appeared at the contract signing, and they usually were the sole adult representing the apprentice.[50] If no adult custodian was available to turn the youth over to an artisan, city officials normally served as substitutes, and on occasion, the notary would state that the official was acting as "the father of minors" (*padre de menores*) when he performed this function. The use of this title was especially prevalent when the youths were said to be orphans. The status of orphan in the apprenticeship contract might refer to youths whose parents had died, but it also referred to the many migrant youths, often Indian, who left families in the sierra or coastal provinces to find work and training in the city.[51]

Elders and city officials sometimes reported that the youths had expressed an "inclination" to learn a trade and had requested to become apprentices. Notaries even occasionally imported a post-Reformation Catholic language of free will into the contracts by stating the apprenticeship was of the youth's "spontaneous volition."[52] Yet at other times, apprenticeship was an instrument used to bend a male youth's will. So it was with the "orphaned" Indian youth Josef Segundo Gutiérrez, who had left his mother and his home in the Andean community of Huánuco. In Lima he had lived with "irregularity" for a while before the alcalde ordinario deposited him in the workshop of a local tailor.[53] In fact, apprenticeship was so closely associated with punishment that another youth, an español, was placed in an "apprenticeship" to study with a private teacher because he was "going about tattered and lost (*roto y perdido*)."[54] By using apprenticeships as schools and reformatories, adults further contributed to the diversity of children's living arrangements in the colonial capital.

The 1700 census and apprenticeship contracts have allowed us to peer into Lima's private residences and workshops and to see colonial households as both familial hearths and sites of labor for slaves, servants, artisans, apprentices, and wet nurses. Multiple strata of adult authority coexisted and sometimes overlapped inside the city's homes. In the end, the colonial ideology of rule that emphasized the separateness of caste groups and its hierarchies of social class and gender was lived in highly intimate settings and thus had to be reproduced socially rather than physically.

In addition, a Spanish paradigm of patriarchal authority was grafted onto a city where children were raised and trained by diverse adults, not necessarily reared in rigidly defined patriarchal nuclear families. Even the presence of español men, the ideal-typical patriarchs, vied with the ubiquity of other adults in the homes where youths lived. Single motherhood was far from a foreign phenomenon in any type of colonial family, and Lima's children more frequently lived in households without men than in homes without women. Furthermore, the prevalence of multiple-generation and multiple-family dwellings, as well as households with slaves, servants, and apprentices, made for a diverse urban universe of child rearing. The entrenched image of the colonial Spanish American family headed by a strong, European father surrounded by his wife, children, and dependents was partly fact, but clearly, it was also partly fiction in colonial Lima. What remains to be seen is whether the constellation of adults present in children's lives eclipsed the law's emphasis on the rights of the father.

ADULTS, CHILDREN, AND THE COLONIAL COURTS, 1650–1750

When adjudicating matters that involved minors of age, Lima's judges were forced to contend with the fact that the everyday functioning of adult authority often spilled outside the parameters established in law. During the period 1650–1750, both ecclesiastical and secular officials recognized that child rearing practices did not always neatly fall within written prescriptions concerning male authority over children and the rights of padres de familia. Yet adult authority was expressed, legitimized, and arbitrated in distinct manners in the legal spheres of church and crown.

In the courts of the Catholic Church, limeños directly tackled the contradictions between their child rearing practices and patriarchal laws, particularly in annulment suits where children blamed adults for forcing them into unwanted vocations and marriages. When accusing elders of abusing their authority, litigants openly debated the meaning of patriarchal authority in a city where multiple adults reared children. In contrast, in Lima's royal courts, city inhabitants instead used silences, legal contrivances, and linguistic contortions to align colonial child rearing practices with patriarchal legal norms. During the period from 1650 to 1750, colonials sought the intervention of secular officials primarily to ratify the generational transmission of colonial class status, to consolidate the privilege of wealth among children of the propertied classes. Even if these adults privately raised propertied children in a manner that did not fully conform to the principle of male generational right, they rarely challenged the principle openly when practicing the law in the king's tribunals.

Reverence and Fear: Adult Authority in the Ecclesiastical Courts

The ideal functioning of relations between colonial Spanish American adults and children was not prescribed only in civil law, and secular courts were not the only institutions that mediated intergenerational relations. Colonials referred to the Catholic Church as "our Holy Mother" and considered the institution an integral member of the family of political society. They marked the passage of hours by its chapel bells, days by its saints, and time in their own lives by its sacraments, from baptism to the last rites. They also sought justice in its tribunals, turning to church magistrates to mediate disputes involving sacraments or conflicts with those who enjoyed ecclesiastical immunity.

Although lawyers from the Real Audiencia often represented Lima's minors of age before church tribunals, canon rather than civil law theoretically governed ecclesiastical legal proceedings. Canon law endowed priests with the power to reach deeply into the everyday lives of colonials, particularly by regulating sexuality and marriage. Young children whose parents battled in annulment and divorce proceedings might find their futures resting squarely in the hands of church officials, especially when wives who were placed on "deposit" in institutions or private homes during trials wished to retain custody of children.[55] Often it was the very *fact* of children—that they had been conceived during a marriage—that ecclesiastical judges considered critical in their judicial decisions. But the particulars concerning the obligations of fathers and mothers and details about children's lives typically did not deeply concern seventeenth-century church authorities, who instead were intently focused on the relations between the adults involved.[56] Their goal was to preserve the sanctity of "the married life" (*la vida maridable*) by bringing extramarital affairs to a quick end and shepherding wandering spouses back to the hearth whenever possible.[57]

Ecclesiastical judges displayed keener interest in generational matters when youths had reached adolescence and prepared to "take state" as adults in the colonial world. In recent decades, several studies have exposed the multiple dimensions of parental authority in colonial Spanish America by examining *disensos*, or objections parents and other elders registered in order to halt children's marriages.[58] As Patricia Seed has argued, until the Spanish Bourbon king Charles III issued a watershed 1776 decree requiring parental consent for marriage, the church held near-exclusive jurisdiction over conflicts regarding marriage choice.[59] Backed by the Council of Trent's doctrine on the sanctity of individual free will, church officials in Spanish America could guard children's free choice of vocation and spouse, even against the protests of parents and other elders. In ruling on cases involving elder-child conflict over marriage, the church figured as a patriarchal legal entity that stood above both father and king in issues associated with sacramental rites of passage.

There is scant record of parents rejecting their children's marriage choices in seventeenth-century Lima.[60] Yet this did not mean that Lima's elders refrained from arranging marriages or from placing children in monastic houses in order to promote their families' economic and social standing.[61] In the seventeenth century, ecclesiastical authorities often arbitrated suits that betrayed contentious interactions between elders and children surrounding the decision to marry or to enter a regular order as a priest or nun. But children, not parents, were the plaintiffs in these suits. Petitioners requested release from the sacramental vows they had taken as minors of age because they claimed they had professed marriage or holy orders under duress from their elders. Using a canonical condemnation of forcing another person to take holy vows, children in Lima commonly protested the actions of elders only *after* they had complied with adults' wishes by becoming priests and nuns or husbands and wives.

An examination of more than 150 marriage annulment cases and petitions to annul monastic vows (called *nulidades de voto*) from the period 1620–1750 offers fresh insights on the interplay between gender and social class in decisions surrounding marriage and vocation. Women and girls—the majority of whom were doñas—requested marital annulments at a rate between three and four times that of males during the period.[62] On the other hand, priests sued to trade in their monastic habits for secular life far more often than did nuns.[63] The reasons for this gender disparity are complex, sometimes springing from the economic needs of priests' families, other times from the cultural dictates of honor, which gave men greater opportunities to flee unhappy marriages and discouraged them from admitting marital problems in court.[64] But for the purposes at hand, the most important aspect of intergenerational relations these court records reveal is how litigants, lawyers, and church judges negotiated the disjuncture between patriarchal models of authority and the colonial realities of child rearing.

Spain possessed a long history of civil and ecclesiastical prohibitions against forcing individuals to take sacramental vows.[65] Among the categories of force that could vitiate sacred oaths, the fear of authority, termed "reverential fear" (*el miedo reverencial*), assumed a privileged place during the Middle Ages.[66] For fear to be reverential, the person using force was required to be a hierarchal superior acting against a subordinate, and the fear was to derive from an individual's natural dependence on the authority figure who compelled him or her to take vows. Litigants in seventeenth-century Lima often described the nature of this kind of fear in the same way it had been articulated by Pope Alexander III in the twelfth century: *metus qui posset in virum constantem*, or the "fear that would befall a constant [steadfast, unshakable] male."[67]

Yet the concept of miedo reverencial had developed over centuries in a lurching, piecemeal way and had never crystallized into a formal pronouncement on who held the authority to inspire such trepidation, even during the Council of Trent.[68] The council's decrees referred to reverential fear only in its chapter on vows of profession to the regular orders, vaguely describing it as "inflicted by a person vested with the authority to do so."[69] Though respected canonists such as Tomás Sánchez attempted to identify more specifically who held authority powerful enough to inspire reverential fear, colonial legal experts did not completely accept his inclusion of men other than fathers as valid authority figures.[70]

The complexity surrounding canon law on reverential fear was more than an intellectual puzzle for scholars and moralists. It was a pressing issue for many families in seventeenth-century Lima. The litigants who claimed that they had professed vows while seized by fearful reverence, all of whom had been under the age of twenty-five when they went to the altar or entered monasteries, explicitly referred to their youth as a factor that mitigated their free will, even when they met the age requirements for entering religious life or marriage. Both types of litigants accused a wide range of adults of forcing them to take sacramental vows. When young married women and priests filed annulment suits arguing that they had taken sacramental oaths while afflicted with reverential fear, they often asked judges to determine whether fear of adults other than fathers could dissolve the bonds of their vows.

From the perspective of church judges, who saw it as their responsibility to protect free will in sacramental vows, the definition of patriarchal authority presented a particularly problematic issue because, especially in marriage annulment cases, fear of fathers was rarely at issue. More often than not, litigants blamed mothers or other female elders who raised or financially supported them for pushing them into life decisions. Throughout the seventeenth century, judges read the petitions of litigants such as Josef Torres de Picón, who testified that his mother had treated him with "a great deal of subjection" and forced him into a Dominican monastery when he was sixteen. He further described how he "possessed a lot of respect and fear of my mother, because she had imposed it upon me since I was of few years [of age]."[71] Judges then turned their attention to the objections of defendants and their lawyers, such as the attorney who flatly stated that a woman "is not one of those people who can incite fear," since women were "very weak and pusillanimous."[72]

Brides seeking marital annulments claimed that their mothers (as opposed to female guardians) were solely responsible for inflicting reverential fear in no less than thirty of sixty-four suits, while they named men as the sole perpetrators in only six cases. Perhaps women were more concerned about their daughters' marriages than were fathers, as the details in certain cases suggest. Some fathers attempted to disengage from conflicts over marriage altogether. Doña

María Francisca de Báldez recalled how she went to her father for protection when her mother attempted to force her to marry. Her father rebuffed her, she said, because "he did not want to insert himself in a single thing and [said] that my mother would do as she wished and what seemed right to her."[73]

Male elders tended to be more interested in forcing adolescent males into the priesthood. Fathers were accused of acting alone in perpetrating force against their sons in almost a quarter of nulidades de votos. Nonetheless, even the majority of litigating priests named women as the primary parties who forced them to enter monasteries, often indicating that their mothers or other female elders had used the institutions for punishment when the youths dallied too long in taking on adult responsibilities. Juan de Espinoza, for one, accused his mother of forcing him to take holy vows because she had grown frustrated at his lack of concern for his studies. "Look what you have done," he recalled her shouting. "Now you will have no choice but to continue your studies, because you are going to be a priest!"[74]

Wealthy married women living with husbands certainly figured as principal antagonists in the tales of reverential fear litigants told in ecclesiastical court. But even though two-thirds of the litigants in marriage suits were doñas and dons, the honorific title barely masked the threadbare economic existence of some litigants' families. Often the hardship of raising children alone compelled single women to force their children into marriages or monasteries. One mother admitted that she had arranged her daughter's marriage to a suitor who owned 4,000 pesos in cash and real estate in the Plaza de Guadalupe because he was willing to take her daughter's hand even though this single mother could not afford a dowry.[75] Widow Luisa Moço confessed that she had used physical violence against her son when she placed him in the Convento Grande of Santo Domingo, because, "being so poor that I had to wash clothes with my own hands, I obligated him to be reduced to this state to be relieved of this work."[76]

Like Luisa, many mothers admitted to having orchestrated dramas filled with menace and violence to force their children into sacramental vows. As litigants recounted being pinched, imprisoned, or threatened with poisoning and even suffocation, they essentially argued that it was might that made right: even if mothers did not technically possess patria potestad, the fact that they threatened their children with violence nonetheless meant that the youths could be "afflicted" under their "dominion" and "power."[77]

As we have seen, a mother was tacitly recognized in Spanish civil law as possessing an accessory authority over children, subsumed under the patria potestad of fathers. Thus testimony concerning mothers' dominion should not be too surprising. But it is certainly striking that litigants in the ecclesiastical courts of Lima would use the term "potestad"—a concept generally reserved to refer to the authority of fathers, masters, and kings and that was expressly denied to women—to refer to a mother's power.

Doña Juana de Herencia began her 1681 marriage annulment case by describing herself as living under the potestad of her mother. Her attorney interrogated witnesses about the nature of her mother's authority. In his second question he asked the witnesses if they were aware that doña Juana was "under the patria Potestad of doña Ysabel de Vera, her mother, and being a girl of the mentioned age, that her mother wanted her to marry Gabriel de Santillán, and that doña Juana denounced [the marriage]."[78] There seems to have been no correlation between doña Juana's social class and the fact that her mother was said to have possessed patria potestad. Even plebeian litigants who did not use the honorific title "doña" might refer to a mother's power by using the term "potestad."[79] Crucially, however, litigants and lawyers reserved the term only for women who raised children without the presence or financial support of fathers or other male elders. Furthermore, the word only appears in marital annulment suits brought forward by female litigants; no husband or priest ever referred to his mother's authority as "potestad." Mothers' authority could become equivalent to masculine generational authority only in the absence of men.[80]

Even such a restricted interpretation of women's power over children as potestad faced systemic opposition in the ecclesiastical court system. The task of church attorneys (*promotores fiscales*) and lawyers of the monastic orders (*promotores* or *procuradores*) was to block annulments in order to protect the indissolubility of sacramental vows. Given that litigants often accused adults other than fathers of force, these legal agents frequently sought to win their cases by vehemently rejecting the implication that women could possess sufficient authority over children to inspire reverential fear.

The key argument the Dominicans' lawyer put forward in the case of Gerónimo de Solis, who had claimed that his mother had forced him into a monastery during his father's absence from the city, was that no one other than a father was capable of inspiring the degree of reverential fear necessary to invalidate marriages or religious professions. The procurador general of Santo Domingo maintained that, in order to invalidate vows, force "had to [originate] from a person to whom the litigant is subject, and not just anyone but a superior like a father or judge or someone else of this quality."[81]

Beyond arguing that women did not qualify as superiors, church and monastic attorneys also contended that women were too kind, or alternately too capricious, to elicit the kind of trepidation in children that could be classified as reverential. "Experience demonstrates," stated one monastic defense lawyer, "that mothers are benevolent with children."[82] Another warned church judges against entertaining any claim to reverential fear that involved nuns accusing female elders, since "in a woman there can be found neither the violence, the authority, nor the maturity (*mayoría*) to cause the fear that would befall a constant man."[83] When making counterarguments to these gendered renderings of valid authority, attorneys representing the priests and wives were often no more flattering to women. One lawyer argued that mothers were, in fact, more capable than fathers of inducing reverential fear in children, "since, ordinarily, women, by their very nature, are more cruel than men" and "because a man is not as relentless as a woman, and it is easier to convince him with reason."[84]

Even if the nature of women's authority over children ignited a special controversy in the church court system, litigants continued to accuse women, as well as a wide variety of elders who were not their parents, of forcing them to the altar or into the monastery. Parents and stepparents made up the majority of elders accused of pushing children into matrimony or monastic houses, but several litigants accused other adults who had raised or supported them, such as brothers, uncles, aunts, patrons, slave masters, and priests.

Slave children fell subject to the authority of adults other than their parents due to their very condition as chattel, yet the Catholic doctrine of free will theoretically extended to slaves as well as to free individuals. Spanish American slave owners who either prevented their slaves from marrying or forced them into matrimony could be challenged before church authorities, although not always successfully.[85] Yet in 1693 the eleven-year-old slave Gertrudis de Jesús won her suit against the Jesuits who owned her when the priests compelled her to marry another slave.[86]

It seemed clear enough to church officials in this case that slave masters qualified as authority figures capable of inspiring reverential fear. It was imperative, however, that free litigants who accused adults other than their parents prove that their fear derived from the debt of filial obedience they had incurred in their childhood homes. They often stressed that they considered the adults who raised them to be fathers or mothers. Because doña Leonor de Arrebulo had been raised in the home of her brother, her lawyer contended that "she respected him as a father, and thus had no way of refusing" his insistence that she marry.[87] When a priest who had been raised in the same home as orphan

Ynés de Rivera was interviewed for her marriage annulment suit, he described how their guardian, scribe Juan Márquez de Toledo, had called Inés "daughter" and how she had referred to him as "father."[88] These descriptions breathe life into the patterns of child rearing found in the city census and notary contracts. Children in colonial Lima were often raised outside biological families, and the time nonkin adults and children spent living together inspired filial feelings in children and, they believed, endowed adults with parental prerogatives regardless of blood relations.

Church and monastic defense attorneys, ever vigilant to classify fathers as the sole individuals who could exert the kind of power that could incite reverential fear, refuted the accusations against these other adults just as stridently as they did accusations against mothers. Even the power of the priest Josef Martínez, who had raised Francisco de Córdova in his cell in the monastery of Santo Domingo, did not meet the procurador's criteria for an adult capable of filling a youth with fearful reverence. Francisco said he "had lived on [the priest's] expenses and was subjected to him, seeing as how I had neither father nor mother in this city," and witnesses corroborated his claim that he held the same fear and respect for Martínez as if the priest had been his father. The attorney of the Dominican order protested that Francisco's accusation against the priest was "in vain," since the priest was "not one of the persons who, in conformity with law, can induce the just fear that would annul an action of this nature." Nonetheless, the vicar of the archbishopric ruled on the case and declared Francisco's profession invalid.[89]

In fact, as in the preceding case, church and monastic lawyers frequently fought a losing battle in annulment suits. In the twenty-nine suits to annul monastic vows that contain judicial decisions, judges declared religious professions invalid fifteen times. Women acted alone in perpetrating force in six of these cases, and in three more both parents acted together. Church judges granted annulments in an even greater number of marriage suits. Judges ruled for plaintiffs in twenty-one of twenty-eight verdicts handed down in reverential fear cases, and in fifteen of these decisions, litigants had accused female elders of compelling them to marry.

Seventeenth-century judges almost never explained their decisions, but it is obvious that they were not swayed by arguments about the inability of elders other than fathers, including women, to inspire reverential fear. Even women unrelated to children were judged capable of exercising a kind of generational authority over children—an authority derived not from gender, biology, or legitimacy but from simply having raised a child. One promotor fiscal inadvertently admitted as much during foundling doña María de Arriaga's marital annulment suit. He argued that, because doña María had lived in the city's foundling home rather than in the home of the woman who paid for her rearing, the plaintiff could "not even claim crianza" as a basis for the woman's authority over her.[90]

We should remember, however, that the authority over children that these judges acknowledged in their decisions was not as much a legal right as it was a negative power. Eventually church officials in Rome would regard church magistrates in Lima as far too generous in this negative interpretation of adult authority. Appeals of several cases involving Lima's Franciscan priests—most of whom claimed that elders had forced them to enter monasteries and that their reverential fear lasted for years, preventing them from seeking annulments—reached the Vatican late in the seventeenth century. Pope Innocent XI (1676–89) issued a papal brief on the matter of Lima's annulments in 1683 in which he scornfully referred to the "abuse" of the precept of reverential fear in Peru's tribunals. The pontiff reiterated a Tridentine decree that required any priest of the regular orders who wished to annul his vows to do so within five years of profession, and he overturned the rulings of Lima's judges in several cases where priests' vows had been determined to be invalid. Included among them were annulment suits in which priests alleged they had entered monasteries out of reverential fear of their mothers.[91]

The ruling from the Vatican made a delayed impact in Lima. References to the papal brief did not appear in the city's ecclesiastical court system until more than a decade had passed. Even as late as 1698, a Franciscan priest named in the papal brief claimed that he had not heard of the ruling, since it was never read aloud in his monastery.[92] But by the turn of the century, news of the pope's censure surely had reached the regular clergy in Lima's monasteries and had circulated through the city at large. After 1701 the stream of monastic annulment suits alleging force and fear slowed to a trickle, and they almost disappeared after 1725.

Local church authorities also became reluctant to grant marriage annulments based on the excuse of reverential fear after Innocent XI issued his brief. In fact, the number of all marital annulments and divorce cases declined drastically during the early eighteenth century. The source of this decline appears to have been an increasing disinclination on the part of judges to accept cases, rather than a decreasing litigiousness among city inhabitants.[93] Amidst this decline, allegations of fear and force all but vanished from the court record. On the rare occasion in which ecclesiastical courts heard marriage annulment cases based on reverential fear in the following years, litigants proceeded with a new caution, and the verdicts in their trials were decidedly less favorable than they had been.[94] In addition to a waning willingness to hear cases of annulment and divorce, church officials in Lima were dissuaded from intervening in domestic matters on behalf of children in other areas as well. In a 1741 papal encyclical, Benedict XVI attempted to halt priests from performing secret marriages against fathers' wishes, instructing them to inquire as to whether the couple was exchanging vows in secret in order to hide their marriage from "a father who forbids it."[95]

By the middle of the eighteenth century, then, the church had stepped back from its central role in adjudicating intergenerational conflicts, including those surrounding reverential fear. As the church retreated, the circle of adults who were legally recognized as possessing authority over children contracted, leaving only medieval civil laws emphasizing the power of the father.

Between Rights and Rearing: Adults and Children in the Secular Courts

When church judges ruled in favor of annulment petitions based on reverential fear, they did not so much sanction the authority of adults other than fathers as attempt to curb the abuse of an authority that they acknowledged existed de facto rather than de jure. In the king's courts, however, Lima's litigants only rarely engaged in such frank arguments about the definition of adult authority. Instead, when they appeared before secular judges in matters surrounding children during the period 1650–1750, they submerged daily practices of child rearing into the paperwork of patriarchal public dealings, at times even masking the power that women privately exercised over children.

Whereas canon law jealously guarded children's free will, Spanish civil laws jealously guarded patriarchal control of children's property. Most codified civil law about minors of age centered on the appointment of guardians who would manage patrimony in children's names until the minors reached the age of majority or married. In a sense, the very purpose of Spanish family law was to ensure the transmission of class status. In the case of a father's death, the courts were to serve as the channel through which property passed to a male guardian or mother, who acted as the wife to the king in the reconstituted family. Royal courts thus intervened in the affairs of children in a manner that quite deliberately favored elite men as the source of authority in the public sphere. However, the practice of civil law camouflaged the multiple dimensions of adult power exercised in the city's homes.

An examination of 213 guardianship contracts and more than 200 civil cases involving minors of age reveals that, until 1750, the propertied classes entered the city's secular courts or visited notaries for contracts related to minors' business far more often than did the ordinary denizens of the city. (An explanation of the sampling procedures for guardianship contracts can be found in Appendix B.) The almost universal prevalence of the titles "don" and "doña" in guardianship contracts and civil cases involving minors of age attests to the elevated social status of individuals who used the legal system in matters pertaining to children during the period 1650–1750.

Disputes over property inspired most city inhabitants to draw up guardianship documents during this period. As Figure 2.4 demonstrates, in almost half (91) of the 194 sampled contracts for the period 1645–1750, guardians were simply court-appointed public advocates (curadores ad litem) for minors who were involved in litigation over financial matters. The adults whom judges named might be relatives and notable individuals from the community, but most often they were legal officials such as procuradores or the Defensor de Menores, many of whom were named specifically to represent the minors in inheritance cases (53).

No father ever appeared before a notary to achieve official guardianship during the period; his right to manage the property of his minor children needed no court sanction. But mothers seeking guardianship did need official approval. Recall that if fathers died ab intestato, mothers could act as guardians for their own children as long as they did not remarry. In the majority of contracts in which mothers were named guardians found in the sample (28), mothers assumed the role because father had died intestate. Yet even when fathers had named their children's mothers in their wills and testaments (20), the women of Lima needed local judges to bestow their patriarchal imprimatur on their guardianship. They usually did not seek such approval unless there was a pressing reason to do so, as there was for doña Andrea de la Roca, who assumed legal guardianship of her five children in 1647. Although her husband had named doña Andrea as their children's guardian in his will, she did not seek official approval until she wanted to sell some of the land the youths had inherited.[96] Thus what compelled most women to file for official guardianship was the need to conduct public, fiduciary business in the name of minors of age.

In only a quarter of all of the contracts did adults other than court-appointed

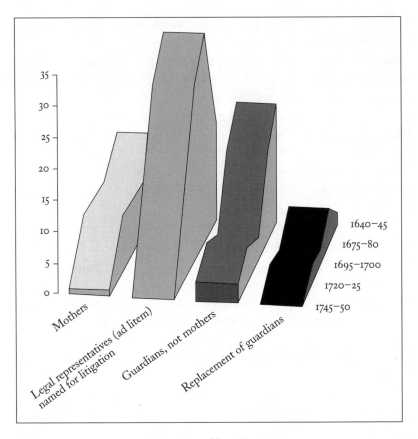

FIGURE 2.4 Guardianship Contracts by Type, Lima, 1640–1750.
Source: AGN, PN, Sample of Tutelas and Curadurías

legal representatives or mothers receive guardianship for purposes not expressly related to litigation over minors' property. The majority of these guardians were prominent men who used the title "don," and in only three cases was a woman other than a mother approved as a guardian—an act that was technically illegal.[97] Sometimes these adults assumed guardianship because the death of both parents had left children orphaned. Yet we cannot assume that all or even most of the minors who received these nonparental guardians were orphans, since contracts often indicated that a father had died but made no reference to the child's mother. In fact, it was clear in certain instances that men assumed guardianship of children even if a mother was alive.[98] The appointment of guardians to children with living mothers highlights a central feature of child rearing in colonial Lima: custody and guardianship were separate responsibilities that did not necessarily overlap.

In written law and according to moralists' treatises, becoming a guardian implied assuming the role of caretaker.[99] In practice, however, an adult usually did so solely for the purposes of litigation or to oversee the division of an estate from which a minor of age inherited, not necessarily to carry out daily, domestic responsibilities. This was true regardless of the minor's age. In fact, the very language of the standard contract reveals that guardianship was not designed to confer custody to an adult but, rather, to assign public economic responsibility for a minor. All of the contracts contained some variation on a boilerplate clause that obligated the guardian, whether a mother or someone else, to "conduct collections, sales, [and] rents, to lease out properties, to provide procurators' salaries, and to come to the defense of the said minor in civil litigation (*pleitos*)."[100] Nowhere in the formulaic language of these contracts did guardians agree to perform the more intimate kinds of responsibilities for their wards that Spanish laws mandated they should, such as providing them an education, taking them into their homes to raise them, or ensuring that they lived in some other socially respectable environment. During this period, limeños thus used guardianship to officially legitimize their control over children's wealth rather than to bestow custody or regulate minors' personal care.

Because the purpose of the contract was public legal representation and the management of finances, clear indications about how and where Lima's wards were reared is rare in the notary record. An unusual guardianship contract filed in 1673 indicates that most of this kind of information probably never reached the historical record. Eight-year-old Pedro de Quirós was an illegitimate orphan, an *hijo natural*, whose mother had died shortly after he was born. The widow doña Eugenia de Núñez took the infant into her home and, as the notary stated, had "raised and supported [him] . . . with much love and good will, without any [personal] interest, and keeps him in her house and company and loves him as a son." Doña Eugenia had acted as the only mother Pedro had ever known, and perhaps this is why the judge permitted her to become the only female guardian not biologically related to her ward I identified in contracts spanning the period 1645–1750. What compelled her to seek this distinction? She wanted to represent Pedro in a suit to collect the 400 pesos he was owed by unnamed parties living in the valley of Pisco.[101] If not for this fact, information about Pedro would have faded from the historical record along with data about many of colonial Lima's propertyless orphans.

Just as guardianship contracts recorded legal matters primarily pertaining to Lima's propertied minors, the bulk of civil litigation reaching Lima's Cabildo and Audiencia from 1650 to 1750 almost always involved the top strata of the city's social hierarchy. Many of the legal matters secular judges supervised were not really "cases" at all but simple records detailing the division of estates and auctions. Others were *cuentas de tutela*, or guardians' uncontested accountings of transactions involving minors' property; over time, these were increasingly overseen by the Defensor General de Menores.

Slightly more than half of the cases involving children during the period can, however, be classified as civil litigation rather than simple court oversight of minors' finances. These cases tended to center around two types of issues. Predictably, both involved property. Many secular suits concerning children involved disputes over the official title of "guardian," and in most cases the primary litigants were men. For much of the colonial period, even litigation surrounding claims to tutela, or guardianship of prepubescent children, principally pivoted on the administration of minors' inheritance rather than on the physical custody of children.[102]

Another major category of litigation centered on the inheritance claims of illegitimate children. These were suits on behalf of minors of age who sought recognition as hijos naturales. During the seventeenth century, most illegitimate children did not seek recognition during the lifetime of a parent. As María Emma Mannarelli has shown in her study of Lima, only after a parent died did most litigants seek parental recognition in order to tap into the wealth and partake of the honor of their lineage.[103] Because of this, many already were adults at the time the suits were initiated, and thus this litigation tended to be focused on economic matters rather than custody, child rearing, and education.

Among the suits that did involve younger illegitimate children, the case of doña Francisca Angelina brought forward in 1673 provides a typical example. She and don Juan Martel Melgarejo had conceived two children, María and Martín, out of wedlock. From his deathbed in the Andean town of Cajatambo, don Juan Martel had named one man as his executor and another man to serve as tutor to his illegitimate children. The executor of the estate, acting on behalf of don Juan's legitimate family, withheld the financial assistance that the father had verbally promised María and Martín as he was dying. Doña Francisca Angelina could not "comfortably sustain" the children on her own, so she decided to sue for their recognition and inheritance.[104]

Children born from unions between unwed partners who faced no canonical impediment to marriage at the time of conception held a legal right to a maximum of one-fifth of a parent's estate if they could demonstrate that adults had recognized these children as their offspring (*filiación*).[105] In Spanish America, upholding natural children's claims to inheritance was an integral part of the process of reproducing colonial hierarchies by transferring class standing among elites, even when their children were procreated outside church-sanctioned unions.[106] Illegitimacy alone would bar *naturales* from a gamut of social privileges when they became adults, whether or not elite fathers or (less frequently) mothers recognized them as their sons and daughters. Being cut out of inheritance could further compound children's dishonor by making it difficult for them to grow up in a manner that corresponded to the status of their progenitors.

To gain inheritance, *naturales* sought to prove that their parents had at some point recognized and financially provided for them. This frequently was expressed quite simply, as a litigant would claim that his or her father acknowledged paternity by "supporting me, rearing me, and calling me his child."[107] But proving paternal acknowledgment was not always enough. In a 1755 case concerning a seven-year-old natural named don Juan José de Ayesta, the Defensor de Menores indicated that children's right to inherit hinged as much on social class status as on civil legal rights derived from paternal acknowledgment. To the Defensor, that Juan José's father recognized him as his progeny was not the only germane issue in the case. Equally important was that both of his parents were of "good birth" and that his mother had been "honest" until seduced by his father.[108] Colonial judges often considered illegitimates' claims for inheritance according to this nexus of gendered sexual honor and color-class lineage. They sometimes ruled that an estate be divided to provide inheritance to *naturales* over the objections of legitimate widows and children and, meanwhile, turned down the requests of lower-caste litigants or ruled against children in cases where the sexual honor of mothers was in question.[109]

Therefore, the caste and class origins of illegitimate children and the circumstances of their parents' sexual relationship determined whether offspring shared in their ascendants' wealth and prestige. It was not unusual for elite fathers to admit to having children with lower-caste women, even with slaves. Nonetheless, to announce as much in a public document remained socially risky. For this reason, one elite limeño changed his will in 1696, only two years after he had first dictated it. He feared that admitting that he had sired a mulatillo named Manuel with a slave woman, along with his bequest of 300 pesos to his son to be used toward his freedom, would "provoke scandalous bad example."[110]

As in Manuel's case, inheritance could be more than an elite affair.[111] It was of enormous consequence to this slave boy, since paternal recognition would have been a legacy of freedom. Inheritance also touched the lives of free plebeian children, illegitimate or otherwise. In seventeenth-century testaments from Lima, parents from the middle or lower socioeconomic ranks of the city legally recognized children conceived out of wedlock. Sometimes parents left their offspring artisan goods such as tools and shop wares; sometimes they left them nothing except the acknowledgment that the children were their progeny.[112] During the period from 1650 to 1750, only on rare occasions would the failure of an ordinary inhabitant to leave a will and testament prompt others to appear before the tribunals to dispute guardianship, since the cost of going to court would easily exceed the value of modest property and sentimental items.[113] Overwhelmingly, the courts heard suits over guardianship, parental recognition, and inheritance in which the financial stakes were high.

Thus the case of María and Martín Melgarejo, the naturales whose mother attempted to force an executor to make good on their dying father's promise to bequeath to them, has revealed the significance of social class and caste in civil suits over minors of age during the period from 1650 to 1750. Property was the common denominator in most litigation and contracts involving minors of age during the era. Even though limeños placed a sizable social value on lineage, they typically did not use the court system to justify children's claims to genealogical honor. Instead, family honor, derived from determinations about parents' sexual behavior, lineage, and caste origins, justified children's claims to inheritance. Furthermore, the civil court system was not used to regulate the rearing of the young or to determine who rightfully held authority over the city's children. Rather, limeños used it to transfer and control wealth and social position among the city's elite.

The Melgarejo suit is instructive in another way. Strictly speaking, the suit was not a matter of adult authority or custody, yet it revealed a critical, though hidden, disparity between laws and practices surrounding adult-child relations in colonial Lima from 1650 to 1750. The case was officially filed under the name of the children's male guardian, but the mother, doña Francisca Angelina, initiated litigation and filed many of the petitions herself. In fact, the children's guardian, theoretically their public representative, remained mute during the majority of proceedings. Furthermore, doña Francisca Angelina revealed during the trial that she was raising the children in her home even though their father had named a third party as the children's tutor.

The Melgarejo litigation exposes the gap between the patriarchal theory that underlay laws on minors of age and actual child rearing practices in colonial Lima. Even if a child's "person" nominally fell under the tutela of a male elder, a woman frequently held the child in her custody.[114] The disjuncture between guardianship and custody applied even to mothers, since, while the *Siete partidas* specifically stated that orphans should be reared in their mothers' homes if they were alive, custody did not translate into official guardianship or legal authority.[115] While women faced a series of restrictions in achieving guardianship over children that men did not, they were still expected to raise youths. The women who reared Lima's children—mothers, aunts, nuns, and grandmothers—might even go so far as to bring suit for minors, but as in the case of the Melgarejo minors, the litigation frequently was registered under the name of male guardians or relatives.

If limeños saw any contradiction between the fact that women were privileged as custodians and men were favored as legal guardians, they rarely openly discussed it in the royal courts during the period 1650–1750. In fact, they rarely discussed the details of child rearing at all. Evidence of children's upbringing emerges instead from offhand comments, silences, and linguistic slips in litigants' petitions, as well as from the exceptional case involving a minor of age in which a woman acted as a primary plaintiff. When a father sued to regain custody of his daughter from his mother-in-law in 1725, he made no mention of finding a woman to care for the girl if she came to live with him. The grandmother's attorney nonetheless stated that his client "is her legitimate grandmother and will not only carry out her instruction and regimen but will do so with complete esteem, which could never happen with a [woman who was a] stranger (*otra extraña*)."[116] The use of the feminine noun for the word "stranger" in this case exposed a common presumption: child rearing was women's work. No one believed that a man—even a father—would alone take on the daily care of a child if he achieved guardianship. It was implied, however, that if the grandmother were awarded guardianship, she would continue to perform the work of rearing the child herself.

That we must search for grammatical evidence to uncover information about child rearing practices in these cases demonstrates how deeply women's centrality in the process of social reproduction was taken for granted, and how thoroughly secular legal practice subsumed women's role in domestic governance into patriarchal formulas. Women's labor in child rearing was an accepted, and generally unchallenged, fact of adult-child relations in colonial Lima.

The ability of these elite women to properly raise propertied youths was likewise generally uncontested. In civil cases during the period, terms such as "rearing" (crianza) and "financial support" (alimentos) appeared primarily in the inventoried lists of expenditures made on behalf of a minor of age and conveyed nothing specific about how the ward was raised.[117] Although Spanish law stated that parents and guardians were beholden to instill *buenas costumbres* in children and "teach them to read and write," most adults entangled in disputes over guardianship before the mid-eighteenth century did not offer proof of their ability to provide instruction or virtuous enclosure to children as justification for their claims to the management of minors' property. Just as it was assumed that women would perform the work of child rearing, it was also understood that those elite inhabitants of Lima who used the secular legal system could provide the proper education and impart the manners of high society to future generations.

When viewed as a group, civil suits involving minors of age during the period 1650–1750 tell us that limeños aligned the realities of child rearing in colonial Lima with what was written in the law when appearing before civil magistrates. If patriarchy pervaded the exercise of authority over children in colonial Lima, it must be understood as a dominance that extended beyond the private power men exercised in their day-to-day interactions with women, children, and other dependents. Instead, patriarchy featured as a legal practice in which colonials funneled the child rearing labors of diverse individuals, including mothers, through a legal philosophy of male right.

Civil laws regarding minors of age had been written in the interest of controlling property and the transmission of social rank through generations. From 1650 to 1750, the civil courts of colonial Lima were primarily the domain of the propertied elite—or at least those who sought to attain, maintain, or control wealth. Even women who sought and achieved guardianship did so in order to manage children's assets or to represent minors in litigation over property, not to gain public approval of their gendered rights or their role in rearing children. Nor did they seek basic financial support for child rearing; rather, they argued that the children had a right to relatively large inheritances. In short, when adults entered the secular court system or appeared before notaries during this period, they did so to consolidate Lima's elite colonial class rather than to assert political or "natural" rights over children. In order to achieve their aims, they complied with patriarchal legal norms on paper, even if multiple individuals reared the city's children in practice.

Covarrubias's definition of the law serves as a pointed reminder that legal history takes place between written prescription and actual practice. When we compare the demographic patterns described in the beginning of this chapter with legal activities involving minors of age, a fundamental disjuncture between patriarchal laws and the colonial practices of rearing children emerges. The legal principle of patria potestad endowed male heads of household with ultimate rights over the property and person of their children and other dependents. Yet adults other than the ideal-typical Spanish father or master—including widows, nonwhite wet nurses, or master artisans—often took on the actual labor of raising Lima's young.

The point is not that legal records hide "truths" that other historical sources such as censuses or apprenticeship contracts divulge. Legal authority over children was negotiated in the very interstices between laws and everyday practice. It is of great significance that, for example, men were privileged as legal authority figures in the civil justice system but women often acted behind the legal scenes. It is also of great significance that restricted definitions of adult authority were not universally applied in all judicial arenas. In the church courts of the city, limeños openly struggled to square patriarchal rights with other salient concepts that structured notions of intergenerational relationships and power, such as the Catholic doctrine of free will. When colonials aired cases before royal judges, however, they tended to press the realities of child rearing into the confines of civil laws that required men to serve as the public face of the family.

Yet even in the secular courts, limeños quietly revealed that a history of adult power existed outside codified ideal family types and even outside the courtrooms of the city. When they offered clues about custody practices, and even when they remained silent on who did the work of raising the city's young, Lima's inhabitants indicated that colonial social reproduction operated in a way that diverged from the orderly vision of household governance enshrined in law. Nevertheless, when Lima's elite litigants entered civil courts, their success often rested on conforming to these laws, for conformity offered them the ability to pass their status to children and to reproduce colonial hierarchies in the next generation. As the following chapter reveals, Lima's inhabitants reproduced these hierarchies not only by upholding patriarchal codes in the secular courts but also by replicating the ideal-typical model of the patriarchal family in the city's institutions, where generations unrelated by blood joined together across the divisions of colonial society.

Whether Son or Stranger

3

Institutions for Child Rearing

I
nstitutions such as religious houses, hospitals, and schools
were as important to Spanish colonial rule as were tribunals
and palaces, and they were as central to the lives of Lima's
ordinary inhabitants as the private residences of the city. This is because many
institutions served as social workshops in which early modern Iberian culture,
religion, and political ideologies were reproduced among a colonial populace,
and particularly a young colonial populace. Adults took charge of rearing
children who were not their own inside buildings founded and maintained
under the auspices of church and crown, and in doing so they passed on the
mores and social distinctions of their own generation through the education
and rearing of the next.

Similar to what we have seen taking place inside the city's private residences,
child rearing inside Lima's colonial institutions constantly created and re-
created a social proximity between adults and children of divergent caste categories. But a close examination of nunneries, a school for Indian "nobles," and the
city's foundling home during the seventeenth century and the first half of the
eighteenth century shows that the similarities between institutions and households did not end there. Institutional practices of child rearing and the authority
adults exercised over students, slaves, and abandoned children followed the
ideal-typical model of the patriarchal family. In turn, children developed filial
ties of dependency on adults other than their parents. To a certain extent,
limeños could find a legal basis for these attachments, since the *Siete partidas*

described raising a child as one of the greatest good acts that a man could do, "because every man is moved by a great affection toward he whom he raises, whether son or stranger."[1] In the end, however, the great affection that bound these children to the adults who reared them did not bridge the social distances between city inhabitants. Indeed, the intergenerational dependencies limeños developed in the city's institutions in many ways served as pillars of colonial social hierarchies.

NUNNERIES AS NURSERIES

Theoretically, religious houses isolated individuals from secular society, providing refuge and seclusion for those who had dedicated their lives to the Christian God. Yet the same commingling between social classes, castes, and generations that occurred in the city's households during the period 1650–1750 also occurred within its sacred spaces, particularly inside colonial nunneries. This was because convents and lay religious institutions for women served as more than cloisters. They also were the childhood homes of a significant number of Lima's inhabitants, from slaves to elite women.

Eighteen religious institutions appeared in the 1700 census: buildings housing monasteries and their schools, houses for "repentant" and "religious" laywomen (*recogimientos* and *beaterios*), and observant convents for professed nuns. Ringed by tall walls jutting backward from elaborate facades, the largest of these institutions engulfed entire city blocks, creating "cities within cities."[2] While these walls physically separated convents from secular society, many aspects of the world beyond the cloistered interiors could not be kept at bay.

The social and economic rhythm inside these cities within cities pulsed in tandem with that of the "city without." In some cases, religious institutions functioned in ways that directly responded to the breakdown of gender order on the outside. Widows retreated to convents upon their husbands' deaths, and married women sought shelter from abusive husbands in the company of other women in convents and recogimientos. Furthermore, husbands, secular judges, and ecclesiastical authorities sometimes "deposited" women into institutions as a form of punishment or containment.[3] Thus, the secular world of marital conflict often entered religious houses as the cultural baggage women brought with them when they entered spiritual seclusion.

Other aspects of the secular world also seeped into convent complexes. For example, in the convent of Santa Clara, young novices were charged with the job of serving as *porteras*, guarding the convent's entrance and keeping watch at the iron grille through which nuns met with visitors. But these adolescents were prone to chatting with Lima's passersby, disrupting prayerful piety with the noisy news of urban life. Their gossiping drew an ecclesiastical scolding in the mid-eighteenth century, and the nuns were ordered to put older women in charge of watching the doors.[4] In addition, because some young women and girls entered convents to avoid marriages arranged by their parents, family quarrels frequently broke through convent walls. In 1758 the prioress of the Monasterio del Prado testified to church officials about the repeated problem of men—fathers, brothers, and lovers of the women inside—forcing their way into the cloisters.[5]

Material matters, too, were highly integrated into the spiritual life of female monasteries. Ironically, to take vows of poverty as a professed nun required money—money to enter and money to construct and maintain a cell. In turn, monastic orders frequently lent money to community elites, creating what Kathryn Burns has dubbed for the case of Cuzco a "spiritual economy."[6] What is more, servants and slaves, who were considered worldly possessions, were more numerous inside large convents than were those who had taken holy vows. In Lima, nuns often employed convent slaves as street vendors, hired them out for temporary jobs, or donated them to others to serve. As a consequence, slaves and servants often departed from the monastic complexes at dawn through side entrances (*puertas falsas*) and returned in the evening with their *jornales*, or daily earnings.

Just as money and slaves circulated in and out of these institutions on a regular basis, so, too, did the social norms of colonial society. Convents and monasteries discriminated on the basis of caste and social class, and their internal structure formed what historian Luis Martín calls "an aristocratic pyramid of unequals, clustered into rigidly defined and mutually exclusive social classes."[7] In a kind of dress reversal that inverted the colonial color-class hierarchy, elite nuns, most of whom were españolas, wore distinctive black veils to set them apart from their white-veiled subordinates, who often were non-white.[8] Nunneries also housed a variety of other women and girls with graduated positions in the convent. In addition to slaves and servants, who fell at the bottom of the hierarchy, there were *seglares* (laywomen and girls), including *educandas* (students in convent schools), *novicias* (novices), and *donadas* (usually nonwhite religious women who did not take binding holy vows).

More children lived within female convents than in male monasteries, yet we only need to recall the renunciation of holy vows submitted by the Dominican priest Francisco de Córdova, whom we first met in Chapter 2, to be reminded that boys, too, grew up in the confines of monastic life, living under the authority of priests who acted as their substitute fathers. Fray Josef Martínez had raised both Francisco and another boy in his "cell and company" in the Convento Grande of Santo Domingo, and both youths eventually became Dominican priests.[9]

Nevertheless, the existence of schools for male youths and the absence of female slaves and servants in male religious institutions ensured that there would never be as many children in male monasteries as there were in nunneries. In the mid-sixteenth century, educational institutions including seminaries, various *colegios* (schools for adolescents, between modern primary and secondary education), and the Royal University of San Martín provided elite male youths spaces for formal learning. These educational institutions were closed to the students' female counterparts, who instead commonly relied on private tutors, called *amigas*—or more colloquially, *migas*—to learn rudimentary reading, writing, and needlework.

In an effort to expand educational, spiritual, and social opportunities for elite women during the second half of the sixteenth century, city notables established a rash of lay schools for girls that were not attached to convents. In the seventeenth century, a new set of schools for girls opened, including Santa Cruz de Atocha, a school for white female foundlings, which was established as an appendage to the city's foundling home, the Casa de Niños Expósitos. But by late in the century, only two female lay schools existed in Lima, while there were seven male colegios. Convents such as La Encarnación (est. 1573), La Santísima Trinidad (est. 1584), and Santa Catalina (est. 1624), which housed classrooms run by the nuns within the convent complexes, made up the difference for female education.

Nunneries and their schools had reached the peak of their popularity, and thus the zenith of their occupancy, at the end of the seventeenth century—precisely when census takers were knocking on city doors to gather information for the Numeración of 1700.[10] A full one-fifth of the city's female population lived in religious houses, and the census placed the populations of the individual female *conventos grandes* in Lima at anywhere from 300 to more than 1,000 individuals. Unfortunately, it does not list the ages of convent residents, but a close look at one of the city's largest conventos grandes gives us some idea of who inhabited the cloisters. Of the 1,041 female inhabitants of the Monasterio de la Concepción, only 251 were professed nuns of the black and white veils, who, by order of the Council of Trent, were required to be at least sixteen years of age.[11] Younger girls could enter the convents in any other capacity—as seglares or novices, servants or slaves, or donadas.

Given the wide age span of convent inhabitants, the "aristocratic pyramid" of female religious life was based not only on caste and class. It was also formed on the basis of generation. Not surprisingly, social hierarchies inside the nunneries conformed to the most "natural" model of authority: the family. Monastic life was filled with family metaphors. Nuns were "brides of Christ," "mothers," and "sisters." The family ordering of convent life could take genealogical as well as generational form. Families developed long-standing financial and spiritual relationships with certain convents, and daughters, aunts, nieces, and grandmothers of elite lineage created "family clusters" in their convents of choice.[12] Thus many girls entered monastic houses with their cousins and sisters, and others came to be cared for by older adult female relatives.[13]

Beyond being bound to the orders through biological kinship, girls who had been raised in the convents as servants or orphans also became part of the imagined kin of the nunneries. In the *autos de ingreso* (acts of entrance) for novices and donadas, nuns made special note when the petitioner had been raised in the convent. Because these young women were already part of the imagined clans of the orders, the nuns consistently stated that it was especially appropriate (*conveniente*) that they be formally accepted into their novitiates.[14]

The most common ages at which seglares entered convento grandes such as Santa Catalina were between seven and twelve years.[15] Many of these girls came to the convent for an education and spiritual training and left when they were old enough to marry.[16] Others, even the very young, entered to become nuns. Because the Council of Trent condemned the practice of forcing girls younger than sixteen to enter convents, these little novices had to officially announce their intentions.[17] Eight-year-old doña Clara de Roxas y de las Montañas walked through the doors of Santa Catalina in 1628 with her fifteen-year-old sister, apparently with plans to take the black veil. In accordance with the Council of Trent's regulations concerning the ages of entering novices, the nuns of Santa Catalina asked Clara to testify upon entrance that it was, in fact, her volition to join the convent, just as all older novices would. The nuns reported that the little girl answered yes.[18]

In addition to the female youths who entered to learn, to profess, or to conserve their virtue until marriage, nuns also raised infants and toddlers of both sexes in religious institutions. During an inspection of Santa Catalina conducted in 1695, Madre Leonarda de San Joseph listed ten children under age seven living in the convento grande. As we shall see shortly, she may have been underrepresenting the number of young children in the convent. Her report nevertheless can serve as a brief typology of the kind of children growing up in the city's cloisters. She counted three nursing daughters of female slaves belonging to nuns, one "white girl" being nursed by another slave, and three four-year-old slave girls, each, respectively, belonging to nuns of the Ordoñez, the Prieto, and the Riasocia families. She also counted two elite children. One was a granddaughter of a professed nun; the other was the niece of a gentleman named don Luis Roxas, who probably had a family or financial connection to the Dominican sisters.[19]

Madre Leonarda, in short, listed some children related to monastic families by blood but also a substantial percentage of very young slaves. In fact, the majority of infants and toddlers populating the cloister usually were slaves and nonwhites. During an inspection of Santa Clara also undertaken in 1695, the *subpromotor fiscal* of the convent found twenty-three children between the ages of one and six living in the convent.[20] Of these children, only seven were white (and thus called *niños* and *niñas*). The rest were children of some degree of African descent, who were referred to with diminutive forms of their racial categories. Among the "mulatillos" and "sambitas," six were slaves.

Some of these children of African descent seem to have spent all of their time in the cloisters, but as one portera of Santa Clara testified, other nonwhite children came and went freely from the convent. A coterie of three or four "mulatillos y negritos" slept in other residences, entering the convent in the daytime either to serve the nuns or to spend time in the company of their mothers. Another nun stated that four "little slave girls" (*esclavitas*) between the ages of two and five regularly trotted into the convent in the morning but left at midday.[21] As these small children entered and exited from the side door onto the Calle de Santa Clara on the far northeastern border of the city, the noise and playful activity they generated surely distinguished the female religious houses from the more solemn all-male monasteries in the city, where children, female slaves, and servants were far more scarce.

During inspections, nuns also identified some children who spent all day in the convents. They referred to many of these children simply as slaves or servants belonging to the black-veiled inhabitants of the convents, without reference to the presence of biological mothers living among them. It is difficult to believe these children—some of whom were infants, while others were as young as three and four years of age—performed services for these women. Nuns, instead, seem to have viewed raising slave or servant children as a labor exchange, albeit one that favored the adult women. The women provided children "education" or "indoctrination" in return for future service. Doña María Ferrer of Santa Catalina engaged in a typical exchange. She petitioned for license to keep an Indian servant in the convent, explaining that her parents had given her the *chola* "in order that I might indoctrinate her and be served from her" (*se serviese de ella*).[22]

Indoctrinating servant and slave youths in Christianity, as well as educating them in the less spiritual arts of needlework, cooking, and fetching, was a wise use of the nuns' time, for it ensured them good, perhaps even loyal, service when slaves and servants became adults and the nuns grew to be old women. Yet, as nuns "mothered" some of these children, they also seem to have nurtured an intimacy with them at times strong enough to inspire them to sign freedom papers. For example, in 1665 a black-veiled nun of the convent of La Purísima Concepción freed the infant daughter of her slave, Valentina, who, she reported, "has born me a *quarterona* named Juana [who is] the age of one month, and for having been my good slave and because I raised [Valentina], and as a consequence of being grateful to her for her service, I am paying her by conceding liberty to her daughter."[23]

Little Juana was born to a slave woman living in the cloisters, but many infants of all races came in alone, entering quite literally through the walls of a convent. Abandoned infants, known as *expósitos*, were passed to the care of nuns on a large revolving tray built into the convent gate for receiving packages. These little children usually appeared on the *torno* in the dark of the night. A good number—although it must be stressed not all—were the illegitimate offspring of adulterous or extramarital unions, abandoned in order to prevent the public scandal and shame they would bring their parents, especially their mothers.[24] Nuns sometimes knew of the "scandalous" origins of these children but never revealed them publicly so long as parents financially compensated them for keeping their secrets and quietly raising their children.[25]

Yet not all expósitos came surreptitiously into the convents under the cover of darkness. Sometimes they entered via the foundling home of the Casa de Niños Expósitos, also known as the Casa de Niños Húerfanos or Casa de Nuestra Señora de Atocha. In her count of the children living in Santa Catalina in 1695, Madre Leonarda mentioned that a slave nursed a "white girl" in the convent. It is likely that the slave was working as a wet nurse, either for an elite family or for the foundling home, which hired lactating women to nurse abandoned infants in exchange for a weekly stipend. Other female foundlings from the Casa received charity from city benefactors who supplied the dowries necessary for them to enter convents and profess as nuns. Such was the case with three foundlings who together entered Santa Catalina in 1703 as novices. All carried the tell-tale surname Atocha—derived from Our Lady of Atocha, the patroness of abandoned children—which marked them as foundlings as though it were their lineage.[26]

Surviving relatives or other guardians also turned to the nuns for help raising youths whose parents had died, as did the uncle of Jacoba Gomes Calderón in 1705. He asked the nuns of Santa Catalina to care for his orphaned niece because, as he said, he could not afford to support her and his four legitimate children at the same time.[27] Orphans like Jacoba found themselves at a disadvantage when being reared in a relative's home. If times were economically tight, certain kinds of blood became thicker than others, and young kin not considered part of the immediate family would be sent away to live in institutions such as nunneries.

Thus colonial limeños counted on the women in religious institutions to provide alternate families for children as diverse as elite maidens, slaves, foundlings, and orphans. This reliance served a gendered function as well as an economic one. Priest and alcalde ordinario of Lima don Andrés Flores de Parra claimed that he had taken in the orphan doña Ana Flores "to do service to our Lord." In 1668, however, he had decided to turn to the Dominican nuns for help in raising her. "You will raise her much better in said convent than in my house," he reasoned, "where there is no other woman who might care for her (la asiste) than the slaves in my service."[28] The implication was that nuns could better care for a young girl than could a man—or, more accurately, than could a man's female slaves.

Don Andrés may have believed that the nuns were especially well suited to care for elite female children. But boys—although fewer in number than girls and often younger—also inhabited the cloistered female world of convents. In 1695 the nuns of Santa Catalina claimed a least three boys living among them, all under age five. The childhood history of Antonio Aliaga, a black orphan in La Concepción, gives us some idea of how little boys could end up living among the nuns. Antonio's mother, a slave, initially had raised him. When she died, he passed to the guardianship of his mother's owner until she was killed in the earthquake of 1687. Antonio was then packed off to live with a priest, who later placed him in the nunnery.[29]

The frequency with which children were circulated through the convents began to alarm ecclesiastical authorities almost immediately after the institutions had been founded. As early as 1631, archbishop Fernando Arias y Ugarte complained that Lima's convents had become more nurseries than nunneries, and he ordered that girls younger than eight years be sent back to "their mothers or persons who brought them."[30] Several decades later, don Melchor de Liñán y Cisneros, who from 1678 to 1681 served simultaneously as archbishop of Lima and the viceroy of Peru, enthusiastically relaunched the campaign to expel children from female monasteries and set his sights on wet nursing practices in the cloisters. He issued a series of orders barring all children younger than seven years from religious houses, and he specifically expelled nursing infants from observant convents.[31] Liñán y Cisneros in part expressed annoyance at the disturbances that crying infants and frolicking toddlers created within institutions ostensibly dedicated to silent reflection. But he also provided another rationale: "Repeated edicts have ordered the Mother Abbesses and the rest of the Prelates and Nuns in the convents of this city to allow neither girls nor boys to be raised in them, because of the grave disadvantages which follow from [this practice], as much in the observance and the state of Religion as because the continuation of their rearing diverts the love that [the nuns] should have for their Husband."[32]

The nuns were not willing to surrender their children to the secular world so easily. That Liñán y Cisneros was forced to reiterate Archbishop Arias y Ugarte's prohibition more than a half-century after it was first issued reveals how intransigent the nuns could be in holding on to children in the convents. In fact, during the 1695 inspections of Santa Catalina and Santa Clara, nuns provided conflicting testimony concerning the number of children in the monastic houses, with almost every nun offering a different count.[33] The nuns' insubordination would continue into the next century. In 1755, ecclesiastical officials throughout Spanish America again sought to expel children from female religious institutions.[34] Following the ruling, the *provisor* of Santa Clara required Abbess doña María Luisa Galindo to provide a list of all children younger than twelve years old living in the convent.

She provided a count of thirty-six children—all girls of some degree of African-descent aged ten years and younger. But the abbess could not let the matter pass without pleading with him to rethink his plan to expel the children. "I cannot fail to place into Your Illustrious Lordship's consideration the torment and pain that it occasions me to see the nuns so anguished and afflicted to make these sacrifices," she pleaded, "which is why I beg Your Illustrious Lordship to feel the pain of these poor women and use your mercy and [do] the will of God."[35]

The prolonged tension between church authorities and the nuns over the issue of convent children revealed a struggle over women's material and generational power within the nunneries. As we have seen, children's presence in the convents was tied to a series of economic activities within the cloisters. Raising future novices would eventually generate dowries when the girls professed; raising illegitimate children would bring quiet financial recompense from parents who wished to keep the existence of offspring a secret; slave children themselves were considered property and were, logically, a valuable source of labor; female servants and slaves nursed infants in the convent for a wage. Perhaps the nuns' desire to keep children in the cloisters was rooted in preserving these various forms of income. But the arguments made by both Abbess Galindo and Archbishop Liñán y Cisneros at the end of the seventeenth century revealed another, less material side to the debate.

The abbess's pleas to the provisor of Santa Clara conveyed the nuns' deep emotional attachment to these children. In turn, the archbishop's concern that cloistered women's love for children might conflict with their love for their "husband," Jesus Christ, suggests that church officials found this kind of emotion to be subversive to the proper gendered ordering of convents. In renouncing family life, women who took holy vows, in theory, were bound to submit themselves completely to male authority, that of both a male god and the male church hierarchy. Ecclesiastical officials regarded the nuns' mothering as dangerous because it endowed women with an authority that vows of chastity were supposed to strip from them. The nuns, for their part, were determined to continue actively participating in the colonial politics of social reproduction.

The nuns would even oppose lay inhabitants of the city in order to keep children in the convents. Because the walls of religious institutions were sturdy barriers to the reach of secular authority and blocked the nuns' lives from public scrutiny, colonial adults who wanted to conceal children found nunneries to be ideal hiding places for them. As a result, throughout the seventeenth century, the nuns periodically found themselves embroiled in disputes involving the children living among them. And sometimes the nuns themselves were the instigators of conflict.

Historian Luis Martín describes the case of a girl kidnapped and put in the convent of La Santísima Trinidad against her mother's wishes as having "no parallel in the long history of colonial nunneries."[36] However, such incidences were not altogether unusual. The nuns sometimes defied the wishes of children's own families in order to retain children under their power. In 1642, eight-year-old doña Catalina Rosada was the object of a complicated dispute between two grandmothers; one was a maternal grandmother, and the other was her stepmother's mother, who litigated with the permission of the girl's father.[37] As we saw in Chapter 2, during this period most civil legal activity over minors of age was nominally between men. Secular judges were unaccustomed to hearing custody cases between women, and it was obvious in the decision in this case. The judges of the Real Audiencia sought to rule in favor of Catalina's father, but because the dispute clearly was between the grandmothers, they came up with a Gordian solution. They awarded custody to Catalina's maternal grandmother, doña María de la Paz, who lived in Lima, with the stipulation that she turn Catalina over to her father, who lived in the northern coastal town of Ica, who would place the girl with his mother-in-law. But rather than comply with the court's decision, the maternal grandmother, doña María, entered young Catalina, fittingly, into the convent of Santa Catalina.

Once Catalina was in the convent, the nuns refused to turn her over to secular authorities. The scribe charged with the case reported that the mother superior dismissed him when he came to get Catalina, telling him "she had asked the little girl if she wanted to be a nun, to which she responded 'yes.'" The scribe was then sent on his way. When the news of Catalina's hasty religious vows reached Ica, the girl's step-grandmother was indignant. Filing a complaint with the authorization of her son-in-law, she demanded that the ecclesiastical court use its authority to force the abbess to turn the girl over to secular officials, pointing out that "at such a young age she cannot be a nun according to the Holy Council of Trent, nor does she possess the capacity to make [such a] choice." The scribe returned to the convent only to face incompliant nuns yet again. After putting him off with claims that the girl was on spiritual retreat, the nuns finally stated that they would not turn the girl over until more testimony was taken in the case.

These nuns restaged their delaying tactics by refusing to submit a young woman to her family seven years after the incident with Catalina, when a widow attempted to remove her stepdaughter from the convent because she could not afford to pay for her upkeep as a novice or the dowry required for her to profess as a black-veiled nun. The nuns dismissed yet another court scribe sent to the convent, blocking him from speaking to the abbess because, the portera explained simply, she was "indisposed." The abbess eventually was censured for turning away a representative of ecclesiastical authority and finally gave a statement to officials. But she showed little remorse when she alleged that the widow was hiding assets that could be used to keep her stepdaughter in the convent.[38]

In both instances, the nuns might have been staging valiant efforts in defense of the novices' right to choose a cloistered life in the service of God. But nuns sometimes kept children in convents for far less noble reasons. They retained youths in their service until a debt was paid, or more frequently, they disputed the free status of the children raised among them.[39] Within a spiritual economy of slave emancipation, colonial slaveholders often extended liberty to their young slaves only as long as they remained in service to the convents, opening a unique arena of legal disputes between slaves, relatives, and nuns.[40] Ana de la O's former owner had granted freedom to both Ana and her daughter, María, with the stipulation that María would achieve emancipated status only if she remained with a nun in the convent of Santa Clara. Yet in the eighteen years since this concession of conditional liberty, Ana stated, the nun had blatantly disregarded her daughter's freedom by treating her as her slave. Ana did not want to withdraw María from the nunnery, since this would only raise perplexing legal questions concerning the young woman's free status. However, she did attempt to ensure that her daughter was treated as a free individual within the convent walls. If the nun did not acknowledge her daughter's liberty, Ana warned that she would have to remove her from the convent, and "there will be a beautiful young woman exposed to the dangers of the secular world (*el siglo*)."[41]

Conditional liberty thus translated into precarious freedom for former slaves who had been emancipated as infants but were forced to grow up in the city's nunneries. The vague distinction in the social reproductive process of exchanging "education" for "service" among nuns and nonwhite children also contributed to confusion about the free status of many of the convents' children, especially for those being secretly raised in the cloisters. In 1663 Feliciana Salinas, the illegitimate daughter of a slave woman and an elite man, petitioned the ecclesiastical court to force her aunt, a nun in Santa Clara, to recognize her as a free person rather than to continue treating her as chattel. She testified that her father had placed her in the convent so the nun "might raise me and educate me as his daughter." The nuns could be as evasive of legal authorities in cases involving youths they considered to be slaves as they were in their battles over girls they wanted to see profess as black-veiled nuns. When served with notice of Feliciana's suit against her, the nun initially refused to appear, claiming she was sick.[42]

The nuns' dogged displays of defiance when confronting church officials and family members suggest that they regarded their role in rearing Lima's youths as a defensible privilege. They clung to their role as "mothers" just as tenaciously as they worked at preserving the caste distinctions of the larger colonial world inside the convents, and they viewed their generational superiority over diverse castes of colonial children as natural. Within the cloisters, under the nuns' watchful eyes, children learned the skills that allowed them to fulfill their caste destinies: refined young ladies were raised in the moral seclusion of recogimiento; elite novices brought money to the convents and guaranteed loans to preserve the economic status of their families; and servants and slaves were bound through fictive kinship bonds to a lifetime of servitude to their female masters. Thus the intimacies created between castes in the small living spaces of nuns' cells did not dissolve the hierarchies of colonial society; they reinforced them.

The same was true in terms of gender hierarchies of the city. In fact, convents were spaces that exposed the inherent tension between women's gendered subordination and generational superiority in the patriarchal family model. We might imagine that, because convents were female spaces, nuns were free to redefine elements of the colonial patriarchal order, such as marriage and family, and to create what Martín once called "islands of women."[43] But rather than redefine family, nuns replicated generational forms of authority inside convents. From the nuns' perspective, the presence of children was more than appropriate to the proper order of convents. Indeed, it was necessary. As was shown in Chapter 1, a mother's authority over children was implicitly accepted as legally valid within the hierarchical family order only as long as it did not conflict with that of the padre de familia or slave master. An adult woman's generational authority was a functioning element of patriarchy, contingent upon but separate from men's control of women. In the end, it was this aspect of the nuns' child rearing activities that most troubled church officials, since their generational power over children distracted them from their gendered role as submissive brides of Christ.

Because the nuns' mothering involved not only nurturing but also controlling convent children, as well as their education and their labor, it should come as little surprise that it occasionally provoked clashes with the lay inhabitants of Lima as well as church officials. Yet, critically, none of the litigants who brought suit against nuns over their children used the repeated ecclesiastical prohibitions against child rearing in convents to argue that children did not belong there. Instead, most provided specific reasons, such as economic hardship or mistreatment, to justify their decisions to remove children from the cloisters. Only the nuns' repeated evasion or outright refusal to follow secular legal protocol spurred their ire. During the period 1650–1750, most lay limeños seem to have shared an almost unshakable conviction that convents were proper places for raising children, even in the face of official attempts to limit the presence of youths in female spiritual houses.

EDUCATION AS CONQUEST:
THE COLEGIO DEL PRÍNCIPE

Just as the reproduction of colonial hierarchies relied on celibate, cloistered women to assume the role of mothers, so too did priests assume the role of fathers to Lima's children. Nowhere was male participation in the colonial processes of social reproduction more pronounced than in the Spanish missionary project to convert and "civilize" the indigenous populations of the Americas. We may recall Richard Trexler's "hegemonic ploy" described in Chapter 1—the imperial ideology through which Spanish colonials "cast nations as generations," and placed the king in the role of patriarch of the Americas.[44] This ploy extended beyond discursive pretext. It involved concrete and organized efforts, particularly on the part of that most familial of holy orders, the Franciscans, to hispanicize a generation of Indian youths through internment and conversion. It was, as one historian of the Franciscans in Mexico writes, "education as conquest."[45]

Research on sixteenth-century mestizas in Peru has shown that institutions such as the *casa recogida* of San Juan de la Penitencia in Lima and Santa Clara of Cuzco—a combination convent, orphanage, and school—were the first Peruvian experiments in "education as colonialism."[46] One step chronologically behind the early colonizing efforts of the Franciscans in Mexico, these institutions nevertheless kept pace with their general spirit. Efforts to educate the maiden daughters of Andean noble women and Spanish conquistadors were patriarchal political ventures aimed at instilling Spanish culture in the first truly colonial generation of women.

Institutionalizing mestizas in order to teach them buenas costumbres, or the proper, "civilized," and Christian behavior of the Spanish upper classes, was a gendered practice in which women were singled out as key figures in the establishment of a colonial elite in early Spanish America. Young mestizas were at times wrenched from their Indian mothers to be entered into recogimientos and convents. But we should not conceive of the institutionalization of colonial youths as a practice only involving women and girls. The internment of mestizas was but a phase in a longer series of colonial enterprises that targeted youths of noble indigenous blood, whether that Indian blood was mixed with Spanish blood or not, and whether the youths were male or female.

92   Institutions for Child Rearing

In a string of royal orders issued during the first decades after conquest, the king fretted over mestizo children whose Spanish fathers had been killed in the civil wars that plagued the postconquest Andes.[47] As we have seen, in Lima panic over wayward or vulnerable mestizo youths led to the establishment of schools and institutions as well as the creation of an official guardianship post, the Defensor de Menores, which placed Spanish men in control of the wealth they inherited. As court-appointed guardians took over management of the children's property, the children themselves also were personally "remedied." Mestizo boys were to be placed in productive apprenticeship posts or schools, and girls were to be sent to "virtuous houses."[48]

This royal concern with protecting and controlling mestizo children distracted official attention from Indian children, leaving the task of teaching *buena policía*, or Spanish Christian political civility, to local Spaniards. These Spaniards, however, sometimes used their educational mission as a ruse to force Indian children into servitude in their homes and estates.[49] In the early seventeenth century, royal officials addressed this neglect and again turned their attention to the institutionalization and education of Indian youths. As with the establishment of the colonial post of the Defensor General de Menores, inheritance again was the central issue driving royal officials to institutionalize colonial children. However, by the seventeenth century, the legacies that royal officials sought to control in children's names were more political than monetary.

The establishment of the Colegio del Príncipe—a school for the sons of Indian nobility that was also popularly known by a variety of names, including the Colegio de Hijos de Caciques and the Colegio del Cercado—reflected a reawakened interest in hispancizing young native leaders in order to nurture their loyalty to the Spanish state. The school had been in the making for decades, but Indian uprisings in the sierra in the early 1600s, including one in Huarochirí, just east of Lima, made Spanish officials skeptical about the success of the first thrust of colonial missionary efforts.[50] The viceroy Francisco de Borja y Aragón, the Príncipe de Esquilache (1616–21), decided that the time had come to transform plans to establish schools for Indian nobles, formulated almost a half-century earlier, into a reality.[51] When the first twelve students entered Lima's Colegio del Príncipe on New Year's Day in 1619, officials openly expressed their hope that the school would curb apostasy and rebellion in indigenous communities.[52] In fact, a jail for Indian "idolaters" operated next to the colegio for years.

In addition to being part of the wave of extirpation campaigns that rolled through the Andes in the first decades of the seventeenth century, the founding of the Colegio del Príncipe was designed to assert state power over the archbishops and the regular clergy of Lima.[53] Although run by the Jesuits, the Colegio del Príncipe ultimately fell under the authority of the state. The *fiscal protector general de los indios*, an official of the Real Audiencia, was charged with making periodic visits to check on the students and to evaluate their education. The symbols surrounding the school were designed to highlight the power of the Spanish crown. Twelve, the number of students initially enrolled by the viceroy, held symbolic power, since it was the number of Jesus' apostles as well as the number of legendary Franciscans who first entered Mexico. This was perhaps a subtle suggestion that the efforts of the regulars were failures and that state officials had to reinitiate them. The official uniform of the students was planned with exquisite care to highlight the power of the students' royal benefactors. The cacique scholars were clad in Spanish-style garments, and they wore sashes bearing a silver emblem emblazoned with the coats of arms of the kingdoms of Castile and Leon across their chests. Below this appeared the coat of arms of Viceroy Príncipe de Esquilache himself, for whom the school was named.[54]

The cacique pupils thus bore sartorial symbols of the colonial state, and the Spanish crown eventually paid their tuition as well. According to viceroy Francisco de Toledo's original plan for the school, each student was to receive a "royal" scholarship of 114 pesos annually. The source of these scholarships was, however, the local Indian community treasuries, or *cajas de comunidad*. By the early seventeenth century, officials began to realize that requiring bankrupt Indian communities to pay for the Spanish education of their future leaders might engender some resentment, and they devised new plans "so that they send [the students] with more pleasure and ease."[55] Ultimately, the funds for the colegio came in the form of loans derived from creative financing through the Caja General de Censos, a branch of the royal treasury holding income from liens.[56]

The school's constitution required the pupils to live apart from their families and villages. Students entered the colegio around the age of ten and remained until they were old enough to marry or inherit their positions of community leadership. They were restricted from leaving the school, which faced the busy plaza at the heart of the Indian district, except with permission from the viceregal government or to attend one of the many public functions in the city square as a group.

Inside the school, these noble Indian pupils lived a cloistered life and followed a daily schedule synchronized to Spanish Christian time. The youths were to pray upon rising from and retiring to bed, to hear mass daily, and to confess regularly. While the Jesuits would be free to establish the students' curriculum, the priests were specifically commissioned with teaching the students to read and to write, especially so that they could read *vidas*, or spiritual biographies of saints, and could serve as "living examples of Christianity and virtue for their subjects and the rest of the Indians." The constitution even regulated the food that the students were to consume, meal for meal, including holidays. The one exception to a diet primarily comprised of Spanish dishes made of fish and bread was a serving of potatoes at the midday meal. The Andean staple was to be served "as much because they are in the habit of eating it, as in order that they do not lose [the habit] when they return to their lands."[57]

The school, in sum, was designed to teach the boys to "conduct themselves civilly like Spaniards in all things" (*en todo se procedan políticamente como los Españoles*).[58] In order to inculcate buena policía, the pedagogical rule of the day was to require unbending acceptance of teachers' authority (*magister dixit*). Lessons could be enforced with a paddle if necessary, for as the old Spanish saying went, "*letra entra con sangre*" (letters enter with blood).[59]

Yet for almost a century and a half, the viceroy's grand hispanicizing aims for the school continually met with a more tempered reality. Twenty years after its establishment, the school reached a record enrollment of 22 students. Soon, however, the number of matriculated pupils dropped to an average of between 10 and 13. In 1700, 14 students boarded in the school, but during other years, only 1 Indian child lived among the Jesuit priests in their house on the Plaza del Cercado.[60] In addition to declining enrollments, the pupils' social status dropped as well. Over time, the Jesuits increasingly drew students from the lower ranks of the Indian political hierarchy, and it appears that the school even began to admit indigenous urban commoners. As the number and rank of the students dropped, the quality of their education also gradually diminished. Although the school for Indian nobles theoretically was to be run in a manner similar to the other Jesuit schools of *primeras letras*, the quality of education had declined by the turn of the century to such a point that it lagged far behind other schools in the city.[61]

By 1762 the school had so departed from its original design that its very purpose was called into question. Don Manuel de Gorena, a minister of Lima's Real Audiencia and judge of the Caja General de Censos, argued to the viceroy that the school had run its course and should no longer benefit from state funds. Rather than an institute of learning, he claimed, the colegio had become little more than a private residence where the Jesuits indoctrinated common Indians from the Cercado. The Indian youths in the colegio, he proposed, instead should take lessons in the public classroom (*aula pública*) that the Jesuits also operated out of their monastery.

After receiving Gorena's statement, Viceroy Manuel Amat y Junient (1761–76) asked the Jesuits to justify their right to continue educating the boys. Much like the abbess of Santa Clara who was required to defend the presence of children in her convent in 1755, rector Manuel Josef de Pro focused his elaborate arguments on the emotional and political reasons the school existed. De Pro avoided touching on the economic benefits that running the school afforded the Company of Jesus and made no mention of the many haciendas they held in the name of the school.[62] Instead, he argued that although there were only four students in the Colegio del Príncipe, these pupils still needed exhaustive education in a "Christian and political life." Any Indian living in the provinces, he reasoned, could learn to read and write sufficiently. The purpose of the school was not simply to instruct the students but to transform them politically and culturally. According to the Jesuit, such a civilizing effort should not be administered by a "foreign hand" (*mano agena*) but properly should be the handiwork of the priests, who supervised the youths with "the diligence that a padre de familia would exercise."

There was something explicitly colonial in de Pro's reference to priests as padres de familia and in the way he contrasted the Jesuits' paternal authority to the foreign hand of their native communities and their own parents. He conveyed in no uncertain terms the generational nature of the ongoing colonial project to civilize Peru's indigenous inhabitants. He was also clear in expressing his conviction that the royal state was ultimately responsible for carrying out this project. He reminded the viceroy that the students of the Colegio del Príncipe wore the uniform and the coat of arms of the king, "which signifies his special protection." In his conclusion, he appealed to the "zeal of Your Excellency and the truly Paternal Love that these miserable Indians deserve."[63]

The viceroy ruled in favor of the Jesuits, and the colegio remained open. Ultimately, the logic for the existence of a school such as this had little to do with the number of students it matriculated or even the efficacy of Jesuit efforts to educate their pupils. (Indeed, Gorena reported that one student failed miserably when asked to demonstrate his ability to write.) Endowing a great multitude of caciques' sons with an education on a par with that offered to the Spanish nobility never had been the true purpose of the Colegio del Príncipe. Rather than a Spanish-style school, it was a paternalistic project that removed

Indian children from their parents and communities in order to produce successive generations of hispancized, "civilized" local indigenous leaders.

Underlying the argument in favor of the Jesuits was a suspicion that the intimacy that developed between the father-priests and future native leaders still served as the crucial emotional adhesive that could bind Indians to the Spanish crown. That the viceroy ruled to keep the boys with their Jesuit fathers indicates that he deemed it still necessary to separate Indian youths from their own communities and families. The colegio's symbolic role in colonial social reproduction and its ongoing efforts at education as conquest were, in the end, more important than offering its students an "education" in a strict sense. In ratifying the rhetoric of paternal love between the priests and their pupils, the viceroy revealed a basic colonial fear: centuries after conquest, the Spanish Father King still had not truly won the hearts and minds of the native inhabitants of Peru.

DOING THE JOB OF PARENTS:
THE CASA DE NIÑOS EXPÓSITOS

During the early seventeenth century, Peruvian officials and elites were preoccupied with transforming their capital into a city that could rival the best urban centers in Catholic Western Europe. Establishing schools and convents would not be enough; the city would need a foundling home. In 1602 Luis Pecador (Luis the Sinner), a wealthy, elderly blind man who had dedicated his life to works of piety, petitioned the king for permission to found such an institution in Lima. His mission was to institutionalize "orphaned" infants who had been left at the doorways of churches and private residences, and in the streets. "We even have retrieved them from manure heaps," he claimed, "and other times they have been found eaten by dogs and in the rivers and aqueducts."[64] The horrifying image Pecador painted in his petition inspired the king to quickly approve the establishment of Lima's foundling home, the Casa de los Niños Expósitos. A *cofradía*, or religious brotherhood, was created for its financial oversight in the same year, and in 1605 Paul V issued a papal brief providing final authorization.[65]

Infant abandonment was by no means a social problem exclusive to Spain's colonial cities. In fact, the practice of "exposing" children dates back to Western antiquity. One historian has argued that the common Western European term for abandonment, "exposure" (*expositio* in Latin; *exponer* in Spanish) did not convey vulnerability, as would a direct English translation. Instead, it simply meant "putting out of the home," without any attendant sense of placing an infant at risk.[66] Whether or not danger to a child's life was involved, through the centuries Western European parents unable or unwilling to care for a child for any of myriad reasons would follow well-established patterns of disassociating themselves from their offspring. They placed their children in the care of others, dropped them at the door of a church or the home of a wealthy neighbor, or simply left an infant to meet his or her fate on a city street or country road, hoping a charitable individual might stage a rescue.

From the end of the Roman Empire through the Middle Ages, exposing children fell into some disrepute as a social practice. Medieval Catholic moralists began to associate infant exposure more closely with sinful sexual activity or parental irresponsibility. Yet none specifically condemned parents for deserting children or envisioned a social world in which exposure would not take place.[67]

Spanish laws concerning abandonment conveyed a similar sense of resignation about the inevitability of the practice. The *Siete partidas* indirectly failed to condemn parents who abandoned children in that it charged only parents who possessed sufficient economic means with the legal responsibility to raise and provide for their own children.[68] In a seventeenth-century treatise on secular and ecclesiastical law, Machado de Chávez summarized the conventional stance on abandonment the following way: "It is a general rule that when parents are oppressed by necessity, or when their lives or honor are in danger, and they expose children at some Hospital, or at outside doors (*puertas agenas*), they in no way sin, because they do so in this manner so that the child is not in danger."[69]

By the time Machado de Chávez wrote, the "outside doors" of Spain and its colonies were becoming especially crowded with abandoned children. The number of infants left at Seville's foundling home, for example, had increased tenfold during the early decades of the century.[70] It was in this context that *sevillano* Luis Brochero published his 1624 tract, *Discurso breve del uso de exponer los niños* [Brief discourse on the use of exposing children], in which the author addressed the question of who held responsibility for raising abandoned infants.[71]

Synthesizing earlier authors' positions on the matter, Brochero asserted that the church, the king, and the republic all shared responsibility for rearing children who had been orphaned or abandoned. Drawing heavily on Roman notions of the emperor as *pater patriae*, he traced the king's responsibility for these children to his political role as a father to his kingdom. Brochero cautioned the Spanish monarch that the title "padre de la patria" should not be mere "vanity" or simply a "trophy of power." Instead, the designation commissioned the king with guardianship of all children of the republic, especially expósitos.[72] This, Brochero claimed, was "a principal work" of monarchies in Spain and throughout the world. In practical terms, this meant that every member of a kingdom should assume a role in rearing abandoned or orphaned infants. Brochero interjected into his discussion a universalizing claim that, to a large extent, shaped the social world of child rearing throughout the Spanish empire: all Spanish subjects were responsible for caring for children in need, Brochero told his readers, simply because "they are your children" (*pues son hijos suyos*).

The belief that child rearing was not the sole responsibility of children's biological parents but, instead, was a joint spiritual and civic effort uniting all members of the Spanish empire under the Father King served as the ideological frame around which foundling homes in cities such as Seville and Lima were built. These "hospitals" for exposed children were created with the express purpose of providing a salutary, sanitary, and secret option for parents who wished to abandon their children.

Thus, Luis Pecador's gruesome description of Lima's discarded children being devoured by dogs in the streets, which is often repeated in modern histories of the founding of the Casa de Niños Expósitos, must be placed within this larger context of civic preoccupations and Christian notions of charity.[73] In early modern cities with staggering rates of infant mortality, concerns about a proper death and burial followed immediately on the heels of birth. There was no more grave disregard for the spiritual well-being of (Christian, white) individuals than to allow them to die in original sin, only to have the bodies in which they were to be resurrected torn apart by beasts. Just like Pecador, Brochero also described unbaptized, abandoned children ravaged by dogs in the streets of Seville.[74] In 1712, Cuba's *casa cuna* reportedly was founded to prevent parents from throwing their children in wells or abandoning them in the streets "so that dogs would tear them apart and eat them," and the viceroy of Río de la Plata evoked similar images when he created a foundling home in Buenos Aires in 1779.[75] Behind the repetition of this centuries-old trope lay a warning about a Christian kingdom's duty to secure babies' spiritual success in the next world. It tells us not that cruel parents tossed their children to the dogs in colonial Spanish America but, instead, that the spiritual welfare of infants was a major preoccupation of the era.[76]

When Pope Paul V approved the request to establish Lima's Casa de Niños Expósitos, the pontiff expressed a special concern with the infants' baptismal state, and this concern extended into the parishes of the city.[77] Only twenty years after the casa opened, the priests of the Parish of the Cathedral, in whose religious domain the foundlings fell, complained that the cofradía allowed priests of other parishes to baptize and bury these children. City inhabitants who removed infants from the casa also carried the babies to their own parish priests to receive the sacrament of baptism and, sadly, sometimes returned for last rites and burials only days later. The priests of the cathedral parish, frustrated that other parishes were collecting fees and creating confusion about whether the children had been baptized, insisted on performing sacraments for these children free of charge.[78]

Aside from the issue of spiritual control over administering sacraments to children abandoned at the casa, the responsibility for financing the foundling home was split among various entities, including private individuals, the church, and increasingly, the state. Each member of the casa's cofradía was to contribute 30 pesos to the institution every year on the day of Saint Thomas. In addition, the casa was a major recipient of legacies left in wills by many of Lima's inhabitants. The testaments contained in the city's colonial civil cases give the impression that orphans and foundlings—especially white, female orphans—were among the most popular beneficiaries of elites' charitable legacies throughout the colonial period.

The casa also obtained regular financing from the royal exchequer. In 1637 the foundling home began to receive, by order of the viceroy, a quarter of the annual royal intake from the property income from the Teatro de las Comedias.[79] As the number of children abandoned at the casa grew, the institution's resources tightened, and the state was forced to provide relief. By 1671 Viceroy Conde de Lemos had alerted the king that expósitos were dying in record numbers; wet nurses had to nurse three or four infants at the same time because the number of children inside the foundling home had so increased. This prompted the Council of the Indies to donate 250 pesos a month to the casa from the Ramo de Sisas, a branch of the royal treasury derived from taxes on agricultural products.[80] Shortly thereafter, the earthquake of 1687 struck, leaving the casa in shambles. The children ate in a roofless dining hall for decades after, and this prompted even greater investment on the part of the state.

Foundling home officials barely held on to their institution as the earthquake literally shook the foundation of the casa, but once the tremors passed, another crisis loomed. At the beginning of the eighteenth century, Lima was in the early stages of a demographic explosion. This swelled the number of impoverished inhabitants, which consequently filled the cradles of the casa with more babies. As the casa's director reported in a request for even more state funds in the early eighteenth century, the occupancy of the casa was soaring "as much because of the misery of their parents as because of the increase in city inhabitants (*vecinos*)."[81] The first Spanish Bourbon king, Philip, underscoring what he viewed as the especially critical task of caring for "recently born" infants, ordered Peru's viceroy Marqués de Castelldos-Rius (1707–10) to increase funding from the royal treasury, "since, to the contrary, it would be necessary to close the casa."[82]

The casa did not shut its doors, however, and Lima's inhabitants continued to abandon their children at the institution throughout the eighteenth century. They did so for reasons of both honor and economics. Ann Twinam's exploration of illegitimacy throughout colonial Spanish America has demonstrated the connections between infant exposure and gendered codes of sexual honor for colonial elites.[83] María Emma Mannarelli's study of illegitimate children in Lima in the seventeenth century also shows that exposure hid a high incidence of extraconjugal sexual relations among elites. On the basis of the rate (54 percent) with which the designation of *padres no conocidos* (parents unknown) appeared for español children in baptismal records from three of the city's parishes, Mannarelli suggests that the phenomenon of exposure was predominantly, although not exclusively, "white."[84]

Yet the correlations between caste, illegitimacy, and abandonment, which were undoubtedly strong, should not lead us to view infant abandonment as only a product of sexual codes of honor among elites. Elsa Malvido's study of infant abandonment in Tula, Mexico, in the late seventeenth and early eighteenth centuries shows that, among the Indian peasantry, rates of abandonment were tied not to church proscriptions against sexual activity outside marriage but to agrarian economic cycles.[85] When the director of Lima's foundling home linked economic misery and population increases to rates of abandonment circa 1712, he indicated that, as in Tula, some of the city's expósitos were simply victims of their parents' dire economic circumstances.

In the end, because the backgrounds of the majority of expósitos were, by definition, shrouded in secrecy, it is difficult to assess the degree to which economic and demographic factors interacted with cultural mores concerning sexual relations and, in turn, affected rates of abandonment and baptism. Rather than tracing the reasons for exposure to either cultural or material causes, perhaps we should note that colonial subjects themselves were far from unanimous in their opinion about whether infant abandonment was due to promiscuity or poverty. This is because a sizable number of children in the foundling home did not seem to be the offspring of elite parents who were struggling to maintain family honor.

In theory, the casa was established to serve primarily español and Indian children. In practice, however, it admitted children of all castes. Its constitution nominally "prohibited" the acceptance of "negros, mulatos y *zambaigos*"—all groups of African descent—yet it recognized that children of these racial categories might turn up at the door of the foundling home nonetheless. To reject these infants, its constitution stated, would constitute an "inhumanity." They were to be admitted, fed, clothed, and taught to read and write, and they were to accompany the other children of the casa in public burials or processions. But girls of African descent could stay in the casa only until they were nine years old, and then they were to be deposited in a casa recogida or convent to serve, submitting any earnings to the casa until they reached age twelve. Male children who appeared to be of any degree of African descent were to be admitted, but after age fourteen they were to be turned over to an artisan or to the infantry, where they would serve until they were twenty. Later, the constitution was amended so that boys would remain in the employment of their outside patrons until age thirty, a stipulation that placed these youths in a kind of indentured servitude for their adolescence and most of their adult lives. This amendment also meant that parents who exposed a free child who might be labeled "black" or "mulato" would be committing their children to a period of slavery.

Constitutional statutes concerning children of African descent differed from those concerning Indians. The casa's director was allowed to place indigenous youths in apprenticeship posts or in casas recogidas without official intervention by the corregidor or the protector de indios. But he was also charged with periodically checking on these youths to ensure that they received honorable upbringings and were given the appropriate religious education. The constitution provided no such insurance to youths of African descent.

From the time it was founded until the late eighteenth century, the casa therefore provided cradles, wet nurses, and an education to a diverse array of colonial children. Entering the institution in numbers between 30 and 170 in a given year, foundlings were placed under the control of an abbess, learned rudimentary reading and writing, and spent their days employed in a workshop, where girls would sew and boys were occupied in handicrafts.[86] Yet while the building itself could serve as the home to more than fifty children at once, the goal of the casa was not to raise the children inside the institution but to find individuals who would take the children into their private residences. The casa's budget provided women 8 pesos a month to nurse and raise the children until they were weaned. For nonwhite children who had reached the age of about eight years, the ultimate goal was placement in a school, an apprenticeship post, or domestic service. Thus the ordinary, often poor, inhabitants of Lima who lived outside the casa assumed much of the responsibility for rearing the *botados* (literally, little cast-asides), as the children were popularly known.

The lives of some of the little girls who were withdrawn from the foundling home can be reconstructed from their petitions to enter Santa Cruz de Atocha, the school for white foundlings that operated beside the casa. These petitions serve as short biographies of the abandoned children and chronicle their circulation through various homes until they petitioned to once again become institutionalized as adolescents. The sixty-six expósitas whose applications for admission to the school are examined here, it should be noted, are not representative of all of the female foundlings left at the casa. Santa Cruz de Atocha, run by the Holy Office of the Inquisition, was exclusive. In order to enter the school, the girls had to meet three criteria: they had to be españolas, to have been baptized, and to be "true orphans," that is, to have never met their parents and to possess no information about them.[87] Upon exiting the school, these girls would qualify for dowries so that they could "take state" (*tomar estado*) as nuns or wives. These petitions therefore cannot tell us what happened to male children or nonwhite children left at the casa's door. Neither do the girls of Santa Cruz represent the scores of elite children who were nursed and nannied by hired amas de leche. Nevertheless, their stories showcase the two facets of colonial child rearing that we have seen in formal institutions such as convents and the school for Indian noble youths: intense emotional bonds developed between adults and children who were not kin, but these affective ties could not bridge the social distance of colonial hierarchies.

An ironic feature of the history of childhood in colonial Lima is that high rates of child mortality, rather than thwarting emotional attachments to infants, often created affective bonds between hired wet nurses and foundlings. The strong grief associated with the loss of an infant inspired many women to offer their services to the foundling home. When María Navidad's baby was stillborn, her friend mestiza Mariana Gamboa took María to the casa. There María served as the godmother to a baby girl and later took the child home to raise her until the age of seven.[88] The motives for replacing a dead infant with an abandoned child or an orphan were physical as well as emotional. One woman had removed an infant from the casa "because the boy child that she gave birth to had died, and it caused illness in her breasts."[89]

In addition to emotional relief for grieving mothers and physical relief for lactating women, the casa also provided economic relief to the city's poor women. Lorenza de Zavalla, an Indian emigrant, reported that she had arrived in Lima with few skills to earn a living in the city. Presumably because Lorenza had recently given birth, a friend informed her of the potential to earn a wage by nursing an abandoned infant from the casa. The newly arrived woman frankly stated that her decision to nurse one of the foundlings derived as much from her desire "to practice charity as to gain the small stipend" that the casa provided.[90]

Removing a baby from the casa did not necessarily mean the ama de leche committed herself to raising a child into adolescence. Over a third of the sixty-six petitions for entrance into Santa Cruz report that the girls were dispatched from one adult to another, and many traveled serpentine paths of custody during the first decade of their lives. In the eleven years before Paula de Atocha Ynclán petitioned for entrance to the school, she had circulated through a number of living situations. Originally raised by a mestiza woman who later died, Paula was returned to the casa. The nuns of the Monasterio de Descalzas then removed her again. After a one-year stay with the nuns, Paula fell into the custody of "one Chepita Honores," a woman who was apparently so indigent that an affluent española named doña María Ynclán was "moved by charity" to take the girl from her.[91]

In a period when rates of child mortality in European and Latin American foundling homes could climb to 80 percent and almost never dropped below 40 percent, the frequency with which the casa's botadas reported that their wet nurses passed away speaks to the inescapability of death as a factor in colonial child rearing.[92] If, like Paula, an abandoned infant were lucky enough to survive, she might still have to face the death of her caretaker before reaching adolescence.[93] In other cases, girls suckled by slaves would be passed on to the slaves' owners when the slave was sold away from the city.[94] Thus the insecurity of slavery and the pervasiveness of death among wet nurses made arrangements between caretakers and botadas unstable, creating an environment where various adults shared responsibility for these children.

The poverty of many wet nurses also contributed to child circulation. When wet nurses transferred custody of the botadas to other adults, they usually did so after the girls had been weaned and the casa had stopped paying them a stipend. It is difficult to determine how many girls were returned to the found-ling home after they finished nursing, but the petitions make it obvious that amas de leche often looked to private individuals to take over the girls' upbringing. In many cases, the individual was a friend, relative, employer, or master of the wet nurse, usually a woman. These caretakers consistently reported to school officials that compassion and a desire to perform an act of charity (*limosna ordinaria*) had moved them to raise the girls without recompense.

In some cases the "charitable" actions of elite women actually veiled practices associated with what Ann Twinam calls "private pregnancies."[95] Elite parents saved themselves from public scandal by passing their illegitimate children through clandestine networks, sometimes to nuns and sometimes to the care of servants or slaves. In such situations, exposure might begin at a foundling home but eventually channel children into the residences of relatives and friends of their biological parents. Some children even ended up back in the homes of their own parents, who would claim to be raising these "orphans" as an act of private beneficence.

Yet it should be remembered that many women who could not have been the mothers of foundlings also claimed that they took children from wet nurses as an act of charity. It was not uncommon for these new guardians to express an only partially veiled disgust at the conditions in which the botadas had been raised. As in the case of Paula de Atocha, who was taken in by a doña because of her custodian's poverty, the city's elite inhabitants often removed girls from the care of poor or slave families.[96] But plebeian families, too, took over the work of rearing the botadas. When a servant from the Monasterio de la Encarnación had finished nursing little María de la Asención, a free mulato mason named Thomás Aquino Santa Cruz, "seeing the neglect (*poca asistencia*) and vulnerability (*desamparo*) in which María de la Asención was kept," took her into his home.[97]

The constant circulation of foundlings and the instability of their makeshift families did not seem to translate into emotional distance between abandoned children and the adults who raised them. Colonial custodians commonly spoke of the "great love and affection" that the foundling girls inspired in them (*el mucho amor y cariño que me cobró*).[98] Amas de leche expressed particularly deep emotion for the children they nursed, often by pointing out that they had been present when the infant's umbilical cord fell off. It is possible that this was a culturally significant moment, an early rite of passage, but most likely it conveyed the idea that the wet nurse had been present in the child's life since only very shortly after birth, a fact that seemed to carry a great deal of sentimental weight.[99]

Perhaps predictably, affection grew even stronger the longer the girls stayed with their custodians. If they did not return the girls to the foundling home after weaning, wet nurses and other custodians stated that it was because the emotional bonds between adult and child made giving the girls back "not worth it" (*no tuvo valor*), meaning not worth the potential emotional anguish returning them would cause. The adults saw themselves as foster parents— perhaps even adoptive parents[100]—to the girls. Manuel Loyasa, a *tintorero* (dye specialist) from Huamanga, and his wife, mulata Melchora de los Reyes, raised María Josefa del Sacramento until age eleven, in his words, "doing the job of parents."[101] Others reported that, in providing for the girls' education and care, they were raising them as though they were their own (biological) children (*como hija suya*).[102]

Despite custodians' professions of "great love and affection" for the botadas, when stipends ran out, economic pressures could strain sentimental attachments. Single women, whether slave or free, who decided to keep the girls past weaning would have to stretch meager daily wages often insufficient to support even themselves. Many of the women who sought to enroll girls in Santa Cruz expressed deep regret for not being able to support their charges any longer and clearly stated that poverty alone was the reason that they were forced to return the girls to institutional care.[103] They were often not exaggerating the indigence the girls would face if they were not admitted. Paula de Atocha y Molina spent the first eleven years of her life begging on the streets with her *zamba* wet nurse, Rosa Molina—at times soliciting alms alone because of Rosa's frequent illnesses.[104]

Marriage could relieve economic pressure on a poor single woman raising a foundling, since a couple, particularly if childless, had more resources to support an orphan than did a woman alone. Although free black shoemaker Juan Antonio de Echenique considered returning Severina de Atocha y Echenique to the foundling home once she stopped nursing, the "great love and fondness" that he and his wife had developed for the girl sapped their "courage to separate her from our company."[105] He proudly reported that he continued to raise Severina respectably for eight years and was even able to pay for a tutor (miga) to provide her education. In fact, Severina had become so much part of their family that she took Juan Antonio's last name, compounding it with "Atocha."

On the other hand, marriage might endanger a botada's position within a reconfigured family. Many of the humble men and women who raised Santa Cruz's foundlings professed to love the girls as their own children, but when they had their own biological children, the demands of raising a child not their own, particularly one that merited special care and education because of her higher caste standing, could become too onerous. Twelve-year-old María del

Carmen testified in 1777 that an Indian woman named Petronila Martínez had raised her since shortly after her birth. However, Petronila had since married a local barber and no longer could "contribute to my support and instruction with the zeal and care that she had when she was unmarried . . . since she directs all of her attention to the assistance of her Husband and Children, and to this is added the assembly of journeymen and apprentices in the Shop."[106]

María del Carmen indicated that living in this large artisan household put at risk the status her whiteness might otherwise afford her, for she claimed the economic "straits" of the family imperiled her "decency" and might "spoil" her "customs." María's fears of losing her precarious foothold on status in Lima's social hierarchy were telling. Affection could not surmount the social distance between nonwhite ama de leche and white expósita. Wet nurses and other custodians may have filled the "office of parents," lovingly rearing these abandoned girls and treating them as if they were their own daughters. Yet the girls who petitioned to enter the school of Santa Cruz de Atocha—and the plebeian and slave adults who often cared for them—realized that no amount of financial sacrifice or emotional attachment could provide them with what the school offered: the possibility to "tomar estado," to take a position as a member of the racial elite in Lima's colonial society. In the end, some strangers could never be the same as sons.

CONCLUSION:
THE COLONIAL FAMILY RECONSIDERED

The family indeed was the nucleus of colonial society but not because most parents reared their children in their private homes. Instead it was a working metaphor through which the adults and children of colonial Lima, even those who lived in institutions, understood and articulated intergenerational relations of power and ties of affection. As we have seen, adults as diverse as nuns, priests, and elite women expressed their authority over the city's youths through a language of generational authority—an authority based not simply on age but also often on colonial notions of caste superiority that were naturalized according to a family model. The Jesuit priests who educated Indian youths, for example, came to see themselves as their pupils' true padres de familia, while nuns battled church officials to keep children living among them.

In accordance with Luis Brochero's image of a proper republic, a diverse array of colonial elders performed the king's paternal work as they did the job of parents, providing for young urban inhabitants economically and facilitating their entrance into adult society. But doing the job of parents did not necessarily mean that caregivers bequeathed to these children their own social status. The affection child rearing created between Lima's generations in convents, schools, and foundling homes did not blur caste and class distinctions. In fact, these bonds ultimately served the demands of colonial control. Nuns who raised slave children benefited from their wards' labor; the Jesuits acted as fathers to Indian noble youths in order to thwart native political and religious rebellion; plebeian wet nurses turned the abandoned babies they nursed back to institutions in order to protect the girls' social standing as racial elites in colonial society. Thus, Lima's institutional child rearing practices ultimately ensured that children would occupy positions appropriate to their caste and gender when they became adults.

In short, limeños generated colonial differences through cross-caste intimacies inside institutions. This was the nature of social reproduction in Lima. Still, child rearing practices designed to reproduce colonial hierarchies and to maintain order were not fail-proof. Some youths rebelled against adult authority and defied social norms; others found themselves vulnerable to violence and disorder even within their own homes. For many of these youths, the long arm of criminal law would replace the webs of household and institutional authority that fixed their place in colonial society. It is to the subject of how the criminal court system dealt with these minors of age that we now turn.

Minor Offenses

Youth and Crime in the Eighteenth Century

I n many ways, Lima's foundling homes, schools, and religious houses functioned to enclose children, sealing them off from the streets outside.[1] But even while adults raised children or benefited from their labor inside the city's institutions, private residences, and workshops, these sites were not fortresses, and they could not contain all of the city's youths. As Alberto Flores Galindo put it, for many of Lima's children, the most important centers of colonial socialization were the "neighborhood, the street and the alleyway."[2]

One afternoon in 1782, while the sun descended behind the building of the Cabildo, a young española ambled through the cobbled streets around *plaza mayor*, which were always crowded with vendors. She had ventured out in search of a pair of stockings. Stopping at the market stall of a fourteen-year-old español for her purchase, she exchanged the requisite pleasantries with the young merchant. When she reached into the purse she carried strung around her neck, she discovered she had been robbed of 56 pesos. The culprit, it was revealed, was Josef Tunco, a youth between ten and twelve years old, who had hidden beneath the stall and furtively emptied the bag while the customer and young merchant chatted. An adult bystander detained Josef and turned him over to nearby "ordinary justice," as the Cabildo's police and judiciary were called, and he was deposited in the public jail only steps from where he had committed his crime. Inside the interrogation room, the *sala de crimen*, Josef confessed not only to this robbery but also to a series of purse snatchings perpetrated against other young girls who walked through the plaza alone.[3]

Young Josef Tunco's misdeeds draw our attention to institutions where we may not expect to see colonial children: jails and the criminal courts of the Cabildo and the Real Audiencia. This chapter analyzes the interactions between the colonial criminal justice system and minors who were victims and suspected perpetrators of crimes. An examination of medieval Spanish laws concerning criminal legal minority, commentaries from eighteenth-century elite publications, and criminal cases heard before the lower-instance court of the Cabildo and the high court of the Real Audiencia reveals how legal categories and juridical discourses came to life as youths faced colonial officials in interrogation rooms and prisons.[4]

Observation of the laws in action in the city's eighteenth-century courts shows that age was of critical importance to colonial officials as well as to the ordinary inhabitants of the city. Most importantly, youth served as a universal criterion for awarding suspects the benefits of legal protection. But relatively simple Spanish laws about age and crime often worked themselves out in a more complex colonial reality. The court protections afforded to minors of age collided and combined with colonial socio-racial, class, and gender hierarchies, particularly those derived from unwritten normative regulations concerning honor. Even when, at the end of the century, intellectual shifts in the concept of childhood and new ideas about the state's role in reforming youths began to infuse legal discussions of youth and crime, Lima's courts continued to dispense privileges and punishments to minors according to a distinctly colonial logic.

LAW AND PUNISHMENT
FROM THE HOME TO THE THRONE

Fathers possessed, as an element of patria potestad, the right—even the moral and civic obligation—to punish their children. In fact, moralist Machado de Chávez asserted that fathers sinned if they refrained from "boldly correcting" their children's "excesses and vices."[5] But a patriarch, he said, should never be "excessive" or "unjust" in his punishment of subordinates, whether slaves, wives, or children. The right to punish children did not consist of *castigo atroz*, which referred to extreme corporal penalties or capital punishment, because such punishment could be handed down "only [by] the Judge, who enjoys public authority within the Republic."[6]

Machado de Chávez's commentary brought into relief several tensions in

Spanish criminal law. The first was the contingent nature of a father's authority in reining in wayward children. It was the public authority of judges on whom the maintenance of Spain's organic, civil order ultimately rested, and they alone possessed the ability to inflict death or physical suffering on criminals for the good of the republic. But judges, no different from fathers, were to temper sentences with moderation and a spirit of paternal correction, especially in regard to youths.[7] The king and his judges, then, were to be both paternally benevolent and supreme disciplinarians.

Laws treating minors, who were considered the most worthy of paternal treatment at the hands of judges until legal categories were created for Indians, most pointedly highlighted the contradiction between the merciful and the punitive character of the colonial criminal justice system. Individuals under age twenty-five were unique beneficiaries of court paternalism in criminal law and enjoyed special legal protections when accused of crimes. These included the right to the assistance of a legal guardian (curador ad litem), who would provide bonds or otherwise administer financial matters for the minor, and the assistance of a legal advocate in court (*defensor*). In Lima, both roles commonly were taken up by a procurador (legal expert for hire) or an abogado (court-recognized attorney) named by the judge to represent the minor in court proceedings. In principle, legal representation by a lawyer was afforded to all accused individuals under age twenty-five, regardless of sex, natal status, or race. But Spanish law did not regard all minors of age as equally culpable for their actions. Criminal responsibility varied according to age, and sentencing was calibrated to social rank.

Children younger than ten and a half years were not to be tried for criminal actions.[8] The *Siete partidas* did not offer an explicit rationale for this, but the common belief, based on the Roman concept of *dolix incapax*, was that small children were incapable of the combination of malice and regretful recognition of wrongdoing (*dolo*) necessary to be held accountable for their crimes. Legal commentators and moralists generally attributed this lack of criminal accountability to children's absence of moral understanding rather than to a paucity of intellect and reason, as would be the case at the end of the eighteenth century.[9]

After age ten and a half, youths entered what one legal expert called "the age of discretion." Then youths began to discern "good from bad, just from unjust," although they still lacked a perfect understanding of the morality of their actions.[10] This intermediate stage was explicitly recognized in Spanish criminal law. Between the ages of ten and a half and seventeen, youths could be charged and tried for criminal actions, but they were not to be sentenced as adults.

Again, the *Partidas* failed to detail the underlying reasons for mitigating the sentences of minors of age, stating only that sentencing should be left to the discretion (*arbitrio*) of judges and stipulating that minors' punishment should be "lighter than that [given] to older individuals who commit the same infraction."[11] In failing to prescribe specific punishments for crimes committed by minors, the *Partidas* allowed magistrates to draw from local custom and individual circumstance rather than binding them to codified law. Individuals between the ages of seventeen and twenty-five no longer merited lenient sentencing but continued to receive the advocacy of a court-appointed lawyer.

The idea that minors held limited criminal responsibility overlapped with a general body of Spanish criminal law based on the ranked privileges of certain members of society. According to the *Siete partidas*, sentences for crimes should vary according to the social and civil status of the convicted, for judges "never should crudely punish the slave as he would the free, the lowly man as he would the hidalgo, the young man as he would the old man, the servant as he would the hidalgo or other honored man."[12] Preferential sentencing was consistently upheld in legislation for the American colonies, buttressing and, in turn, reinforced by the color/class hierarchies of colonialism.[13]

Thus, in Lima's criminal justice system, the privileges of legal minority had to compete with the privileges of caste and social class. Neither laws nor legal commentators offered a solution for cases in which the theory of preferential sentencing conflicted with legal entitlements derived from the youth of a criminal suspect. These ambiguities in the laws on minors allowed each generation of Spanish subjects, and each dominion in the Spanish empire, to interpret legal codes according to its own social values and perceived needs—in other words, to determine whether the king would be a clement father or a stern disciplinarian. Lima's judges, lawyers, and young victims and suspects did exactly that in criminal trials throughout the eighteenth century.

THE CASES

To be arrested in colonial Lima meant, first, that the *alguacil mayor* (sheriff) would draw up an order calling for the seizure of a suspect's person and property. Suspects then would be detained and locked in a humid, dark cell in the royal prison or public jail. There they would await, often for months, the opportunity to deny in a formal interrogation (*confesión*) the charges that the police, neighbors, and strikingly often, their own friends and families had leveled against them. The interrogation was officially launched when the suspect was questioned about his or her identity: name, ethnicity, origin, occupation, and age. If the suspect reported that he or she was under age twenty-five, the interrogation would be suspended and a lawyer and guardian were named to the case. The lawyer then was required to be present in the sala de crimen to support the client during questioning and to file subsequent petitions and arguments.

Surviving Cabildo criminal records, which span the years 1714 to 1813, contain the dossiers of 336 people who were arrested for crimes in the city and brought before the first-instance court of the Cabildo. Ninety-nine of the individuals detained by the Cabildo during the period—just shy of one-third of the total—were minors of age. Given the connections modern investigators have established between youth and crime, this percentage may not strike us as unusual. But we should recall that the association between youth and crime is a historical construction. In Western Europe the conventional wisdom that youths were inclined to delinquency, and even the concept of juvenile delinquency itself, began to emerge only during the last decades of the eighteenth century.[14] Therefore, the number of minors who confronted the courts of the city as suspected criminals is remarkable, even when we take into account the fact that the Cabildo was a first-instance court and many of the crimes it tried were petty infractions. If we add to this the number of youths who appeared in court as victims of or witnesses to crimes, the proportion of youths who had direct interaction with the colonial legal system becomes even more significant.[15]

Alternate Forms of Punishment

Certainly not every minor who broke the law could be found awaiting sentencing in the deplorable conditions of the city jails. There were undoubtedly many more juvenile delinquents than those whose cases wound up in the historical record. Many young lawbreakers would never be caught, and others were deemed too young to be formally prosecuted. Still more, particularly those implicated in less serious crimes, could have been dealt with extrajudicially by colonial officials or might have been turned over to their parents, guardians, or masters for punishment. It is also easy to imagine that many conflicts between youths—fisticuffs, petty thefts, and childish pranks—were taken to be of moral rather than legal consequence and were simply handled by parents and guardians without appeal to legal officials.[16]

Laws specifically established for the New World, however, demonstrated a royal preoccupation with controlling precisely those youths who lacked adult supervision. A string of Spanish kings expressed concern that the colonies would attract vagrants and "incorrigibles," namely Spaniards and mulatos, who might live among indigenous populations and exploit them through crimes and deception. Vagabonds were to be forced to learn a trade, while incorrigibles were to be banished to military outposts in the Americas, the Philippines, or Africa.[17] In the sixteenth century, the growing concern with mestizo orphans in the Americas was also worked into the law, and over time, the term "orphan" would become analogous in many ways to "vagrant."[18]

As we have seen, Lima's officials detained these orphans and rootless youths throughout the colonial period, sometimes serving only as labor brokers for them, but at other times as judge and jury. Indeed, it was not unusual in other colonial capitals, such as Mexico City, to find adolescent delinquents placed in artisans' workshops without a formal trial.[19] When the alcaldes of Lima carried out similar sentences, they often acted as "fathers of all minors" by committing boys to several years of labor and learning with an artisan who held the right to physically punish and detain the youth. During the Bourbon years, the state's anxiety about errant youths extended from the transient and orphaned to include the simply poor and mendicant. Lima's new *alcaldes de barrio* (neighborhood police officials) were ordered to step up a campaign against vagrancy and pauperism by seizing any beggar's child over age five and placing the child with a master artisan.[20]

Punishment through apprenticeship was an option for parents as well as local officials. For example, the mother of thirteen-year-old Manuel de la Cruz Veleban committed her son to "six forced years" (*seis años forzados*) in a tailor's workshop in 1796.[21] Parents also used a variety of other colonial institutions to punish youths, even when the youths had never been formally convicted of crimes.[22] Marcelo Matunano's parents had city officials incarcerate him in the Presidio of Valdivia, witnesses stated, "in order to rein him in from certain youthful pranks (*mocedades*)."[23] Slave minors who gave their owners trouble might be placed in *panaderías*, the infernal bakeries of the city, where they would work side by side with slave adults who had been sent there by master and judge alike. Workshops, panaderías, and presidios would be the destiny of youths from the bottom of the colonial social hierarchy. As we saw in Chapter 2, the parents of obstreperous español boys would make reformatories out of monasteries.[24]

The Strategic Ambiguity of Age

In spite of such informal solutions for the punishment of youths, young limeños nevertheless found themselves facing the law through the bars of cells and testifying before colonial officials. Cases reaching the Cabildo and Real Audiencia offer us a wealth of information about legal attitudes and practices concerning minors, subjects who had legal grounds to demand the benevolent paternalism of colonial judges. Yet a caveat must be made concerning the statistics derived from the extant criminal cases brought before the "ordinary justice" of the Cabildo. The Cabildo criminal series, like much colonial documentation, is incomplete. Entire years as well as an unknowable number of individual cases are missing, and paperwork often abruptly ends just before a sentence was handed down, leaving no trace of information about whether the suspect was freed or hanged. But the Cabildo cases are a complete series, and while they do not offer solid numbers of arrests and sentences, they do allow impressionistic statistical analysis of crime and youth in the viceregal capital. When read with the cases from the Real Audiencia, they permit us to look through the bars of the city's jails and gain an unparalleled view of the daily lives of youths, how they became involved in crimes and perceived their own actions, and how the courts enacted their paternal responsibilities.

The first general pattern that can be gleaned from the surviving Cabildo cases is that youths could not always avoid formal encounters with the law by relying on informal mechanisms of punishment, such as placement in a workshop or monastery. Almost a third of the total number of suspects processed were minors of age, and teenagers between ages sixteen and twenty comprised almost 20 percent of suspects arrested.

While determining the age of a criminal suspect was a standard part of legal protocol, officials in Lima did not always follow prescribed practice.[25] In 29 percent of individual arrests—that is, in 103 cases—the age of the accused was not noted. Where ages were registered, almost 42 percent of the suspects were minors of age, and 65 percent of the individuals arrested were under age thirty. This suggests that the determination of age was not a mechanical gesture on the part of officials but, instead, was practiced, at least in part, with the intention of ascertaining whether the suspect was young enough to merit special treatment and, above all, the advocacy of a court-appointed lawyer.

Nevertheless, the Cabildo only reluctantly provided suspects the benefits of legal minority. In fact, eschewing their role as protectors, court officials took advantage of the fact that many inhabitants of the city had no idea exactly how

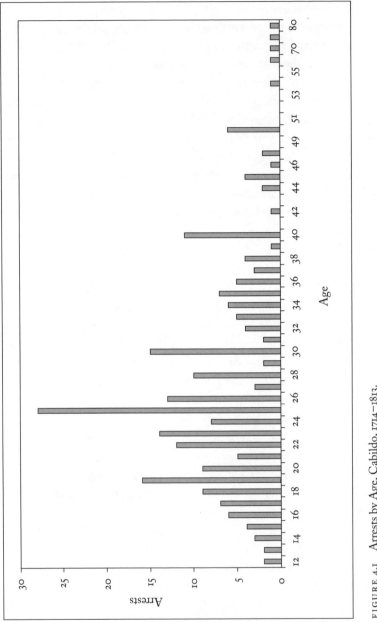

FIGURE 4.1 Arrests by Age, Cabildo, 1714–1813.
Source: AGN, Cab., C. Crim.

many years they had been alive. Suspects whose origins were at best distant memories or who had no kin in the city who could recount the stories of their births—such as *bozales*, or first-generation African slaves, and Indian immigrants to the city—were especially vulnerable when they had to report their ages. In these instances, the court scribe, in the presence of the alcalde ordinario, would simply assign ages to suspects based on their appearance (*al parecer* or *por su aspecto*). Frequently, ages were given as rough approximations, such as "between nineteen and twenty years old."

It is not difficult to imagine that this process could be highly subjective. Court officials tended to round ages to five- and ten-year intervals. What is more, as Figure 4.1 demonstrates, suspects time and again conveniently appeared to be twenty-five or "twenty-five years or more."[26] Thus, in assigning ages, officials frequently prevented suspects from receiving special juridical consideration and left them without legal counsel unless they qualified for that of the protector de indios or—and this was less probable—the protector of the poor.[27]

Perhaps predictably, suspects often reduced their own ages in their testimony in order to garner lenient sentencing or the counsel of court-appointed advocates. Seventeen was the magic number in many of these cases, since judges could impose regular sentences on convicts after they reached this age. When the slave Bernardo Tagle was arrested for breaking and entering with the intent to burglarize in 1772, he reported that he was sixteen years old. However, his baptismal certificate disclosed that he was over twenty-two.[28] In response to suspects like Bernardo, the *agente fiscal*, the equivalent of a crown attorney, spent considerable energy challenging the criminally accused over the issue of how old they were. But he, too, could find such a strategy backfiring in a city where so few defendants knew when they had been born.

The agente fiscal's first line of legal attack in the homicide case against don Tomás Loiaza de Quieroga was to argue that the suspect was older than seventeen. In 1728 don Tomás shot and killed his playmate, slave Juan Esclavo, as Juan waited to be given his daily tasks in the receiving room of the house and panadería of Tomás's mother. Claiming to be fifteen years old and calling himself an hijo de familia, Tomás testified that he had accidentally pulled the trigger on a shotgun while the two friends played. The prosecutor called for Tomás's baptismal certificate to show that the suspect was old enough to incur regular sentencing. When the paperwork was presented, the crown's lawyer was foiled. Tomás had been born in 1715 and was only thirteen years old.[29]

In the event that a baptismal certificate was not readily available, prosecutors would go to great lengths, even forcing suspects to undergo physical inspections, to verify the ages of accused criminals. The court asked don Francisco de la Rua, a physician and professor of anatomy at the Royal University of San Marcos, to examine and determine the age of Juan de Torres, a free mulato from Santiago de Chile, who confessed in 1773 to a series of break-in burglaries throughout the city.[30] After delivering a circuitous disquisition concerning "Nature" and the solid and liquid properties of the human body, Dr. de la Rua finally concluded that he really had no idea how old Juan was but guessed that he was "not too distant" from seventeen years old. The physician's judgment ultimately was of little help to either the prosecution or the defense. But the fact that the court called for the medical examination of suspects' bodies demonstrates how much weight was given to precise age in legal matters and reveals how jealously court officials worked to withhold protection from accused criminals.

When certain crime victims were minors of age, the courts also became highly interested in how old they were and called for certificates of baptism and physical inspections just as they might when a suspect claimed to be under twenty-five. Many of the offenses committed against minors reaching the high court of the Audiencia were rape cases, generally perpetrated against girls or young women.[31] While some legal commentators understood the sixteenth-century law code *Leyes de toro* as prescribing capital punishment to those who raped girls under the age of twelve, no Spanish law drew a distinction between the rape of children and of adults based on age per se. Instead of age, the courts classified sexual crimes according to a complex set of gendered criteria including a woman's prior sexual behavior and consent to the sex act.[32] *Estupro* was literally taken to mean the rape of a virgin, but there existed a crucial difference between *estupro con violencia*, or rape with violence, and *estupro con seducción*, rape by means of seduction and kidnapping, known as *rapto*.[33] This typology was intended to differentiate rape from other cases in which young women were "seduced" into consensual sex or in which young couples would steal away without their parents' permission and exchange marriage promises before engaging in intercourse.[34]

In the case of the rape of a virgin, court officials regarded a physician's examination as necessary to prove not only that a "violent" rape had occurred but also that the girl had been, in fact, sexually inactive prior to the assault. When a six-year-old girl was raped by her mother's *compadre* (co-godparent), the medical examiner made sure to note that her hymen had been ruptured only recently, in case there was any doubt about her sexual purity.[35] No fewer than four medical experts examined eight-year-old *china* María Josefa de Liñán after she claimed she was raped by a boy and his father's slave when the three children played together in the courtyard of an *aposento* (complex of single-room apartments). María Josefa's mother introduced her daughter's baptismal certificate as evidence in the case without explanation. This likely was a preemptive move to prove how young her daughter was and thus protect her from the character attacks she knew would soon follow. In fact, the defense called on a variety of neighborhood witnesses to testify that young María Josefa was of loose morals (*de mala naturaleza*) and had lost her virginity eight months before the incident.[36]

We will return to this case later, but it should be noted that as her mother battled tirelessly to seek retribution from her daughter's young rapists, María Josefa appeared to be getting younger. Initially the mother referred to her daughter as seven years old. Even after María Josefa's baptismal certificate was presented and showed that she was over eight years of age, her mother continued to call her *mi hija menor de siete años*, which in Spanish can mean both "my seven-year-old minor daughter" and "my daughter who is less than seven years old."[37] María Josefa's mother may have been ambiguous on purpose. Reporting that victims of sexual crimes were younger than they were helped to portray them as more innocent.[38]

Just as parents like María Josefa's mother progressively reported lower ages for minors who were victims of crimes, defense attorneys also lowered the ages of minor suspects as cases dragged on and the youths grew older. Indeed, almost everyone played the legal game of exploiting the ambiguity surrounding age. To excuse their actions, accused rapists could counter by inflating the ages of their victims. A horrifying example is that of Justo Manrique, from the coastal city of Ica, who kidnapped and raped a five-year-old slave girl. Finding the girl bathing alone in a stream, he put her under his poncho, told her he was taking her to see her mother, and galloped north toward Lima. When arrested, Justo claimed that he had heard the girl was seven and a half years old, which would have made her old enough for betrothal according to canon law. He said he had thought it appropriate to force sex with her because, when he asked her if she wanted to marry him, she consented.[39]

Clearly, court officials were not alone in manipulating the reporting of ages in criminal cases; both suspects and accusers also altered ages in order to influence the outcome of criminal trials. At the core of this colonial age ambiguity was the state's conflicted role as protector and castigator. Logically, suspects and victims would report ages that would place them in legally defined, protected categories. Meanwhile, the courts—including the agentes fiscales, the scribes, and the alcaldes who oversaw the assigning of ages during interrogations—attempted to establish that criminal suspects were not minors of age and therefore were not entitled to minority's privileges.

The manipulation of the ages of rape victims also exposes other meanings of age in the criminal courts, and these meanings were not specifically addressed in legal codes or ad hoc bodies of law. When elders reported lower ages for the girls and suspects claimed that they believed their victims were older than they were, they were referring to an informal, gendered legal minority of sorts. Parents assumed that judges would consider girls under certain ages—usually around eight years or younger, rather than younger than twelve, the official age of female puberty—as sexual innocents. Girls entering adolescence, particularly nonwhite plebeians girls, became vulnerable to accusations against their sexual honor, and thus cases against accused rapists would be increasingly complicated. In his prosecution of six-year-old china Rosa Sánchez's accused rapist, the agente fiscal pointed out that "the rape victim is not of soiled reputation (*mala fama*), and no stain can fall on her conduct at such a young age."[40] Such a comment would seem to us to go without saying. But in colonial Lima, it could not.

Weak Patriarchs: Patterns of Arrests and Accusations

By reducing sentences or ensuring that suspects received legal counsel, criminal judges did act as protectors, however reluctantly, for accused criminals whose ages fell within the legal boundaries of minority. They also undoubtedly dealt summarily with minors accused of particularly minor offenses. Yet they were also more than willing to allow the trials of some young suspects to proceed to formal hearings. Certain groups faced Cabildo judges in these formal cases more frequently than others. Rates of arrests and formal trial in the city varied according to the sex and socio-racial status of individuals, and this was true of cases among minors and nonminors alike.

For example, white females (españolas) comprised the group least likely to be arrested in both categories. Rarely was a Spanish female of any age arrested and brought to court for a crime, and only three in total were imprisoned.[41] A married fifteen-year-old, doña María Manuela Ramírez, was the only española minor in the surviving cases who appeared before the first-instance city court, and her case was prosecuted as far as it was only because her accuser wanted to convict María's impoverished husband for facilitating his young wife's thievery.[42] It may seem, then, that by virtue of their sex, women answered to private

TABLE 4.1   Cabildo Arrests by Caste and Gender, 1714–1813
(in cases where both race and sex are registered; n=258)

	Total				Minors				Nonminors/NG			
	M	F	T	%	M	F	T	%	M	F	T	%
Español	74	2	76	29.5	19	1	20	24.1	55	1	56	32
Casta	94	23	117	45.3	30	13	43	51.8	64	10	74	42.3
Slave	39	17	56	21.7	11	3	14	16.9	28	14	42	24
Indian	6	3	9	3.5	4	2	6	7.2	2	1	3	1.7
Total	213	45	258	100	64	19	83	100	149	26	175	100

Source: AGN, Cab., C. Crim.
Note: M=Male; F=Female; T=Total; NG=Not Given

authority in the home rather than representatives of the king when they broke the law. Yet forty-five women did stand trial before the Cabildo, and more than half of them were castas. This suggests that arrest patterns were not conditioned solely by the sex of suspects but also by their racial or economic standing.

Cases involving minors of different castes diverged from criminal trials involving adult suspects in slight but telling ways. Minors of age who were white and male were arrested with somewhat less frequency than their adult counterparts. White males constituted 24 percent of the total number of suspects arrested within the minor group, compared with 32 percent of arrests among adults. Arrests of slave minors also were lower than arrests of slave adults. Slave minors made up nearly 17 percent of the minors' cases, compared with 24 percent among nonminors.

We are left, then, with two groups of minors with greater rates of arrests than their adult counterparts: Indians and free castas. The Indians who stood trial before the Cabildo were almost always minors of age. It is unclear why these youths appeared here and not before the Indian corregidor (provincial magistrate). Perhaps it was due to the types of crime in which they were implicated; the majority of arrests were for the relatively minor crimes of poaching and the illegal sale of agricultural products. It is also likely that Indians appeared before the Cabildo because they were migrants only temporarily in the city. Rather than call on the corregidor of Lima or of their provinces of origin, the Cabildo chose to deal with the crimes of these indigenous youths rapidly and, often, leniently. For example, Pedro Gómez y José García, indigenous youths from Caraballo and Huaylas, were arrested for transporting stolen mules.[43] Both were given a commuted sentence of fifteen days of public works.

The total number of Indians appearing in criminal trials in Lima is too small to allow us to draw definitive conclusions about indigenous minors and crime.[44] Nevertheless, if we turn for a moment to a sentence that Lima's corregidor handed down against an Indian minor, we glean something of the logic behind the leniency in the sentencing of indigenous criminals. In this case, a twenty-two-year-old Indian confessed to having robbed various items of clothing from a local shop. Quite significantly, the young man was represented by the protector de indios, not by a court-appointed lawyer or by the Defensor General de Menores. The protector argued in his client's defense, "Who would deny that because of my client's circumstance of double minority, due to both his age . . . and to his Indian condition (*condición Yndica*) that he should not be subject to the full rigor of the Laws but instead be treated with the greatest possible equity?" Despite the suspect's admission to having committed the crime, and with no real explanation by the corregidor, the young man was absolved of all charges against him.[45] The minority status of Indian youths was thus a compound minority that in theory afforded them the most benevolent treatment in sentencing by judges.

This leaves the castas. Poor casta minors of age had as many opportunities to commit crimes as did other groups, including young slaves. As with the free castas, the survival of urban slaves often depended on their daily earnings (jornales) from freelance labor or market activities, and thus neither group lived and worked under the constant vigilance of adult superiors. Why, then, should casta youths face the courts more frequently than slaves? The reason can be found where private patriarchal authority ended and the public power of the colonial state began, in judges' imagined role as substitute father to Lima's youths.

Just as city officials acted as "the father of all minors" when placing orphaned and vagrant youths in apprenticeships, the police and criminal judges may have been more disposed to flex their public paternal muscle in arresting and criminally prosecuting casta youths, who were assumed to be less likely to have patriarchs at home who could control and "correct" them. In seventeenth-century Lima, castas had the highest rates of illegitimacy in the city, and thus casta children would be the group most likely to be fatherless.[46] Illegitimacy and the dissolution of families also was high among Indians and slaves. But unlike Indian youths, castas did not enjoy the special privileges of double minority, which might secure them extrajudicial or lenient sentencing. Furthermore, despite many slaves' relative autonomy in their daily economic activities, judges could be certain that slave youths eventually would have to answer to private authority in the form of a master rather than a father.

The courts even seemed hesitant to hear criminal cases that involved slave minors for fear of treading on the patriarchal rights of their owners. In one case, a lawyer argued that the Cabildo had overstepped its authority in trying a fourteen-year-old slave for robbing his master. He stated that his client "enjoys the privilege of not being judicially accused . . . because he should be considered as a member of the household (*familiar*) whose punishment is to be practiced at the discretion of his master."[47]

Just as delinquent minors who came from households with strong español patriarchal figures appeared less frequently before the courts as criminal suspects, a close examination of the families of young victims of rape demonstrates that strong patriarchs were less likely to bring cases to court as accusers, as well. Of the twenty-eight cases of rape committed against minors that I identified in the Real Audiencia and Cabildo series, the majority (eighteen) were brought forward by single or widowed women, mostly but not always mothers, who were raising the girls. Even when male heads of household brought charges, almost inevitably it was revealed during the course of the trial that they were castas or were married to casta women, had been absent from their homes when the rape occurred, and/or were economically struggling plebeians. Together these cases create a composite profile of a weak patriarchal figure in families of girls who were raped.[48]

Lower-class and -caste parents often were unable to shelter their children from the streets beyond their homes; plebeian girls and boys played together in the patios of large housing complexes, ran errands alone in the streets, and worked without adult supervision. The tight quarters in which Lima's inhabitants lived could place poor girls in close contact with potential sex offenders. One day in the late 1770s a man living in an aposento near doña Hipólita Pérez ordered the woman's eleven-year-old female servant to fetch him some chocolate. When the girl returned with his request, the young man locked her in his room and kept her imprisoned for hours.[49]

But what ultimately placed girls like Hipólita's servant in the greatest danger was not the fact that they lived so close to potential sex offenders but the gendered contradictions of colonial culture. The expectation that females had to be enclosed (*recogida*) to be virtuous conflicted with plebeian economic reality. Recall the case of María Josefa, whose mother filed petition after petition to bring her daughter's two adolescent rapists to trial. Her mother poignantly summarized her plight when she warned the judge that, if he refused to levy a stiff sentence against the wealthy español youth who, with his slave attacked her daughter, such boys would prey on "all girls of such a young age, whose senses do not warn them of danger, and whose care by their Mothers, employed in providing for themselves and for them, do not permit them the [care] that those [parents] of greater means exercise with their daughters of all ages and states, which is why frequently the poor People who live in rooms or flats are reduced to seeing their tiny sons and daughters living in the streets for the better part of the day."[50]

When elders brought a case of rape and seduction to the attention of judicial authorities, they risked being accused of "prostituting" the girls in order to sue defendants for the dowry that convicted rapists were required to offer their victims.[51] Many defendants and their attorneys also alleged during the case that the victims' families were racially or class "deficient," and thus disorderly.[52] Thus rape cases ensnared the victims' mothers, fathers, and other guardians in legal thickets that often wound around their own caste, social standing, and methods of household governance rather than whether the rape had occurred.

Fathers in particular seemed to find this kind of scrutiny repugnant, for it implicitly challenged their masculinity and patriarchal authority. Perhaps this, more than anything else, helps explain the dearth of españolas as prosecuted criminals during the period and why so few strong patriarchs brought sex crimes against their daughters into the courts. Indeed, the wording in the petitions of those relatively few español men who appeared before criminal judges to accuse other men of raping or seducing their daughters indicates that they found the process to be a humiliating experience.

When español Melchor Navajas accused a mulato youth of his daughter's "seduction and corruption," he in turn also faced accusations. The defense claimed that his wife was not an española, as he had claimed, and that he, often absent from home, did not properly supervise his daughter, who habitually left her house accompanied only by her younger brother. Though he continually proclaimed his standing as "a Spanish gentleman," he was forced to concede that his daughter was not quite the elite maiden he portrayed her to be, and he wrote that "all women (well, except for the barmaids who serve at the counters of taverns) are in possession of the right (*acción*) to request satisfaction for their honors, and so for them are their fathers. . . . The rapist always deserves punishment, even if the maiden is humble."[53]

Don Melchor also warned that "if the Plaintiff (*Suplicante*) were permitted to take vengeance by his own hand, he already would have taken it. [But] he knows that such is the business of the Señores Judges, and especially of Your Excellency [the viceroy]."[54] The same mix of masculine bluster, social class insecurity, and humiliation at appearing before criminal judges appeared in a similar accusation filed by Fernando Espinosa, a peninsular from Burgos, Spain, against a young limeño named Luis Rubina. "My honor has been gravely injured," he wrote, "and although I have no noble coat of arms (if only I did!), I am at least an honorable man, and if now I have had the continence to appear before the powerful and righteous Justice of Your Highness, I could, on another occasion, compelled by this same honor, commit an act that would injure both Luis Rubina and myself."[55]

In a study of crime in late colonial Buenos Aires, Susan Socolow noted that in the very act of appearing before magistrates to report acts of violence committed against his wife or lover, a man was "publicly admitting his vulnerability, and the fact that he was too weak to seek his own retribution."[56] Such a claim is supported by the profiles of adult accusers in Lima, as the infrequent white father who pursued criminal prosecution of a daughter's rapist alluded to private, violent means of seeking vengeance when expressing deference to the public authority of the criminal courts. Instances in which strong patriarchs relied on extrajudicial means of avenging their daughters' loss of honor would have left few traces in the court records.[57] Therefore, just as the courts more frequently tried nonelite criminal suspects, nonelite girls appeared frequently in the criminal record as victims—not simply because they were at greater risk for sexual attack, but also because weak patriarchal families had less to lose when seeking the fatherly protection of judges when their children were victims of crime.

"The Bridle that Holds Them Back": Crime and Honor among Minors

Overall, youths in colonial Lima were accused of committing a full spectrum of crimes. They beat, stabbed, and shot one another, and they committed acts that might be categorized as crimes "against authority," such as the illegal carrying of weapons by nonwhites and the manufacture of counterfeit currency.[58] Minors of age were prosecuted for property crimes, such as stealing horses or breaking into churches to filch elaborate and expensive ornaments, more frequently than were their adult counterparts. But what is striking about the content of all of the cases, including property crimes, is the degree to which young suspects constructed their own statements about the circumstances of their arrests on the normative institution of honor.

Minors were seldom prosecuted for crimes based solely on slander and insult (*injurias personales*), but they nonetheless fully participated in the culture(s) of honor that so shaped the interactions of the inhabitants of colonial Spanish America.[59] While their lawyers emphasized the mitigating effect of their clients' youth on their criminal culpability, young criminals often defended themselves by asserting their social position relative to others, including adults.

Let us revisit the story of Agustín de Castro, the Spanish youth we first encountered in Chapter 1, who refused special treatment in the court system because he was a minor of age. In 1742, sixteen-year-old Agustín was arguing with a youth named Agustín de la Vega over the possession of a mule and the boundaries of his pastoral lands on the outskirts of the city. Juan José Gallardo, a mestizo muleteer, observed the altercation as he passed by on horseback and decided to get involved. Upon hearing de Castro call the other youth a *cholo*, Juan José reprehended him, saying that de la Vega was not a "cholo but a boy just like you." Such a comment not only undercut the youth's sense of manhood; it offended his racial honor by insinuating that his age was more important than his whiteness. Agustín de Castro retorted, "Look at what [trouble] the mestizo brings with him." But slighting Juan José by pointing out that he was mestizo did not satisfy young de Castro. After stewing for a moment, he mounted his horse and went to find his father. The two galloped off after Juan José. Catching up with him, de Castro stabbed the older man in the chest, killing him, he claimed, in "defense of my honor and that of my father."[60] While historians of violence in Latin America have long noted that men involved in duels often asserted generational superiority over their opponents, none has considered the results when a nonwhite elder might try to assert his authority over a younger man of higher social standing.[61] If the outcome of Juan José's attempt is any indication, giving orders or even advice to a younger but whiter man could be dangerous business.

Being older, then, did not automatically confer more honor on every individual. Neither did youth prevent limeños from trying to share in honor's benefits, or better said, in the benefits that the multiple kinds of honor, obtained through a variety of means, provided. Elite español minors—like all other castes and social groups—normally did not initiate criminal charges on their own, although they frequently sued in civil courts. Don Antonio Zubiaga, however, was an exception. He contracted a defensor to bring criminal charges

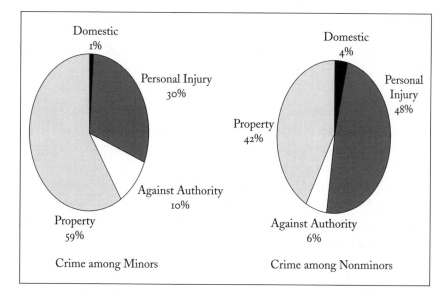

Domestic
1%

Personal Injury
30%

Against Authority
10%

Property
59%

Crime among Minors

Domestic
4%

Personal
Injury
48%

Property
42%

Against Authority
6%

Crime among Nonminors

FIGURE 4.2   Cabildo Cases by Crime Type, 1714–1813

against another youth who had insulted "his honor and good reputation" after he had lost an earlier civil claim.[62]

Plebeians espoused their own versions of an honor not based on racial purity and social precedence by birth (*honor*) but instead achieved through hard work, discipline, and social conduct (*honra*).[63] While a fourteen-year-old español named Luis de Ciudad did not use the word, his work-based honor was insulted when a master silversmith employed the youth as an apprentice rather than as a journeyman. In retaliation, Luis stole three pieces of worked silver from his patron and sold them for a profit.[64] Even male slave minors might refute allegations against them by claiming that they were honorable (*honrrado*), based on their employment and public reputation.[65]

Girls of all castes and classes also coveted their virtuous reputations and sexual purity. When the slave Simona Laredo, ten to twelve years of age, stood in the street of La Trinidad whistling for her sister to come out of her master's house so they could eat the midday meal together, she was insulted by a young black slave whom she did not know. The boy yelled, "Who the devil is this whore (*putona*) who is whistling?" "What is this, to make such an insolent comment to me, when I had never even slept with him?" Simona saucily responded when she recalled the affront. The exchange of insults between Simona and the slave boy turned into a scuffle, and several days later Simona returned to the street to defend her honor. She stabbed the boy with a knife that she claimed she carried to peel fruit.[66]

In spite of her young age, Simona believed that her honor rested on her sexual comportment, as much as it would for an elite or older woman. But the violent actions she undertook to defend her honor shared more in common with the recourses undertaken by Lima's plebeians, who appeared in court for settling their disputes with brawls and knives, than with those carried out by elite women, who were known to sue their verbal assailants for offending them but seldom appeared in court following physical frays.[67]

In Simona's defense, her court-appointed attorney asked the judge to consider not only his client's "young age" but also her "fragile sex" as proof of her lack of forethought (*menos advertencia*) and requested that the court take into account "the repeated provocation with which she was insulted by the negro."[68] A person with no honor cannot be provoked. Thus Simona's defense suggests that colonial judges would have recognized a type of honor as the legitimate possession of young slaves. But colonial officials—lawyers as much as judges— were not inclined to conceive of plebeian or slave honor as the same as the genealogy-based honor commanded by españoles. When one defense lawyer appealed a rather harsh sentence that the Cabildo handed down against his sixteen-year-old mulato client, the attorney explained, "If honor is the base of Monarchical Government, this should be understood as the greater or lesser elevation of Individuals according to their rank. The *plebe* has no glory, but fulfilling its duties, enjoys public esteem. All of this is lost . . . when a sentence is imposed that strips [public esteem] from [plebeians] and releases the bridle that holds every man back from his wicked inclinations."[69]

Although elites believed plebeian notions of honor served as the bridle that held them in their place in the hierarchical society of the Spanish empire, as it turned out, honor was also something that even the youngest city inhabitants had to defend, and it was the defense of honor that brought them into the city courts. Slave girls, by virtue of their gender, earned honor through their sexual conduct, but they avenged attacks against it by violent means not usually employed by elite white women. Plebeian boys earned their honor through "fulfilling their duties," especially by being diligent and skilled workers. In doing so, they expected adults in their trades to accord them occupation-based honor. When it was denied to them, they might, like Luis de Ciudad, retaliate by robbing their patrons.

The fact that young limeños construed their own place in the social world of Lima through the same codes of honor as did adults meant criminal judges had to levy sentences on minors with care. As the lawyer in the above appeal implied, stripping even a thieving slave of public esteem during the early years of his life would not be so much unjust as dangerous, for it would shred the developing ties of public reputation and social rank that bound all individuals to the colonial order. Without these ties, youths would careen into lives of crime. As we shall see, these kinds of arguments intensified at the end of the eighteenth century, as the colonial criminal justice system became increasingly sensitive to new philosophies about childhood and rehabilitation.

THE HANGMAN'S NOOSE OR THE SILVERSMITH'S SHOP: LATE COLONIAL PUNISHMENTS

A Spanish traveler arriving in the viceregal capital in 1738 contended that not even one-tenth of the city's population was comprised of whites, "being excessive the number of black men and women, mulatos, Indians and other such riffraff (*gentalla*)."[70] The Spaniard's remarks, though clearly exaggerated, had some foundation. Eighteenth-century censuses of the urban population in Lima reveal that between 1700 and 1790 peninsular and creole Spaniards (*blancos*) decreased from 56.5 to 38 percent of the city's population. The relative population of black and Indian inhabitants also fell. Who, then, populated the capital? It was the racially mixed group of the castas—mulatos, zambos, and chinos, as well as mestizos—that grew in number throughout the century.

In the 1700 census, the only category for people with some degree of African descent was "mulato." By the end of the century, there were at least six such categories.[71] This pluralization of categories was related only in part to the real increase in the mixed-race population of the city. From the perspective of elites, the growth in the number of free people of color in the city reflected ruptures in the colonial socio-racial order. Elites fractured caste categories into ever more specific groups in an effort to define and segregate the nonwhite population by means of classification.[72]

These fears of caste disorder coincided with the policing reforms implemented under the Bourbon monarchy. A central goal of the Bourbon Reforms was to wash Spain's cities clean of vice, crime, and mendicancy.[73] Though this campaign was born in the Spanish metropole, efforts at *policía* took on a decidedly colonial character when implemented in Lima. News of the rebellion of Túpac Amaru II in the Peruvian highlands and revolution in Haiti reverberated throughout the capital city in the 1780s and 1790s, agitating concerns over local plebeian riots and slave rebellions. Upper-class anxiety about crime and the dissolution of social control, along with seemingly ceaseless royal edicts attempting to rein in vagrancy, crystallized in a series of urban reforms. The alleyways of the city were lit with gas lanterns in order to expose criminal activity, and the countenance of local policing changed dramatically throughout the last decades of the century. A local "peace force" (*serenazgo*), demanding "voluntary" donations for new police patrols, made rounds through old neighborhoods christened with new, orderly jurisdictional names. One of these patrols included among its ranks a Lieutenant Colonel for the Prosecution of Vagrants, Thieves and Ne'r-Do-Wells.[74]

Crime in the city was thought to have reached epidemic proportions, and as Flores Galindo comments, the "popular classes and the dangerous classes" were becoming synonymous.[75] I would add that "dangerous classes" and "youth" also became equated as discourses concerning crime increasingly began to turn on the question of how criminals were made. Youth, colonials began to believe, was a particularly dangerous stage of life. One lawyer representing a minor of age voiced the common belief that criminal tendencies were forged in adolescence: "Men normally fall in the first years of their lives, when they are released from the yoke that they need to contain them," he stated in defense of his young client.[76]

On one hand, this brewing anxiety about the criminal tendencies of youth inspired judges to sentence minors more sternly. Yet at the same time, another set of discourses reawakened the tension that lay deep within medieval laws on crime and minority. Emergent Enlightenment ideas elevated childhood as a state of innocence and youth as a stage of life during which social values and practices become indelibly imprinted on human beings. These notions pulled Lima's legal officials in another direction. More than ever, magistrates were encouraged to "correct" wayward youths rather than to seek retribution for their misdeeds, since harsh sentences might turn merely troublesome youths into career criminals.

Before the last decades of the eighteenth century, lawyers usually underscored the lack of malice and forethought and the imperfect comprehension of their clients in order to argue for their reduced culpability. At the end of the century, attorneys continued using these arguments but sprinkled them with references to the "docility" and "greater reliability" (*fidedignidad*) of the young, as well as their greater potential to be "corrected" into proper subjects of the empire. The lawyer for the slave youth Simona, who stabbed a boy for insulting her, advised the alcalde that "the Law confers her . . . more docility in order to correct and reform her future actions." In another case, a lawyer openly warned the judge to "not impose a sentence that will make [my minor client] incorrigible in the future [rather] than moderate him in the present." This lawyer even took his argument so far as to deny the punitive function of justice entirely in cases involving minors, asserting that "laws [on minors] were not established for vengeance, but to benefit the delinquent himself and to ensure public security."[77]

But outside the courtrooms of the city, a new "enlightened" emphasis on education and child rearing was laying roots deep into a purely local terrain fertile with fears of fissures in the generational and racial order. Contemporary commentators in Lima's burgeoning press announced, "In Peru, youths squander their time, and achieve nothing more than ridiculous slang and few principles of Philosophy."[78] The creole periodical *Mercurio Peruano* published an article from "foreign papers" with the paranoiac subtitle, "For the deterrent of youths too accessible to bad example." It recounted the fictitious tale of a youth who, after a night of "hard liquors" and gambling, found himself arrested for a homicide that he had not committed.[79] Such were the dangers that lurked in the streets for youths who were too likely to be overcome by passions and vices. In fact, guides to child rearing counseled parents to impart moral lessons unrelentingly, even to older children, for inconsistent instruction would give rise to "those defects and pernicious evils which are the vices that are beginning to ferment" during adolescence.[80]

These articles on proper child rearing were intended to be used in the courts as much as in the city's homes. In 1790 *El Diario de Lima* issued a series of articles concerning the topic that, it was underscored, would be of as much use "to Judges" as "to the Citizen (*ciudadano*), to the Father, to the son, to the Husband, to the Wife, to the master [and] to the Slave."[81] As we will see again in Chapter 6, the wheels of justice went into high gear in the late colonial period, as courts processed a greater number of civil as well as criminal cases involving minors of age. But even though observers and writers sounded alarms about the criminal tendencies of youths during the late eighteenth century, their warnings were more imagined than real. Juvenile delinquency does not appear to have increased in any discernible manner. The total number of individuals of all age groups arrested did increase significantly during the 1780s, the decade of the most strident police reforms, but the proportion of minors among suspects tried before the Cabildo remained relatively constant during the period from 1714 to 1813.[82]

Nonetheless, frantic discourses concerning the hazards of juvenile pastimes, from dance to games of chance, smoothly combined with official campaigns against crime and elite fears of racial disorder, leaving their mark on late colonial criminal proceedings.[83] For example, one slave owner cleverly played on Bourbon concerns about vice and vagrancy when he sought a tough sentence for an eighteen-year-old mestizo named Blas Changay, who had abetted a ten-year-old slave in robbing 10 pesos from his master. Blas, the owner said, had pushed the young slave into robbery "in order to acquire by such reprobate means what he needs to spend on games and the other vices to which he dedicates himself . . . since he cannot sustain himself as a vagrant without known occupation."[84] Without a stiff sentence, he predicted, Blas would spread like a scourge through the city, encouraging other slaves to steal from their masters.

Criminal defense lawyers representing minors of age thus had to battle the coalescing image of derelict, unemployed, fun-loving youths who lacked respect for private and public authority. The public hanging of eleven crooks at once in the city square in 1772 made their jobs even more difficult: several of the thieves dangling from the ropes were minors of age. A year later, Gregorio Guido, a lawyer representing a youth accused of robbery, attempted to distance his minor client from the still-vivid memory of the public spectacle of the executions.[85] He argued, "If among the Thieves who were executed last year in this Capital there was a minor, this is because there occurred certain and true violence in the most enormous sense, and it was necessary to use the complete Rigor of the Laws for public deterrent and the tranquility and security of the Republic. And there is none of that here [in this case]."[86]

Criminal judges faced a contradictory mandate. On one side, they were besieged with the perceived dissolution of social order because youths were out of control; on the other, they faced emerging ideas about the state's role as reformer of impressionable children. Unfortunately, the incomplete nature of many of the cases thwarts any attempt to statistically analyze sentences handed down in criminal cases tried by both the Cabildo and the Real Audiencia. However, it does seem that the courts responded to the new trends in sentencing quite selectively. Some minors, such as Josef Tunco, were absolved because of "a lack of evidence," a claim that may have covered the court's decision that the youths were simply too young to provide consistent testimony even in their own confessions, and were thus too young to be sentenced.[87] This, too, was the outcome of the trial against the knife-wielding slave girl, Simona Laredo. Her master was forced to pay for the medical treatment of the boy she had stabbed, but she was spared sentencing "in attention to her minority."[88]

It is of particular interest that the alcalde who handed down the sentence against Simona referred to age and not gender as the basis for his leniency, even though her lawyer had specifically mentioned that she should be spared the full weight of the law because of her "fragile sex."[89] In only one case did a Cabildo judge mention that he had considered the sex of a suspect a reason to provide a merciful sentence, and this was the case against a white female minor of age. As with arrest patterns, it appears that caste, even more than gender, was the crucial variable affecting sentencing.

Indeed, at the end of the eighteenth century, as judges decided for whom they would act as clement father and to whom they would mete out stern discipline, they fell back on the traditional principle of preferential sentencing. To illustrate, let us compare the cases of two immigrant youths. The first was a seventeen-year-old mulato from the coastal city of Piura who had come to the city to apprentice himself out as a tailor; the other was a fifteen-year-old español youth from Buenos Aires who had no occupation. The *ronda*, a patrol set up during the Bourbon police reforms in the city, apprehended the mulato apprentice, Josef Manuel Mora, for snatching hats off the heads of pedestrians in the plaza mayor, a game that was designed to embarrass but not physically hurt its victims.[90] Upon arresting the youth, the patrol discovered he was carrying a knife. The sentence against him was severe: six years at the Presidio of Valdivia. We previously encountered his lawyer's appeal, in which the defensor argued that hard sentences turned youths into hardened criminals. The Audiencia only partially agreed in this case; its final sentence was a public whipping of twenty-five lashes and banishment to Piura. A judge added the additional warning that "under no motive nor pretext" should Josef Manuel "return to this capital."[91]

Fifteen-year-old Valentín Cadenas was also apprehended by the ronda, in his case for having stolen meat from a slave on the outskirts of the city shortly after he disembarked from the ship that had brought him from Buenos Aires. Valentín first was given the opportunity to work off his punishment for pay on an estate that employed other poor español youths. However, his patron fired him for "bad conduct" shortly after taking him on. Before departing the estate, Valentín relieved his patron of a bricklayer's knife, which he promptly sold on the docks of the port of Callao. After his employer alerted city authorities, Valentín finally was officially arrested and put in the public prison to await sentencing. But rather than being banished or publicly whipped in the plaza, as were many other young criminals in Lima, the Defensor de Menores took over as Valentín's guardian. Concerned not with punishing the youth but with "providing him a trade according to his inclination," the Defensor turned the boy over to the head of Lima's silversmiths' guild as an apprentice. The master silversmith, who had not been consulted, protested the sentence vehemently, complaining, "The said youth is disorderly and somewhat sticky-fingered (*algo ligero de manos*), which is why he finds himself in prison." But the silversmith's objections were in vain. A contract for apprenticeship was signed, and the youth had a new patron.[92]

The special treatment Valentín enjoyed might have been an extreme case, but soft sentencing for español minors was certainly not unusual. When the pickpocket Josef Tunco was let free, no mention was made of the 56 pesos he stole in the plaza. The married fifteen-year-old española who admitted to robbing her neighbor of 200 pesos was absolved with the light warning to "moderate and contain from here forward similar actions that might accredit her little confidence and disorderly conduct."[93] On the other hand, the ten-year-old slave convicted of stealing only 10 pesos from his owner—a charge he denied—was sold 100 leagues away from the city to toil on one of the coastal haciendas, a sentence that many slaves of the day associated with death.[94]

These and other cases suggest that discourses of social disorder and Enlightenment principles of reform were channeled through a justice system that continued to implement sentences to youths according to the rule of preferential sentencing. Bourbon social policies attempted to find a productive space for all individuals in order to promote order and maximize crown revenue. Lima's courts would find such productive spaces for español youths within the walls of the city, regardless of their prospects to be "corrected." On this the judges would insist, even forcing private subjects to take on the role of "substitute fathers" for rootless white youths. Yet casta or slave minors often were banished from Lima, expelled from the court's jurisdiction, and distanced from its protective shelter and role in reform. There was no place in the city for these young criminals.

CONCLUSION

The definition of legal minority may have been fixed in codified laws on crime, but in practice its definition was more subjective than the laws revealed. In eighteenth-century Lima, the meaning of minority issued forth from a complex combination of factors. Some were based on caste; others, on reputation and honor; and still others, on colonials' presumptions about household governance. The variation and subjectivity in the attitudes of limeños toward youth are evident in the way they used, and sometimes abused, the ambiguities of age in the city courts—in the concentration of arrests of "twenty-five-year-olds" and in defendants' and accusers' manipulation of ages in criminal trials. Such divergent constructions of legal minority were also obvious in sentences, where an Indian youth might enjoy the benefits of a "double minority," a slave might be turned over to his master for punishment, a casta youth could be sentenced to years of uncompensated labor "for the king" in a presidio far away, and an español who clearly showed early signs of a life of crime might be given a home within the city.

Preferential sentencing never meant simply throwing the book at errant nonwhite youths. It meant carefully imposing sentences that reinforced colonial hierarchies while still ensuring that all of the city's youths and their families could respect the courts and profit, even in a small way, from colonial justice. If we take into account judges' double mandate to be both clement patriarchs and stern disciplinarians, we may begin to understand not only the tension in the rules governing the criminal tribunals of the Cabildo and the Real Audiencia, but also something critical about Spanish colonial rule itself. Plebeian, male minors of age tended to end up in the city's jails as criminal suspects more often than did the elite or female youths. But rape cases also show us that nonelite families and women raising children stood before judges as accusers more often than did elite families headed by strong patriarchs.

Evidence that the sons, daughters, servants, and slaves of weak patriarchal households were more prone to appear in the criminal justice system, whether as accused criminals or as plaintiffs seeking formal as opposed to extralegal justice, speaks volumes about how state paternalism functioned. The counsel of court-appointed lawyers was only one of the special protections—"corporate privileges," in a sense—the state provided to needy or "unprotected" colonial subjects. In many ways, intervening in families where patriarchs were absent or unacceptable was the very raison d'être for laws on minority, and as a result it should come as little surprise that the court used its power more frequently and punitively against youths who lacked what was deemed to be acceptable private authority at home. The final irony may be that it was the parents and guardians of such children who were most likely to seek protection from colonial judges.

Although scholars often use criminal records to understand social norms by examining crime as deviancy, criminal records involving minors of age in eighteenth-century Lima tell us more about patriarchal debility than about deviancy.[95] Far from social marginals, most suspected criminals were fully socialized into gender and racial hierarchies even at a young age. To be a girl just eight years old signified sharing in a sexual system of honor, as well as vulnerability to its counterpart of masculine sexual violence; to be a young apprentice meant to share in plebeian honor based on work and discipline. Lima's judges, like judges elsewhere in colonial Spanish America, considered the reputation and honor of the parties involved in criminal trials to be crucial factors when issuing their sentences, and this was no less true for minors of all social ranks than it was for adults.[96]

At the end of the eighteenth century, judges also had to factor into their decisions new ideas about youths' unique potential to be rehabilitated and about childhood as an innocent state of life. But it would not be easy for defense attorneys to convince Lima's magistrates to experiment with new Enlightenment ideas about treating juvenile delinquents with leniency when the judges were reading city newspapers filled with reports about rebellion, revolution, and youths gone wild. New concepts of childhood and rehabilitation ultimately left only traces on criminal court sentences in the late eighteenth century. In contrast, new philosophies of child rearing saturated the legal arguments judges read and the sentences they handed down in late colonial civil proceedings over custody and child support. But before we examine how transformations in colonial concepts of childhood and authority were forged in Lima's civil court system, we first must explore how these new ideas circulated through the palaces, streets, and homes of the city.

The Colonial Child Reborn

Reform and Enlightenment in the Late Colonial Period

etween 1790 and 1791 a compilation of royal edicts on children was published in Madrid, a Peruvian's revolutionary invective against Spanish colonial paternalism turned up in London, and a pair of articles on the weakening of patriarchal control in elite households appeared in a Lima newspaper. Each of these texts captured and circulated a late eighteenth-century rebirth in political thought on childhood and patriarchal rule, although each also embodied a distinct aspect of this particular renaissance.

In 1790, several of the key edicts that the Spanish Bourbon monarchs Charles III (1759–88) and Charles IV (1788–1808) had issued on children, parents, and the state were pulled together for publication as a *circular*.[1] Each royal edict incorporated an Enlightenment era emphasis on education into a revived tradition of Spanish royal paternalism by commissioning local officials with the special task of supervising children's education so, as one law put it, "they might learn some trade or useful occupation." In addition to stressing economic productivity as the ultimate purpose of education, these royal edicts promoted state intervention into the process of social reproduction. Local sheriffs were deputized with "correct[ing] the education, sloth, and the vicious natures that parents pass on to their children," and in another law, the king ordered local judges to use their benches to "make up for the apathy or negligence of parents" in order to limit "the notoriety and damage that sloth brings to universal industry, on which communal happiness depends."

A year later, Juan Pablo Viscardo y Guzmán, a Peruvian Jesuit living in forced exile in Britain, composed a treatise that drew from a different strain of politicized notions about the king as father. During Hapsburg rule, royal paternalism had justified Spanish colonialism as a kind of tutelary guardianship, but Viscardo argued in his famously revolutionary "Letter to Spanish Americans" that the Bourbon monarch was a "distant father" and a "perverse guardian, who is accustomed to living in pride and opulence at the expensive of his ward." America was a "son" who would be "a fool if in the conduct of his concerns he always waited for the decision of his father. . . . The son," he proclaimed, "is set free by natural right."[2]

At the same time that this exiled Jesuit rallied his American compatriots to assert their natural rights as mature citizens, a local correspondent in Lima wrote two allegorical articles on child rearing for a new creole periodical, *Mercurio Peruano*.[3] This pseudonymous author described his own home, where gender and generational order had fallen into a critical state of disarray. What lay at the root of this patriarchal crisis for the creole correspondent was the manner in which radical Enlightenment ideas concerning the politics of childhood undermined Lima's traditional colonial child rearing practices and caste hierarchies. The introduction of new pedagogies into his home had weakened his authority over his daughter, wife, mother-in-law, and most dangerous of all, the slave woman who raised his child.

In late colonial Lima, childhood was becoming increasingly politicized terrain. This politicization involved multiple actors—from radical Enlightenment thinkers to local colonial officials, and from Spanish Bourbon kings to Lima's own parents and children. It also occurred in episodic bursts of royal activism and retreat as well as local acceptance and rejection of new Spanish policies and broader European philosophies. To capture this dynamism, we might loosely borrow a phrase from an early Bourbon era royal adviser and call the interplay between social reform, local responses, and emerging Enlightenment philosophies of childhood and political authority a "new politics of the child."[4]

As the 1790 circular makes clear, royal efforts to increase state control of domestic governance comprised a central subset of the new politics of the child. During the late eighteenth century, the Spanish state became increasingly attentive to children—to their education, their rearing, and their control. Bourbon monarchs instituted self-proclaimed "enlightened" social policies, including educational reforms, the implementation of programs to raise children as potential producers for the state, jurisdictional changes giving royal courts more legal sway over domestic matters such as marriage, and policies on foundlings and wet nursing. Yet even while some elements of these reforms grew from the cultural and intellectual environment of the late eighteenth century, in other respects the reforms were as old as the colonial enterprise itself. Particularly when instituting policies aimed at children and youths, Bourbon officials entrenched the traditional ideology of monarch as father as they reached deeper into the lives of colonial families.

Lima's upper classes, increasingly threatened by the rebellion and revolutionary philosophies that characterized the age in which they lived, often celebrated the state's renewed interest in royal paternalism. They hoped that the crown could contain the potential for the dissolution of their own control over the city by vesting more power in parents and in the secular state. Many—particularly creole elites—considered themselves enlightened (*ilustrados*) and read, admired, and critiqued the works of Europe's radical philosophes. They embraced new pedagogies and philosophies of childhood and even instituted their own social measures without prompting from Madrid. Nonetheless, enlightened state intervention into domestic governance had uniquely dramatic consequences in the colonies.

It became increasingly clear to Lima's elites that the king's campaign to bolster his own, centralized authority came at the expense of their control over the politics of child rearing. Some enlightened social policies complemented traditional models of generational hierarchy and child rearing practices in the city. But, ultimately, the Bourbon Reforms aimed to increase imperial control, not colonial control. Local elites discovered that many new policies on children proved antagonistic to traditional modes of colonial child rearing, especially those that reproduced caste differences by creating quasi-familial ties of dependency between the city's children and the myriad adults who raised them.

While Lima's local elites fended off rulings from Spain that they deemed detrimental to vital features of colonial social reproduction, they also had to contend with the radical ideas of European philosophers that tied child rearing to revolutionary politics. European Enlightenment discourses, which unfavorably equated monarchical subjects with children and associated race with place, portrayed creoles as corrupted and stunted by their New World environs. Ultimately, when colonial elites grappled with contemporary ideas about education and child rearing, they were also struggling with the larger political implications of empire-wide reform and new political models of authority. If the relationship between adults and children was undergoing reconsideration in the late eighteenth century, so was the relationship between the Father King and his colonial subjects.

Scholars who have sought a single philosophical inspiration behind the administrative, military, and economic reforms enacted during the reigns of Charles III and Charles IV have, it seems, searched for an elusive treasure. They have employed the terms "centralism," "regalism," "enlightened despotism," "new imperialism," and "absolutism" to describe these imperial policies in the American colonies, and one historian even called the Bourbon Reforms a "second conquest" of the New World.[5] But other historians emphasize how regionally disarticulated the policies were and point to their varied outcomes as proof that the quest for a coherent reform ideology may be futile.[6] A weak, grasping Bourbon state, they tell us, forced the creole elite to "thwart" or "water down" one ill-conceived or ad hoc policy after another until Spanish Americans finally reached the point of exhausted alienation from the crown.[7]

While the social reforms of the Bourbon years have rarely been analyzed as a whole, historians studying individual policies, such as new marriage laws or legislation on foundlings, suggest that social reforms followed the same pattern as the crown's economic and administrative reforms. Generally, these studies describe social reforms as riddled with contradictory goals, particularly in terms of their racial and patriarchal ideologies.[8] But close scrutiny of reforms aimed at children and youths indicates that the contradictions in Bourbon social policies did not reside in their philosophical inspiration as much as in their impact on colonial society.

When viewed from the vantage point of royal intentions rather than from the perspective of colonial elites, the social reforms of the late colonial period do not appear particularly piecemeal or inconsistent. As historian Scarlett O'Phelan Godoy has argued, Bourbon social measures instituted in Peru, which targeted everything from hygiene and education to technology and popular culture, formed an "integrated project" based on "orchestrated objectives."[9] Indeed, Bourbon policies, especially those aimed at children, often displayed the distinctive marks of broader European Enlightenment philosophies.

With their social reforms, Bourbon officials tackled several key areas associated with children, including education, economic utility, secular control of domestic life, and the demographic growth of empire. Each policy objective radiated from a central hub: the enhancement of the king's power and wealth. Given the common portrayal of Enlightenment thought as radically anti-monarchical, to describe these policies as enlightened might seem incongruent.

But it should be remembered that the Enlightenment was a multifaceted cultural and intellectual movement that produced discussion, debate, and criticism more than orthodoxy.[10] And it was neither coeval nor coterminous with revolutionary thought. Monarchies in France, England, the Germanys, and czarist Russia sponsored enlightened projects, which ranged in goals from direct challenges to traditional epistemologies and institutions to more modest attempts to tweak older economic and political models.[11] To draw too bold a distinction between the Enlightenment and enlightened absolutism risks falling into a teleological trap in which all political developments in the eighteenth century must lead to revolution against the Old Regime and all economic developments must result in industrial revolutions in order to merit the label "enlightened."[12]

The Spanish Bourbons' enlightened social reforms produced uneven and unintended results in the colonies, making them in this respect similar to their economic and administrative policies. But this did not occur because the social policies were ideologically inchoate. Unlike other reform measures, Bourbon social policies on children were often empire-wide, rather than regional, in scope. As we shall see, the crown encountered resistance in implementing its social measures precisely because these policies often were poorly tailored to the colonial regions of the empire.[13] Therefore, just as Bourbon absolutism rankled the creole elite by haphazardly revising the economic and administrative relationship between king and colony, it achieved equally counterproductive political effects with its universal social policies on children.

During the last decades of the eighteenth century, the inhabitants of Lima watched as the king tightened metropolitan control over the colonial economy and, in many ways, remade their city. The creation of the viceroyalty of Río de la Plata, with Buenos Aires as a new commercial hub and port (1782), not only reduced the geographical size of the viceroyalty of Peru; it eroded the power and opulence of its capital city, once the resplendent centerpiece of Spain's dominion in South America. When the administrative map of Peru was redrawn, the political influence of Lima's officials, and of creoles in particular, contracted.[14] A policy to centralize the bureaucracy filled governmental posts with peninsulares and institutionalized long-standing social biases against American-born Spaniards. Meanwhile Iberian immigration swelled the city's upper-class ranks with *chapetones*, as peninsular Spaniards were sometimes called, while the power of the city's merchants also shrank. The new official economic philosophy of *comercio libre*—which, more than a strict policy of free trade was a rejection of the former inefficiency of Hapsburg mercantilism—resulted in a relaxing of colonial trade restrictions in the 1770s and 1790s, further undermining the economic privileges Lima had long enjoyed.[15]

Some members of Lima's upper classes applauded what the reforms brought, especially the establishment of cafés and commercial centers, and they celebrated their relatively unfettered access to some manufactured items from Europe.[16] But they also looked on as the reforms fueled violent popular uprisings just beyond the foothills to the east of the city. The most severe outburst originated high in the Andes, where more extractive methods of tax collection and a coercive system of distributing credit and goods to Indian commoners (the *reparto de mercancías*) spawned the bloody rebellions led by Túpac Amaru II and others in his name.[17] The threat of rebellion must have seemed ever greater as Lima's literate inhabitants read spirited attacks on monarchy from the banned books that were smuggled into the city, or when they turned the pages of the local newspapers and found out about revolutions in North America, in France, and particularly, in Haiti.[18]

Elite limeños thus came to understand the social projects of the Bourbon years in an environment swirling with anxiety about the unraveling of colonial order—a threat that, to some degree, crown reforms had helped foster. Still, since a principal objective of Bourbon social policy was the fortification of the patriarchal state through attention to children, many royal policies seemed to offer elites hope for restoring control.

The enlightened social reforms of the Bourbon state promoted four discrete, though often overlapping, tenets, including education, utility, secular legal expansion, and a physiocratic concern with orphans and foundlings, each of which are explored in detail in this chapter. In theory, the official promotion of patriarchal social control, in its private and (secular) public forms, would breed "useful," economically productive imperial children who would, as adults, bring greater benefits to the Spanish state. But as we have seen, child rearing practices in Lima relied on the efforts of diverse adults, some of whom were not ideal-typical patriarchs. Local elites especially benefited from these practices, since they had long relied on others to do the work of child rearing but nonetheless had been rewarded with children's labor and the prerogatives of patriarchal power, even over children who were not their own. Examining late colonial social policies reveals that, by strengthening the ideology of the Father King, the Bourbon monarchy ultimately upset these delicately balanced contingencies of adult authority in Lima, creating a patriarchal crisis for the city's creole elite. The final section of the chapter explores this crisis, demonstrating that, at the end of the eighteenth century, Lima's creoles began to see themselves as trapped patriarchal protagonists, facing the unraveling of the colonial order from within and without.

EDUCATION

Local elites and officials began preening Lima's schools and educational practices according to emerging Enlightenment fashions during the early decades of the eighteenth century.[19] Still, it might be argued that Spanish enlightened absolutism, at least in terms of social policies aimed at children, made its official debut on 27 February 1767, the day Charles III expelled the Jesuit order from the colonies. Rumors of the priests' participation in Iberian riots during the preceding year provided a convenient pretext for the king to take decisive action against the independent order, which simply did not fit into his plans to reap the greatest possible amount of revenue for the state and to limit the economic influence of the church.[20]

Some Spanish American officials worried that the exodus of the priests would spell ruin for colonial schools. Even a staunch opponent of the Jesuits, the bishop of Córdoba, worried: "In view of their absence I do not know what we are to do with the children and youth of these countries."[21] But royal officials had no intention of abandoning the task of educating colonial children. In fact, replacing Jesuit-run schools with state-sponsored institutions for youths was a priority for the Real Junta de las Temporalidades, a branch of the royal government founded to manage the exiled priests' property.

In Lima the transfer from Jesuit educational patronage to royal control could be traced on the city map. The urban plan was reconfigured after two great events—the earthquake of 1748 and the expulsion—and state-run institutions opened in buildings that once housed Jesuit schools and monasteries.[22] The Colegio del Príncipe was one of the first to change hands during the period. After being closed for several years while the Junta de Temporalidades concentrated on the occupational instruction of poor and orphaned vagrants, the school was finally moved from the central plaza of the Indian district to a building formerly occupied by a Jesuit school for elite Spanish boys.[23]

It was as if, by simply moving the colegio into a building that once educated the español elite, the entire cultural mission toward Indian pupils had been reoriented. In addition to instructing cacique boys, the junta hired teachers of primeras letras and Latin to teach a broad variety of children in a public classroom (*aula pública*), fusing the ostensibly separate schools of the Jesuits. In June 1771 the junta hired three teachers to instruct the pupils, "so that the Public no longer goes without the teaching and instruction of the primeras letras, so recommended by his Majesty in his royal orders." Although the state was a poor economic steward for many of its schools and sometimes failed even to pay its teachers, the colegio's curriculum was clearly directed at providing pupils an education comparable to the kind offered in schools for elite español youths.[24] Whereas Indian pupils had barely learned to read and write when the Jesuits ran the school, after the expulsion some went on to study at prestigious institutions.[25] A few even were able to pass the public exams necessary to study philosophy, mathematics, and "Oriental languages" at the state-run center of Enlightenment education, the Real Convictorio de San Carlos.[26]

In 1803 the colegio's students petitioned for greater funding, requesting uniforms and scholarships in order to stay in the school beyond the normal period of matriculation. Rector José Silva advocated on their behalf. "Make them useful," he implored, "to those of their nation." Silva claimed that before the Jesuit expulsion many Indian students abandoned their studies early in order to marry or to succeed their fathers as community leaders. Now his students were studying ethics and philosophy and could return "to their pueblos and instruct and edify them with their doctrine and example, with better success than when they went back to fulfill cacicazgos, which do not have the domination now that they did in earlier times."[27] Instead of a cultural holding pen where youths' minds were imprinted with the repetitive reading of the lives of saints and the recitation of memorized prayers, it was hoped that the Colegio del Príncipe would graduate indigenous scholars.[28]

Changes in the Colegio del Príncipe reflected a broader transformation in pedagogical theories—an emphasis on reason, science, and learning through experience—that circulated far from the Andean communities to which these Indian sons would return. From John Locke to Jean-Jacques Rousseau, Enlightenment philosophers accentuated the importance of an early and comprehensive education because they believed developing intellect, reason, and experience during childhood was decisive for one's future as a citizen.[29] The 1762 appearance of *Émile*, Rousseau's enormously popular tract on education, provided a capstone to a culminating idea that children were closer than adults to nature.[30] Children, Rousseau believed, should be allowed to follow their innate rational instincts without being subjected to austere moral rules and rote memorization, and they should be educated by tutors rather than wet nurses or mothers.

As with so many other masterworks of the French Enlightenment, Rousseau's works were received in Spain with what John Lynch describes as a mixture of "outrage and condemnation, excitement and praise."[31] But the ideas he espoused were clearly influential, finding their way into classics of the Spanish Enlightenment such as Gaspar Melchor de Jovellanos's "Memória sobre educación pública."[32] Jovellanos, an intellectual with ties to the royal court, believed that "nothing is more . . . accredited by experience than the liveliness with which ideas inspired in our childhood imprint themselves on our souls, and the facility and tenacity with which they are received."

Jovellanos argued that adults wasted valuable time teaching youths buenas costumbres, which he defined as "presenting themselves, walking, sitting and rising with grace, speaking with modesty, and greeting with affability and courtesy." Instead of imparting these courtly manners, which early modern Spanish moralists had viewed as the primary purpose of education, Jovellanos advocated teaching children *buena crianza*, which he defined as the "science of virtue" and the "philosophy of action."[33] In practical terms, what "good rearing" entailed was a comprehensive, challenging, rational education in ethics and civility.[34]

The distinction Jovellanos drew between buenas costumbres and buena crianza was crucial to the Spanish variant of an enlightened education.[35] Because the goal of education was to provide the state with useful adult citizens, crianza could be imparted to a wider array of the Spanish empire's young subjects than had former models of indoctrinating youths in courtly costumbres. The most important goal of education was the enrichment of the monarchy, and the best means through which it could be achieved was to follow the philosophes' program for exposing children to rational thought while preserving the main tenets of Catholic moral ethics.

Indeed, Jovellanos rejected the radical secularism of many Enlightenment thinkers and instead emphasized the power of reason to "enlighten the spirit and rectify hearts." He distanced himself from French philosophes, by now inextricably linked in the minds of Spaniards to revolution and regicide, and whom he called "enemies of all religion and all sovereignty, conspiring to bring ruin to the altars and thrones of all institutions." It was obvious to Jovellanos that radical notions of equality lay nestled inside Enlightenment philosophies of childhood, education, and politics. So he struggled to excise these subversive political implications from the Spanish practice of enlightened education in order to avoid violating the traditional order created by social hierarchy.[36] "Every man theoretically may be born equal and free," he wrote. But every man was also born "subject to some species of authority. . . . Society cannot exist without hierarchy, nor hierarchy without a graduated order of distinction and superiority; inequality not only is necessary but essential to civil society."[37]

It was easier to theorize about how to use Enlightenment pedagogies without endorsing their underlying political implications concerning equality than actually to do so. When the Spanish Bourbon monarchy embraced the educational ethos of the Enlightenment, it often failed to reconcile its equalizing tendencies with colonial hierarchies built on caste. The inherent paradox in Bourbon absolutist educational policy was evident in Charles IV's 1792 announcement concerning the founding of the Colegio de Nobles Americanos, a secondary school for creole "nobles" ages twelve through eighteen, to be established in the Spanish city of Granada.[38]

"No objective occupies my sovereign attention and paternal endeavors like that of procuring, by any accessible means, the greatest happiness of all of my vassals, wherever they exist," the king wrote. Importantly, the colegio would admit "the children and descendants of pure Spanish Nobles, born in the Indies . . . *without excluding* the children of Caciques and Indian Nobles, nor of Noble Mestizos" (emphasis mine). The purpose of establishing the school, where students were to "rapidly progress" through studies in theology, military arts, law, and politics, was that "nothing is as important as the universal diffusion of *las luces* [lit., 'the lights,' or the Enlightenment], and in no way can this be assured except by perfecting the system of human studies in the growing generation."

Lima's creole Enlightenment newspaper, *Mercurio Peruano*, published the king's announcement along with an approving commentary on its goal of providing "the youth of the Americas the education necessary for the man and citizen." Describing past Spanish kings as "conquerors of the throne," it feted Charles IV as "Peacemaker of his Pueblos, the restorer of letters . . . Father of America." *Mercurio* lauded the king's matrix of admission as a signal that "trying to find differences between the children of the same father is in harm and dishonor to the State" and an "odious rivalry." But the editors stumbled over the provision that made the school open to mestizos as well as creoles and Indian nobility. They referred only to the opportunity the king gave "the Noble Indian" to enroll in the school, regarding it as a recompense for "the sheen of blood, the fatigues of his efforts," but they made no comment on the king's decision to accept mestizo students.

Lima's creole elites may have been uncomfortable with the king's inclusive definition of noble pupils, but they were not necessarily hostile to the educational ethos he espoused. In fact, efforts to "restore letters" to colonial society often originated at home rather than from royal policy penned in Madrid. An Enlightenment focus on rational forms of education and child rearing prevailed among Lima's educators and colonial officials even before the Jesuit expulsion and the establishment of new royal secondary schools. As early as 1759, Esteban de Orellana published his new *Introducción de la Lengua Latina*, which condemned corporal punishment and drew from the ideas of European philosophers such as Locke and the Portuguese pedagogue known as Barbadiño in promoting pedagogies based on "experience, practice and the vitality of language."[39] Throughout the remainder of the eighteenth century, officials in Lima's schools began to assign learning materials that mirrored Orellana's recommendations. For example, rather than memorizing traditional texts, students educated in the Casa de Niños Expósitos were assigned Francisco Amado Pouget's catechism, which incorporated similar instructional methods.[40]

Pouget's work was also assigned to the female students attending the Colegio de las Amparadas, a school founded in 1766 by royal order of Charles III and attached to a recogimiento under the control of the Junta de Temporalidades. The school's constitution was drafted under the supervision of Viceroy Manuel Amat y Junient (1761–76), an avid supporter of Enlightenment philosophies.[41] The ranked system of candidacy for admission to the Colegio de las Amparadas reflected the particularly gendered design of certain Bourbon social reforms, as royal officials increasingly worried about educating and training children from weak patriarchal households. The primary candidates for entrance would be the daughters of the repentant women who entered the recogimiento. Next in line were orphans, followed by those without fathers, those without mothers, and finally, those whose parents could not support them. Apparently girls fitting this description were numerous, since by the 1790s the Casa generally housed more than 100 interns, of which orphaned girls and educandas—both casta and española—comprised the majority.[42]

The school's admissions policies and the pupils' daily regimen also displayed certain features of the caste ecumenicalism the king exhibited when drawing up plans for the Colegio de Nobles. Although casta girls worked as servants in the school, each pupil, regardless of caste, received not only lessons in traditional gender costumbres but also a rational education, or crianza, that was tailored to her as an individual. The students' days were filled with lessons in honesty, chastity (*pudor*), and modesty, as well as instruction in the "rules of urbanity and buena crianza, no less than buenas costumbres; for which, the temperament and inclinations of each girl [should be] observed and, with each, frequent conferences held." Teachers were admonished to refrain from whipping toddlers or chastising pupils in front of their peers in order to avoid inciting "an incorrigible disposition."[43]

This last requirement gestured toward a new disciplinary tenet that we have already seen at work in Lima's late colonial criminal trials. The belief that excessive punishment would turn children into unruly adults—what historian Pablo Macera has called a "condemnation of the empire of force"—circulated among Lima's pupils as well as among teachers and officials, causing trouble in some of the city's schools.[44] Although the students at Santa Cruz de Atocha, the city's school for white expósitas, were occasionally insubordinate in the seventeenth and early eighteenth centuries, Inquisition inspectors normally reported that the girls lived "pacifically" with their superiors.[45] In the late colonial period, however, the pupils of Santa Cruz waged open battles with school officials, repeatedly forcing the retirement, resignation, and dismissal of their teachers and female rectors. The girls even wrote a letter to the inquisitors who supervised the institution in 1799 to complain of the abuses they suffered at the hands of their *rectora*, who treated them not like "children but field slaves (*negras de chacra*)." "We know how to obey," they said, "when there is reason to do so."[46]

Male students attending the Real Convictorio de San Carlos, where students were instructed according to Spanish Enlightenment pedagogies, also wrote a formal complaint to colonial officials about their rector. Some of their grumblings would be familiar to students today: bad food, poor instruction, and mean teachers. But the first accusation these pupils leveled against their schoolmaster was the most politically provocative, since they indicated that new notions of childhood and royal paternalism could undercut the traditional authority of colonial elders. The rector, the students reported, who "in no way understands how to carry forward the laudable crianza of Youth," behaved "tyrannically" and "thinks of himself as the Monarch." They informed officials that they attended school to learn rather than to obey, and that their superiors should treat them with respect rather than rigidity. Only the king, the students of San Carlos suggested, had the ultimate authority to discipline them.[47]

Gone, then, were the days of "magister dixit" and "letra entra por sangre," as schoolchildren in Lima interpreted crianza as a mandate to demand less severity. Gone, too, were the days when city parents would tolerate the long-standing practice of using educational institutions as cash cows rather than places of instruction. Because they had to provide most of the tuition and daily support for the pupils, ordinary parents whose children attended new state-run schools insisted, in the name of crianza, that school directors take their roles as educators seriously. In 1806 fourteen fathers of male students enrolled in the Colegio de Desamparados, another school run by the Junta de Temporalidades, filed a formal complaint over the lack of supplies their children received.[48] They rhapsodized about the days when the Jesuits "provided paper, ink and quills without requiring any compensation." Although the rector retorted that the budget allotted by the state was insufficient to provide students' basic materials, the fathers accused him of running the school like a business. For evidence, they pointed to a practice that, in fact, had been quite common under the Jesuits: school funds were used to purchase a hacienda rather than being spent on the pupils. School monies, they asserted, should be spent to "educate these poor boys who, because of the lack of an aula pública (free public school) have been left without crianza, without knowing the rudiments of the Catholic Religion and without the other civil maxims with which they are made useful to the state."[49]

If crianza, imparted through formal schooling, was designed to make children useful to the state, it could become something that limeños believed all of the city's children—including the poor—deserved. In fact, many correspondents in the local press saw an opportunity to push for public educational programs when Napoleon's occupation of Iberia left the Spanish empire with a liberal constitutional *cortes* instead of a king from 1808 until 1814. The Constitution of 1812 dissolved the Inquisition, and Lima's newspapers published a flurry of articles and letters proposing that its resources be used to found schools. Among these was a letter from someone who called himself the Defender of Widows and proclaimed to the editor of *El Investigador* that what the city really needed was establishment of a free public school.[50] Poor widows, he reported, had been turning up at the door of the Colegio del Príncipe requesting that their children be enrolled. The Defender of Widows claimed that they were turned away and were told that "they do not teach for free. . . . And this is a free school!" "Make the Enlightenment (*Ylustración*) beneficial," the writer entreated readers, "so that by means of these principles all individuals be called to Citizenship [and] know how to read, write, etc."

Lima's elites, like this correspondent, used the local press, which emerged in the 1790s, to encourage the application of Enlightenment pedagogies in the city's homes as well as to urge the opening of schools. One of the principal activities of the Sociedad de los Amantes del País, a creole economic society formed in Lima in 1790 and modeled on similar associations in Spain, was the publication of its paper, *Mercurio Peruano*, which ran from 1791 until 1795. The editors of *Mercurio* saw themselves as a new young generation of ilustrados who would use the paper to enlighten the rest of the inhabitants of Peru.[51]

Mercurio Peruano had company. Papers established by peninsular Spaniards, such as Jayme Bausate y Mesa's *Diario curioso, erudito, económico y comercial de Lima* and Franciscan priest Juan Antonio de Olavarrieta's Sunday paper, *El Semanario Crítico*, also appeared in the 1790s. Purchasing the papers from a store across the street from the modish Café de Bodegones, elite colonials would gather, read the articles aloud, and then hold *tertulias* (salons or public discourses). The list of subscribers to the papers included many of Lima's bureaucrats and high-ranking legal officials, including the Defensor de Menores and abogados of the Real Audiencia.[52]

Each of these papers was to fulfill an edifying function for Lima, and instilling new pedagogical and child rearing practices in city inhabitants was high on the contributors' agenda. Correspondents and writers broached an almost limitless array of topics related to childhood, from guides to pregnancy to a report, cribbed from "a modern journal" in Paris, about the great success that French pedagogues were experiencing in teaching students to write with both their left and right hands.[53] In some cases, their articles were only thinly disguised local versions of the writings of classic Enlightenment thinkers such as Rousseau and Voltaire. Voltaire's *Nanine*, a 1749 work about convents and female education, surely provided the impetus for the *Diario*'s article titled "Inconveniences Resulting from Enclosing Señoritas in Convents When They Are Close to Puberty."[54] The article recommended removing young women from convents, which were described as "most horrific jails" where parents placed their daughters under "a pretext of perfecting their education." These sunless sanctuaries from rational thought, the article stated, "muted nature's voice" and deprived young girls of their natural youthful happiness.

Beyond criticizing the well-established practice of using convents for female education, articles in the *Diario* treated the "art" or "science" of child rearing in the home and served primarily as guides for women. Conventional Enlightenment invectives against overly indulgent mothers, swaddling, and coddling appeared in its series "Instrucción de las costumbres," which began on 10 October 1790.[55] Like Jovellanos, the *Diario* was cautious about advancing the philosophes' argument that children were fully rational. Yet, as one article in the series explained, "if it is an enormous error among parents to assume, as the ilustrados call for, children to be rational, almost from birth speaking to them like formed men even before they know how to talk, it is equally great [an error] (*if not perhaps greater*) to postpone over a long time the discovery of the seeds of reason" (emphasis mine).[56]

Practicing rational methods of child rearing in the home, local intellectuals believed, would benefit the empire as a whole, since domestic education directly affected imperial governance. "Domestic politics," the *Diario*'s editor announced, "is a branch of the public [sphere and] has a great influence over all public matters." If children were poorly educated, they would be unfit to perform the labor associated with building a strong monarchical state. "It is of major importance to Families and the state," the *Diario* announced, "to have men of solid constitution, robust and dauntless, who can one day be useful to the Patria."[57] This concern with merging domestic and imperial politics to create useful subjects, with ensuring the strength of the state through the physical and intellectual vigor of the inhabitants of the empire, became a central leitmotif of late colonial reform projects.

UTILITY

By the early nineteenth century, the concept of utility and a Bourbon obsession with the detrimental effects of laziness and vice had become tightly intertwined with educational practices. For example, one city inhabitant touted the fables attributed to Félix María Samaniego as ideal reading materials for the city's pupils because they turned the philosophy of utility into a story that any child could comprehend.[58] In Samaniego's parable of the pig and the ass, the ass envies the indolent life of a spoiled, lazy pig until the day he witnesses the pig slaughtered. The poem ends with the donkey realizing, "If this is how laziness and spoils end / to work and whip I shall attend."[59] Providing students these kinds of didactic warnings against idleness was clearly intended to steer Lima's children toward developing a work ethic that would make them industrious adults. Yet many Bourbon reform projects sought to create producers for the state through more than just clever poems.

The advisers to Charles III and Charles IV were inspired by the ideas (and policy failures) of French physiocrats who advocated free trade and who believed that land and agriculture were a vast, untapped source of wealth for the state.[60] As a result, many Bourbon policies on children were based on the idea that the empire's economic productivity was linked to its demographic size.

The Spanish Bourbons, like other enlightened absolutists, made improving public hygiene and lowering infant mortality rates a centerpiece of their social policy.

The Expedición Filantrópica was a model scientific experiment in physiocratic royal paternalism. This early nineteenth-century vaccination campaign was a pet project of Charles IV, who sent Spanish orphans who had been exposed to smallpox parading through the American colonies to provide blood to inoculate colonial subjects. The orphans arrived in Lima in 1805 to supply transfusions for select members of the city's population. Children from the Casa de Niños Expósitos and Indians from the Cercado were gathered up, their arms injected with smallpox-tainted blood, and a local paper reported that more than 1,000 of the city's inhabitants were immunized during one week in November.[61]

Physician José Hipólito Unánue voiced the creole reaction to such policies in a speech given at the Royal University of San Marcos to celebrate the event. He contrasted the royal paternalism at work in the vaccination campaign with slave revolution in Haiti, where "colonial blood runs in torrents, spilled by implacable barbarous hands."[62] Peruvians, he proclaimed, although "busy burying the children smallpox kills . . . can proclaim that Lord Charles IV is the father of the Americas . . . Friends, the KING, your lord and father, said to the poor savages, I send you this remedy that will free you from smallpox. . . . Just as the paternal cares of our good monarch are engraved in the breasts of our rustic Indians, they are [engraved, too,] on the chest of our most cultured citizens." The circulation of Spanish blood through the veins of colonial orphans and "poor savages," he implied, created blood ties of loyalty between nonwhite subjects and the Father King. The vaccination campaign was more than a medical project; it was an antidote for race rebellion and anticolonial revolution.

Other city elites also projected their own social concerns on Bourbon policies and saw the king's drive to promote utility as an opportunity to increase their own control over the city's poor and marginalized inhabitants. Particularly in the case of Lima's poorhouse, local elites found that they could capitalize on the king's new interest in children, exerting their own paternalistic authority over the city's impoverished inhabitants by interning young vagrants and the poor in the name of the Spanish monarch.

As was the case with so many Bourbon social reforms throughout Spanish America, local elites in cities like Mexico City and Lima, not officials in Madrid, initiated the project to intern paupers in urban poorhouses. Nevertheless, Charles III forced the local founders of Mexico City's institution to reframe their original proposal, which was aimed primarily at adults, and to redirect the project at parentless children. Presented with the outline of the poorhouse in 1764, the king withheld formal approval for several reasons, among them his "dismay" that the Mexican institution was designed for adult "beggars and idlers instead of including foundlings and orphans," whom he considered to be the most deserving of Bourbon paternalism.[63]

In Lima the campaign to incarcerate urban beggars and destitute women was also local in origin and predated that of Mexico City by six years. Don Diego Ladrón de Guevara, an enterprising Spanish émigré from Navarre, first proposed establishing a combination technical school and prison for the adult poor who filled Lima's streets in 1754.[64] In his proposal to found the poorhouse, Ladrón de Guevara did worry that some of the city's impoverished inhabitants "(particularly women) take poverty as an occupation and their children work in it from the time they are small." But Ladrón de Guevara was the director of Lima's Casa de Niños Expósitos, which, unlike the Mexico City foundling home, had weathered chronic budget problems and never shut down after it was opened. Thus his poorhouse was designed to intern primarily adult beggars who would manufacture clothing, coarse cotton cloth (*tocuyos*), and linens at the institution's *obraje* (rudimentary textile factory).

Although Viceroy Conde de Superunda (1745–61) and the Cabildo approved the request to found the institution in 1758, not until the Jesuit expulsion emptied city buildings and made space for state-sponsored projects such as the poorhouse did Lima's Hospicio de Pobres open its doors.[65] By this time the king's interest in abandoned and poor children had become increasingly clear, and city officials sought to bring the poorhouse project more in line with royal concerns. In a 1770 order, local officials announced that "one of the principal objectives of our Sovereign in the application of these houses . . . has been to establish Hospices for the aid and maintenance of the poor invalids, beggars, and for the recogimiento and instruction of Youths, who, without Parents, occupation or destination, wander (*vagan*) through the City and Provinces of the Kingdom."[66] In its new incarnation, the poorhouse was to function as a youth reformatory as well as an institution for adult paupers, and its name was changed from Jesús el Nazereno to the more secular and child-centered Hospicio de Pobres, y Recogimiento de Jóvenes Huérfanos, y Vagantes. Established in the very building formerly occupied by the Colegio del Príncipe, it physically took the place of one of the former Jesuit sites of social reproduction.

In its early years the poorhouse was reported to have housed up to ninety-five inhabitants, although it is difficult to tell who the interns may have been.

What is clear, however, is that the institution languished only two decades after it opened. In 1791 the director was compelled to request greater state financing, complaining of the "few funds" available to the institution and reporting that the building housing the poor was in such dilapidated condition that a wall had collapsed. If Lima's poorhouse had become increasingly oriented toward interning youths after the Jesuit expulsion, plans to renovate the institution in the 1790s only further intensified its patriarchal character.

The decayed state of Ladrón de Guevara's brainchild inspired a small group of enlightened elites, some of whom were Basques living in Lima, to form a board of directors entrusted with rejuvenating the poorhouse by reviving its technical school. The Sociedad de Beneficencia, as the group called itself, adopted two priorities: first, the "employment of . . . poor peoples" and, second, the "particular aid of women," especially poor españolas, the majority of whom "dedicate themselves to sewing without even earning enough to make ends meet."[67] They worried about a class of fraudulent poor women who were called *pordioseras* because they cried *"por Diós"* when requesting alms and who instructed children in the arts of professional panhandling. These women, they reported, taught the youths lessons "as pernicious in morals as prejudicial in politics (*la pólitica*)."[68]

In its proposal, the Sociedad de Beneficencia drew heavily from the imagery of royal paternalism and claimed that the enrichment of the monarchy was its ultimate goal. Metaphors likening the monarch to father also filled *Mercurio Peruano*'s essays about the poorhouse. The same year that the Sociedad de Beneficencia was formed, *Mercurio* published an article promoting a reform of the institution. It described the "paternal love" the urban poor received in the poorhouse and concluded by quoting Caesar's martial epigram: "The monarch is always prince by his authority, always father by his tenderness."[69] Saving the institution, its author predicted, would elicit "a cheer from all pueblos," "a general cry acclaiming the king as the true 'Father' of the Patria."[70]

Clearly, symbolic royal paternalism at times served the local elite—both creole and peninsular—well. Lima's upper classes and royal officials could invoke the traditional image of the Father King in order to pledge their loyalty to the new colonial political order amidst the dizzying events of the Age of Revolution and, perhaps most importantly, to justify their own social measures in a city that they felt was threatened by disorder. But the new politics of the child involved more than simply using intensified discourses of royal paternalism to promote elite social control; it also meant that the authority of the king increasingly overshadowed the power of local patriarchs in the city. While on the throne, both Charles III and Charles IV asserted their royal authority over domestic governance, particular in matters pertaining to child support and marriage choice. In order to bring all imperial subjects more centrally under royal control, the state invaded territory once the exclusive terrain of local elders and the Catholic Church—jurisdictional control over marriage.

SECULAR CONTROL OF FAMILY LIFE

During the late eighteenth century, a number of royal edicts drew the institution of matrimony into the civil, rather than purely sacramental, realm of law. A royal ruling on divorce and alimony, a ruling about bigamy trials, and most notably, a 1776 edict on parental consent for marriage all transferred conflicts surrounding marriage and children from ecclesiastical to secular jurisdiction. These changes elevated the secular courts, and thus the royal state, to the position of supreme arbiter of family life.

In the 1780s the king issued two rulings that limited the church's jurisdiction over the economic aspects of divorce litigation and over bigamy suits. A divorce case from Lima prompted the first ruling. Doña Josefa Castañeda had sued her husband, don Rodrigo del Castillo, the Marqúes de Casa-Castillo, for divorce in the ecclesiastical tribunal of Lima. The church judges granted the divorce and ordered the marqúes to return doña Josefa's dowry, to hand over the profit from the property she brought into the marriage (*gananciales*) and to pay her alimony (*alimentos*). Yet when the case reached the Council of the Indies in 1787, its ministers determined that Lima's ecclesiastical tribunal had overstepped its jurisdiction when it demanded financial compensation for doña Josefa. Ecclesiastical authorities, it stated, "should only hear cases of divorce, which is spiritual and the exclusive privilege of the Church, without becoming mixed up . . . in temporal and profane matters concerning support, attorneys' fees, or the restitution of dowries, which are rightful and exclusive to the secular Magistrates."[71] The next year a royal edict made bigamy a criminal offense that, under certain conditions, was to be heard by secular courts.[72]

These rulings nudged marriage from church to crown domain. By asserting secular jurisdiction over alimentos—which referred both to alimony and to child support—the first ruling also put suits involving the children of divorcing parents onto the dockets of secular judges. As we shall see in the following chapters, this meant that children's futures were increasingly determined by

Lima's civil court system. But no ruling concerning marriage and children better illustrated Bourbon patriarchal absolutism than the Pragmatic Sanction on Unequal Marriages, issued in 1776 and extended to the American colonies in 1778.

The ruling required minors of age to obtain elders' consent in order to marry and forbade priests from performing marriages without the approval of elders, principally fathers. If children married "unequally" or over elders' "rational" objections, elders could appear before secular judges to halt the nuptials and to levy civil punishments on their children by disinheriting them or denying their daughters dowries.[73] While historians have long pondered what precisely compelled the king to issue the edict, the sanction itself states that the intention was "the conservation of the rightful and orderly authority that is due to parents for their intervention and consent in the marriages of their children, and of the greater good and utility of the children themselves, for their families, and for the State."[74]

In asserting state control of intergenerational disputes over marriage, the Pragmatic Sanction came close to infringing on the two-century-old Tridentine philosophy of free will in marriage choice. Still, Charles III avoided violating Catholic doctrine by drawing a stark line between parental coercion and consent. The king explained that elders who opposed their children's marriage choices on self-interested, irrational grounds would find no shelter in the Pragmatic Sanction, nor would those who forced children into unions when the parties felt no affection for each other. The king's decree, therefore, did not so much alter the authority that canon law had bestowed on elders to regulate marriage among minors of age as increase the secular courts' supervision of elders who wished to exercise that authority.[75] Marriage was defined as a key civil institution on which the good order of the state depended, and the edict aimed to bring children more fully under the authority of elders—and elders more firmly under royal authority.

Only shortly after the Pragmatic Sanction was issued, Lima's adults began to appeal to secular judges to prevent their children, grandchildren, wards, and even younger brothers and sisters from marrying partners they deemed unfit. In several instances, elders argued that a marriage would be "unequal" because the youths were of different castes; others objected to marriages because the bride and groom were considered too young, because suitors were unemployed, because fiancées were sexually promiscuous, or simply because their children were defiant.[76] In one case, a father opposed his daughter's marriage to a young man he claimed was "unequal by custom" because the youth enjoyed dressing in an effeminate style and was publicly accused of being a *maricón* (queer) and committing sodomy.[77]

Just like Lima's elders, adults throughout Spanish America used the edict in attempts to prevent children from marrying for a patchwork of reasons.[78] Their enthusiastic use of the crown's decree has led some historians to regard the law as a conservative social measure that supported elite patriarchal control, particularly on the matter of race.[79] Yet it was not only parents who used the Pragmatic Sanction to impose their will on children's marriage choices. Lima's children sometimes used the edict to sue their parents over opposition to marriage. What is more, elders could not rely on the consistent sympathy of the secular courts, since the verdicts in these suits came down as frequently in favor of children as on the side of elders.[80]

In official circles, the Pragmatic Sanction was not heralded as benefiting elite, or even patriarchal, control. Instead, colonial officials complained that the sanction was poorly fitted to the contours of a caste-based society. The reaction to the ruling in the colonies is instructive for understanding a central dynamic at work in the new politics of the child: secular magistrates followed the edict, hearing a stream of cases of elder dissent. But even as the authority of the courts grew, many inhabitants of the colonies began to realize that the edict was not designed to bolster the power of elite parents, only to increase royal control over all of the empire's subjects.

Although colonial officials and elders read race into the king's references to inequality and published local versions of the law that dealt more specifically with the theme, the king himself had failed to define both equality between partners and what might constitute a "rational" objection to a minor's marriage choice.[81] In fact, a close consideration of the language on race in the Pragmatic Sanction reveals that the crown was more concerned with asserting its own patriarchal power over domestic matters than with dictating which castes could form unions with one another. In the 1778 edict extending the Pragmatic Sanction to Spain's American colonies, the king did specifically exempt or make special provisions for minors of age of African or Indian descent.[82] However, these provisions, far from betraying a racial motivation for the ruling, instead displayed a notable lack of sensitivity to the racial situation in the colonies. The edict equated most colonial subjects of African descent with slaves and crudely characterized Indians as migrating tribute payers who would encounter greater ease in finding a priest than a parent to obtain consent.[83] The Pragmatic Sanction produced a great deal of confusion when applied to the colonies, in part because of these racial exceptions and in part because the edict's vague language and silence on several legal matters opened a Pandora's box of questions in the colonial setting. Colonial officials would repeatedly petition for clarification on the ruling in the coming decades.[84]

Charles IV issued another *cédula* on the matter in 1803.[85] In this royal order, the king lowered the age at which children were considered minors for the purposes of marriage but stated that all of these newly defined minors of age, "of whatever category (*clase*) of the State [to which] they pertain," were required to seek their elders' consent to marry. He also ruled that fathers in particular no longer had to explain themselves before the courts.[86] Although colonial elites had been pressing for clarification for years, Steinar Saether argues that this modified ruling was not issued in response to their concerns but instead was the product of a "pan-European, enlightened and patriarchal political ideology" and paralleled similar rulings in Austria and France.[87] Indeed, even when the king removed all racial exceptions to the ruling in 1803, he still failed to address specifically the subject of interracial marriages.

For this reason the 1803 edict clearly dissatisfied the archbishop of Buenos Aires, who protested that it still did not suffice "in countries where negros and mulatos of all classes abound."[88] The Council of the Indies, which seemed to be still reluctant to issue a blanket ruling about mixed-race marriages, responded that if a noble of "notoriously clean blood" wished to marry someone of "another caste," local secular courts should hear the case. Inequality was still to be determined by local officials according to regional custom rather than on the basis of a universal set of caste-based qualifications. Finally, in 1805 the council delivered a ruling that specifically defined as unequal marriages between nobles and individuals of African descent.[89] But it had taken almost three decades for the ministers to soothe elite colonials' concerns about race.

During those decades, Lima's periodicals registered skepticism about Bourbon marriage law on a more enlightened plane. They ran articles on the new state-centered philosophy of marriage that struggled to reconcile the policy with contemporary discourses concerning youth and romantic love.[90] In January and February 1791 the *Diario de Lima* published a series on youth, marriage, and parental dissent, beginning with a reprinting of the 1776 Pragmatic Sanction and subsequent rulings on marriage choice.[91] Rather than applaud the ruling for bringing greater order to society through generational (or even racial) control, the periodical ran an advice column written by "el Filósofo," who counseled young women to use reason and consider their future happiness when making marital choices.

El Filósofo generally advised his female readers to do as their parents wished by waiting until they were older to marry or by selecting a suitor who was more prudent than passionate. But he appealed to readers as rational individuals rather than promoting their blind adherence to traditional authorities, including parents. The *Diario* even published a poem that mocked the official discourse on marriage choice:

More [ridiculous] than that a father, whipped up
by passion, wishes to obligate
his children to marry
only because of the state
[is] that because God has ordered that
children be obedient
toward their parents and relatives
they carry out his order.

Inverting the conventional notion that youths were overly influenced by emotion and passion in marriage decisions, the poem suggested that fathers' "passions" instead were irrational, while youths could be persuaded to act rationally. And the traditional authority of fathers was not the only "ridiculous" aspect of the new official policies on children's marriage choices. The use of the word "state" (*estado*) in the poem bears a double meaning. In Spanish, as in English, "estado" means both civil status, as in "the state of matrimony" as well as "government." Thus, the poem did more than mock the idea that children should marry according to parental desires. It also mocked the idea that marriage should satisfy the desires of the king.

The *Diario de Lima*'s satirical response to the issue of children's marriage choice reveals that elites' use of state-centered paternal discourses when implementing their own social policies was more instrumental than sincere. City inhabitants incorporated tenets of Bourbon thought when convenient, but they also incorporated other strains of Enlightenment thought, such as an emphasis on reason, individualism, and happiness, into their version of the new politics of the child, even when they did not harmonize with policies coming from Spain. Still, even if Bourbon marriage policy discomfited local cities by neglecting concerns about race, and even if it appeared ridiculous to local commentators because it reduced romantic love to royal interest, it did not quite bring Lima's elites and the king to an impasse. The new Bourbon approach to abandoned children, however, did.

The journey toward this impasse began in 1767, when the director of the Casa de Niños Expósitos sold a six-year-old mulato foundling named Cayetano María to don Francisco de Ormaza y Coronel for 100 pesos. As a condition of the sale, Cayetano María, like all male children of African descent abandoned at the Casa, would achieve free status when he reached age thirty.[92] Seven years later, Ormaza became embroiled in a drawn-out battle over the custody of Cayetano María with a woman identified as a "negra called Chavela," perhaps Cayetano María's mother. Turning first to Pedro Antonio Echeverz y Zubiza, the Audiencia minister responsible for overseeing the foundling home, then to the viceroy, Ormaza attempted to settle the matter once and for all.

When the ruling in this case is analyzed alongside a 1794 royal cédula that granted legitimacy status to foundlings, it becomes evident that the new official Bourbon stance on children often undermined colonial elites' efforts to sharpen social distinctions in the late eighteenth century. While the Bourbon king promoted greater social acceptance for abandoned children because he believed foundlings were an untapped labor resource that could be used for the state, local elites, beset by a sense that they were losing control of their city, embarked on a campaign of social exclusion.

Recall from Chapter 3 that the destinies of children abandoned at the Casa were plotted by caste and charted to channel the children into their "proper" positions in colonial society when they reached adulthood. According to the letter of the law in its constitution, the director of the Casa de Niños Expósitos had no right to sell children of African descent, only to place them in apprenticeship posts or servants' positions in "virtuous houses." Yet for male foundlings of African descent, apprenticeships were tantamount to enslavement during the first three decades of their lives. Because raising expósitos was a social and financial expense for private individuals, the city inhabitants who took foundlings into their homes made their charitable acts worthwhile by recouping their investment in the form of the children's slave labor.

Undoubtedly, the changing demographic situation in Lima also contributed to the practice of enslaving abandoned children of African descent. As we saw in Chapter 4, the city underwent significant population growth during the eighteenth century, and more than one observer noted the diminishing proportion of white inhabitants in Lima. In fact, the proportion of inhabitants of the "pure" castes in the city dropped, while the population of mixed-race residents grew throughout the century. And the mixed-race population was increasingly likely to be free rather than enslaved.[93] This means that the once-tidy correlation between African origins and slavery had loosened, and Lima's elites grew alarmed.

Elites looked inside as well as outside their class and saw their social control of the city jeopardized. They closed ranks in response to the growth of the mixed-race population and the increased permeability of social circles ostensibly reserved only for those who could claim limpieza de sangre. They demanded more proof of noble status and a greater transparency of racial origins before they would accept as their peers individuals who had shadowy pasts, and as Ann Twinam has shown, they gave greater currency to legitimacy as proof of status.[94] If an individual's origins were not known, the tendency among local elites at the end of the eighteenth century was to assume "the worst." This presumption would apply especially to expósitos, whom the elites considered to be the products of religiously and racially impure unions; if they appeared to be black, they were considered slaves.

But Bourbon officials had other ideas, as the ruling in Cayetano María's case demonstrates. Audiencia minister Echeverz reported to Viceroy Manuel Guirior that when he first investigated Cayetano María's case, he learned that the boy was one of many foundlings of African descent abandoned at the Casa who were presumed to be slaves and sold as apprentices. The Casa's director, don Diego de Ladrón de Guevara, regularly affixed notices on city walls announcing that the foundling home would receive infants "without distinction and without examination"—meaning without regard for race. Many city elites, including the editors of *Mercurio Peruano*, would later regard the director's color-blind receptiveness as a mark of his great charity.[95] In hindsight, however, financial rather than charitable concerns may have inspired Ladrón de Guevara to admit all infants to the Casa, since nonwhite infants could be sold for cash and generate income for the foundling home. In fact, while investigating Cayetano María's case, Echeverz discovered that local courts had been hearing "various complaints from the wet nurses of these sold expósitos" during Ladrón de Guevara's tenure as director.

Echeverz confronted the director of the foundling home, and Ladrón de Guevara explained that the institution's constitution granted him the ability to sell exposed children as long as their bondage lasted only for a limited term. Yet when Echeverz read the wording of the constitution, he realized that it did not allow the director to enslave children of African descent. "Neither the law of Nations (*Gente*) nor the law of Nature can permit that a house of asylum and refuge, erected for the conservation of these innocents, might become, to their harm, a penalty so harsh as that of slavery," he concluded. Echeverz recommended that some of the youths continue in apprenticeships as a "precaution" against "laziness" until they complete their *primera edad*, meaning until they reached adolescence. But he compelled the Casa to return all of the money it had collected to those who had purchased the foundling boys.[96]

When Ormaza appealed the case, Viceroy Guirior not only upheld Echeverz's ruling; he limited to twelve years the length of time that male expósitos of African descent could remain in apprenticeships. He also required artisans who accepted foundlings as apprentices to pay the Casa a stipend and the boys a salary, and he ruled that work contracts involving foundlings should contain no language or clause that could be interpreted as a sale. As for Francisco de Ormaza, Viceroy Guirior severely rebuked him for his participation in the commercial trafficking of expósitos and ordered him to repay the Casa more than 100 pesos—more than the amount that Ormaza had paid for Cayetano María seven years earlier.

Ormaza did not allow the matter to rest and continued to appeal the ruling even after it had been posted on walls around the city. In his protests, he drew less on his position as a property holder and instead made a case based on his standing as a member of the racial elite of colonial society.[97] He insisted that all abandoned children were not the same. "I am not speaking of Indians," he clarified, "because they are as free as we are. I speak of the rest of the castas, either those who are born subject to bondage or those who are born free. The Casa was not established for them, and only by the pure affection of humanity have they been accepted. Their subjugation until the age of thirty, not to a rigorous enslavement, but to an *almost filial subordination* in favor of the very Casa that educated them or of the person to whom they have been assigned for a stipend, is not [designed] to do them injury" (emphasis mine).

By stressing the subordination of castas to the patriarchal authority of the adults who raised them, Ormaza revealed that traditional social reproductive processes in the city, which rewarded colonial elites with children's labor in return for their rearing, clashed with the new, inclusive Bourbon paternalism toward foundlings. He also voiced the growing elite espousal of social policies that would promote elite caste insularity and the fortification of rigid barriers to prevent individuals from ascending the colonial hierarchy. He insisted that it should be impossible to raise the "condition" of a child through abandonment. To rule otherwise, he warned, would be to unleash the "danger" of a species "prejudicial to the Republic" and to allow "the republic to raise and educate at its bosom individuals who will rip [it] asunder."

If local elites presumed the worst failing clear evidence of an individual's origins, the viceroy and the Audiencia minister were prepared to presume the best. While in his original ruling Viceroy Guirior did not abandon completely the colonial precept of distinct life paths for different castes of foundlings, he was adamant that abandoned children should never end up as chattel. He did not revoke his decision, and during the years following the ruling, the Casa's next director exercised caution in signing children of African descent into apprenticeship posts. For example, when a twelve-year-old mulato foundling named Baltazar Atocha entered an apprenticeship with a master tailor in 1779, his contract clearly stated that the foundling home director was prohibited by decree from selling expósitos as slaves.[98]

Two decades later, a royal edict on foundlings even further undermined colonial elites' efforts at social insularity with respect to expósitos. In 1794 Charles IV issued the striking ruling that all exposed children would be considered legitimate. The ruling, while certainly a defining piece of Bourbon social legislation, did not spring from thin air. Local judges in the empire had made decisions on the education and care of foundlings that, like the verdict in Cayetano María's case, increasingly treated abandoned children as future citizens by minimizing the legal limits they faced due to their natal status.[99] Furthermore, old ideological currents of royal paternalism also ran through the edict. Its wording echoed the sentiments of Luis Brochero, the sevillano who wrote a tract about expósitos almost two centuries earlier: "As they lack knowledge [about] and the care [of] their natural parents," the royal order read, "it falls to my dignity and Royal authority to consider them as my sons and daughters."[100]

Yet a marked shift in the official stance on children had taken place under the Bourbons. The 1794 cédula exhibited a sensibility that infancy was a critical stage of life and a concern with education characteristic of Enlightenment thinkers.[101] In various versions of the law, the king laid out the details of the foundlings' rearing and education, with special emphasis on how long the infants should nurse. The notable accent on the innocence of children in the cédula is another indication that the king had been swayed by the Enlightenment notion that children were closer to nature and still untainted by the corrosive effects of adulthood and even by the sins of their parents.

The edict also demonstrated a concern for the demographic size of the state typical of the physiocrats who had counseled French king Louis XV, and many provisions in the ruling directly paralleled the arguments that Claude Piarron de Chamousset had advanced in his influential 1756 tract, *Mémoire politique sur les enfants*. Louis XV had instituted several royal programs designed to lower his country's rates of infant mortality, and Charles IV drew from these programs as models.[102] The Spanish king discussed at length the issue of the "great distances" that the European infants traveled from the city to the countryside, where they were placed with rural wet nurses—another matter of physiocratic anxiety. Indeed, preserving the lives of this "numerous population of vassals" was one of the primary motives of the king's ruling.

Still, by extending legitimacy to foundlings, Charles IV treated abandoned children far more inclusively than his absolutist counterparts ever had. What compelled him to do so was what Joan Sherwood calls a "new economic paternalism." To convert abandoned children into industrious adult subjects, the king rejected the tradition of treating them as stains on family honor and instead "envisaged the foundling as a component of the state and separate from the family—a unit to be utilized for the public good."[103] The king lashed out against the long-standing assumption that foundlings were illegitimate and their subsequent exclusion from schools, official posts, and elite circles. He perceived the "scorn" and "humiliation" to which expósitos were subjected as detrimental to the economic health of the empire, since it rendered these children "lost to the state." Foundlings, he wrote, "have been taken for bastards, spurious [children], and the products of incest and adultery; it being so the contrary, because legitimate parents often tend to expose them . . . in the majority when they see that in any other manner they cannot preserve their lives." The expósitos, he implied, were not illegitimate but poor, and thus carried no stain of moral impurity. Rather than to marginalize the foundlings, the king sought to bring them into the imperial fold, where "because of their innocence, lack of protection, and my paternal vigilance" they could receive the same opportunities to become economically productive citizens as any other "gentleman" in the empire. Their "conservation and sound education," the king wrote, "can produce serious benefits for the state."[104]

Just as his father had with the 1776 Pragmatic Sanction on Unequal Marriages, the king failed to take into full account the effect that the edict on expósitos would have on his colonies. He offered no acknowledgment that erasing the presumption of moral impurity would mean erasing the presumption of racial impurity and thus destabilize the genealogical-racial categories integral to the caste order of colonial society. He simply extended to these children the social benefit of the doubt. Yet, colonial elites believed that in doing so the king also permitted parents to improve the social condition of their offspring by abandoning infants to his royal paternal care. Some opposed the king's new inclusive treatment of foundlings by arming their institutions against these newly legitimated children.

To protect the integrity of traditional caste hierarchies in the face of the king's edict, the director of Lima's School of Navigation refused to accept the city's foundlings in his institution.[105] In 1801 don Juan José de Cavero, the director of the Casa de Niños Expósitos, attempted to use his young inmates' new status to enroll them in the exclusive school for nautical studies. The director of the School of Navigation pointed out that the 1794 ruling contained an exemption for any institution that required entrants to prove they were the progeny of "true marriages." He argued that, according to the constitution of his school, its pupils were to be not only legitimate but also "indispensably white." The foundlings of the Casa, he suggested, may have been "legitimate" according to the 1794 ruling, but they spent their time "rubbing shoulders with servants," living in an institution that failed to segregate them from ordinary plebeians, and "beating the streets asking for alms." Thus they remained the social equals not of white children but of commoners.[106]

Officials who, like the director of the School of Navigation, were responsible for educating español pupils might have most vehemently rejected the ruling, but they were not alone. The director of the Colegio del Príncipe also tried to keep the association between foundlings, illegitimacy, and denigrated caste status alive after the royal grant of legitimacy as he waged a decades-long battle against the director of Lima's foundling home over its students' symbolic placement in the plaza mayor during public events. The colegio's director was dismayed that his "noble" Indian pupils stood below the foundlings on the rafters constructed for viewing autos-da-fe, bullfights, and public processions. The physical placement of his students, who were "illustrious vassals," indicated a "diminished [social] position" relative to abandoned children, whom he equated with the "lowliest plebeians."[107]

Strikingly, even while the director of the Casa de Niños Expósitos sought to enroll the foundlings in exclusive schools and jockeyed to elevate his students' status over Indian youths at public events, he also rejected a central tenet of the 1794 royal ruling. In the early nineteenth century, don Juan José de Cavero began a campaign to require parents to pay the foundling home when they abandoned their children. He decided to publish some of his correspondence with the archbishop on the matter, in which he contradicted the king's assertion that infant abandonment was the result of poverty rather than promiscuity. During his tenure as director of the Casa de Niños Expósitos, which began just after the 1794 ruling, the number of infants abandoned at the institution's door had soared. Cavero believed that most of these children were the progeny of immoral unions whose parents possessed sufficient means to support them.[108]

Although Cavero retreated into the notion that foundlings were degraded by their parents' sins rather than race, his protests reveal that even those colonial elites closest to foundlings detected in the 1794 edict a troubling tendency to stress the equal lot of children by means of their shared innocence, as well as a reckless royal disregard for proof of origins. For them, the equalizing tendencies of the edict held the potential to raze the very socioeconomic pillars of colonial hierarchies. In some places they had proof that the edict could undo that most basic of colonial institutions: forced Indian labor. According to Cynthia Milton, Indian children in Ecuador were increasingly labeled as foundlings and thus ascribed the status of legitimate after the 1794 ruling. On this basis they were exempted from mandatory labor duty over the loud protests of local elites.[109] Instead of innocence by virtue of youth, colonial elites repeatedly underscored the danger inherent in children of unknown origin. Rather than equality, colonial elites sought to reinforce the inequity built into the colonial social structure and to preserve traditional means of identifying children's status.

As they had with other reforms, colonial elites demanded that the Bourbon state clarify the racial implications of the policy on foundlings. But rather than refer the matter to local courts as they had with the Pragmatic Sanction on Unequal Marriages, members of the Cámara in Madrid refused to actively enforce the royal fiat on foundlings as early as 1797, only four years after its promulgation.[110] In 1805, when a case concerning a foundling's admission to Mexico's Colegio de Abogados reached the justices, they decided that considering all foundlings to be legitimate was ultimately incompatible with the promotion of caste order in the colonies.[111] The ministers referred to expósitos as potentially the offspring "of punishable and damnable sexual relations or of dark quality and infected origin." In short, the Cámara was forced to recognize that rather than producing "serious benefits for the state," the 1794 ruling was a "grave prejudice" to colonial elites.

In the end, the history of the king's edict on foundlings took a familiar course. Time and again, Bourbon social policies sidestepped the issue of race in favor making sure that no young imperial subject was lost to the royal exchequer. Time and again, local elites protested that reform policies concerning children were too inclusive or failed to differentiate among colonial castes. A new economic paternalism, they continually reminded the king, could not be applied universally to all children of the empire without careful consideration of the precarious social situation of colonial elites. It was within this dialectic of absolutist reform and local elite reaction that Lima's creole intellectuals began to reflect deeply on what emerging Enlightenment ideas regarding children and authority conveyed about their own political and racial kinship to Spain.

THE CREOLE FAMILY CRISIS

Since the child was often a metaphorical stand-in for the royal subject in Enlightenment writings, new pedagogies served as more than advice books for how to raise children. They were also antimonarchical philosophical tracts. Lynn Hunt, for one, has described the collapse of France's ancien régime as a Freudian "family romance," in which regicide was tantamount to patricide and revolutions created nations comprised of citizen-brothers rather than child-subjects.[112] The family romance narrative of revolution had been scripted in writings like Viscardo's *Letter to the Spanish Americans* and, most famously, in Rousseau's *The Social Contract*, where the idea that, at a certain stage, children must "be released from the obedience that they owed to the father" held clear political connotations.[113]

It was one thing for Spanish Americans who were loyal to colonial rule to refute these challenges to royal paternalism while the king actually governed the empire. But the French invasion of Spain in 1808 made the political kinship between creole elites and the Father King much more distant. Intellectuals in Lima strained to sustain the patriarchal model of monarchy in the young king's absence, and they began to torture the metaphor of king as father. Reporting on the establishment of a constitutional cortes in Spain in 1809, one article in the royalist paper *Minerva Peruana* summarized the news thus: "a king, who freely abdicates the crown, and later will return to reclaim it, and a child who holds it amidst an upheaval in the pueblo, and who will later return it."[114] In a letter to the editor, another contributor recounted how he had been heartened to hear a group of slave children singing songs praising the Spanish king while they gathered kindling in the woods. "Without these songs," the author reflected, "these babes would not know the name, even of the existence, of their monarch." But soon enough, he hoped, they would "know him and love him," since it could not be much longer before the king returned to the "breast of his children, who pass the time of their toils by intoning his name."[115]

As if the new political connotations of childhood and Napoleon's occupation of Spain were not enough to heighten local elites' sense that the traditional family model of colonial authority was becoming increasingly complicated, and perhaps even untenable, elite creoles also had to face another challenge. During the eighteenth century, European Enlightenment philosophers and scientists leveled a racial and political critique of the inhabitants of the New World that connected childhood, racial degradation, and revolutionary politics.

Europeans had long imagined the native inhabitants of the Americas as feminine and infantile, but in the eighteenth century this image of Indians shone with a new, scientific patina. Guillaume-Thomas Raynal's *Histoire philosophique de . . . duex Indes*, a collaborative effort by twelve Enlightenment philosophers published in the 1770s and 1780s, drew from the scientific theories of George-Louis Leclerc Comte de Buffon and Corneille de Pauw, who argued that the land mass known as the New World was relatively "young" in geological time and its inhabitants were biologically and culturally underdeveloped.[116] In Raynal's *Histoire*, the infantilization and feminization of Indians had clear political connotations: "The men there are less strong, less courageous, without beard or hair, degenerate in all signs of manhood. . . . The indifference of the males toward that other sex to which Nature has entrusted the place of reproduction suggests an organic imperfection, a sort of infancy of the people of America similar to that of the individuals on our continent who have not reached the age of puberty."[117] This characterization of Indians bore a striking resemblance to contemporary European commentary on Lima's creoles published elsewhere. For example, an anonymous visitor to Lima characterized creoles as "natural cowards and effeminate, and as a consequence weak and incapable of withstanding work with constancy."[118]

The portrayal of creoles as effete, weak, and infantile could be traced, in part, to wet nursing practices in the colonies. Many enlightened Europeans believed the climate of the New World and the milk of Indian nurses transmitted racial characteristics. In fact, the bonds that colonial child rearing practices created were considered to be as strong as those of blood.[119] Even Juan Pablo Viscardo argued that wet nursing created a kind of colonial consanguinity when he wrote that creoles had become "almost the same people (*popolo*)" as Indians because they were "suckled by their women."[120] Arguments such as these could easily be taken to mean that Spanish America was incapable of governing itself because its inhabitants, including creoles, were like children, still unprepared for the break from the Father King that philosophes such as Rousseau prescribed.[121]

As a result, the use of nonwhite wet nurses attracted biting satirical attention as well as sober concern in colonial Lima. In fact, the elite practice of relying on nonwhite women to raise children became a lightning rod for political commentary about colonial society. The intimacy forged between colonial servants and español children was cast as a danger, a degenerative force, corrupting and stunting the colonies. The idea, in essence, was that the milk passed from nonwhite subordinates to creole infants debased the colonists and made them, in effect, biologically "go native."

If Michel Foucault saw the eighteenth century in Europe as an era of increased adult scrutiny of children's sexuality, Ann Laura Stoler has expanded the observation for nineteenth-century colonial settings, asserting that this monitoring of children had everything to do with the highly imperial concerns of miscegenation, acculturation, and degeneration. Colonial policymakers possessed an "overwhelming concern with the dispositions of very small children and the malleabilities of their minds. All attended to the importance of breeding self-disciplined children and to the dangers of servants in the home."[122] Anxiety over sexual relations was one of the reasons that the proximity between servants and elite children in the colonial household moved to the center of colonial concerns, but it was only a part of a more generalized preoccupation with what John Locke had described in the late seventeenth century as domestic "contagion."[123]

Newspapers in Lima at the end of the century provided a venue for examining such notions about colonial servants and their young charges. Enlightenment thinkers in Europe, and even monarchs such as the king of Spain, disparaged wet nursing as harmful in terms of education and hygiene, and self-proclaimed ilustrados and intellectuals in Peru generated their own articulations of the criticism.[124] Ideas about the degenerative influence of nursemaids were not, of course, completely novel at the end of the eighteenth century. As noted in Chapter 2, early modern Spanish writers encouraged mothers to breastfeed their own children. But the concern over wet nurses in late colonial Lima was more than a mere revival of these earlier admonitions. It was produced by shifting family models of political legitimacy during the late eighteenth century and a coalescing image of creoles as racially degraded and politically stunted.

Within this context Lima's creole readers turned the pages of the *Semanario Crítico* in 1791 and found an invective against their child rearing practices laid out, quite literally, in black and white. Juan Antonio de Olavarrieta, the peninsular Franciscan who published the paper, observed how Lima's elite mothers passed children to wet nurses—"foreign mothers," in his words. This was no less than a "sinful, vile commerce" in which the wet nurse transmitted "seeds of vile corruption" to children through her milk.[125] In addition to biological contamination, Olavarrieta pointed out that Lima's inhabitants had a tendency to leave the children in the care of lower-caste women as they grew older, exposing them to pernicious cultural influences. He repeated basic Enlightenment truisms: these women filled children with fears of the boogeyman (*el coco*) and of fairies, elves, devils, witches, and spells. Furthermore, the children of the city began speaking with a "ridiculous" language because their vocabulary and pronunciation were ruined by "the tendency to feign and diminish vowels that is the philosopher's stone of all wet nurses."[126]

Lima's ilustrados, particularly those associated with the Sociedad de Amantes del País, bristled at Olavarrieta's ideas. It was not that the Sociedad was filled with staunch defenders of black and Indian wet nurses; it was that its members suspected that behind the Spanish priest's invective lay a more general, and damning, European condemnation of American-born Spaniards. Dubbing the priest *el Frayle de las Amas de Criar*, or the Wet Nurses' Priest, writers at *Mercurio* accused Olavarrieta of attempting to re-ignite factionalism between creoles and peninsulares. This animosity, they said, had long since been "extinguished, to the point that Europeans and Americans see ourselves as sons of the same father."

Creole elites in Lima glorified the new Bourbon paternalism when it equalized their position with peninsular subjects. But the phrasing here also prefigured *Mercurio*'s commentary on the creation of the royal Colegio de Nobles Americanos, and particularly its proclamation that permitting native noble boys to enroll in the school would extinguish the "odious rivalry" between Indians and creoles, who were the "sons" of the same Spanish Father King. Extinguishing differences among all of the king's subjects meant much more than simply asserting creoles' equality with peninsulares. Creoles only had to look to their own experience with Bourbon policy to understand that it might as easily imply a demeaning creole equality with the king's nonwhite subjects.

The Sociedad de Amantes del País claimed that Olavarrieta's criticism of the practice of using nonwhite amas de leche demonstrated his ignorance of local customs and of enlightened science itself. The priest had misunderstood *Mercurio*'s publication of Father Pedro Nolasco Crespo's observations on body fluids, an article that, in part, had inspired Olavarrieta's comments on the transmission of customs through the breast milk of wet nurses. "Dear priest, it would have been better if you had stayed quiet in your Monastery . . . than to have come from so far away, and gotten yourself involved in a critique of a noble and wise Country, before familiarizing yourself with the streets and the customs."[127]

Olavarrieta responded in print, admitting that *Mercurio Peruano* did, in fact, inspire his treatise on child rearing. But he had written in reaction not to Pedro Nolasco Crespo's articles but to two different letters to the *Mercurio's* editor. Olavarrieta blamed articles authored by an individual assuming the pen name "Eustaquio Filómates" for disparaging the "honorable houses of the city."[128] The articles to which the priest referred were satires of creole domestic life that, when closely analyzed, reveal that child rearing was a well-understood allegory for broader political concerns about patriarchal governance and Spanish rule in an age of Enlightenment.

Filómates's letters were based on one of the most critical European literary works about Lima published during the period. The poem *Lima por dentro y fuera* (Lima, inside and out), written by Spanish poet Esteban Terralla y Landa, described the city as a nightmare of social reversals.[129] Lima was in chaos on the outside because inside its homes the colonial family was in a state of critical gender and generational disorder. Women ruled men, slaves ruled their masters, and children ruled adults. Just as had other European authors of the age, Terralla y Landa believed American-born boys to be effeminate and degraded by colonial child rearing practices.

City inhabitants reacted fiercely against the poem and even publicly burned copies of it in a bonfire in 1790.[130] But the idea that creole households were in crisis did not float away with the smoke. A year later, the *Mercurio* ran the first of the two letters to which Olavarrieta would later turn when accusing the Sociedad de Amantes del País of "disparaging the honorable houses of the city." Filómates's "Educación: Carta sobre el abuso de los hijos que tuteen a sus padres," which took the form of a letter to the editor, directly borrowed its title from Terralla y Landa's verse "De la mala costumbre que usan los hijos en tutear a los padres y demás duedos."[131] Given the scandal surrounding the Spaniard's poem, it is safe to assume that the readership of *Mercurio Peruano* would have recognized the reference.

Filómates not only borrowed his title from Terralla y Landa; he rewrote the poet's dystopic vision of elite domestic life, adding local color and elements of irony that were meant to entertain and provoke readers familiar with the city. Like Terralla y Landa's poem, where sassy broods ruled parents, wives ruled husbands, and uppity slaves ruled their masters, the correspondent similarly described his own elite household as a place where social order had been turned on its head.

In the first letter, Filómates pointed to the very grammar household dependents used in addressing their elders as indicative of a political inversion of patriarchal order. The narrator lamented that his daughter, Clarisa, had adopted the "pernicious habit" of referring to her elders by using the familiar *tú*. The origin of this insubordinate behavior was his mother-in-law, Democracia, who had taught her granddaughter to use the linguistic form "common among all classes of citizens." Upon hearing his young daughter freely demanding adults to "give me candy, give me this, gimme! (*dáme caramelos, dáme esto, dáme*)," Filómates finally chastised the little girl. Democracia intervened, charging, "Your Mercy does not love your children; you are more tyrant to them than father." She went on, "Your Mercy who wants to teach others buena crianza, should know first that it is audacious to want to correct general custom."[132]

Although Filómates based his letter on Terralla y Landa's poem, he did not merely parrot European characterizations of Lima. Instead, he suggested that it was new Enlightenment philosophies of childhood and eighteenth-century transformations in political ideologies that had created a patriarchal crisis for the city's creole elite. In the Filómates clan, children, slaves, and women—or all members of political society—had begun to think of themselves as equals of the father. The origin of disorder was the mother-in-law, Democracia, who accused the father (king) of tyranny simply for trying to establish order.

The names chosen for the family members are revealing: Filómates is a name that translates into "child killer"; Democracia is an obvious choice for the reviled mother-in-law; and Teopiste, the mother, personifies religion. But it is the name Clarisa that had the most illustrious Enlightenment pedigree. It was assigned to the heroine in the widely read novel by Englishman Samuel Richardson, *Clarissa, or the History of a Young Lady* (1748)—in which the young heroine is delivered from dependence on her patriarchal family—as well as in a Frenchwoman's 1767 literary response to the novel, Jeanne-Marie Leprince de Beaumont's *La nouvelle Clarise, histoire véritable*.[133] The first of Filómates's letters, then, was in direct dialogue with a broader Enlightenment literature that focused on the replacement of patriarchal monarchies with societies of free and equal individuals.

But in Lima, *las luces* were always refracted through a distinctly colonial prism of racial dimensions. In his second letter, Filómates turned to another, particularly colonial danger lurking in Lima's households. Titling this epistle

"Amas de leche," Filómates described how, upon returning home from a twenty-two-month junket to Cuzco, he discovered that María, the once-humble slave wet nurse he had purchased to care for Clarisa, had been transformed into the de facto head of the household during his absence. In fact, Clarisa had become so intimate with María that she slept, ate, and played with the slave and even called her "my mama," displacing the affection due her mother, Teopiste. The correspondent appreciated the "services of a negra who raises children with care and tenderness." But he decried how the "openness and familiarity" between creole families and nonwhite wet nurses permitted the slaves to feel as though they could "lord over (señorear) everyone in the family," and he classified wet nurses' rearing as "always a detriment to the buena crianza of innocent little children."

Perhaps these articles were a double satire, and *Mercurio* cleverly presented the dethroned creole paterfamilias to its readers to satirize not only Lima's domestic disorder but also elite fears of racial disorder. Yet while equalizing Enlightenment pedagogies could threaten traditional patriarchal households everywhere, they would have particularly dramatic consequences in a society where generational proximity between races engendered colonial hierarchies. There is a niggling sense of sincerity in Filómates's attempt to identify social problems and to offer enlightened solutions, and it is in this sincerity that the creole family predicament becomes most obvious.

Mercurio editor José Rossi y Rubi added a comment to Filómates's second letter, published on 21 January 1791, praising the educative value of the articles and wondering, if this was the condition of Filómates's family after his absence, "what disorders there might be in those families where the father hardly pays a bit of attention, and the mother cares not at all. . . . We do not speak only of Lima: all of Peru and all of America are included in the declamations of our correspondent and our comments."[134] What is more, the story the author recounted may not have been completely fictional. Jean-Pierre Clément identifies Filómates as Demetrio Guasque, an archivist of the viceregal Cámara who, like the fictional Filómates, had been absent from Lima for twenty-two months before returning in 1790.[135]

As Julie Greer Johnson has pointed out in her study of Spanish American satire, the literary device is meant not to be didactic as much as to inspire the reader to think critically about the "interpretative distance" between the hyperbolic image it presents and reality.[136] Put another way, satire is only effective if it contains an element of recognized truth. Filómates's letters may have been fiction, but they offered a social critique that could be achieved only by portraying accepted realities about the colonial order writ large. Other articles on child rearing in Lima indicated that the idea of colonial degeneration and disorder was not merely a useful pretext for creole ruminations on patriarchy and new political philosophies. It was a problem to be solved.

In November 1791 *Mercurio* published a stinging satire, a "Letter about queers (*maricones*)," which treated perhaps the most inflammatory European criticism of the American-born inhabitants of the New World: the charge that creole men were effeminate.[137] The letter stirred a response from friar Tomás de Méndez y Lachica. Writing under the pen name "Teagnes," he expressed a fear that the sardonic article would not be effective in eradicating the "vice" of sodomy among the "lowest class, against whom the satire, with all of its acrimony, has less force than the cautious care of judges employed in rooting it out." The priest regarded the issue of gender "degeneration" as a scientific fact and set out to determine whether the feminization of men and the masculinization of women in Peru was an "anomaly of nature," a "defect of the climate," or a "vice engendered through education."

Méndez y Lachica decided that the culprit was nurture rather than nature, and he concentrated his discussion on the feminization of Peru's male children.[138] The "defect," according to Méndez y Lachica, occurred because Peruvian boys were "abandoned in the hands of a wet nurse."[139] Echoing Locke, the priest wrote that "excessive maternal love" during early education ensured that the child "has no other lessons than the manners of the [feminine] sex; and since in her he encounters all of the flatteries of misunderstood love, the reciprocal tenderness brings to his tender soul customs which do not conform to his condition." Inspired by a reputed Indonesian practice recorded in Raynal's *Histoire*, Méndez y Lachica recommended that Peruvian boys be removed from women's care until the age of six or seven so that male colonial subjects would no longer be "weak," "corrupted," and "effeminate."[140]

At the heart of the new politics of the child, then, was an Enlightenment quandary for local elites in Lima. To prove themselves enlightened, they had to concede that their child rearing practices led to creoles' infantilization and racial degradation. Teagnes's letters revealed his conviction that creoles, these native sons of Peruvian soil, had in fact become degenerate, effeminate, and perpetual children of the Father King. He also sought solutions in the writings of the same European Enlightened philosophers that had cast the problem as degeneration in the first place.

If, in the midst of this Enlightenment crisis, creole intellectuals in Lima continually reinscribed the relationship between Peru and Spain as paternal, it was because they had reason to fear that the alternative to accepting their role as children of the king was to be written out of the Spanish American family romance altogether. A late colonial painting from Lima depicts America as a woman suckling parasitic Spanish noble boys while two noble Andean couples sit below. At their feet, America's Indian sons lie groaning in hunger despite the paradise of Old and New World bounty that surrounds them.[141] The caption at the bottom reads, "Where in the world has it been seen what we are looking at here . . . / Her own sons groaning and the Strangers suckling" (Donde se ha visto en el Mundo lo que aquí estamos mirando . . . / Los hijos propios gimiendo y los Estraños mamando).

The painting's anonymous artist presented Spanish colonialism not as the corruption of Europeans at the breast of a wet nurse but, instead, as the Andean motherland's abandonment of the colonial subject, who is represented by Indian children. This was a sharp departure from artistic tradition. At the time of contact, the New World was frequently represented in art and literature as a virgin woman to be penetrated and possessed by virile European conquerors.[142] After the establishment of colonial rule in Peru, quite predictably, it became conventional to portray Indians as children and Spaniards as adults.[143] Yet in the above painting, there were no adult Spaniards, and America had become a mother rather than a virgin. The Spanish Father King was conspicuously missing from this artistic portrayal of colonialism, and nowhere were creoles explicitly to be found. If the true political children in Peru's family romance were Indians, and if, ultimately, their political maturity would erase creoles from the picture completely, this was enough to keep many of Lima's local elites loyal to the paternal political model of monarchy well into the nineteenth century.

CONCLUSION

It may be tempting to view the new politics of the child as a simple matter of enlightened reform and reaction, in which the state acted according to a new ideology and the colonial elite reacted.[144] It is true that broader European absolutist trends and Enlightenment philosophies of child rearing inspired many Bourbon social policies, and that the king frequently pushed social reforms too far for colonial elites in Spanish America. However, to recognize that both the king and local elites formulated their own versions of new philosophies and policies of childhood—that the interaction was comprised not of a unilateral imposition of European ideas on the city but of a new

America Nursing Spanish Noble Boys, anonymous Peruvian artist, late eighteenth century. (Used by kind permission of the anonymous owner.)

politics of ideas on childhood—means that we must refrain from reducing the period to a simple thesis-antithesis dynamic, and from portraying the king as a liberalizing reformer and colonial elites as conservative reactionaries.

The Spanish Bourbons expressed an enthusiasm to engage, though not always adopt without alteration, emergent philosophies based on reason and equality over ideologies founded on tradition and caste distinctions. Certain tenets of these philosophies were evident in the creation of the Colegio de Nobles Americanos and the reforms instituted in the Colegio del Príncipe, where erudition, rather than cultural mimesis, became the goal for young Indian nobles. A heightened sense of the vulnerability and impressionability of children became evident in many other schools as well and was even articulated by students themselves when they wished to improve their treatment by adult superiors. New pedagogical ideas were pervasive, extending beyond formal schooling and reaching the domestic sphere via the newspapers that demonstrated a marked interest in enlightening Lima's mothers about new child rearing practices.

At the same time, the correspondence between what historians term "the Enlightenment" and the Bourbon Reforms was not perfect. Various aspects of the Bourbon social reforms grew directly from enlightened absolutism; others were new growth blossoming from the long-dormant branches of Hapsburg philosophies of social organization and rule. The Spanish Enlightenment itself was the product of alchemy between traditional Catholic humanistic theology and new, rational, scientific models, a mixture then applied to economic and political problems.[145] In their broadest sense, Bourbon policies that intensified royal paternalism were not radical or intended to upset the caste-based hierarchies in the colonial regions of the Spanish empire. But the innovations these policies did contain—the emphasis on education, the dominance of notions of utility, and even the importance of childhood itself—transformed how limeños thought about child rearing and royal authority.

In late colonial Lima, state officials mediated generational disputes over marriage choice while local elites scoured the streets for poor women, children, and youths and carted them off to work in buildings where priests had once educated Indian noble boys. Notices announcing that it was illegal to purchase black foundlings as slaves were affixed on the outer walls of buildings lining city streets, in plain sight of the poor widows who marched to the doors of schools to clamor for their children's education. The Spanish king never before must have seemed more powerful, present, and paternal to the city's young inhabitants and the adults who reared them.

In turn, Lima's elites and officials did not simply await an implemented state reform before forming a response to emerging ideas about childhood and paternalism. They demonstrated an acute awareness of new philosophies about charity, child rearing, and education and, in many instances, had already considered and experimented with social policies aimed at youths years before official royal edicts were written. Such was the case with plans to create useful youths by creating a poorhouse, and it was true, too, of new policies concerning race and foundlings.

There were, however, distinct differences in the way the Enlightenment was experienced in Madrid and Lima. In Spain, practicing the new politics of the child meant that the king and his advisers incorporated some of the ideas of philosophes and physiocrats into social policies and rejected others. But in Lima, creole elites accepted and rejected not only new European philosophies but also Spanish reform measures, ever watchful of how they might undermine the colonial order. In the end, many of the most innovative social reforms instituted during the years 1770–90 would be reversed in the face of their resistance.[146] In the years following rebellion in Spanish America and revolutions in France, North America, and Haiti and, most importantly, because of reactions in the colonies, the Cámara and Council of the Indies recoiled from some of the king's more pathbreaking, and potentially disruptive, social policies on children.

In late colonial Lima, elites contended with the hegemony of monarchical measures that deprived native sons of political and economic control while seizing on those policies that granted greater authority to elites and elders. They ruminated over the potentially empowering and intrinsically antimonarchical ethos of new political philosophies as they educated their children as rational beings. And they intellectually wrestled in print, in salons, and in cafés with the implications of European strains of rational, scientific thought, some of which—like ideas about wet nursing—were essentially hostile to the New World. The rise of the new politics of the child was neither philosophically nor causally straightforward. Instead, it was an uneven, complicated process through which social reproduction was vested with deep political meaning. As we will see in the final two chapters, the fresh political valence of child rearing was not lost on the ordinary inhabitants of the city.

The New Politics of the Child
in the Late Colonial Courts

6

W
hat little autumn Lima can claim comes in April, when, during the evenings, the hot, humid cloud that blankets the day gives way to a cool mist constituting the city's winter. It was on such an April evening in 1760 that little doña María Francisca Mudarra y Cavero—known simply as Francisca—was kidnapped by two wet nurses and a man dressed in women's clothing.[1]

Between 7:00 and 8:00 in the evening, three women of African descent appeared at the lavish residence of Francisca's aunt, doña María. Don Gerónimo de Mudarra, a wealthy vineyard owner, had placed his infant daughter there when his wife died of complications during a second pregnancy. When doña María came to the door that evening, one of the visitors explained that the baby's father had contracted her services as a wet nurse. As she and María discussed the arrangement, one of the individuals, who had been standing behind the others, suddenly stepped forward, pulled off a hood, and revealed himself to be a man. Several other men, all later described as negros, appeared from the mist, rushed in through the door, and flanked the kidnapper as he snatched the baby and fled the residence. María dashed outside, accompanied, as would be any respectable elite woman, by two servants from the house. She stood on the cobblestone street, crying for help as the kidnappers vanished into the haze.

Although don Gerónimo worried that his daughter was being passed clandestinely from house to house among plebeians and mixed-race thugs, he knew who ultimately was to blame for doña Francisca's disappearance. He had, after all, been involved in a dispute over the custody of his child and the possession of her inheritance with his dead wife's family, including her politically influential cousin, the Marqués de Casaboza. Beginning in the first-instance court of the Cabildo in Lima and finally ending in the Council of the Indies in Madrid, the dispute between the adults in doña Francisca's life would last for sixteen years. During its course, the family saga would reach operatic proportions. Insults would be exchanged and swords would be drawn, the Council of the Indies would chastise members of the Audiencia, and don Gerónimo would even allege that the marqués had replaced Francisca with a look-alike double. By the time it ended, the contest over who possessed rightful claim to the custody of this one little girl would be recorded in thousands of pages of written legal arguments.

If law were the only measure of adult authority, there should have been little reason to dispute the rightful custody of doña Francisca. Don Gerónimo and her mother had been married in the Catholic Church, and thus their daughter was considered legitimate. The fact that this father sued for her return indicated that, unlike some parents in colonial Lima, he was more than willing to take care of his child as she grew into adulthood. In fact, he was willing to fight to do so. Most important from a strictly legal perspective, don Gerónimo possessed patria potestad, a right that indisputably granted a padre de familia control of the property and person of his legitimate minor children, except in rare cases.

What, then, should we make of the fact that the patria potestad of a wealthy *hacendado* such as don Gerónimo could be contested at all? Many recent histories of gender relations in colonial Latin America provide a ready answer. Patriarchy, their authors contend, is no less than an ongoing process of asserting male right in which gender power was constantly negotiated.[2] Patriarchy as negotiation—or perhaps more accurately, since colonial histories of gender relations often draw from court battles, patriarchy as contest—provides a formula with which historians can calculate the gendered variables in the daily interactions between colonial Latin American men and women.

In particular, historian Steve Stern contends that balancing between "absolute" ideas of male authority and culturally constructed notions of the reciprocal rights between genders was a central calculus at work in late colonial Mexican cases of domestic violence.[3] As we shall see, in the custody disputes that pitted adult limeños against one another, central points of contention included the fulfillment or breach of gender rights and obligations. Women often took men to court to force them to fulfill their obligations in supporting their children, while men voiced their absolute rights as padres de familia, rights derived from codified Spanish law.

But an examination of the history of guardianship and custody cases in late colonial Lima also reveals that negotiations over patriarchy, such as the one that involved Francisca Mudarra, took place on grounds wider than the gendered terrain contoured by male-female relationships. This is why don Gerónimo could be locked in a struggle not with his child's mother but with another man who could claim authority over his daughter. It also explains why the case was not settled on the legal bases of lineage and legitimacy alone. Conflicts over the legal right to guardianship and custody of children could spring from interpretations of laws or cultural norms concerning gender rights, but at the end of the eighteenth century, they were also increasingly inspired by new ideas about children and adult authority.

As we have seen, during the period from 1650 to 1750, laws favoring fathers often hid cultural practices and real-life social relations that invested women and other men—biological parents as well as wet nurses, patrons, and priests—with overlapping spheres of power over children. In the late colonial period, litigants and their lawyers began to claim that this power over children was more than cultural convention. It was, they asserted in their suits, an authority based in right rather than a privilege based in custom.[4] In the new politics of the child, legally sanctioned authority over children could be earned or lost by raising children in conformity with enlightened principles of childhood, as well as by relying on the secular courts' new mandate to intervene in domestic matters for the benefit of the state.

Thus, the traditional practice of civil law, in which actual colonial child rearing customs were concealed in favor of maintaining patriarchal fictions in the courts, eroded during the late colonial period; the old politics of the child gave way to the new. Amidst changes in ideas about childhood and patriarchal authority in the domestic realm, and emboldened by royal policies that provided the secular courts greater jurisdiction over disputes that involved minors of age, colonial magistrates began to mediate between overlapping and contentious claims to authority over children brought by an ever-widening cross section of Lima's population.

This chapter looks at this late colonial transformation in conflicts over the guardianship, custody, and financial support of Lima's free children in two parts. First, late colonial litigation is situated within the general expansion of the powers of the secular judiciary during the second half of the eighteenth century. Lima's secular magistrates, acting on their own accord or spurred by royal edicts that charged courts with supervising the education and care of children and slaves, increasingly heard cases over children brought forward by colonial adults of all walks of life.

The second section, which constitutes the heart of the chapter, analyzes the content of guardianship contracts and civil cases aired before Lima's Cabildo and Real Audiencia during the late colonial period, when the courts moved away from only overseeing cases over children that involved property and the city's elite, as they had during the period 1650–1750. The types of adults who litigated over children, the kinds of suits they brought, and the arguments litigants and their lawyers put before secular magistrates in disputes over children changed dramatically at the end of the eighteenth century. This transformation bore the distinctive marks of the new politics of the child. Its cardinal tenets—including secular control over matters of domestic governance, the promotion of utility, and the emergence of rational pedagogies and new philosophies about childhood—found their way beyond the edicts, essays, and school constitutions in which they made their first appearances in Lima. They became the arguments ordinary colonials employed when engaged in litigation over children.

These arguments can be placed under four distinct rubrics, although litigants and their lawyers seldom relied on only one in pleading their cases. First, limeños began to translate the emotion elders felt for children into assertions about their natural rights as parents—rights derived from the sentiment that they expressed and manifested toward the young. In addition, the quality of the education that children received also became a key criterion in arguing for and awarding custody and guardianship to litigants. A third element of the new politics of the child, a concern with discipline and social control, placed new stresses on parents, whose treatment of children fell under increasing court surveillance. But Bourbon discipline was more than a state social control project. Tapping into the local social control efforts that promoted order, utility, and the policing of the city, limeños also initiated formal appeals to even the high courts of the city to help them control their own children. The increased secular mediation of disputes over the financial support of children (alimentos)—a by-product of Bourbon policy to increase state jurisdictional control over marriage—comprised the fourth element of late colonial legal disputes over children. It was in ruling on these cases that the colonial state made its most significant incursion into the private patriarchal sphere.

By asserting royal paternalism and applying the new politics of the child from their benches, the crown's judges sometimes became the unlikely allies of patriarchal subordinates in legal battles against men who had law on their side. New concepts about children and authority were not, however, simply crude implements with which women sought to strip men of patriarchal rights over children. Men did not make their arguments based only on their absolute right of patria potestad. Instead, they often adopted the same criteria as did their legal opponents. In order to counter challenges to their paternal authority, they referred to their natural rights and emotions for children, and they sometimes eloquently justified their ability to provide their children an appropriate education. Indeed, a broad array of colonials—patriarchs and subordinates alike— became familiar with ideas about the intervening role of the state in family matters and the importance of providing youths the education and discipline to make them good citizens. In the end, in addition to being both official policy and elite philosophy, the new politics of the child was a popular politics as well.

THE CONTEXT FOR COURT CONTESTS

Several factors brought about a transformation in litigation over children during the late colonial period. To begin with, the number of civil cases involving minors of age increased during the end of the century alongside all civil cases aired in the secular judicial system. A review of proceedings in the Audiencia series in Lima's national archive, for example, indicates that the amount of civil litigation grew considerably between the seventeenth and nineteenth centuries, just as we saw in Chapter 4 with criminal trials. Disaggregating the average number of cases within the periods in figure 6.1 helps to pinpoint the decades of change more precisely. During the first half of the eighteenth century, the average number of civil cases heard by the Audiencia was about 16 per year and was only slightly higher than the average of 11.23 during the preceding century. But after the 1750s, the number of cases brought before secular magistrates increased at a remarkable rate, climbing to an average of 51.98 per year.

We cannot know for certain if the increase in cases found in the archive today means that colonial inhabitants actually used the civil court system more actively at the end of the colonial period. The increase may be due to population growth in the city, or it could be primarily a remnant of Bourbon officials' better record keeping. The city population did increase throughout the century; for every inhabitant in 1700, 1.4 resided in the city in 1790. Yet if the population grew steadily, the number of civil cases seemed to skyrocket. For

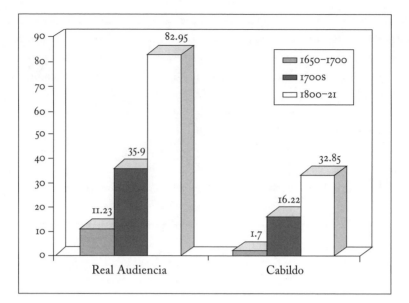

FIGURE 6.1 Average Number of Civil Cases per Year, Lima, 1650–1821.
Source: AGN, RA, C. Civ.; AGN, Cab., C. Civ.

every civil case brought forward in the first half of the eighteenth century, 4.6 were filed during the second half of the century.[5]

Even if the increase in the quantity of civil cases housed in the archives does not conclusively prove that colonials sued one another more frequently in the late colonial period, the changing profile of litigants in disputes over children tells us that a qualitative change in the use of the courts occurred nonetheless. Suits over the control of minors' property and attempts to force propertied parents (especially fathers) to recognize and bequeath to illegitimate children were a mainstay of cases over minors of age in the period from 1650 to 1750. These cases continued to enter the court system after 1750. But they sat on the desks of lawyers and scribes beside an increasing number of "bread and butter" suits—litigation between adults over children possessing little or no claims to inheritance.[6] Wet nurses, separated parents, the parents and relatives of slave children, and battling relatives, as well as myriad other adults who had raised children, began to appear before the scribes that lined the streets off the city square. Unlike their predecessors, these litigants did not lay claim in a child's name to thousands of pesos, slaves, real estate, or haciendas. Instead, scribes penned arguments to persuade judges to award litigants child custody, to free their enslaved children, to garner modest financial support with which to raise the young, or to force another elder to compensate them for what they had already invested in child rearing. In other words, it is not simply that there were more cases over children. The nature of the cases changed as well.

These late colonial transformations in civil litigation over children involved the employment of new legal arguments in court as well as the introduction of new kinds of suits. As we shall see, litigants and lawyers made arguments during civil litigation that reflected the same Enlightenment ideas that were circulating in other social arenas in the city, such as schools and periodicals. Many of Lima's lawyers, dozens of judges, and most notably, the Defensor de Menores subscribed to the "enlightened" periodicals being published in the city, which ran articles dedicated to instructing Lima's adults on raising "rational" children. These articles, like royal orders or other printed matter, were read aloud in the streets.[7] In addition, limeños followed the news of scandalous court cases, and, at times, lawyers published especially clever arguments for public consumption.[8] Based on these clues, we might imagine that those who read particularly compelling legal arguments passed along reports to individuals involved in disputes over children, generating more of the new kinds of litigation. As the old Spanish proverb goes, "Lawsuits are like cherries; have one and many follow."[9]

New legal arguments were often deployed in a secular court system that held a much wider ambit of authority over domestic cases involving children than it had in the past. Jurisdictional changes at all levels of the Bourbon judicial bureaucracy transformed the types of suits aired in court over children at the end of the eighteenth century. Lima's alcaldes, the Audiencia, the Council of the Indies, and even the king himself expanded the reach of the secular courts into family life throughout the late colonial period. As the royal state encroached upon the city's households by hearing the civil aspects of marriage disputes—particularly in cases concerning alimentos, which referred to both alimony and child support—the city's secular judges presided over a greater number of disputes over the custody and care of children.

This expansion was by no means smooth. Until the late 1780s, the Council of the Indies remained hesitant to rule on disputes over alimentos because of their proximity to divorce cases, and thus to ecclesiastical jurisdiction. It threw out the Mudarra–Marqués de Casaboza case when the suit was appealed to Madrid. The council chided the viceroy and members of Lima's Audiencia for becoming involved in the dispute and ruling against the father. Since it was revealed during the course of the trial that Francisca's mother had filed for divorce just before she died, the Spanish judges believed the case fell under ecclesiastical jurisdiction.[10] The council again admonished the oidores of the Audiencia of Lima—and this time even fined Viceroy Amat y Junient—for becoming involved in a suit a woman filed against lawyer don Blas Quiroz for failing to fulfill a marriage promise and neglecting his two illegitimate children. Limeños were well aware of the Quiroz affair. It became something of a cause célèbre in the city, and Lima's late colonial litigants occasionally cited it as a kind of precedent.[11]

Judges in Lima displayed an inclination to intervene in marital disputes earlier than officials in Madrid, but the Spanish magistrates would eventually change their minds. As explained in Chapter 5, the Cámara finally shifted its position concerning secular jurisdiction over alimentos suits in 1787, bringing metropolitan policy more in line with local practice in Lima. This time, rather than reprimand the secular courts for overstepping jurisdictional bounds, the Cámara reproached the city's ecclesiastical tribunal for interfering in a suit over alimentos and a dowry following the divorce of Josefa Castañeda and Rodrigo del Castillo. In this ruling, the council announced that secular courts had exclusive jurisdiction over alimony and child support cases.[12]

In addition to these formal jurisdictional changes, the late colonial period also witnessed increased bureaucratic specialization in judicial hearings. Lima's Defensor de Menores began to preside over a wide and diverse body of cases, often far removed in content from the inheritance issues generally associated with the city's elite children. It was evident in other regions, too, that the role of Spanish American Defensores de Menores had expanded from overseeing property to protecting the well-being of a vast array of children. For example, upon the creation of the new intendancy of Río de la Plata in 1776, the Argentine Defensor was commissioned with protecting both minors and the indigent and took on child welfare cases in addition to property disputes.[13]

The Bourbon drive to garner quick revenue for the war-plagued Spanish state also affected how laws on children were applied in the colonies. In 1795 the crown published an American version of a price list (*arancel*) for *cédulas de gracias al sacar*, or royal dispensations of honors and privileges. The royal government would offer Spanish Americans willing to put up the cash—and to put up with the slow and invasive process of telling their life stories in court— with what birth had not, such as legitimacy and limpieza de sangre. Included among the privileges listed for sale on the 1795 price list was a dispensation of guardianship to remarried widows, who could pay to avoid losing custody of their children and control over their property. Drawing from a 1773 Castilian price list that included dispensations for widows' guardianship, the 1795 American arancel charged remarried colonial widows 6,000 pesos to retain custody of their children.[14]

Although a few women in the Spanish empire did purchase the gracias in the late eighteenth and nineteenth centuries in order to retain guardianship, Lima's colonial widows did not seem to flock to file for this dispensation.[15] Its availability nonetheless affected prevailing interpretations of women's rights and authority over children at a more general level. The legal definition of "mother" in Joaquín Escriche's 1851 dictionary of Spanish law and jurisprudence indicated that, while patria potestad still was not the domain of women, for all practical purposes the sale of dispensations meant that widows might enjoy the same authority to retain custody and manage the assets of their children as did men.[16] By feverishly trading legal privileges for pesos, the cash-strapped Bourbon monarchy had undermined long-standing laws restricting women from enjoying full legal authority over their children.

Thus, during the late eighteenth century, specific Bourbon provisions widened the jurisdiction of the secular courts, expanded the role of the Defensor de Menores, and altered gendered definitions of adult authority over children. More than merely shifting disputes over children from church to state courts in Lima or generating more of the old kinds of disputes over children, the new politics of the child allowed a new kind of litigant to bring a new kind of litigation into the city's courts.

PRACTICING THE NEW POLITICS OF THE CHILD

Love, Law, and Nature:
New Discourses of Authority over Free Children

Colonial limeños had long raised their children in a manner that did not exactly correspond to the procedures printed in codified law or enshrined in the texts of the legal scholars and moralists whom they reverently called "the Authors." Recall from Chapter 2 that civil cases during the seventeenth and early eighteenth centuries revealed a quiet but key disparity between law and practice in terms of child custody: men might retain the legal title of "guardian" or fathers might hold authority over their children based on patria potestad, but in fact, women raised children. In the late colonial period, female litigants and their lawyers began to translate this cultural assumption, which formerly had been tacitly understood but not overtly argued as a basis for authority, into legal arguments about women's right to child custody and financial support.

Don Gerónimo, father of the kidnapped infant Francisca Mudarra, made a point to promise that his sister would raise his daughter when he filed his suit to achieve guardianship of the girl. In fact, the Defensor de Menores who reviewed the case, Domingo Larrión, based his legal recommendation in part on whether a woman would care for Francisca. He believed that don Gerónimo possessed the legitimate right to the "administration of the person and property of his daughter by reason of patria potestad, which can be denied to no father." However, Larrión saw a "difference between the person of the minor and her property." The custom of placing children in female custody, he wrote, sprang not only from a law that required mothers to provide alimentos to children under age three but also from the fact that "the tenderness of children demands an assistance, prolixity, and care that is purely womanly, domestic, and familiar, which no man can accommodate."[17]

Larrión distinguished between men's property rights and women's right to raise children in part because, in the late eighteenth century, emotion became a critical criterion in determining what best served a child's interest. Judges began to deem claims for custody worthy of an official audience if the litigant expressed affection for the child in question, and courts considered the possibility that the written law might run contrary to the "love that nature inspired" and, thus, to natural rights. What is more, maternal love was believed to engender maternal right, and maternal right was configured as a natural right. This configuration permitted women to clamor vocally for legal recognition as guardians and for custody of their children. Yet, as we shall see, while allowing women to make arguments in defense of their own rights to authority over children, the stress on the emotional bonds between adult and child also influenced how men made arguments in the court system.

In his influential study of family life in England, Lawrence Stone asserted that "there developed much warmer affective relations between husbands and wives and parents and children" in the late eighteenth century.[18] Stone's assertion that parents actually *felt* more love for children is impossible to prove. We have seen that, throughout the centuries, colonial elders, whether parents or not, spoke of the affection that children "inspired in them" despite high levels of infant mortality and child circulation, and despite the acceptance of certain levels of violence against children within the domestic sphere. But at least in colonial Lima, family members did articulate emotion more openly in court after the middle of the eighteenth century. At this time, the fact that an adult loved a child seemed to acquire a denser social and legal weight in tipping custody decisions. This weight was not simply a calculation of the affection adults felt. It was derived from philosophies about sentiment's relationship to nature, and nature's relationship to right.

The affective transformation in language is evident even in the mundane guardianship contracts city notaries drafted at the end of the century. What was once the simple protocol involved with naming and approving guardians became more elaborate as officials such as the Defensor de Menores and the parties involved used the procedure as an opportunity to reflect on what best served the emotional interests of children. For example, Defensor General de Menores Felipe Aylvando explained why he thought it appropriate to name the uncle of José Bernardo and Buenaventura Marín as their guardian in a 1799 contract. When the original guardian named in their mother's will renounced the responsibility, the Defensor had considered naming several of the children's adult relatives. Initially, he said, he had passed over their aunt, doña Josefa Marín, because she was a married woman, indicating that laws restricting women other than mothers from serving as guardians might be circumvented as long as the women were single. But upon deliberation, the Defensor had changed his decision in light of her "honor, judgment, and conduct"; because she had no children of her own; and significantly, because he believed "she would instill in them her natural goodness and tenderness." The Defensor openly revealed that he had slipped around the illegality of naming a married woman as a guardian by appointing her husband in her name: "Her sex had at one time excluded her from tutela," he wrote, "but her husband, don José Montiel Dávalos, has all of the qualities necessary to be charged with the office."[19] The Defensor still followed an established practice of nominally awarding a man guardianship while a woman would raise orphaned children, but he now made his reasons for doing so known.

Ideas about tenderness and natural goodness as well as love became important determinants in battles over guardianship and custody waged in secular court as well as in simple guardianship appointments. Late colonial magistrates were willing to test the boundaries of guardianship law by factoring in how deep litigants' feelings ran for the child. Fifteen-year-old doña María Mercedes Vásquez de Vásquez wanted her stepfather to serve as her curador when her mother died because of "how much during my mother's life and after her death he has done to attend to me, and is now doing to attend and care for me with singular caution and esteem."[20] But her uncle challenged the stepfather for guardianship by explaining, "I have loved her and do love her and [have] a solid interest in her best state." The uncle attempted to convince the judges of the Audiencia that Spanish law was inherently suspicious of stepfathers. Surely, he said, María Mercedes's stepfather would favor his own biological child over her in business dealings—"since everyone knows that parents love their own children more . . . by means of Nature itself." But the Audiencia ultimately confirmed María Mercedes's choice as administrator of her property.

Because affection between adults and children, which was often discursively linked to nature, became a criterion for awarding custody, women as well as men (or perhaps even more than men) could argue that they had a right to custody of minors of age. In the late eighteenth century, ordinary colonials expressed a belief that the natural love that mothers felt for their children (*el amor de madre*, or "a mother's love") translated into women's natural rights over children. Doña Feliciana Bustamante invoked the new legal significance of love when she requested to be named tutora of her own natural daughter in 1777. "It is indispensable that the guardianship of my daughter be conferred to me," she stated. "Although this office is not the property of women, it is dispensed in favor of the mother and the grandmother for the love that they hold for [the children], and for this end." The Defensor de Menores granted her guardianship "because the *buena crianza* that said doña Feliciana gives to her minor daughter is clear to the Defensor."[21]

Litigants also began to argue that, since motherly love for children did not end when mothers remarried, the law in the *Siete partidas* that deprived remarried widows of guardianship was unjust. Recall that as long as a widow received legal confirmation to do so and did not take another husband, she could legally be recognized as guardian for her children. If she did remarry or if the father named another man as guardian, a widow theoretically lost control over her children.[22] At the end of the eighteenth century, the dispensation of gracias al sacar to widows may have weakened this law. Yet Bourbon legislation never appeared as a basis for remarried widows' arguments about their authority over children in late colonial Lima. Instead, these mothers argued that legal codes conflicted with their natural rights as mothers, which were above written law.[23]

Doña Paula de Silva objected to what she believed was the profligate life-style her daughter, Gregoria, led in her sister-in-law's household, where the girl had moved when her father died. The father had left a testament stating his desire that his daughter be raised in his sister's home, but doña Paula, since remarried, petitioned to have Gregoria removed from the household to a convent to prevent the girl from marrying. She was, she said, "using the rights (*derechos*) that maternity grants me in order to avoid harm and seek the good of my children." Worried that the judge would rule that she had lost authority over her daughter when she remarried, doña Paula argued, "Even though they are natural rights[, they are] never extinguished by a mother's marriage to someone other than the Fathers."[24] She asked for the man who since her remarriage had been acting as curador to her daughter to express his support for her decision to move Gregoria to a convent, which he promptly did.

The remarried widow doña Josefa Escudero also expressed misgivings about the justice of a law that stripped her of her right to custody of her son and management of his property. When doña Josefa took another husband, guardianship of her son, Antonio, was transferred to his grandmother.[25] When the grandmother passed away, doña Josefa stepped forward, deciding that, since all of her son's closest remaining kin were male, it was up to her to raise her child. Antonio, she said, was at the "tender age that demands the most detailed and meticulous circumstances, for which the care of men is not adequate." Even if a benevolent desire to protect minor children from the financial malfeasance of remarried widows and stepfathers underlay the law, she asserted, "the appreciation of my person and the love that nature inspires in me as mother of the pupil are particularities that disarm the presumption of evil handiwork."

Although codified law did not support her case, doña Josefa argued, the "laws of good reason and humanity" did. These laws, she said, supported the dictum that "no one better than a mother can carry on the care of a pupil, and nothing will make a more lasting impression than her inattention and lack of care." Doña Josefa even went so far as to claim that the law granted mothers the "faculty to establish guardianships for orphans, and only they exercise the office of patria potestad." Thus, through an equation that linked gender custom to the contemporary concepts of natural rights and reason, a mother could claim that she possessed patria potestad. Unable to resolve the issue, the judges of the Audiencia, on recommendation from the Defensor de Menores, placed Antonio with a third party.[26]

Late colonial women such as doña Josefa could link maternal emotion to legal rights over children even as they utilized a new vocabulary of the laws of "good reason." Emotion was the opposite of reason in some Enlightenment philosophical formulas, but the increased value of sentimentality and a condemnation of human cruelty, especially to slaves and children, underpinned their connection in the late eighteenth century.[27] Enlightenment philosophies at once defined reason as a masculine domain and advanced a gendered ideology of love, in which maternal sentiment was elevated to the sacred realm of nature, from which all basic rights were generated.[28] Women may not have been deemed equal to men politically, but their authority as mothers if not citizens ultimately was conceded as a natural right.[29]

When putting forward their new legal interpretations of authority over children, late colonial lawyers and litigants claimed that justice was inherently rational, and they sometimes denounced strict adherence to the law—rather than to precepts of reason—as irrational.[30] For example, when doña Antonia Hernández became pregnant with Teodoro Martínez's child, she argued that laws favoring fathers could be irrational. In response to her suit for child support in the amount of 4 reales per day, Teodoro strictly interpreted a law in the *Siete partidas* to read that women must take on full financial responsibility for children until they were weaned.[31] The suggestion that a father did not have an obligation to support infants struck doña Antonia as unreasonable. "It is one thing that children, in these days, cannot be ripped from the tender breasts of their mothers, and it is another, very different thing that the father is [free of] obligations for the whole time. One is just, the other would be irrational."[32]

Women also began also to contrast their own loving natures with the tyranny of the men they sued over their children's custody and support. Doña María Ignacia del Castillo claimed that the alcalde "only has to lay eyes on the statement" of her husband to see all the evidence he needed to prove her husband's "tyranny and cruelty."[33] Flora Guerrero accused her child's father of "indolence, tyranny, and the failure to comply with his obligation" to his son.[34] Another mother claimed that her son ran away from home because his father was a "tyrant."[35]

Women in colonial Lima had long accused husbands of abuse and failure to provide for their families before crown and church authorities. But litigants' increased references to fathers as tyrants were a distinctly late colonial phenomenon. It is worth noting that in the seventeenth-century annulment cases we examined in Chapter 2, children accused parents of coercing them to marry or take religious habits, but in no case did they refer to elders as tyrants as such. The word was absent even in the few secular cases over fathers' obligations and custody of their children that occurred before the end of the century—including in the 1769 Mudarra case, where it was revealed that his wife had attempted to deprive her husband of guardianship in her will because of his "hatred" for his daughter. The ubiquity of the term "tyrant" in late eighteenth-century political discourse, then, appears to have made it readily available for women to use in court cases.

It is possible that Lima's litigants and lawyers adopted the word without its attendant political meanings. But there is evidence that this change in language was only one element in a rising public disdain for abusive patriarchs in Enlightenment discourse. In the late eighteenth century, young men who were accused of seducing young women commonly began to argue that the girls had fled into their arms because their fathers and stepfathers were cruel and tyrannical.[36] In the early nineteenth century, Mexican newspapers often ran articles criticizing abusive husbands, and around the same time, novelist José Joaquín Fernández de Lizardi expressed his belief that men who mistreated their wives were, among other things, "tyrants" and "despots," far from the "civilized man who knows the laws of humanity and honor."[37]

These references to love, the natural rights of parents, and tyranny in late colonial court battles over children invite us to return to the home of the fictional Filómates, where patriarchal order was coming undone, and there to draw some parallels between literature and law. When Democracia accused this padre de familia of trying to "correct a general custom," she echoed a contrast between austere laws and common colonial practices of child rearing that was becoming more pronounced in late colonial legal petitions. When she accused Filómates of failing to love his children, her allegations conjured up the same stress on love and sentimentality for children Lima's parents and custodians expressed in the courts. In telling him that he was "less father than tyrant"—a term so politically fraught in the period—Democracia, like Lima's mothers who went to court over their children, suggested that tyrants should lose their authority over children.

The Rights of Fathers Erased Forever: Discipline

The ascendancy of the secular legal system as the ultimate arbitrator of intergenerational relations, as the patriarch of last resort for both parents and children alike, was a key feature of Bourbon plans to rebuild imperial society. Recall that in 1790 the king had drawn together edicts on matters concerning parents and children, circulating them with the intent to encourage secular judges to ensure that youths "are good Citizens, and avoid crimes and scandal."[38] Throughout the colonial period, limeños had asked alcaldes to place their sons in apprenticeships or even to send them to presidios precisely for this purpose. However, in the late colonial period these requests took on a more official nature. Elders asked for the intervention of even viceroys to control their children by calling upon the heightened Bourbon contempt for vagrancy and vice.

Doña Manuela de Lara appealed directly to the Audiencia concerning her wayward brother in 1793.[39] Although their "illustrious parents" gave them "the crianza and education that corresponded to their status by birth," her brother José was given to gambling and drink and consorted with "inferior and poorly versed people." Doña Manuela petitioned the judges to send José to a presidio in Africa because, she said, "he will not be subjected to reason or other oversight that might refrain him." The Audiencia sentenced him to spend two years on the next marine ship leaving the port of Callao. In a similar manner, shoemaker Manuel Palacios went all the way to the viceroy to punish his adult son. Throughout his son's life, Manuel had repeatedly sought the help of various officials in the city, and at one point his son had been sent to the Presidio of Valdivia. Manuel had become desperate and, "despite being a father," decided he simply could not handle his progeny. He asked the viceroy to send his son to a panadería until he could be put on the next ship leaving for Spain.[40]

Anxiety about laziness and vice was especially pronounced when parents used the courts to control male children, who could be shipped off as soldiers and sailors and forced to become economically productive for the state. But the misdeeds of female youths also concerned some parents. Don Diego Robledo was having trouble with his two daughters, Rufina and Felipa, and so he, too, went to the legal system for help.[41] Because he had encountered difficulties with his offspring before, he had placed the younger Felipa in a convent. He was convinced that Rufina, already married and separated from her husband, had posed as her sibling in the convent so that Felipa could break out of the cloister, roam the streets, and attend public celebrations. With Felipa still missing from the convent, a court official questioned Rufina about her father's accusation. She protested that she had no idea of her sister's whereabouts. "Either the rights of fathers over their children have been erased forever, or I have done something to make the paternal piety of your Justice come here in vindication of his respect, to punish a crime that the Father himself has committed," she responded.

Rufina's response slyly suggested that the authority of fathers had been weakened by the state's interest in enforcing its power over families. Like Rufina, other limeños were beginning to marvel at the level of state intervention into domestic affairs. While some parents might find the royal state helpful in containing their children, others found its paternalistic intrusions into Lima's households alarming. When the eighteen-year-old priest José Rivera asked the alcalde to force his father to pay for his upkeep in the monastery, he made sure to point out that it was legal for a son to sue his father for alimentos, "according to the laws that inspire and order Fathers to [provide] this care to their minor children." Yet José's father was incensed by the suit and claimed that it and all similar cases reaching the courts were "persecutions of filial disobedience."[42]

José's father worried that the state was making parents, rather than wayward children, the targets of the Bourbon campaign to instill discipline and order. Lima's judges may not have disagreed, since their disciplinary responsibilities had come to involve monitoring parents. In fact, the Bourbon kings specifically commissioned judges to "make up for [parents'] apathy or negligence." It should not be surprising, then, that certain kinds of colonial parents might be judged more apathetic or negligent than others. In eighteenth-century criminal trials analyzed in Chapter 4, the Bourbon judicial system used its punitive faculties with somewhat greater frequency against youths who were deemed to be dangerous by virtue of caste and lack of patriarchal authority at home. Although the case record does not contain evidence that the secular courts were used to discipline a sizable number of parents in the colonial period, the emergence of certain kinds of cases in the latter half of the eighteenth century suggests that the secular judicial apparatus was specially deployed to protect, not just punish, children who lived in weak patriarchal families.[43]

One such child was a little boy who had disobeyed his mother as they traveled on the road that linked Lima to the port of Callao in 1817. Following the same route on horseback that day, don Ramón Saldano saw a commotion in the distance. Approaching, he witnessed a "china" grabbing a young boy, shaking him upside-down, forcing a kerchief to his face, and demanding, "Now you will tell me where the key is!" Don Ramón intervened, mounting the boy on his horse and turning the youth's attacker over to the alcalde.[44]

The alcalde who initially heard the case took custody of the child, put him to work at various tasks around the plaza, and placed María Socorro Díaz in the royal prison, submitting her case to the Audiencia. From within the prison, María Socorro gave her statement. She reported that she had gone to the port town that day with her son to collect some debts. Entrusting the six-year-old with some coins and the key to their room, which she wrapped in the kerchief, she turned to wash her feet in the irrigation stream (*acequia*) that ran along the side of the road. When she returned, the boy gave her the kerchief, which was now empty of its precious content. Asking what had happened to the key and coins, the boy finally confessed that he had thrown them into the river. "Bothered," she said, "I tried to castigate him as a Mother."

María Socorro turned the concept of natural maternal rights to her defense, explaining that she was merely punishing her son, not threatening his life: "It stretches Nature for your Lordship to hear such a thing, that a mother would take the life of her son or would even try." "I am," she proclaimed, "his mother and incapable of such a crime." As she worked concepts of the natural love between mother and son into her statement, she also relied on intensified paternalistic discourses of justice to make her case. She pleaded with the oidor, "Your lordship is not only Judge but Father, and from the simple confession I have offered you will see I am not a criminal." The Audiencia released her from prison, but its justices warned her to treat her son with the "moderation that corresponds to his minor age and his innocent state" in the future.

María Socorro's criminal trial, while handled relatively summarily and without elaborate arguments, suggests that Lima's high court considered the most routine disciplinary interactions between parents and children as matters fit for a formal case. The new politics of the child, however, provided more than a mandate for judges to supervise suspect parents. It also provided litigants facing these secular judges new avenues of defense against allegations that they mistreated children. Although she faced a judicial system more vigilant about child abuse and parental misconduct, María Socorro exploited emergent discourses about mothers' natural love and heightened discourses of state paternalism to escape punishment. Accused criminals also utilized other new discourses associated with the new politics of the child to defend their treatment of children. For example, in one case a woman testified on behalf of her sister, who was accused of beating her four-year-old daughter to death, by conceding that her sister indeed had physically punished the child. But, she said, this was only because the girl had been raised by a disorderly wet nurse, that most maligned of all educators in the new order of things. The girl, her aunt claimed, had "come back from the lactation nurse so badly taught that she only proffered obscene words, and the punishment [her mother meted out] was proportional to the need to correct her."[45]

According to this woman, bad teaching, not parental abuse, had killed the little girl. In the 1790 circular, the king empowered police and judges to supervise parents to "correct the education, sloth, and the vicious natures that parents pass on to their children." When engaged in late colonial litigation over children, many adults realized that proving that they were following the king's recipe for preventing "the notoriety and damage that sloth brings to universal industry" by being attentive to children's education and training would be critical to their legal success. As a result, education itself became a key ingredient in many late colonial battles over children.

Education

In his seventeenth-century treatise on canon and civil law, Machado de Chávez had considered various authoritative opinions concerning parents' responsibility to educate children. "The Doctors concur," he summarized, "that parents, by virtue of being so, and having the necessary means, are obligated to give the child over to studies, encouraging him in his lessons and spending whatever is necessary in conformity with the quality of his property and responsibilities." However, Machado de Chávez recognized that "many circumstances can impede" the fulfillment of this obligation. If a parent could not or would not provide a child with education, or if the education parents provided was not sufficient, the law suggested the intervention of another man, presumably a magistrate. "When there are doubts," he wrote, "the only remedy the law provides is to leave the matter up to a good man (*buen hombre*) to decide."[46]

In the late colonial period, the good men of the courts were increasingly called upon to decide whether elders were providing a proper education for children. Late colonial litigants abandoned the subtle allusions to education, always calibrated to the "quality" of the child, that were used in court cases during the period 1650–1750. Instead, plaintiffs and defendants made outright linkages between adult authority and instruction, and they forcefully argued that they would provide children with an education superior to that which their opponents could offer.

Education became a polysemic concept that turned up everywhere in late colonial battles over children. While viewed as a prerequisite for good parenting among colonials of all backgrounds, it also could be a code for the kind of honorable behavior that only the elite could afford. Nonetheless, just as plebeians espoused their own versions of honor, adults from lower ranks of colonial society expressed aspirations for their children through the language of education. Education also served as a yardstick with which the maturity and rationality of minors could be measured, and it was a gloss for the civility of urban life.

The language of education began to mix with the issue of honor in legal conflicts over illegitimate children. Honor had always been an element in suits of the type that transpired between the Boza family and doña María Luisa de Armas of Chancay, a coastal city just north of Lima.[47] As a young woman, doña María Luisa became romantically involved with the son of an Audiencia minister, don Antonio Boza, and gave birth to a girl named María Josefa and a boy named Manuel. After his son died, don Antonio had taken over the responsibility of rearing his grandchildren, treating María Luisa with "honors, respect, and good conduct, as if she were a married woman." Yet because María Luisa initiated inheritance litigation against the children's aunt, who was the executrix of the younger Boza's estate, the amiable relations between the legitimate and the illegitimate Boza families soured. The aunt planned to take ten-year-old María Josefa to live in don Antonio's residence in Lima or to deposit her in a convent. Doña María Luisa refused and sued to retain custody of her daughter as well as to gain a portion of Boza's estate for her children.

A scribe recorded doña María Luisa's arguments during the early phase of the suit, while she was still acting without the services of an attorney. Education—both her own and that which she provided her children—figured as centrally as her honor in her petitions. She called for a *probanza*, or the examination of character witnesses, in order to prove her good conduct and to show that "I have always dedicated myself to the best education of my children." Her neighbors testified that she sent her children out every morning, conducted by a servant, to be taught by a miga (female tutor). Manuel and María Josefa would return punctually at midday and then go out again to be tutored in the afternoon. That the door to María Luisa's home remained closed so that the "other minors" of the neighborhood would not enter and "pass vices on to her children," they reported, was proof of their proper "instruction." After the witnesses were interviewed, María Luisa made a point of stating that, were she to lose the inheritance case, she would be deprived of resources to ensure the "political and scientific education of my children."

The importance of education was not limited to the political and scientific instruction that doña María Luisa's children received. It pervaded the woman's presentation of herself as a proper mother.[48] She argued, "I am a woman capable of giving a good education to my children, not only in doctrine but by example. . . . If I were a woman given to pleasures, given to the spectacles and vices of youth, I might be able to tolerate that the executrix put my daughter in a convent. . . . But the studies I have pursued and pursue in my life [consist of] comporting myself with the utmost decorum." Doña María Luisa's suitability to maintain custody of her daughter, derived from her own "studies," made it unconscionable that her daughter would be "exposed to the education of a [female] stranger (*una extraña*)." The alcalde who heard the case in the first instance upheld doña María Luisa's claim, awarded her custody and 3,000 pesos, and declared the children to be "naturals." When the Boza family appealed the ruling to the Audiencia, the Defensor de Menores reviewed the case and sided with the children's mother, finding even the process of formal review to be "odious" in the case, since the "legal foundations" of the mother's arguments "support the notorious justice of Minors."

María Luisa's victory was not unusual. Judges, often acting on the advice of the Defensor de Menores, tended to favor parties who demonstrated vigilance concerning educating children. In a case involving the custody of his natural son, don Pedro Prieto found that he could sidestep paying his former lover a monthly allowance by suggesting that the boy should be in the custody of neither parent but, rather, enrolled in school.[49] His lawyer, Toribio Ramírez de Arellano, stirred up late colonial judges' enthusiasm for education by suggesting that, since his client's son was eight years old, "the best thing is for the boy to be dedicated to school and studies so he might direct himself toward a career." The alcalde decided that the boy should be removed from his mother's custody and placed in the Colegio del Príncipe, at the father's expense.

Courts might as easily force a mother to give up her son to a school like the Colegio del Príncipe as uphold a mother's claim to custody, depending on where they determined that the child would be better educated. Officials consistently demonstrated a preference for educating children in the capital city, where colonial children had greater access to formal educational institutions and where urban life was characterized by a higher degree of civility.[50] Doña Petronila Gómez, who sued her ex-husband, José Antonio Pro, for support for their daughter, resisted her former husband's attempts to place the girl in his parents' home in the provinces.[51] She scoffed at his plans to move their daughter to the pueblo of Magdalena, since it was at a great "distance from the civilization of the court" and a small town "where there are no tutors who might teach her to pray and *primeras letras*, which are the necessary adornments of women."

Education also became a factor in determining whether minors could legally act on their own behalf. Prior to the end of the eighteenth century, when minors petitioned to be released from minority status or to name their own guardians, they pointed to their honorable conduct and reputation to convince the courts that they were capable of making their own decisions. For example, in 1697 when sixteen-year-old don Pedro Moreda petitioned to manage his own finances without the intervention of a guardian, witnesses testified to the soundness of don Pedro's judgment with statements like "there is no bad notoriety (*nota*) of his conduct."[52] At the end of the eighteenth century, however, education rather than honor signaled a minor's legal maturity. In doña María Mercedes Vásquez de Vásquez's case to name her stepfather as her guardian, her lawyer argued that she had the capacity to decide for herself whom she wanted to manage her property by pointing to the "good education and instruction that, conforming to her quality and circumstances, her virtuous and diligent mother had given her." The Audiencia deemed her in possession of the "knowledge" to make her choice.[53]

Lack of formal education, in turn, was a reason to discredit the legal choices made by minors about guardianship, particularly when they lived outside Lima. Because doña María Ignacia de la Fuente lacked formal education, she was denied her request to replace her guardian. The defense argued that she had been raised in the uncivilized environment of mining communities of Arequipa, and the lawyer described her as "a mass of flesh without more education than that which can be provided in the Mines, where she could not even learn to read or write."[54]

Although the Defensor de Menores continued to oversee issues of property, his own commentary in both guardianship contracts and civil cases revealed that he began to regard protecting the education, rather than the property, of minors as his primary responsibility. In 1780 Defensor Mariano Carrillo stated that he had taken the initiative in naming a guardian for Petronila Dávila de Castillo because he worried that, as a twelve-year-old orphan, she was "without a tutor who might care for the property she possesses and, *what is more*, who might take charge of her education, indoctrinating her with the order (*arreglo*) that is necessary."[55]

This new emphasis on education was not confined only to the wealthy children of the Peruvian elite, whose guardianship entailed the administration of property or who could afford tutors and formal instruction in schools. Colonials of all social ranks began to consider education as the ultimate determinant in judging who ought to receive legal authority over children. Chapter 2 described how master artisans were beholden by contract to treat their apprentices as if they were their children. There was no guarantee that they would actually do so, of course. But here it seems that law reflected a reality at least for some artisans and their master teachers. The intimacy forged in workshops led some minors of age to feel that the artisans from whom they learned their trades were better guardians to them than their kin. In 1806 an Indian minor argued that the gunsmith with whom he had already been working for some time had "always taken care to attend to me and teach me with the greatest care, as if I were his own son." In order to "perfect the trade," he petitioned to name the gunsmith rather than his brother-in-law as his guardian.[56]

Even though a broad array of colonials cited education and training as critical criteria for legal custody and guardianship, limeños continued to arrange their decisions about just how much or what kind of education a child might need along the distinctly colonial coordinates of caste and class. Although her son was already thirty years old, Flora Guerrero decided to bring suit against his natural father, don José Antonio Cueto, in 1791 in order to obtain back child support.[57] Don José Antonio claimed that he had, in fact, supported his son, Felipe, for several years in the city of Ica, paying for a tutor to teach him to read and write. The father said he had hoped that one day Felipe would become a physician or surgeon; but when the boy turned twelve, Flora seized him, and together mother and son fled to Lima.

When she brought suit, Flora gathered witnesses to testify that she took custody of Felipe because his father withheld any education beyond basic literacy. She claimed that because she never received financial support from don José Antonio, Felipe was forced to work in a silversmith's shop and there was left "unprotected, barefoot and uncovered of all clothing." His lack of education at his father's hand during his formative years had turned him "indocile, and now in a more advanced age he cannot be reduced to any application." Don José Antonio's lawyer challenged her claims that the education Felipe had received was insufficient and argued that "a son proceeding from a woman of lower quality—and Flora is one of these from all looks of it—requires no other class of alimentos" than a basic education in reading and writing. Unfortunately, we do not know how the alcalde ruled in this case, but what is clear is that Flora and José Antonio had different ideas of what a proper education for their son should entail. Perhaps Flora, like the española we are about to meet, envisioned education as something more than teaching her son a skill with which he could earn a living but as an opportunity to raise his status.

Doña Teresa Alzamora had given birth to six children during her seven-year extramarital relationship with don Joaquín Navárez.[58] She supported their only surviving son, Mariano, until she decided to enter a convent, at which point she sent the youth to live in the house of his father and his new wife. The fractious Mariano was kicked out of his father's home and sought his mother in the convent. Years later, doña Teresa finally decided to seek recompense for the time that she had spent "doing the job of Father" in raising her son. Petitioning for back payment of child support, she stated that don Joaquín had failed to live up to "the obligations of a Christian father" and had treated his son "like a vile servant," neglecting to provide him "doctrine," and making him "toil with leather" while he went hungry. Don Joaquín, however, countered that Mariano was a disorderly youth who had been influenced by his mother's belief that his occupation as fringe maker (*flequero*) was a "disgrace" and "beneath" her son. He called on friends and neighbors to testify that he had taught his son to read and write and that he had cared for him "with love and affection." In the end, don Joaquín won back custody of his wayward son so that he could instruct him in his trade.

Don Joaquín successfully argued that he could provide his son a respectable education and thwarted doña Teresa's attempts to force him to pay for a child outside his control. Men in late colonial Lima were caught in the same intellectual and legal currents that pushed mothers and children to argue on the grounds of education. Don Joaquín did not simply contend that, if he were to be forced to pay for the youth's alimentos, he had a right to custody of his son; he sought to show that he had been a good father in trying to train and educate the boy and to demonstrate that he had done so lovingly.

Far more than an excuse mothers used to gain child support from fathers, education was a key criterion that all adults involved in court battles over children marshaled to make their cases. The petitions of plaintiff and defendant alike accentuated the importance of providing instruction to children, even if they disagreed over what a proper education meant. Indeed, some colonials—particularly mothers facing artisan fathers—began to conceive of education as far more than simple occupational training. In this legal environment, artisan fathers could find themselves on the defensive, and they strove to demonstrate that they had taught their sons not only how to toil in the workshop but also to read and write. When we consider cases concerning the education of slave children in the following chapter, it will become even clearer that the Enlightenment emphasis on education as reading, writing, and reason rather than work pervaded the arguments of all social sectors of Lima.

Child Support

The final change in court cases over free children in the late colonial period involved new calculations of the financial investment that adults made in raising their children and their economic responsibility to provide for their offspring. When Lima's judges began to receive cases involving child support, these nearly displaced inheritance suits as the primary type of civil litigation over minors of age. In hearing children support cases and not merely suits over inheritance, the secular judges opened the doors of the civil court wide to a greater number of Lima's inhabitants. As a consequence, the profile of litigants shifted from the propertied elite to ordinary city dwellers.

As can be detected in the previous discussions of love, natural rights, discipline, and education, many of the disputes over children that late colonial magistrates heard were, strictly speaking, conflicts over who would pay for the everyday financial support of children. This changed the tenor of the litigation significantly. From 1650 to 1750, to support their inheritance suits, litigants battling over guardianship had been concerned with providing material comforts appropriate to a child's "illustrious" social class. By contrast, in cases involving child support in the late colonial period, the financial inability to provide for even the basic needs of a child drove litigants into the court system in the first place.

Doña Josefa Flores was so poor that she and her orphaned granddaughter begged for their livelihood in Lima's streets.[59] Horrified by the mendicancy of his niece, an uncle—a priest named Manuel Antonio Aramburú—located a married couple in Urubamba, a fertile valley just beyond the city of Cuzco, to care for her. Petitioning before the alcalde, whom he called "my lord Father," Fray Manuel Antonio attempted to convince the magistrate that placement with this new family would generate in his niece "Christian judgment and a temporal occupation [befitting] the honesty of her sex."

Doña Josefa responded, combining new discourses on education with her own unique interpretation of a law that men usually cited in order to avoid paying support to young children. She claimed that, while "fathers have the ability to take their children" after three years of age, "mothers have the faculty to refuse to hand over their children when they do not consider the place comfortable and proportionate to their education." Doña Josefa won her legal battle in part by claiming Urubamba was too rustic an environment for her granddaughter. But she also contended that her poverty should not take precedence over the fact that she was, by blood, the girl's grandmother and thus of closer blood relation. As one woman put it in a different custody dispute, "Blood relations can never be bartered over (*Relaciones de parentesco por afinidad son s[iem]pre inavenibles*)."[60]

The alcalde who decided the case ruled that the girl should remain with her grandmother, although he also ruled that she would receive no financial support from the uncle. In the civil courts of late colonial Lima, class standing alone was a shrinking, though not disappearing, legal ground for depriving an adult of custody. In this case, lineage, the fact that doña Josefa was a woman, and the court's preference for keeping children in the city to guarantee their best education worked together to override concerns about the destitution in which the girl was raised. Another factor leading to the alcalde's decision in doña Josefa's case may have been the investment the grandmother had already made in raising the girl. Josefa did not demand support during the suit, but the alcalde nonetheless ruled on financial support in his decision. Like the alcade, many of Lima's judges began to consider carefully the effort and financial expense adults had spent on children as a signal of their commitment to them. This could mean that limeños who traditionally raised children, especially wet nurses, could be awarded custody if parents had failed to compensate them for raising their children. Sebastiana Avila had turned her son, Tomás de Vergara, over to a free zamba named Agustina Carvajal to nurse.[61] Apparently, Sebastiana never paid Agustina for her services, and so the wet nurse refused to return the child to her. Sebastiana obtained a superior decree from the viceroy ordering Agustina to release Tomás to her custody. "It being certain that my son is a free boy (*un muchacho libre*)," she said, the wet nurse "cannot retain him as collateral, even if there is a true debt." When Agustina resisted and petitioned the alcalde, she argued that she had "nursed and fed him since he was small, without the smallest subsidy" from Sebastiana. Furthermore, Agustina demonstrated that she educated, baptized, and cared for Tomás—all "as if he were her own son." The alcalde agreed that Tomás "would have a better and more Christian education under the shelter of Agustina than with she who calls herself 'mother,'" and he ruled that the boy "continue in the power of the ama who raised him."

Still, Agustina might not have won custody, even with proof of her great investment in the boy, if she had faced an elite defendant. The zamba Juana Gamonal had taken a child from the Casa de Niños Expósitos to nurse, but eventually the baby's mother, doña Josefa Varela, attempted to force Juana to return the infant to the foundling home. The baby was not an expósita, doña Josefa explained, but her legitimate daughter. Doña Josefa said she had only placed her daughter in the Casa because she had been too ill to raise her herself. The judges, however, had reason to suspect that she may have been one of the many poor mothers of the city whom the director of the foundling home condemned for using the institution to raise their children so that they would not incur the expense of rearing an infant. Yet even if doña Josefa had taken a risk in placing her child anonymously in the Casa, she could effectively use her caste standing to redeem custody of her daughter. "A decent child, like the child of the plaintiff, cannot spend any more time in the hands of a zamba," she said, "whose discipline cannot be believed to conform to that which she ought to receive under her mother's supervision." Audiencia judge Manuel Manzilla ruled that the infant be returned to her mother's custody.[62]

As we saw in Chapter 5, during this period the archbishop of Lima had begun to call for greater public censure of parents who abandoned children and failed to compensate those institutions or individuals who raised their young. Although colonial officials and intellectuals began to criticize wet nurses as the source of high rates of child mortality, amas de leche ultimately were able to turn the new politics of the child to their advantage by suggesting that parents who relied on them to raise their children were negligent, and they sued to be reimbursed by parents who failed to pay them for raising their children.[63]

In an environment of heightened litigation over all types of child support, even the least legally savvy individuals found their way into Lima's court system. In the early nineteenth century, an indigenous woman named María Cárdenas came to the capital from Jauja to breastfeed don Josef Solís's illegitimate daughter. When, after eleven months of nursing, the infant girl died and don Josef refused to pay her, María found herself destitute in a strange city. María decide to sue him even though she felt unprepared to speak on her own behalf in legal matters, perhaps because of a weak command of Spanish. "My heart wants to explain [my situation] to your Mercy," her statement reads, "but my language does not aid me, and thus I beseech your Excellency, as Father of the Poor and Helpless like me . . . to provide me patronage." Not only does María's statement attest to ordinary colonials' galvanized use of the court system in matters pertaining to children; it also betrays their relative legal autonomy. Although scribes may have crafted litigants' phrasing or guided them to the most effective legal arguments, the impulse to sue came from the adults who reared Lima's children, not from court officials. María fretted that she lacked the knowledge necessary to negotiate the legal system, but she knew enough to believe she had a case.

The rising number of cases over modest amounts of child support or financial compensation did not necessarily mean that all suits were successful for all litigants. When women sued men for alimentos, they ran a tremendous risk, for fathers could turn support cases into custody battles by asserting their absolute rights as fathers and taking physical control of the children. Although colonial judges often upheld the customary practice of allowing women to retain custody of children older than three years, cultural habit was slippery legal ground. Suing for child support was a risky strategy for Lima's women because fathers could always flaunt the fact that patriarchal law was on their side by citing the *Siete partidas*.[64] Fathers often argued that the law granted them, by virtue of patria potestad, the unassailable right to take physical custody of their children after age three, and even more so if they were forced to support their offspring.

In 1802 doña María del Carmen Campos knew that suing the father of her illegitimate daughter, María Petronila, for back child support meant gambling with her daughter in the legal system.[65] When María Petronila had been born fifteen years earlier, María del Carmen had brought a child support suit against the girl's father, tavern owner don Antonio Vargas. The alcalde had ruled that don Antonio indeed should pay her a monthly stipend, which he did for five years, until he married another woman and was "distracted" by his new family from his paternal obligation to provide financial resources to his illegitimate daughter. Now that María Petronila was fifteen years old and was preparing to "take state," her mother was penniless and could not guarantee her future through a dowry.

Suing for back child support was a desperate move. It might garner a settlement that would pay for her daughter's marriage or entrance into a convent, but if she lost the case, María del Carmen could also lose her daughter altogether. María del Carmen worried that, like other fathers who wound up in court for failure to support their children, don Antonio would try to gain custody of his daughter instead of paying her what he owed her. She warned the judges of the Audiencia that Antonio might attempt to employ the "weak subterfuge of attending to [our daughter] at his side," so as to "frustrate [my claim to] contribution." But, she said, his claims should be dismissed, since he could never "easily educate a girl in the proper way nor inspire in her those instructions particular to her sex."

María del Carmen indicated that fathers repeatedly demanded custody to divert attention from mothers' suits for financial assistance. Other cases in civil record seem to corroborate her accusation, since several fathers raised the issue of custody in direct response to requests to increase the amount paid in child support. For instance, in 1794 don Gabriel Barbadillo issued an ultimatum to his former wife after his marriage had been annulled. She could either accept the 36 pesos a month he offered as support for their two children or turn them over to him to raise.[66]

But when fathers threatened to take custody of children in order to avoid paying support to mothers who reared them, they did not lean on the law alone to prop up their arguments. Fathers of illegitimate children continued to question the motives and chastity of the women who bore them children out of wedlock, as they had in the past. But now they could combine these assaults with other, newer arguments, especially by warning the courts that ruling in favor of illegitimate mothers would contribute to vagrancy and vice. When one father refused to pay support for his illegitimate child, who he claimed "wandered the streets without restraint," he argued that the "delinquency of the mother destroys the innocence of the boy."[67] The Defensor de Menores reviewed the case and determined that the boy would be "better instructed and informed" by living with his father and his new wife than at his mother's side.

Even while judges and the Defensor de Menores began to listen carefully to new claims that could undermine men's absolute rights over their children, patria potestad was still an intractable fact of Spanish law. As such, male authority represented a real challenge for the lawyers and litigants who brought cases against fathers in the late colonial courts. In 1789 lawyer Gregorio Guido preempted a father's assertion of the absolute right to custody of his natural son when he represented doña Baltazara de Alva y Vélez in a suit over her seduction and for the possession of a slave, whose wages would pay for their son's up-bringing.[68] Don Pedro Prieto could not, Guido argued, take custody of the boy, since, as a man who had seduced a woman, the father "lacks patria potestad, *especially since* the boy is at his mother's side in honesty and recogimiento" (emphasis mine). The lawyer attempted to argue that what was relevant in the case was the manner in which the mother raised her son, not only laws about seduction and paternity.

But perhaps doña Baltazara's lawyer had chanced too much in raising the issue of education and rearing. Doña Baltazara ultimately got nowhere with her case for back child support, and as revealed earlier, her son was taken from her and enrolled at the Colegio del Príncipe. Although she stridently resisted enrolling the boy in the school, she ultimately submitted to the court order. Like many mothers who sued for child support in late colonial Lima, this mother not only failed to achieve financial assistance; she lost custody of her child. By stressing the court's responsibility to ensure that parents properly provided for children, the new politics of the child made it possible for women like doña Baltazara to take fathers to court. Yet by privileging education, discipline, and the paternal role of the state, the new politics of the child also gave men new arguments that they used to bolster claims to absolute rights, making them formidable legal foes.

CONCLUSION

Although he argued his case before the ecclesiastical tribunal of Lima in 1790, don Mariano de Espinoza mined every vein of the new politics of the child when he asserted his authority over his ten-year-old daughter.[69] In his statement he even expressed skepticism about his daughter's placement in a religious institution, making his petition particularly noteworthy in light of the secularizing drift in the meaning of an "enlightened" education, a tendency that the previous focus in this chapter on secular court cases tends to obscure.

Don Mariano wanted to remove his natural daughter, Inés, from the con-vent of Santa Catalina, where her mother had placed her under the guardianship of a nun. "Patria potestad is indisputable in the laws," he announced in his petition to ecclesiastical authorities, "and a child can only be outside of it when the father does not present the necessary alimentos. . . . There is none of that here, and thus the Mother of my daughter cannot act over her without my consent." But he did not end with invoking his absolute rights as Inés's father. He continued by equating his daughter's enclosure in a convent with servitude, thus conveying a growing scorn for female convent education that we have already encountered in Chapter 5. "It should not be permitted that this unhappy infant—whom I have loved tenderly, since she is the first [child] I have had—be reduced to the miserable state of servitude," he stated. Beyond denouncing convent life, don Mariano also argued that his rights as father were greater than a mother's natural rights. "The laws commend the education of children to the father in particular," he argued, "giving him more faculties than necessary, above and beyond [those] those which nature gives." In addition, he further bolstered his claim for authority over his daughter with a skillful concatenation of emotion, education, and utility. "No one," he claimed, "will care better than I for my daughter, whom I love with a Paternal love. . . . It [is] my duty to educate her in conformity to the spirit of religion and give her the means with which she might be happy and useful to society."

In one petition don Mariano perfectly distilled the multiple and overlapping sources of authority over children that late colonial limeños recognized as valid. A child's best interest was no longer derived only from laws about male right. It now originated from nature, love, education, and the economic investment an elder was willing to make in a child for the good of society and, ultimately, the well-being of the state.

Lima was a colonial city where traditional processes of social reproduction had always relied on the emotion, effort, and economic investment of individuals who were not padres de familia, particularly on the child rearing labors of women. The new politics of the child provided those who actually did the work of raising Lima's children a language for making claims to legal authority and a space in which they could do so. The Bourbon interest in shoring up state patriarchy entailed bolstering the courts' authority over parents and children in order to produce orderly imperial subjects. Quite unexpectedly, it also opened legal debates about whether authority should always reside with individuals who could claim the patriarchal rights granted by law.

However, the story of the new politics of the child in the late colonial courts of Lima should not be read as a triumphant tale of the equalizing power of Enlightenment notions of rights for women. It is, instead, the history of a shift in how the colonial inhabitants of Lima conceived of the best interest of children and the paternal power of the state. Patria potestad continued to serve as a basis for legal understandings of authority over children. Yet as a qualification for awarding custody and allocating child support, patria potestad was beginning to look more contingent than absolute. Even fathers spoke the language of love, natural rights, discipline, education, and economic investment—in short, all of the elements of the new politics of the child—rather than relying only on law to argue for custody over and control of their children. As a result, a chorus of new discourses about child rearing competed with claims about absolute male rights over children in an increasingly interventionist court system.

Here we might return to the "patriarchy as contest" paradigm with which we began and ask what the late colonial transformations in cases over children in Lima can tell us about the larger arena of patriarchal relations, at the level of both the household and the state, in colonial Spanish America. Historians have argued that colonial Spanish American women asserted conjugal rights by calling on "patriarchal pacts," by appropriating gender ideologies and turning them to their advantage, or by articulating concepts of gender rooted in traditional, community-level cultures of reciprocity.[70] The colonial church, the state, and local elders served these women as "metafathers" in hearing and adjudicating instances of gender conflict, permitting women to limit the power of private patriarchs without attacking public forms of patriarchy. The arguments these women made, Steve Stern suggests, exemplify "the practical language and experience of arguments on gender right in non-feminist or pre-feminist historical settings."[71]

This description of how pluralizing patriarchs mollified the potential for more radical challenges to male power proves valuable for understanding what we have encountered in this chapter concerning the custody and rearing of Lima's free children. Even as they battled over the details of their obligations to and rights over children, in a larger sense, the men and women who raised children in Lima reinscribed the patriarchal family model of political society. They sometimes directly challenged even codified legal principles of patriarchy and asserted their own authority over children in such a way that it undercut masculine privilege and property rights. Yet by doing so before the paternal benevolence of magistrates, they failed to challenge the larger patriarchal foundations of colonial society.

Still, the appearance of new legal arguments about children and adult authority in late colonial Lima—and the very fact that ordinary limeños openly articulated these claims before secular magistrates at all—suggests that certain debates about gender and generational authority are unique artifacts of the end of the eighteenth century.[72] The late colonial period was a moment of intense change in the character of state and private patriarchy throughout Spanish America. In Lima, it was a historical moment also defined by the popular expansion of litigation over children. City inhabitants made it clear in their legal contests that they, too, would participate in the epochal transformations in notions of childhood and patriarchal rights by producing a local version of the same philosophical trends that precipitated the crisis of the Old Regime in many countries in Europe.

In Lima, when colonial litigants cast their complaints about private patriarchs in terms of tyranny, when they spoke of their natural rights over and economic investment in children, and when they sought at once greater discipline and special treatment for children, they demonstrated that the political developments associated with the Enlightenment and the new regalism in Spain were not simply the rarefied musings of local elites and royal advisers. The new politics of the child was indeed an abstract philosophical discourse about human nature, political society, and imperial social control. But it was also a practice through which ordinary limeños and court officials restructured common concepts about childhood and adult authority.

Even as we listen for the reverberations of the new politics of the child in arguments over patriarchal authority in late colonial courtrooms, we should not be deaf to the resonance of claims about gender and generational authority redolent of the earlier colonial period. Certain "rights" subordinates claimed for themselves echoed longer-standing legal customs involving adult authority and children, including the important role assigned to women as caregivers, and the principles of honor, genealogy, and legitimacy—all discernible in the period from 1650 to 1750. Yet the new politics of the child amplified these more traditional expressions of authority over children in the courts. It was as if in seventeenth-century civil cases elite colonials only whispered that women would retain custody of children even if men had the legal title of guardian. But in the late colonial period, ordinary colonials from all ranks of the social hierarchy spoke aloud about their authority over children. In doing so, they began to transform it from a privilege to a right.

The New Politics of the Slave
Child in the Late Colonial Courts

I n colonial Spanish America, slaveholders commonly used diminutive forms of the names of their slaves, whether the slaves
were young or old.[1] "Juan" would be "Juancito," and he thus
would become the simultaneous object of his master's affection and domination. Imagining slaveholders' power as a generational superiority made it seem
natural, familiar, and immutable. But Spanish law also made the social and
legal infantilization of adult slaves potentially unstable. As Chapter 1 demonstrated, codified secular laws tempered the rights of both father and master
with certain responsibilities and offered all patriarchal subordinates the opportunity to use the justice system to ensure that individual patriarchs and masters
did not abuse their authority.[2] What is more, Spanish slave law preserved a
measure of patriarchal authority within the slave family itself. This meant that
there existed a very real legal possibility that Juancito might attempt to assert
his authority over his own child by appealing to the paternal justice of the king
through the courts and, in doing so, defy the authority of his master.

In late colonial Lima, such a hypothetical situation increasingly became
reality. Just as patria potestad became ever more subject to the approval of the
Father King's judges at the end of the eighteenth century, so, too, did potestad
domínica, or the right associated with the control of slaves. What I have called
the "new politics of the child"—the interactions around Enlightenment philosophies and Bourbon policies on children—pervaded a rising number of cases
between adults over the custody, support, and freedom of slave youths. Liti-

gants and their lawyers advanced arguments that rested on Enlightenment ideas of natural rights and the importance of slave youths' education, as well as on the Bourbon preoccupation with creating useful imperial subjects through discipline and economic investment in children. These new criteria for judging authority over children served the parents and relatives of slaves well. Slowly, the litigants who brought suit over slave children chipped away at the paternal facade of African bondage in late colonial Lima.

But the adult relatives who brought suit on behalf of slave minors in Lima were not the sole practitioners of the new politics of the child. Just as both men and women adopted elements of Enlightenment thought and Bourbon social ideologies when battling over free children in court, the legal statements of masters as well as slaves hewed to the new politics of the child, including its most benevolent discourses. New philosophies of children and child rearing produced a shared idiom among litigants and defendants, but they did not produce shared significations. When colonial limeños squared off in court over the city's children, they engaged in small battles over the meanings of large concepts such as natural rights, education, discipline, and financial responsibility.

All participants in legal contests over slave children promoted a patriarchal ideology, but plaintiffs and defendants differed in their interpretations of who could claim ultimate authority as patriarch. The parents and relatives of slaves attempted to cash in on judges' responsibilities as patrons of the poor and miserable, while slave owners often tendered their arguments in the ideology of master, rather than state, patriarchal power. Lima's slave owners sometimes expressed their sentimental attachment to slaves raised in their homes from infancy. They claimed to have assiduously educated these children and to have carefully tended to their upbringing, and they acknowledged that slavery depended, even if only in small measure, on a degree of mutual obligation between master and slave.

Masters thus attempted to subsume the discourses associated with the new politics of the child into the traditional ideological framework of slavery, where power and subordination derived from an organic familial relationship between master and slave. Yet this was an uneasy fit. It became increasingly difficult for slaveholders to maintain the legal fiction of paternalism when, more and more, they were forced to defend their treatment of slave children in secular courts. As masters stood before royal judges in greater numbers, the legal grounds for their authority over slave children shifted under their feet. The paternalistic power they had long enjoyed over slave children, based purely on law and little on the actual measures they undertook to rear and care for the children under their dominion, faced repeated challenges by litigious family members. And it was repeatedly undercut by judges whose rulings often treated slave children first and foremost as children.

THE LEGAL CONTEXT OF
SUING OVER SLAVE CHILDREN

In her 1994 study of slave families and labor in Lima, Christine Hünefeldt called attention to the special significance of legal suits over slave children during 1800–50. For Hünefeldt, who examined some of the same cases I present here, court contests over family members represented one of the many strategies slaves used to obtain "fractions of freedom" and to exert influence over the day-to-day realities of slave life—strategies that ultimately culminated in the abolition of slavery. In her view, the cumulative effect of each individual slave suit was to force limeños to contend directly with larger questions about African bondage and with broader contradictions of the "legitimacy of power" in their society.[3]

It required an especially adroit manipulation of the law for Lima's people of African descent to use the civil legal system as an official implement with which they, on their own behalf or for enslaved members of their families, could loosen the stranglehold of bondage. Their strategies were varied, and not all slaves brought suits before secular magistrates for precisely the same ends. Some slaves or their family members leveled charges of intolerable abuse (*sevicia*) and sought the ability to search for a more benevolent master; some looked to lower selling prices. At other times—and these were often the most emotionally gripping cases—slaves tried to pry themselves altogether free of the bonds of slavery in suits over their liberty.

This litigation was surprisingly often successful. Occasionally, owners simply settled the cases by conceding to a demand, such as sale, realizing that keeping a contentious slave was not economically beneficial. However, judges also ruled for slave plaintiffs in many late colonial civil cases. One by one, slaves and their relatives forced masters to answer to the courts concerning treatment, the integrity of labor arrangements they established, and the fairness of the prices they set.

Still, it is important to remember that litigants who brought civil suits against masters sought only redress for their individual situations, not necessarily to topple the institution of slavery itself. An examination of late colonial litigation over slave children makes it clear that while the parents and relatives of slaves were taking measured steps in what would become the long march toward the abolition of Peruvian slavery, in the immediate moment, they were keeping pace with the tempo of the new politics of the child.

The arguments put forward by the parents, relatives, and masters in litigation over the custody, care, and freedom of children explains why the young were often a focal point of slave litigation. Judges followed the Bourbon mandate to create useful subjects, even of slaves. The new politics of the child meant that colonial officials valued education and special treatment for slave minors, and they rewarded the emotional and economic investment adults made in the children they raised. In short, the introduction of new philosophies of child rearing provided wider legal and philosophical terrain on which litigants could challenge masters' control of slave children. In implementing the new politics of the child from their benches, judges began to disclose the deep conflicts in the patriarchal pact of slavery in Lima. Some of those conflicts grew from the peculiarities of slave life in the urban setting, but others sprang from cracks in Spanish slave law itself.

The Tangled Circuitry of Filial Obligation: Spanish Law on Slavery

Spanish law on slavery had always recognized the existence of contradictory, or at least potentially overlapping, patriarchal authorities within slavery. The slave was envisaged as a man with a family, and so, too, was his master. For example, a slave owed both his master and his family obedience and was even beholden to give his life in defense of each member of the master's family. In turn, a master was prohibited from killing or seriously injuring not only his slave but also the slave's wife and children.[4] Laws on slavery, then, portrayed slavery as a family in bondage to another family, a nested situation of patriarchal power in which the authority of elders and masters overlapped.

Since it was inherited from the maternal line, slavery was a genealogical status. The *Siete partidas*, which provided much of the law governing African bondage in the New World despite being written centuries before the slave trade crested on the Atlantic Ocean, stated that, even if a woman were to be freed and gave birth one hour later, her child would be free.[5] Yet beyond the transmission of servitude, the relationship between a slave parent and child was not legally delineated. Indeed, the law further complicated matters because each child was said to be subordinate to his or her parents by nature, termed as owing a "natural debt." But the law also awarded payment of the natural debt of obedience to anyone who raised a child.[6] Furthermore, servants owed a special filial debt to masters who cared for them from birth, a debt described as "the honor and reverence that they should have toward their father."[7]

The law thus established a tangled circuitry of filial obligation based on natural debt incurred by rearing, genealogy, and subordination through servitude. But it fell silent on what might happen if a slave's natural debt should cross between caregiver, parent, and master. As we shall see in a moment, a late colonial royal edict on African slavery only exacerbated the potential for conflict by more vividly describing the relationship between master and slave as like that between father and child. This history of this ruling, which was aimed at bringing the domestic governance of slaves more tightly under the control of the patriarchal state, reflected the basic elements of the new politics of the child as both official policy and political practice in late colonial Lima.

The Expansion of Slave Litigation

Several studies of Spanish American slavery in the nineteenth century suggest that slaves used the liberal, anticolonial ideas of the movements for independence to make judges their allies in their quotidian struggles over labor, treatment by masters, and freedom.[8] Historian Carlos Aguirre describes how the rhetoric of independence and liberty that circulated through early republican Peru also produced a "juridical awakening" in slaves, who began to file into local courts to confront owners on legal grounds.[9]

There is no doubt that "independence" assumed a different meaning for slaves than for free people in the 1820s. But almost seventy-five years before independence, slave litigation began to increase. Taking my review of the Audiencia's civil case record as an example, the proportion of lawsuits involving slaves swelled notably after 1750. Cases involving slave children grew at a rate that even outstripped the remarkable increase in the proportion of cases involving free children. In the period 1650–1750, cases centering primarily on slave children comprised a small number (around 6.5 percent) of all suits over children. In contrast, during the second half of the eighteenth century, as the number of civil cases involving all children increased, suits involving slave children came to comprise more than a quarter (28 percent).[10]

It was not, then, the noise of artillery fire during South America's independence battles in the nineteenth century that initially awakened Lima's slaves to the promising prospect of suing their children's masters, although it may have roused them more fully. During the last decades of Spanish rule, men and women of African descent, slave and free, along with dons, doñas, and plebeians, had joined the ranks of Peru's indigenous inhabitants, who centuries earlier had "earned a reputation as litigious peoples" because of their propensity to use the courts to defend community interests and to resist poor treatment by officials.[11]

Important to all colonials, the legal system was of particularly acute importance to slaves and their families. The piece of paper containing a contract for freedom (*carta de libertad*) or a court ruling stamped with the king's seal was a precious commodity for slaves, since it provided an official guarantee against an uncertain future, where the possibility of being forced back into bondage always loomed. Former slave María del Carmen Ansieta and her children had been recently freed in her owner's testament, and she was nervous that someone might attempt to challenge their new status. She presented herself before the alcalde in 1792 and insisted that the court scribe draw up a formal document that she could exhibit if their freedom was questioned.[12] Legal contracts and court rulings also served as the textual weapons slaves used to legitimize their use of the courts in the first place, since they always faced the prospect that owners would argue that charges should be dismissed because the slaves lacked the juridical personality (*personería*) necessary to file suit.

Rulings from Lima were not slaves' only admission tickets to the courts. Royal policy crafted in Madrid also helped to usher them into the tribunals. Among its many provisions, Charles IV's Instruction on Slavery, issued in 1789, provided official backing for parents and relatives of slave children who wished to sue masters over child support. The edict was intended to restate in a clear form previous royal policies that dealt with the master-slave relationship, but the instruction placed far more emphasis on the responsibilities of masters than on the obligations of slaves.[13] The only reference to the responsibility that slaves owed to their masters was cast in filial tones. Slaves were to "obey and respect the Owners and Overseers, carrying out the tasks and labors that they are given according to their ability, and venerating [their masters] as *Padres de familia.*" In return for filial respect, owners incurred several of the same duties that parents were obligated to perform for their children: to provide education, basic economic support in the form of food and clothing, training to make them useful, and moderate treatment in work and punishment.

In keeping with the importance Bourbon kings assigned to education as the key to an orderly state, the edict delineated masters' obligations to educate slaves first. Masters were required to instruct slaves in Christian doctrine and see to it that they took sacraments, especially baptism. Next, the king insisted that masters were required to provide basic support not only for male slaves but also for their wives and children, "whether the latter be in the same condition or free," until they were old enough to support themselves with their labors.

The king thus underscored that providing for prepubescent children of male slaves—in effect, doing the job of parents—was the responsibility of masters, not of slave fathers.

Reference to masters' paternal responsibilities to slave minors did not end there. Throughout the instruction, Charles IV reminded masters that they had an obligation to adjust workloads to the "ages, forces, and robustness" of youths and to spare minors younger than seventeen years from the harshest forms of labor. He demanded that owners should avoid giving female slaves tasks "that do not conform to their sex" and issued a graduated scale of fines to be levied against owners or overseers who abandoned minors, the elderly, and the sick. The edict concluded by restating the medieval law on sevicia, or the excessive punishment of and cruelty toward slaves, which stipulated that the slave of any owner proven to be physically abusive would be confiscated and sold.[14]

The 1789 Instruction on Slavery was not necessarily conceived of as new policy. Rather, it was designed to instruct the king's vassals who were slave owners in the law so that existing law might be followed more closely. Yet the edict—and in particular its demand that masters economically support slave children—had more of an edifying effect on litigants and judges than on masters. In the period 1650–1750, the parents of slave children had occasionally filed complaints of sevicia or requests to purchase the freedom of their children, which were the two types of litigation that the *Siete partidas* had permitted slaves to initiate.[15] After the appearance of the Carolinian Instruction on Slaves, they used the one innovation of existing slave law that appeared in the ruling to file suits over alimentos, or child support.

But the edict was not the sole source of the increased litigation over masters' responsibilities to feed, clothe, and educate children under their dominion. Years before the instruction was issued, litigants in Lima brought forward several cases that already showed signs of the new politics of the child. As early as the 1770s, parents and masters wrangled over the meaning of slave education, care, and discipline before the judges of the city's Cabildo and Audiencia. Rather than evidence of the Bourbon state's strength in implementing new policies on domestic governance, then, the 1789 instruction is a singularly telling example of how the new politics of the child was also a legal practice that often operated independently of authorization from Madrid. Indeed, the limits of royal policy in transforming legal behavior in Lima become even more pronounced when we consider that, only six years after the 1789 Carolinian code was published and circulated throughout Spanish America, the king retracted it on the advice of the Council of the Indies.[16]

The 1789 instruction, with its heavy emphasis on masters' responsibilities, rankled the slaveholding oligarchy in the colonies, who watched with trepidation as abolitionary sentiment gripped some revolutionaries in France and engulfed Haiti, and as the British seized a number of Spanish slave ships in the Atlantic. Masters from various parts of the Spanish empire flooded Madrid with protests against the ruling, filling their complaints with apocalyptic visions of slave revolts and society come undone as a result of the king's standardization of slave work and punishment. More to the point, the New Orleans Cabildo described another hazard in the implementation of the code: slaves were pouring into the courts "with infinite lawsuits that excite their natural disquiet and rebellious nature."[17]

But a hasty royal retreat could not rein in what the king had not alone unleashed. Just as in the case of other social aspects of the Bourbon Reforms, such as the Pragmatic Sanction on Unequal Marriages or the extension of legitimacy status to foundlings, royal policies were as much the result as the cause of a new approach to childhood in the Spanish empire. Lima's slaves continued to bring suits against their masters in record numbers even after the retraction of the 1789 instruction. They found in the court system institutions and individuals that facilitated their aims. The Defensor de Menores was energetically advising on cases involving slave minors at this time, often acting as advocate for children against masters. Secular judges, whether officially endorsed by the crown or not, used their benches to guarantee that adults in the city were fulfilling their obligations to children. Even if the Bourbon crown was too weak or too fearful to risk alienating slaveholders as a class by following through with the 1789 instruction, judges in Lima seemed to rule in agreement with its basic premise: children—even slave children—had become a key to the strength of colonial society, and their treatment and care now fell under the surveillance of Lima's secular courts.

PRACTICING THE NEW POLITICS OF THE SLAVE CHILD

Love, Law, and Nature:
New Discourses of Authority over Slave Children

Why were Lima's judges so willing to hear these suits against masters? Why was this litigation, on the whole, more successful for plaintiffs than suits over free children? The answer seems to be rooted in the nature of the households where these slave children were raised. Just as the criminal courts ensnared youths who came from weak patriarchal households, the same pattern appears in civil cases over slave children. In fact, a significant number of suits over slave children in late colonial Lima seem to have been arguments between women.

Women, most of whom were mothers, were the primary plaintiffs in suits over slave children, just as in suits over free children. Female care of children was an integral part of the social world of all limeños, and thus mothers, more frequently than fathers, would maintain familial connections with their slave children, particularly given the fact that slavery made it difficult (although by no means impossible) for individuals to form stable marriages or unions.[18] But the reasons women entered Lima's courts on behalf of slave minors also derived from the particularly gendered nature of urban slavery.

Because slave women often held custody of their children while the infants nursed, conflicts could arise when owners reclaimed the children when they grew older, spurring mothers to litigate in retaliation. Furthermore, in Lima as elsewhere throughout Latin America, female slaves were more likely to gain manumission than male slaves and, once free, could not be restricted by masters from filing legal suits for relatives.[19] In addition, urban slave women were often employed in occupations such as street selling or wet nursing, and they had access to the cash needed to purchase their children and grandchildren, often against owners' wishes. Thus child rearing practices in the city, which depended on slave women rearing their own children, together with urban slave women's unique labor roles and brighter prospects for freedom, led female relatives into the court system over slave children with greater frequency than male kin.

Another, if still impressionistic, feature of court battles over slave children is that elders litigating for slave children seemed to challenge the authority of female slave masters more often than that of male slaveholders. Better statistics of overall slave litigation are still needed to substantiate this impression. Yet the predominantly female profile of defendants in my review of court battles over slave children suggests, as does similar evidence of criminal litigation in Lima's eighteenth-century courts, that women who lived in weak patriarchal situations were dragged into court over the slave children they owned more often than those whose domestic situations approximated the patriarchal ideal.

Because slaveholding women often expressed their relationships to slaves in deeply intimate, familial terms, they also may have made themselves especially vulnerable to legal challenges by raising slaves' expectations that they would emancipate them or their family members.[20] Historians of Latin American slavery have long remarked on how women who manumitted their slaves made expressions—more often than men—of what Stuart Schwartz terms "surrogate paternity," or the emotional ties created by rearing slave children in a master's home.[21] In Lima as elsewhere, cartas de libertad often contained proclamations of reciprocal love between master and slave. For example, doña Tomasa Balcasar freed her fifteen-year-old slave in 1695 "with respect to the much love and volition that I have for Juan Josef, for having raised him and for the good he has served me."[22] These emotional justifications for manumissions often extended through generations in a gendered manner. Masters might reward a loyal female slave with freedom because she had raised their children, or they might grant slaves' offspring freedom as recompense for service. Doña María Antonia Collasos immortalized the way in which child rearing created a chain of emotion between women slave masters, female slaves, and children. She freed both her slave Victoria and Victoria's child, Baltazar, in "attention to the good service and the love the cited Victoria has professed to me, and for having raised for me various children at her breast."[23]

Cartas de libertad, like most notary records, combined legal boilerplate with the repetition of cultural conventions, so we cannot know for certain whether these professions of emotion were genuine. Yet, in civil cases, the sentiments owners expressed were not prescribed by standardized formula. Often litigants, together with scribes, prepared their own statements in petitions, and unlike in contracts, there was no strict formula to follow, only compelling or previously successful legal arguments from which they could choose. Given this, masters' claims of affection for slave children are striking, even when we consider that many masters were in court to refute charges of abuse. For example, doña Petronila Vásquez claimed that she had raised and educated a slave girl named María Ignacia from infancy, treating her "with the greatest possible esteem, loving her with a tenderness *more than if she were my daughter*" (emphasis mine).[24]

Just as in contracts for freedom, quite often statements in civil cases indicated that the deep emotion between master and slave was founded on the fact that the slave had been born in the house or power of a master. One lawyer revealed the common belief that masters especially "loved" slave children born and reared in their houses when he stated that his client, the owner of a slave youth named Faustino, "raised him, and educated him with the same love as he would have if [Faustino] had been born in his home."[25]

Because masters—especially female masters—expressed affection toward slave children and claimed to love and raise them as their own, mothers of slave children could not easily employ the equation between a mother's love and natural rights that women frequently used in legal disputes over free children. As we might imagine, many parents seemed to have loved slave children profoundly and said so in court. However, given that expressions of affection toward slave children were so prevalent among masters, and given that both litigant and defendant were often women, elders representing slave children held no exclusive claim to be better custodians based on emotion.

As a result, the relatives of slave children could be forced to make complicated, and questionable, legal arguments in order to refrain from becoming muddied in the "filthy paternalism"[26] that emotionally joined slave and master. Slave owner doña Petronila Vásquez claimed she loved the slave youth María Ignacia "as her own daughter" when the girl's uncle sued to purchase the girl's freedom for 500 pesos. The defense refused to sell her, arguing that the plaintiff did not possess a close familial relationship with his niece, and even that he was not the girl's true uncle. He responded that all of doña Petronila's claims to authority over the child were based on the presumption of "reciprocal sentiment" between the master and her slave.[27] By this he meant that, while it was possible that doña Petronila loved the girl, if the slave child did not love her master in return, the owner's defense was null. His argument was unsuccessful, and the courts ruled that María Ignacia should remain in bondage. Blood relations and emotional bonds between adult relatives and slave children would not be sufficient to challenge the authority of slaveholders, especially when masters themselves spoke of their deep emotion for slave children and of the family-like bonds that legitimated their authority.

Because masters' claims of emotional attachment to slave children threw up semantic barriers that impeded litigants from turning new discourses on emotion and natural rights to their advantage, many litigants extended slavery's network of emotion and paternalism, "pluralizing" their sources of patronage.[28] In their legal struggles with masters, these adults made appeals rich with the imagery of judges as protective patrons and pleaded for magistrates to exhibit compassion and love in their rulings. Francisca Suazo, a freed *morena*, litigated against the owner of her daughter by claiming, "Humanity has an interest in the patronage of the indigent slave, and in providing the means [for him] to improve his lot[.] Your highness, in his pious love, cannot be indifferent to the delay of this benefit, not even for an instant."[29]

While some litigants bypassed the question of masters' paternalism and instead framed their suits within the ideology of royal patronage of the unprotected, others directly confronted legal blockages by reinterpreting the meaning of natural rights or a mother's rights as a right to litigate. The lawyer for slave Petronila Sánchez defended her right to sue over her son by claiming that she was "stimulated by the ties of blood, which conforms to nature."[30] Tiburcia Arrosarena considered litigation as a responsibility she owed to her enslaved son. "I, as mother of my son, owe it to him to find a good, orderly Master," she stated when a man who claimed to be her son's owner kidnapped him. Acting "according to my maternal love," she said she was using her right to enter court, which was "the only liberty that miserable slaves enjoy."[31]

As we have seen, medieval Spanish laws effectively deprived slaves of per- sonería in all but cases of excessive punishment and false enslavement. A case between Manuela Olaza and her child's owner, doña Juana Hurtado y Sandoval, however, indicates that the medieval restrictions on the types of legal suits slaves could bring on their children's behalf were weakening at the end of the eighteenth century, especially in light of the 1789 Instruction on Slaves. During the early stages of the trial, doña Juana claimed that it was illegal for Manuela to appear in court, since the mother was also a slave. During an appeal to the Audiencia, lawyer Manuel Soriano argued in Manuela's defense. "The rules of humanity," he proclaimed, "have given [slaves] the liberty to request their own conservation." The defense's interpretation of restrictions on slave litigation, he contended, was too literal. "The slave is not a person by disposition of civil law, but he has not lost the rights (*derechos*) that apply to him by nature and that are common to all men," Soriano asserted.

Furthermore, the lawyer reasoned, Manuela had the right to be a party in contracts by default. Since she had "license to work for a daily wage," she could "contract, request, sue, and be sued, of which there are continual examples in the courts, although usually these are verbal cases because of their small en- tity."[32] Soriano's cunning logic proved difficult for the defense to refute. Seizing on the contradictions of urban slavery, in which slaves often lived, worked, and engaged in financial transactions outside a master's home and supervision, Soriano concluded that owners tacitly granted the numerous urban slaves who worked on a wage system certain undeniable civil rights. The lawyer thus countered the written law that restricted slaves from bringing suit with the customary legal practice of recognizing slave's juridical personality in economic matters, a practice that many of Lima's slaveholders relied on to secure cash payments rather than personal labor from their slaves.

Since slaves were never thought to be stripped completely of natural rights by servitude, it is possible Soriano's claim that his client had natural "rights . . . common to all men" could have been made in 1692, or even 1492, rather than in 1792.[33] Yet such phrasing held a stronger political currency in the late eighteenth century than ever before. Neither Soriano nor the magistrates who read his argument would have been blind to the fact that Enlightenment philosophers were caught in an intellectual conundrum over the subject of slavery. And they could not have been ignorant of contemporary debates about rights common to all men in other countries, including the United States, a former colony itself in the process of patching over the inconsistencies of affirming universal freedom and equality in a slaveholding society.[34]

Soriano certainly was no thinly disguised abolitionist. Indeed, in other cases he defended masters just as cleverly as he did slaves.[35] But the manner in which his argument set emergent notions of liberty and natural law against written law was consistent with a broader set of challenges being made in Lima's courts. Educated lawyers were not the only authors of such challenges. They appeared in the petitions that slaves themselves had drawn up to initiate legal suits over their children. The parents of slave children, whether free or enslaved, registered claims about their own rights that sometimes intimated a deeper understanding of the larger political context in which they litigated, and they revealed certain, although attenuated and nascent, liberal notions of equality before the law.

Some petitions began to draw from the very language of medieval Spanish laws, often paraphrasing a preamble to a section on slavery in the *Siete partidas*, which suggested that bondage was a temporary condition rather than an intrinsic state.[36] However, claims about slaves' basic human freedom—even if based on Spanish law—could be too easily interpreted as radical challenges to slavery and the colonial social order itself. Thus litigants' petitions normally linked assertions about slaves' human right to seek liberty to the traditional paternal role of the courts. Josefa Arriaga y Córonel, a free morena, sued for her child's freedom in 1793. "Two powerful motives support my claim," she stated. "The first is that we are all born free [and that] the laws conspire against captivity." The second was that she had no money to bring suit without being declared a caso de corte, a protected legal status that granted her the right to an attorney as a poor widow, which she was promptly granted.[37] When the freed slave child Baltazar and his mother, Victoria, were re-enslaved on a hacienda in Ica, their former master, doña María Antonia Collasos, came forward to aid them. She, too, articulated the same dual premises of the right to litigate against slave masters in her petition. "Liberty is cherished by all creatures of the World," she pronounced just before she appealed to the Audiencia to "protect the poor and defenseless" in naming them a lawyer.[38]

If "liberty" held new political resonance, litigants' cases against masters sometimes also employed the politically charged terms "tyranny" and "despotism," displaying awareness that these terms conveyed a particularly potent critique of the abuse of authority. In 1811 Tiburcia Arrosarena recounted how a priest claiming usufruct rights over her slave son violently grabbed him one day as mother and son walked along the Calle de Encarnación, and she called his behavior "most violent and despotic."[39] In 1815 a man who had put up bond for a slave child during a court dispute petitioned to be reimbursed by the master for caring for the mother and son, who came to him disheveled and hungry during litigation. He told the court, "Slavery does not reach the depth (*orado*) of such tyranny that only I [should] be saddled with obligations for those who are disgraced and made unhappy by it."[40]

Perhaps because of their potentially radical nature, references to the tyranny of slaveholders and the justice of liberty did not find their way into the majority of petitions over slave children in late colonial Lima. More often, those who advocated for slave children introduced another emergent Enlightenment discourse into court: the idea that reason should be the operational basis for law and legal practice. María Josefa Oyague showed a firm grasp of the potent discourse of reason when she appealed to the court to hear a case over the liberty of her daughter and a grandson. "Justice always operates in reason," she stated, "but, at the same time, I will express my feelings."[41] María Josefa thus recognized the contemporary contrast between reason and emotion, yet she commingled traditional visions of justice as paternal benevolence and newer, Enlightenment visions of justice as rational in her petition in order to hedge her legal bet.

In addition, as some of the cases we have seen suggest, both litigants and defendants contrasted custom with reason in court contests over slave minors. One custom—often termed a vulgarity—that proved particularly contentious in Lima's courts involved children who had not been purchased but were born in the house or power of a master.[42] In such cases, masters rather than the market could determine the youths' selling prices. This permitted slaveholders to thwart parents or relatives who wished to purchase children. Increasingly, parents began to argue that slaves possessed the right to *coartación*, or to purchase themselves or their relatives for a fair price, regardless of where they were born.

Petronila Sánchez attacked the custom that permitted masters to determine the market price of slaves born in their power. She had worked for years to save up the 400 pesos she needed to purchase her seventeen-year-old son. When she presented the amount to his mistress, doña Lugarda Márquez, her son's price suddenly jumped to 600 pesos. Petronila claimed that the owner was able to place the purchase price of her son out of her reach "for no other reason than that he was born in her house." "I know well that without placing a suit of sevicia and proving it, a slave cannot compel a master to sell," her statement reads. But any belief that slaves born in a master's house did not have the right to a fair price, she claimed, was "a vulgarity and delirium." "If there is an intention to sell, the slave has an actionable right (*acción*) that the price be equitable [and] rational[.] Justice issues forth from this same right (*derecho*)."[43]

Litigants' assertions of equality, freedom, and rationality in cases over slavery were by no means isolated to Lima and were not limited to suits over children. In a study of slave petitions in late colonial Quito, Bernard Lavallé presents a litany of similar allusions to liberty, declarations against tyranny, and assertions of slaves' rationality. What Lavallé detects in the Quito cases is "an affirmation of a fundamental equality (natural, or rational, depending on the case)" between slaves and free individuals. He maintains that the influence of the "Enlightenment and the French Revolution," while "never cited," was "without a doubt present in the minds of not a few authors of these allegations."[44] Yet the new approach to children produced changes more subtle than this smattering of direct assertions about freedom and condemnations of tyranny. Arguments derived simply from a parent's right to live close to a child, while less politically subversive, proved equally disruptive to the patriarchal order of slavery in Lima.

While many of the suits parents of slave children initiated were offensive maneuvers designed to secure freedom for slave children by setting "rational" prices, other parents and relatives entered the court system defensively, in order to prevent the sale of their children away from the city. Catholic doctrine in principle frowned on sales that would split slave families apart, but in the secular courts of the late colonial period, spiritual matters seemed secondary to parents' assertion of authority and right.[45]

Slave Juana Medina argued that her daughter could not be sold away from Lima simply because her daughter's owner had died. "I am her legitimate, living mother," she said, "and the right and authority I have over my daughter . . . have not perished" with the death of her first owner. Juana clearly viewed her authority over María Teresa to be more binding than what limeños referred to as the yoke of bondage, and she expressed frustration with the "bad faith with which the Executors try to deprive me of a Mother's right and authority over a daughter."[46]

The petition of slave mother María del Rosario Hidalgo even referred to her "dominion," a term normally reserved for masters, over her children. María had successfully sued her former master for sevicia and was sold to a new owner. She now wanted to force the owner of her three children to sell them to their father's master. In her petition she explained how, since the owner "harshly secluded our children from our view, so that they can never come out when we beg [to see them]," he had caused them "pain that, by natural law, inflicts a mother and a father." She went even further in her petition, arguing that her youngest son, a two-year-old, merited no price at all, since the infant "had never known another dominion than my own maternal [authority]."[47]

Mothers were not alone in using the court system to prevent separation between family members. Fathers, too, came forward in the court system to assert rights over their children, especially to protest the sale of their children outside the city. Some used arguments that were similar to those advanced by mothers, as was the case when a father petitioned to find a buyer for his three-year-old daughter when her owner proposed to sell her to a coastal hacienda. This father warned the judges of the "harms that [will be] inflicted on this poor infant if she is extracted from her patria and the proximity of her parents to a distant place where a new owner may not give her the treatment that humanity and reason demand."[48]

Francisco Pimentel filed a similar petition, but he based his argument in written law rather than reason, emotion, and humanity. He drew from a law concerning a father's right to purchase his enslaved children. When his eighteen-year-old son, Matías, was sold to a hacienda in Ica, Francisco protested, referring to a 1563 royal edict that allowed fathers the right to be first buyers for children in bondage. The lawyer representing the new owner rejected Francisco's use of the royal edict, stating that it "was only introduced [into] law for the benefit of Españoles," an argument that was technically correct.[49] In the end, however, the judge set Matías's price at the low amount of 100 pesos, effectively allowing Francisco to purchase his son's freedom.[50]

It is critical to note that when litigants asserted their authority, defended their rights, and denounced tyranny, they did not exclusively draw from the discourses associated with the new politics of the child. As in Francisco's case, litigants reinterpreted old laws in a new context. Parents also frequently spoke in an idiom based on long-standing cultural values, particularly in the culture of legitimacy.[51] In both criminal and civil legal cases over their slave sons and daughters, mothers and fathers used the cultural mores associated with legitimacy to suggest that their authority, too, was legitimate, and thus worthy of legal consideration. At times, when slave parents referred to themselves as the legitimate mother or legitimate father of a child, they were referring to the fact that they had been married in the church.[52] In many other cases, however, references to marriage were absent. "Legitimacy" might mean that they had baptized their children, or it might simply indicate that they had recognized and raised the child as their own.[53] This could be true of fathers as well as mothers.[54] In some cases, parents might substitute other designations in order to achieve the same effect. One mother, for example, identified herself as the "true" (*verdadera*) mother of her daughter in her civil suit against her son's owner.[55]

Newer discourses associated with natural rights, reason, and parental authority did not, therefore, completely displace traditional discourses associated with legitimacy or legal norms that considered slaves the miserable "children" of paternal judges. But, increasingly, the inhabitants of Lima who decided to use the court system to assert their adult authority over children and to challenge the potestad domínica of masters submitted petitions written in a politically and philosophically evocative language of liberty, natural rights, and rationality. Their arguments also manifested other contemporary ideas about how children were to be raised and educated. No less than other inhabitants of colonial Lima, the parents of slaves adopted multiple facets of the new politics of the child, including the quintessentially Bourbon tenets of discipline and order.

Correction or Abuse:
The Bourbon Discourses on Discipline and Utility

In the late eighteenth century, heightened efforts to police Lima were evident to all colonials. In a city where fears of crime and disorder abounded but where a new emphasis on the gentle correction of youths began to dominate legal discussions in matters ranging from punishment to pedagogy, the distinction between disciplining and abusing slave children could only become more tenuous. In cases over sevicia, parents and masters often engaged in debates about how to balance the demands of a new disciplinary regime against the emergent dictum to treat children with special care.

While masters could have defended the punishment they meted out to slave children as simply a matter of policía, instead they often emphasized that they had punished these youths in no other manner than as if they were a loving parent. Many masters even invoked the new condemnation of severity with children that underlay Enlightenment era pedagogies described in Chapter 5. When Cayetana Cepeda argued that the placement of her son in a panadería constituted abuse, the owner of the twelve-year-old boy defended herself by saying that he was a troublemaker who stole a crop of chirimoya fruit from her. Despite this, her lawyer claimed, she had not punished him at all but had treated him "with the contemplation as if toward a son."[56] Because the boy spent all of his time in the street and never paid her his daily wage, she decided to place him in a panadería; thus the punishment was made in the interest of her own economic interests and public order but was also undertaken with paternalistic concern.

Nonetheless, masters' claims to familial, lenient treatment of youths often foundered during their own testimony. One female master, though arguing that she had treated the slave girl she owned with great tenderness, also contended that "masters are permitted to correct the excesses of slaves because it is in the public interest that they are raised with subordination, buenas costumbres, and doctrine: if they do not receive instruction, they tend toward uppitiness (altanería)."[57]

Fray Domingo Noboa, who was accused in 1790 of sevicia, also argued that he had treated his young slave, Josef Tereso, with the "general beneficence, love, and compassion with which I treat all my slaves." The slave's mother, Josefa Cavero, disagreed. The priest, she recounted, had branded Josef, punished him excessively, placed him in a panadería, and now was threatening to sell him to a coastal hacienda. She stated in her opening petition, "I seek no other deliberation than that which is permitted to the judges in order to direct that [punishment] does not stray from the line of fraternal correction." In Josefa's petition, the traditional ideology of masters' paternalism was altered to become a fraternal relationship—a critical move that displaced the master as father and tacitly set mother above the owner in the generational chain of authority. Noboa finally admitted that there were limits to his benevolent treatment of Josef and argued that "the transgressions to which [Josef] has confessed are not of the class [that merit] fraternal correction but demand severe punishment."[58]

In addition to disputing masters' claims that they were merely correcting rather than abusing slave children, parents often objected to children's sale as a criminal sentence. As several of the cases we have seen suggest, the threat of losing their children to sale outside Lima, particularly to work on coastal haciendas, was often what stirred parents and elders to enter the court system against owners.[59] Sale to haciendas was common for slave youths found guilty in criminal trials, and many colonials even equated it with a death sentence. Petronila Sánchez worried that her son, José Andrés, would be sold to Ica "although he has committed no crime." She described that city's coastal haciendas as places "where miserable slaves live and die."[60]

The imprisonment of slave minors in popular penal institutions, including panaderías, *casas de abasto* (storehouses), and *pastelerías* (pastry shops), also spurred parents and elders to litigate. In part, the ghastly working conditions of the bakeries elicited concerns for youths' health. But relatives often regarded the incarceration of slave youths as a risky measure that would turn their offspring into incorrigibles.

Like other limeños, María Teresa Llanos tailored her legal suit over her daughter's placement in a panadería to the burgeoning idea that youths should be punished less severely than adults in order to avoid turning children into hardened criminals.[61] María Teresa complained that her daughter was "treated in a way only appropriate for slaves [who are] scourges, delinquents, and have no hope of correction."[62] Slave mother Mónica Muñoz made the argument even more forcefully. The owner of her seventeen-year-old son, she claimed, worked him relentlessly on the hacienda where he labored, treating him with an "intolerable rigor and [keeping him in a state] of grave necessity (by which means robbers, spiteful [men], and charlatans are made)."[63]

Thus the new emphasis on the malleability of the young and the dangers of harsh punishment—arguments particularly evident in late colonial criminal courts of Lima—were easily imported into civil suits, where litigants used the same logic against masters who punished slave youths or required them to perform harsh labor. The 1789 royal instruction had specifically warned masters against overworking youths, and Lima's judges began to ensure that they did not. In 1805 the alcalde personally followed up on María Josefa Oyague's complaint that her son was being overworked by visiting the storehouse where the young slave was employed. There he admonished the *abastador* to lighten the youth's workload. The situation provided fuel for the lawyer eventually named to defend the slave mother and her son before the Audiencia. Manuel Fuentes Chávez decried the damage that being confined to the institution had wrought on the youth's behavior and development. He "has not been able to acquire the notions and good sentiments of religion to which he was [once] susceptible," Fuentes charged. "On the contrary, there are warning signs that he has been disgraced . . . with vices. . . . In place of the virtues that should characterize a good citizen, he [instead] carries the sensibility of disorder and disarrayed customs."[64] To suggest that hard work turned slave youths into disorderly citizens appealed directly to judges' commission to guarantee public order and to prevent crime in the city.

Even when attacking masters for giving slave youths grueling labor assignments, the parents of slave children in Lima seemed acutely aware that demonstrating their own efforts to discipline their children would be critical to their success in the court system. Like other parents in the city, they attempted to utilize whatever disciplinary apparatuses were available to them to rein in wayward progeny. However, rather than appeal to the courts for help, parents of slave children could simply utilize the punitive resources normally reserved for masters, such as panaderías. Or they could try to discipline their children by turning them over to masters themselves.

Catalina del Castillo told a long tale of the measures that she and various slave masters had undertaken to control her son, Juan Pablo, during his eighteen years of life. She herself had paid one owner Juan Pablo's daily wages so that he could live with her and receive "a good and Christian education." But Juan Pablo "would not follow the order with which an *hombre de bien* (gentleman) conducts himself," so she returned him to his owner. In the following years, a series of masters failed to rein in the youth, even by imprisoning him in a pastelería. However, when Juan Pablo was sold to a priest, Catalina began to worry that her son was being mistreated rather than disciplined. She discovered that the priest was beating Juan Pablo excessively, at times with four rounds of whippings in a single punishment. "Before, I applauded the correction," Catalina said, referring to other masters' attempts to contain her son, but now she had no recourse but to level sevicia charges against the priest and to attempt to purchase the teenager herself.[65]

Catalina's story of her struggles with her wayward son and her strident efforts to use whatever means were available to her to gain control over him demonstrate that parents were not always at odds with masters concerning the punishment of slave youths. Indeed, they sometimes claimed that they were allies in trying to instill the virtues of discipline and work. From the perspective of parents and relatives, however, this alliance did not provide masters the unfettered ability to physically punish a slave youth. Catalina had a clear vision of what kind of discipline was appropriate for her troublesome son—the kind she might applaud—and what constituted abuse. In the end, she, as parent, wanted to discipline her own son.

Purchased Only for Work: Education and Slave Child Labor

A striking feature of late colonial cases over slave children was the degree to which adults began to make legal arguments stressing their ability to provide an education and, in turn, to attack the suitability of their opponents on the same grounds. In fact, this strategy was never exclusive to one side in custody disputes over slave children. Masters no less than other adults proclaimed themselves the rightful guardians of slave children by defending the quality of instruction they offered.

Because slaves were workers by definition, the education of slave youths was often indistinguishable from occupational training. Outfitting slave children with work skills was, of course, a sound investment for any owner. It was an investment for parents as well, although of a different nature. Parents who were slaves were surely eager to see their children earn cash that could enable them to purchase freedom for family members. But, critically, many elders also claimed that they wanted their male children to be made useful so that they could be gainfully employed, whether free or still enslaved. They expressed a hope that their daughters, too, would receive instruction in "honesty" to prevent them from becoming objects of social disdain or seduction.

Given the desire they expressed to see their children educated, parents often criticized masters for neglecting to provide their sons training in a useful, and potentially profitable, occupation. Petronila Sánchez disapproved of how her son's owner, doña Lugarda Márquez, trained her son, complaining that he was a "youth who does not know how to do anything."[66] Doña Lugarda's attorney claimed that, on the contrary, José Antonio was a "famous cook." The lawyer representing Petronila ridiculed the defense's claim, stating that any servant would know the art of "making the most common meals, especially those that are regularly [eaten] by the poor; and this is not enough to call him a cook." In this case, arguing that doña Lugarda had neglected her responsibility to educate José Antonio was a sage strategy for the plaintiff on two counts: it portrayed her legal opponent as a negligent slave owner, and it lowered the youth's purchase price, since he might be considered unskilled.

Legal struggles over the nature of slave youths' education could, however, transcend questions of occupational training. When a poor española, doña Agustina Sotomayor, was accused of neglecting and mistreating her slave, she did her best to prove that the treatment and education she had provided little María Ignacia met the cultural expectations that slaves should be instructed in Christian civility. María Ignacia's mother claimed that the master had not taught the girl Christian doctrine or taken her to communion or to confession, yet doña Agustina maintained that she had "educated María Ignacia with appreciation, using good documents," while her mother only taught the girl "the trade of runaways."[67] The slave owner implied that her authority over a slave generated not from ownership but from the superior education and discipline she could provide the youth. She even suggested that educating slave children might involve instructions in reading and writing, not just behaving submissively. Indeed, at the end of the eighteenth century, expectations about the education that slave children should receive began to extend beyond taking slaves to mass, teaching them prayers, or providing training in skilled professions. In some cases, it even meant providing a formal education.

Lawyer Pedro Angulo Portocarrero refuted Audiencia official don Gaspar de la Puente Ibáñez's claims to having well educated his young slave, Faustino.[68] The lawyer contended that when Ibáñez discovered that Faustino's mother was bringing suit against him, he increased the youth's workload so much that the youth had no time "to establish himself as a *ladino* [Spanish-speaker] and learn some trade." Nevertheless, Angulo argued that Faustino was a motivated young man who still rented himself out during the day to learn the art of tailoring while serving as a coachman for his master at night. "Through all of this (which is not raising Faustino with education and love, as [the owner] states to the contrary), he studied and achieved great savings."

At this point, Angulo's comments expressed nothing particularly remarkable concerning a master's responsibility to see to it that a young male slave learned a trade and became proficient in Spanish. But what came next was far more striking. The lawyer argued that when Faustino was sold to the Audiencia official by his first owner—a nun named Juana—he was forced to leave "the school next to Don Larrión,[69] for which Hermana Juana paid, where he had learned Christian doctrine and how to read in a book. But all of this is forgotten, because . . . he immediately started serving by hand without having even one more day of school, *as he was purchased only for work*" (emphasis mine).[70]

The lawyer's contention that a master had a responsibility beyond simply allowing Faustino to learn occupational skills, and particularly his suggestion that a slave youth might be purchased for something other than work, reveals how deeply the contemporary stress on education in childhood had pervaded all ranks of society in colonial Lima. While the notion that masters owed their slaves sustenance and skills dates from the origins of the slave trade to Spanish America in the sixteenth century, the idea that slave youths should be taught to read and should even be given formal schooling was the fruit of Enlightenment ideas about the importance of formal education for all children.

In this environment, masters were forced to defend themselves by claiming that they had not made work the primary activity of slave children under their dominion. Doña Petronila Vásquez, who fought to retain ownership of her young slave, María Antonia, described her treatment of the girl in the best possible terms. Doña Petronila had raised and educated the girl from infancy, asking her only to keep her company during the owner's illnesses and "at times not even permitting her to take a broom in her hand." María Antonia, she said "has never felt the weight of slavery, but only the privileges of a daughter."[71]

In turn, slave parents also described the virtue of the education that they provided to their children. In some of their suits, litigants expressed a sentiment no different from that found in the 1789 instruction—that educating slave children would transform them into obedient, honorable members of society. As we saw in the case of the mother Catalina del Castillo, who attempted to find owners who could control her son, the parents of slaves were preoccupied with the dangers that obstreperous children might bring on themselves later in life, and their arguments mirrored the same vision of an orderly society as the arguments of their masters. Education was the key to creating such a society for master and parent alike. Catalina's recollections of the great strides she took to provide her recalcitrant son with "the good education that my quality and sex permit" surely would have received sympathetic nods from many mothers of free children of all castes and classes in Lima.

Just like that of the mothers and fathers of Lima's free children, litigants' suitability as custodians of slave children often was based on their level of education and "civility." Lawyer Pedro Angulo Portocarrero had made a point of noting that Faustino's mother, although a slave, was also a *samba letrada*, or a literate woman of mixed African ancestry.[72] Catalina Castillo, too, described herself in terms of education, attempting to show that she was at home in the "lettered city" of the viceregal capital.[73] "Although it may not be obvious," she admitted, "I was not born in this capital, but nevertheless I am well civilized, and as such, with the holy terror of God, this was the mode of my education until my son was raised."

Catalina's reference to her mode of education—constructed in a grammatically curious manner—provides insight into what education had come to mean for ordinary limeños during the late colonial period. Perhaps the best way to understand it is by comparison. Recall from Chapter 6 the petitions filed by doña María Luisa de Armas, the elite española living in Chancay who brought suit over the custody of her illegitimate children in 1793. She made the equally intriguing statement that "the studies I have pursued and pursue in my life [consist of] comporting myself with the utmost decorum."[74] For both the doña and the mother of a slave, education referred not only to the instruction that they provided their children but also to their own studies, or their own behavior and civility and the status they achieved through learning or literacy. Education in the late colonial period was serving a complementary, if not the same, function as the traditional discourse of honor, and just like the discourses of honor, the education of slaves was highly gendered.

In civil cases over their daughters, many parents echoed a sentiment captured in the 1789 instruction, which stated that the work of female slaves should not jeopardize their sexual virtue and indoctrination into proper moral behavior.[75] By breaching the gendered codes of proper work, masters exposed themselves to accusations of abuse. María Antonia Oyague accused her daughter's owner, doña Agustina Sotomayor, of employing the girl in "work improper to moral doctrine and good example, and this constitutes moral sevicia." The charge was based on the fact that the owner forced the "young maiden to work by going into the woods for kindling and other tasks [about] which moderation silences me."[76]

Other mothers, too, stretched the definition of abuse to encompass a violation of codes of honor and decorum for slave girls. Rafaela Araujo made a contention that was frequent in cases involving free children: she argued that men like her daughter's owner, an employee of the Royal Post, were ill suited as guardians of girls, and thus she reasoned that the child should be sold to a woman. Because the owner was often absent from the city, Rafaela explained, he could not educate her daughter, Felipa, and left the girl exposed "to a situation in which she might soon slip and prostitute herself, which are the consequences of lack of care and abandonment in youth."

The owner decided to avoid litigation and sold Felipa to another party. But Rafaela was not finished with her suit. Like other parents who protested when their children were sold without their knowledge, Rafaela objected to the preemptive sale of her daughter, claiming it was performed "without my intervention, necessary in this case, given that I am her mother, and as such have an interest in her best crianza and education, and would have come up with the money" to purchase her. Rafaela was outraged at the "commerce" the owner had undertaken in purchasing Felipa for 100 pesos and selling her only eight months later for 250, "without in this short time having undertaken a single diligence toward her education and teaching." The Defensor de Menores reviewed the case and decided that there was little he could do for Rafaela, since the bill of sale was not false and she had no further claim to sevicia. So the intrepid Rafaela took another course. She found a woman who said that she would pay the new owner 250 pesos and who promised to offer Felipa buena crianza. The Defensor hesitated, noting that the arrangement was, in a certain sense, "the same as leaving her, in reality, a slave with only the name of a free person." Yet the case, heard in 1812, was one of many in which the Defensor began to override the letter of the law in consideration of what was in a child's interest. "For the good of this youth" he wrote, "I will allow [the woman Rafaela chose] to be her benefactor and to continue educating and indoctrinating her at her side, without the mother being able to remove her."[77]

Rafaela's case spotlights the leading role education had taken on multiple stages in court battles over slave youths. Her initial suit was based on the common belief that male owners, often away from the city on business, could not provide young female slaves a gendered moral education necessary to keep them from slipping into vice. Furthermore, she objected to the increase in her daughter's price, since during the short time Felipa was in Castro's dominion he could not have added to her value through education. Finally, providing for the girl's good education was a crucial component of the Defensor de Menores's decision, a component that could override the legal strictures on forcing masters to sell slaves. Educational concerns could even outweigh the obvious contradiction in allowing individuals to be "slaves only with the name of free persons." Felipa may have been a slave, but she was most importantly a child, and providing her an education was judged to be more important than her owner's right to refuse to sell her.

"Their Service Cannot Equal What I Have Spent": Slave Child Support

In no other area of litigation did the parents and relatives of Lima's slave children put forth arguments as intrinsically challenging to the system of urban slavery than in petitioning to be economically compensated for child rearing. The contrast between law and practice within slavery could be stark in several respects, but it was particularly pronounced on the matter of financial support for slave children.[78] The peculiar institution of urban slavery relied, to a great measure, on the child rearing labors of slave women. Therefore, a customary recognition of slave parents' responsibility for, and rights over, children was integral to how slavery functioned and was reproduced in Lima.

At the close of the eighteenth century, colonial magistrates and the Defensor de Menores determined that parents of slave children could sue masters for recompense for the cost of rearing children. Although they might have admitted these cases in order to force owners to uphold their end of the patriarchal pact of slavery, they unwittingly allowed slaves to begin to whittle away at the foundations of the institution of slavery, which had for so long been erected on masters' ability to enjoy the benefits of the social reproductive efforts of slave parents.

There was no one kind of slavery, of course, and the variation in living situations in the city meant that some slaves were raised in the homes of their masters. In at least one case, a female master was said to have nursed a slave infant while the child's mother spent her days engaged in street selling.[79] This intimacy between slave and master served to constantly reinforce the affective and fictive familial bonds between them. Yet slavery was an economic as well as a social system, and the procedures by which slaves' labor was converted into cash in the form of a monthly wage (*mesada*) paid to their owners provided a great deal of flexibility in terms of the custody of slave children.[80] Allowing slave mothers to nurse their own children was convenient and cheap for slave masters and seems to have been a common practice even when female slaves worked and lived outside their home. In the late colonial period, mothers who retained custody and raised enslaved children, providing their basic needs not only during infancy but often until they were adolescents, discovered that they could sue masters in the court system.

Lima's late colonial civil case records contain no evidence of masters punctually coming forward to redeem slave children when they reached age three or were weaned. In fact, most of the cases revolved around children who were in their early teens and already had acquired work skills. Therefore, by the time that masters attempted to reclaim or sell their young chattel, the parents of slave children already had made a substantial investment in their upbringing. In the late colonial period, this investment became fertile ground for acrimonious litigation between the parents of slaves and masters.

The 1792 case brought by Manuela Olaza against her master, Juana Hurtado y Sandoval, was the first in Lima I identified as a suit exclusively over alimentos.[81] Manuela had worked and lived outside her owner's home and punctually submitted her wages to her owner for eight years. During this time, Manuela gave birth to three children and provided their food, clothing, and medical treatment without recompense from doña Juana. What was more, said Manuela, doña Juana refused to rebate her monthly wage during the time that she was nursing and bedridden from a miscarriage. Manuela sued Juana, claiming that, in neglecting to support her and her children, she had reduced the slave mother's personal capital and, by extension, prevented her from freeing herself and her children.

The 1789 instruction ironically had only cast light on the economic contradictions between what were viewed as the natural obligations of slave parents and those of masters. In the preceding case, it was the slaveholder who stated in her defense that parents had a natural obligation to their children. She claimed Manuela's financial outlay was "an affair of natural obligation" and judgments about decisions to feed and clothe slave children fell under the "jurisdiction of [the master's own] conscious," not the jurisdiction of royal courts. This argument did completely convince Lima's judges. First the alcalde, then the ministers of the Audiencia, ruled that Manuela could search for a new owner, although they struck down Manuela's claim for back compensation for child support. While not a complete victory for Manuela, Lima's magistrates signaled that they were willing to hear cases over slave child support and thus created a breach in the court system for radical legal debates about the economic responsibilities of masters and parents.

The mothers of Lima's slave children saw their opportunity. More cases such as Manuela's entered the court record in spite of the retraction of the 1789 Instruction on Slaves. Only five years after Manuela's suit, free morena Paula Marchán faced the possibility that her five children and grandson would be sold following the death of their owner.[82] She decided to sue for back pay of child support as a means of preventing the disintegration of her family. Throughout their lives her children had lived with her and her husband, a saddle maker who, she said, had "invested all of the fruits of his labors in the benefit of his children" until he died, and who had even purchased Paula's own freedom. "Their youth makes it so their service could not equal what I spent," she argued. "It is not right (*regular*) that my husband would invest in raising and maintaining these children until their present ages in order for the heirs [of her dead owner] to take advantage of them as part of the inheritance."

It is noteworthy that Paula did not attempt, as did other parents, to allege the wrongful enslavement of her children—indeed, she admitted she had been a slave when she gave birth to them. Nor did she allege that they had been mistreated in any way. After all, it was she who had cared for them their entire lives. But by the late colonial period, masters' failure to financially support slave children had assumed a primary place alongside other accusations as legal grounds to sue owners. Following the dictates of the 1789 Carolinian slave code, and disregarding its nullification, judges and the Defensor de Menores had become as concerned with the economic investment adults made in raising children as with the finer points of codified slave law. The Audiencia ruled that Paula could purchase all of her children and her one grandchild—six slaves in total—for the low price of 500 pesos.

The parents of slave children also began to make legal ground by contending that owners should not be permitted to raise the selling price of their children based on the economic investment that the parents had made in the youths. Recall the case of Rafaela Araujo, who dauntlessly fashioned a succession of arguments to try to liberate her daughter, Felipa, and finally found a new, female owner to purchase and educate the girl. One of the arguments Rafaela made was that the owner had unfairly profited from her daughter by selling her at more than twice the cost he had paid eight months earlier, "without in this short time having undertaken a single diligence toward her education and teaching." Other parents of the period shared Rafaela's belief that owners should invest something tangible in their young slaves in order to raise their price. They contended that if the owners had done nothing to advance the education or well-being of slave children during the period of ownership, they should not be allowed to profit from their sale.[83]

Almost poetically, the clash between the financial responsibilities of owners and the natural rights and obligations of parents finally came to a head in Lima during the waning days of colonial rule. In 1819 a case reaching the Real Audiencia revealed how the intricate overlays of adult authority that were stitched into the very fabric of urban slavery had begun to come undone. When don Eugenio Barrera, who was master of her fourteen-year-old daughter and her eleven-year-old son, died, María Andrea Barrera brought suit against his heirs for back payment of child support, calculated to the massive sum of 3,456 pesos (figured at the rate of 2 reales per day, or 8 pesos a month).[84] The arguments lawyers put forward in the case brought to bear all of the contemporary ideas about child rearing and the all of the contradictions of Spanish laws on slavery and parental authority.

Lawyer Isidrio Vilca defended María Andrea by arguing, "It is generally agreed upon by every tribunal that the master should financially support [slave children]." But because María Andrea had raised the children, it was "irrational" and "contrary to all natural law" that don Eugenio's widow could profit "by taking usufruct of that which she has not cultivated." "It is clear," he said, that "don Ugenio [sic] extricated himself from supporting the children until they were useful, and it simply cannot be that my client, in addition to the grave pain of seeing them subject to captivity, should suffer the injustice of losing that in which she has invested and cared."

Lawyer Pablo Ramírez de Arrellano advocated on behalf of Eugenio Barrera's widow, doña María Echenique. He claimed that María Andrea had maintained custody and care of the children only "because she wanted to as mother" and with the intention of eventually suing for back child support. Surely, he said, the woman was familiar with "the popular adage—since among people of her class such witticisms are common—'he who gives bread to another's dog loses the bread and loses the dog.'" In his closing argument, Ramírez claimed that the owner had been deprived of the labor of the children, who, he contended were old enough for small tasks. But since she had not benefited from their labor, doña María had no responsibility to provide support for the children. "In the end," Ramírez said, "the obligations between Master and slaves are reciprocal."

By the time the case reached the Defensor de Menores, matters were being settled without his intervention. Doña María Echenique had decided to sell the two children to another purchaser, and the Defensor appeared relieved that she had made the decision, since the case would have put his oft-stated desire to rule in the best interests of minors of age to the test. But this was only one case. In general, the men who served as Defensores de Menores were instrumental in advising the judges of the Cabildo and the Audiencia to take into account not only written law but also the well-being of minors of age—whether slave or free—when they ruled on civil cases. Increasingly, they advocated for children rather than adults, pushing judges to recognize the rights of mothers and the parents of slaves as valid and to limit the authority of fathers and slave owners.

Cases over slave child support eventually compelled Peru's viceroy to make an official statement on the matter. On 21 November 1821, as the wars of independence raged through the Andes, the viceroy issued a supreme decree that made an official policy of what courts had been ruling since the turn of the century: masters were responsible for providing alimentos to slave children.[85] Furthermore, Article Five of the ruling stated that "in retribution for the small expenditures that good masters pass on to mothers during the time of lactation, which lasts up to three years, and during childhood [*infancia*], [which lasts] up to seven years and a half, conforming to Law, they acquire the right of *patronato*," or the right to accumulate sums of money that owners could hold in escrow toward their freedom. The decree was a triumph for mothers of slave children on several points. It officially revived a central tenet of the 1789 instruction: slave owners—not parents—were ultimately responsible for the financial support of slave children. Yet, even more crucially, the decision did not deprive mothers of the right to custody of their young children. In fact, their diligence in raising them would be rewarded with pay that could be used for freedom.

The Defensor de Menores was deputized with enforcing the decree and overseeing all relevant cases, and his official role in protecting slaves expanded ever more rapidly in subsequent years.[86] After Peru's independence, he was charged with summarizing the civil allegations of all slaves, not only children, and providing them with "a legal apprenticeship."[87] Circulating notices around Lima announcing that he would assist slaves seeking to bring suit against their masters, the Defensor de Menores—this individual once charged only with overseeing the division of property of wealthy minors of age—became the most important political proponent of slaves' rights in Peru and was reviled by the country's slaveholders, one of whom dubbed the officeholder "the chief enemy of agriculture."[88]

CONCLUSION

It may seem that, despite the success of some select slave legal practices, the system of bondage that developed in the Spanish colonies ultimately always favored the master. Numerous cases recounting the cruel punishment of Lima's slaves (including children) are cataloged in the archives, and reading them might lead us to conclude, as did Alberto Flores Galindo, that "convivial paternalism" was a convenient myth created by masters.[89] But an examination of parents' and relatives' challenges to slave masters, and their triumphs and failures, reveals that paternalism was more than an ideological shroud that concealed the violence of African bondage. At the end of the eighteenth century, it had become an art of Bourbon judicial statecraft, a mandate to protect children that allowed judges to limit the property rights of slaveholders in the city. It also had become the grounds for a dynamic struggle between elders and masters over Lima's slave children.

The appearance of rival interpretations of slave childhood and adult authority over young slaves was a product of the new politics of the child. The emergence of a language of natural rights, education, discipline, and economic investment in children corroded the bond that legally alloyed a master's potestad over slaves to the king's control of subjects.[90] Ultimately, the new politics of the child provided a means for some limeños to challenge one of the ugliest legacies of Spanish colonialism in the Americas: the bondage of children. Ironically, they made this challenge in the secular court system, the very institution that Bourbon officials had charged with promoting social order through patriarchal control.

To argue that Lima's late colonial litigants, lawyers, and court agents participated in an enlightened politics of the slave child is not to argue that these individuals were budding abolitionists. It is true that after independence Defensores de Menores began to openly voice the Enlightenment foundations that had, for decades, provided part of the basis for their legal rulings in cases involving slave children. "Now that *las luces* have flourished," stated one Defensor, "it is imperative that the rational hand of justice, in the spirit of our patria's laws, providently ministers to the consolation of the captive."[91] But the quest for rational justice for slaves was not the exclusive property of early nineteenth-century republicans. In some ways, it was a quest begun by the Spanish king and the city's own slaves.

No matter how tentative Charles IV was in sticking to his own social policies in the face of elite opposition, his reforms did reveal that the crown had begun to view the education and economic care of slave children as critical to imperial order, as was protecting them from masters' abuse. Ordinary litigants articulated these same ideas in Lima's courts. Yet, particularly in the case of litigation over slave minors, it became clear that the Bourbon monarch could not contain the potential for drastic challenges to the social reproductive process of slavery by selectively harnessing some elements of Enlightenment discourse to the cause of an absolutist order and eliminating others. The child would not be elevated to a new position of social importance without destabilizing traditional colonial child rearing practices and the notion that the patriarchal family was the social structure that housed all relations of power, including those between master and slave. Still, in the end, when the relatives and parents of slave children practiced the new politics of the slave child in secular courts, they accomplished something equally as profound as shaking the traditional ideological foundation of slavery as a paternal relationship. They slowly transformed the slave child into someone new: a child like any other.

Strange Ties and Interior Fears

Conclusion

I n 1795 a dispute over the guardianship and custody of a twelve-year-old orphan took place far north of Lima, in Caracas. Following a series of deaths in the family, young Simón passed to the guardianship of an uncle, don Carlos Palacios. When the boy fled to live with his sister and her husband, doña María and don Pablo, they petitioned the Caracas Audiencia for guardianship and custody. But don Carlos resisted losing guardianship of his nephew.

In his petition don Carlos pointed out that, in his home, the boy was surrounded by a multitude of servants and adult relatives "who are other mothers and fathers to him" and that he treated the youth lovingly. He could not understand what compelled his ward to run away other than to guess that the boy was trying to "shake off the yoke of teaching and discipline." Don Carlos urged the judges to "reduce the boy to reason," since, he said, when dealing with "children of a tender age, who cannot discern what is good or bad for them, it is imperative to subject them to someone who can halt their disorderly inclinations." If Simón were to be permitted to choose his own guardian, he would only learn that he could do as he pleased and become a "capricious youth, a rude man, beholden to no law other than that of his passions."

A court scribe attempted several times to collect the boy from his sister's home and take him back to his legal guardian. Each time he physically resisted, at one point sassily informing the official that "he was not going to go anywhere." In the meantime, don Carlos decided that the best solution was for his nephew to live and study in a school run by a well-respected local teacher.

Doña María and her husband were heartbroken about losing her brother. Don Pablo approached the court again, asking the ministers to rethink their original ruling. In his petition he argued that a public school was beneath his family's class status. "Under the care of a stranger," the youth had begun fraternizing with other boys "not of his quality" and running loose in the streets. Indeed, at this point in the legal dispute, Simón managed to run away from school, stunning the judges. "It boggles the imagination, these ideas of disobedience to Justice he has demonstrated, prejudicial to himself and to the whole community," one minister wrote. The Audiencia ruled that he return to school in order "to rectify his customs and teach him those that correspond to a distinguished citizen."

Doña María asked them to elaborate further on their ruling to keep the boy in the school, so the Audiencia ministers responded, "Youths' education, being one of the matters of most interest to the public good . . . can tend to be undermined as much by too much love and deference of parents, siblings, and relatives as by too much rigidity." They had decided that the school, not her home, was the appropriate place for Simón "as much because of the great love she has for him, as because they are both too young, and do not have enough experience to deal with the occasions that are born from a voluntary education, in which [children] tend to have more liberty."

Doña María and her husband continued to litigate, proposing the youth be moved to a seminary school, but don Carlos would not comply with their desires. Finally, the judges decided to ask the youth what he wanted to do. The scribe who interviewed him reported that the boy, undoubtedly awed by the depths of the trouble he had gotten himself into and "now, more reflective about the benefits of education and learning, is not only ready but soundly desires to return to the house and shelter of his uncle and tutor . . . continuing under the lessons and direction of his teacher, don Simón Narcisco Rodríguez."[1]

So little Simón Bolívar, future leader of South American independence, returned to his teacher to learn the "customs of good citizens." It would later be reported that Rodríguez followed the plan laid out in Rousseau's *Émile* when he educated Bolívar, although this has never been proved. What is certain is that Rodríguez, involved in a pardo conspiracy against the colonial government in 1797, passed on to his pupil a set of distinctly radical ideas and a fascination with Enlightenment philosophies. In 1805, when Simón Bolívar met his former mentor in Paris, the two decided to visit Rousseau's home in Chambéry to pay their respects to the memory of the great philosophe.[2]

The Bolívar custody case was exceptional only in that it concerned a boy who would grow up to be known as "the Liberator." In almost every other way, the case looked very similar to court battles waged in Lima at the same time. It contained evidence of an official concern with education, fears about youthful passions, a stress on the importance of familial love and female care, and even the emergence of nascent notions of citizenship. If the Bolívar case was hardly different from many of the family sagas aired before tribunals in Lima, it also seems to have shared a great deal in common with early nineteenth-century court battles in other Spanish American cities, such as Buenos Aires, Bogotá, and Mexico City.[3] Indeed, at the end of the colonial period, court disputes reflecting new philosophies and practices associated with children became a common phenomenon.

Until the end of the 1970s, most scholars portrayed the Enlightenment in Latin America as an elite intellectual trend without devoting much attention to its effects on ordinary colonials. This is especially true for Lima, where the scholarship on the Amantes del País and its legendary publication, *Mercurio Peruano*, leaves no doubt that the Enlightenment shaped upper-class cultural and political proclivities.[4] But it tells us little about how the pioneering little pamphlet affected or reflected the attitudes of the many city inhabitants who could not read it. More recently, the masses of ordinary Spanish Americans have figured as main characters in historical narratives of the last decades of colonial rule. But this shift has only partially revised our image of the Enlightenment in Spanish America. Historians tend either to link the Enlightenment to a new late colonial disciplinary regime, in which elite and official vigilance of the popular classes grew in Spanish colonial cities, or to dismiss altogether the importance of this intellectual and cultural movement for ordinary colonials.[5] In reflecting on whether the intellectual activities of late colonial elites filtered down to ordinary, poor limeños, Alberto Flores Galindo once boldly asserted, "For *la plebe*, there was no Enlightenment."[6]

It is true that, at times, Lima's popular classes were the objects of enlightened absolutist policies rather than subjects producing new philosophies. Upper-class fears of popular uprisings and suspicions about castas and slaves left their mark on criminal sentencing of minors of age in the eighteenth century, even as judges began to consider new arguments about the importance of reforming potential criminals while they were still young. Particularly in terms of policing the city and disciplining miscreant or vagrant youths, the old colonial hierarchies of gender, color, and social class meant that Bourbon officials and elites applied emergent philosophies of childhood and rehabilitation quite selectively.

Yet the Enlightenment, whether in its local, Spanish, or broader European forms, had an impact on ordinary colonials beyond the policing of the streets. It affected daily interactions in schools, courtrooms, and homes. It provided the rationale for many strident Bourbon social policies that aimed to include, not prosecute, the city's children. And it influenced how laws on custody and child support were applied during the late colonial period. As historian John Tate Lanning pointed out decades ago, Enlightenment philosophies did not always arrive in Spanish America via banned books tacked to the bottom of chairs.[7] In fact, as I have argued in the case of new pedagogies and philosophies of childhood, the Enlightenment often entered the city of Lima in the form of royal edicts on schools, foundlings, and marriage. It was also produced in local form by limeños themselves.

During the last decades of colonial rule, young limeños enjoyed expanded educational opportunities, royal officials promoted the application of attenuated (and state-centered) notions of equality among children, and patriarchal subordinates pressed for recognition of natural rights over children in the city courts. Thus, Enlightenment philosophies of childhood transformed not only the lives of Lima's elite inhabitants but also the lives of ordinary people living in the viceregal capital. As litigants debated the terms and meanings of natural rights, education, discipline, and child rearing in Lima's courts, they ensured that new philosophies of childhood and authority—the new politics of the child—became a process of everyday negotiations of power at the domestic level rather than simply a matter of elite intellectual debate or royal policy.

The new politics of the child certainly did not spawn a complete revolution in how Lima's children were raised. Well into the nineteenth century, Lima's girls still entered convents for education; parents still abandoned their children at the Casa de Niños Expósitos, which became the republican Orphans' Hospital; and elite families still hired women to nurse their infants.[8] New notions of equality among the empire's children and rights for all who raised them did not immediately and completely replace traditional notions about legal protection or cultural constructs such as honor and legitimacy. Yet they irrevocably altered how limeños conceived of their child rearing practices and defined childhood and authority.

For much of the colonial period, the analogy between a father's authority over children and the king's patriarchal power over his colonial subjects concealed and contained the diversity of adult-child relations on which reproducing a colonial order relied. Colonial Lima's homes and institutions contained a dizzying network of cross-caste and intergenerational relationships of dependency, intimacy, and authority. The ideology of patriarchal household governance—based on generation as well as gender—imposed an imaginary order on this diversity, naturalizing the multiple hierarchies that existed in the city. It made it perfectly understandable that a man who bought a black foundling from a charitable institution saw the boy's subordination to him as filial, that priests who reared Indian noble boys saw themselves as padres de familia, and that elite women who tended to the financial affairs of their children forfeited public authority in courts to a man who held the official title of guardian. By continually likening colonial racial hierarchies, labor arrangements, and legal rights to the generational order in a family, colonials also reproduced one of the principal political justifications for both monarchy and colonialism: Spanish paternalism.

At the end of the eighteenth century, however, the Enlightenment and the Bourbons' heightened state intervention into the domestic sphere threw the mutually reinforcing ideological relationship between patriarchal household governance and royal paternalism off balance. This book has traced the legal and social history of childhood and youth over two centuries in order to account for this transformation and, along the way, has yielded several minor histories of social practices and institutions in the seventeenth and eighteenth centuries. The historical trajectories of the Colegio del Príncipe, of the practice of wet nursing, and of the office of the Defensor de Menores—to choose just three examples presented here—encapsulate the transition from an old to a new politics of the child.

The evolution of the Colegio del Príncipe, established in 1619, serves as a microcosm of changing attitudes concerning education—especially toward Peru's young male indigenous nobility—from the sixteenth to the eighteenth centuries. The institution originally was founded as part of an early colonial project to stamp out native Andean religion and to foster political loyalty among the youngest generation of native leaders. The Jesuits' mission to educate the younger generations of Indian nobles was mostly a symbolic exercise in colonial paternalism. Enrolling few pupils and increasingly drawing students from the lesser ranks of indigenous society, the priests pursued a policy of cultural confinement, an attempt simply to isolate their pupils from the "corrosive" influences of native communities rather than to instruct them in the same way that elite español youths were taught. In the meantime, the priests treated the school primarily as a mechanism for converting crown funding into profit-producing haciendas.

The priests' privileges as colonial "fathers" did not go unchallenged. An Audiencia minister doubted that the colegio's pupils could even write, and he made a bid to close the school in 1762. Although he was not successful, his assessment of the Jesuits' educational failings predated a crown edict expelling the order from the American colonies by five years, offering one of many examples of the local origins of Bourbon reform projects. When the crown forced the Jesuits out of the colonies in 1767, the colegio was transferred to complete state control. Its reopening was delayed because educating Indian nobles took a backseat to plans to cart vagrant orphans and widows off the streets, and the very building in which Indian noble sons were housed was converted into a classic Bourbon institution: a poorhouse. When the school finally reopened, the pupils of the Colegio del Príncipe, once destined only to learn the buenas costumbres that would make them "conduct themselves civilly like the Spanish in all things," now were provided buena crianza, a rational education based on Enlightenment pedagogies.

Elite limeños enthusiastically embraced the concept of buena crianza and sought to extend education to a wide array of Lima's youths, including those who had not formerly received formal instruction. This was evident when the self-dubbed Defender of Widows wrote to one of Lima's many new news-papers, *El Investigador*, in 1812 and lamented that the Colegio del Príncipe was still not "making the Enlightenment useful" to enough of the city's children. Those traditionally thought to be unprotected by patriarchs, such as orphans, were imagined to be ideal recipients of new social projects. But, crucially, certain children were left out of the plans to offer buena crianza. At roughly the same time that the Defender of Widows sent his suggestions to the newspaper, the director of the Colegio del Príncipe was continuing a decades-long battle to prevent his students from being confused with the city's foundlings during the public festivals held in the plaza mayor. The Defender of Widows's silence when it came to abandoned children was telling: he was the defender of widows and the fatherless, but not of children whose racial origins were unknown.

Many of Lima's elites reached the limit of their tolerance for new policies, philosophies, and pedagogies when it came to abandoned children or to slave children protected by judges or to mestizo youths who could enroll in the king's school for "noble Americans." Despite royal efforts to provide a measure of social equity to colonial children in order to convert them into productive subjects of the empire, elites in Lima were adamantly opposed to presuming innocence and granting all of the city's children the same social legitimacy. Time and again, they resisted enlightened absolutist reforms because these policies undermined their own control over the children of the city.

The practice and meanings of wet nursing further illustrate the Enlightenment predicament that the creole elite faced as traditional notions of childhood and adult authority shifted during the era. Wet nursing, the use of convents as nurseries, and apprenticeships were colonial social reproductive practices that smoothed the transmission of colonial hierarchies by creating intimacy across castes and down through generations. The customary recognition of diverse adult authority over children and the social proximity between adults and children of different castes, which had served the elite so well for so long, came under attack at the end of the eighteenth century. European philosophers, travelers, and poets speculated that the affective bonds between colonial generations had created domestic disorder in the colonies. They implied that traditional colonial child rearing practices had rendered creoles too feminine, too childlike, and too politically immature—in short, too close to those who had nursed them—to emancipate themselves from the Spanish Father King.

Lima's creole elite may have been tempted to prove this notion wrong if it was not so fearful that a full adoption of emergent Enlightenment political ideologies would inspire subordinates to lay waste to their own paternal prerogatives at home. In fact, while Lima's literati gathered in cafés and salons to debate how new tenets related to child rearing, wet nursing, and education should be applied in the city's households, the parents of slave children, free casta wet nurses, and even elite wives began to slip out of their homes and enter royal courts, where they challenged the patriarchal prerogatives of fathers and masters. It was becoming clear that the kind of patriarchal control that Bourbon kings promoted was not necessarily the control Lima's men could exert over subordinates such as minors, the mothers of their children, and slaves, but the kind that the kings alone possessed.

The history of one legal office is instructive for approaching the question of why Lima's late colonial judges increasingly heard complaints from patriarchal subordinates in issues involving children. The Defensor de Menores was, in many ways, the incarnation of the changing character of the royal state in relation to the colonial family, of the firmer control the Father King began to exert over the padre de familia. The office originally was designed to facilitate the transfer of wealth from the first generation of Spaniards to their mestizo children during Peru's protracted era of conquest. It evolved in the seventeenth century into a charitable post used to protect elite orphans and their property. The transformation coincided with an early consolidation of Lima's colonial elites as a class, marking Lima's maturity as a Spanish imperial city.

But the office had been cultivated in a particularly colonial culture, and its roots in that culture were never severed. During the early seventeenth century, the legal post of Defensor de Menores grew in the shade of a parallel office of legal advocacy for Indians, the protector de indios, to such an extent that the same individual occupied these offices simultaneously in the provinces of Peru. Protecting Indians, no less than protecting mestizo orphans and elite minors of age, was a natural outgrowth of the flourishing of Spanish legal culture in colonial terrain, where many individuals—whether they were categorized as miserables, desamparados, orphans, widows, or minors—were considered to need tutelage and were specially tended to by the Father King.

When put on the market during the cash-poor years of waning Hapsburg rule, the post of the Defensor de Menores became a more prestigious and powerful position, used by creole elites to advance in their climb toward the upper echelons of Lima's bureaucratic hierarchy. The mid-eighteenth-century tenure of Defensor Domingo Larrión marked a passage to yet another phase in the history of the office. Larrión was more active in court cases involving children than any of his predecessors. He delivered a long exposition about patria potestad and the importance of female care in the Mudarra–Marqués de Casaboza case that introduced Chapter 6. Although he recommended that patriarch don Gerónimo de Mudarra be granted custody of his infant daughter, he did so in part because the man had promised that the girl would be raised in the home of his sister. Larrión freely used his secular post to adjudicate a father's authority, and though the Council of the Indies believed that Lima's local magistrates had transgressed ecclesiastical jurisdiction in this case, eventually both the council and the crown would agree that suits over the custody and care of youths—both slave and free—were the domain of the secular courts. The Defensor de Menores's intervention into Lima's households on behalf of the city's children would no longer be left to the personal initiative of men such as Larrión. It would become an institutionalized element of the new politics of the child.

By the early republican period, the Defensor de Menores launched himself ever more deeply into affairs of domestic governance, and his office became a platform of advocacy for adult slaves as well as children. From his desk, the Defensor de Menores of an independent Peru began to write decisions that hinted at how Enlightenment ideas of equality and liberty would merge with traditional notions of privileged protection before the law in the modern period. It was then that the Defensor issued statements that called for national laws to protect slaves by appealing for "the rational hand of justice" to minister to the "consolation of captives." Even in republican Peru, enlightened notions of reason and equality would not be asserted for slaves without appeal to traditional Spanish legal notions of tutelage for those considered miserables, and to notions of paternal protection before the law.

Well beyond the colonial period, the legacy of political paternalism, of the limiting legal protections placed on those defined as dependents, seems to have become a distinctive birthright of Peruvians and of Latin Americans in general.[9] Our own contemporary stereotypes of Latin American machismo, of entrenched forms of patronage politics, and of cultures built around the patriarchal family lead us, unavoidably, to the question of how such colonial traditions withstood the collapse of Spanish rule.

Part of the answer may be conceptualized as what Carole Pateman has described as the rise of "fraternal patriarchy."[10] Upon the collapse of monarchies at the end of the eighteenth century, paternal patriarchy was replaced with a form of modern patriarchy characterized by a fraternity of men that excluded women and restricted them to a domestic sphere. Indeed, the rise of what looks much like fraternal patriarchy occurred in Peru and in many new republics throughout Latin America. As Sarah Chambers has demonstrated for early republican Arequipa, women's domestic efforts were subtly transformed into service for the public good, and this, in turn, limited women's inclusion in the republic as citizens.[11] When Mexican lawmakers deliberated over how to write women into national legislation in the mid-nineteenth century, they bowed to mothers' new prestige as civilizers of future citizens and wondered whether they should retain the medieval Spanish law that deprived widows of patria potestad, a law that the Bourbon government itself had weakened by selling widows the privilege of retaining guardianship when they remarried.[12] Even as Mexican jurists pondered this question, however, the natural rights of motherhood were being relegated to a domestic, rather than public, sphere of authority. The author of *Nuevo Febrero*, a guide to Mexican law, stated that widows could receive patria potestad because it was not "a public charge that would be appropriate and exclusive to men; it is but a domestic authority based on the incapacity of the child."[13]

The relegation of motherhood to a domestic authority—a qualified, and thus depoliticized, power over children—accompanied a growing belief that women were innately emotional, religious, and traditional. In the late eighteenth century, colonial judges considered emotion and natural love as important criteria for awarding women custody of children. But in the nineteenth century, a harder, more inflexible division between female emotionalism and male rationalism crystallized, and women's character could be deemed ultimately detrimental to children.[14] Indeed, the concept already had a certain momentum in late colonial Spanish American courts. As the judges of Caracas's Audiencia indicated in 1797, Simón Bolívar's sister could be deprived of authority over her younger brother at least in part because she loved him too much.

Further research is needed to determine whether the condemnation of women's emotionalism led judges to deny women custody of their children in nineteenth-century Lima or if it otherwise affected republican notions of motherhood throughout Latin America. Despite a spate of recent historical scholarship on gender in Spanish American cities during the decades after independence, it is still unclear how nineteenth-century judges arbitrated adult authority over children. Some evidence indicates that female custody became standard in Lima after the city became capital of a new nation rather than a viceroyalty. Christine Hünefeldt found that only two men in more than 1,000 cases of conjugal conflict in nineteenth-century Lima requested custody of their children.[15] Yet other studies indicate that legal authorities vacillated between protecting the custody rights of patriarchs who could prove "good citizenship" and valorizing motherhood.[16]

Spanish America's long and bumpy transition from colonies to postcolonial republics ultimately may have resulted in exclusive fraternalism, but as this book has shown, for those who lived during the dynamic half-century between 1770 and the end of colonial rule in Lima, it was far from clear how Enlightenment notions of childhood and adult authority, as well as new social policies, would affect the gender and generational order in the city's households. It was even less clear how they would affect larger ideologies of political authority and governance. In this respect, Lima was hardly different from France, where as Suzanne Desan argues, the family was "put on trial" by republican lawmakers after the revolution. Some women, far from being automatically excluded by the legal philosophies of republicanism, found that emerging liberal ideas could, in fact, be quite liberating in terms of traditional gender inequalities.[17]

Feminist and postcolonial scholars have cautioned us against the kind of teleological thinking that trumpets the Enlightenment as an emancipatory movement that inaugurated the "modern era."[18] Yet the civic role of women as republican mothers, as well as their exclusion from full citizenship, was not established in a day but, instead, was worked out over the course of decades. To recognize as much is to break free from another teleology: that which posits modern political marginalization as a historical given rather than a historical process. Late eighteenth-century judges in Peru—and Mexico and, for that matter, revolutionary France—in fact did legislate dramatic changes in house-hold governance when they determined that the adults who reared children possessed rights that previously had been withheld from them. Thus, the transition from early modern patriarchy to modern republican political fraternity was far from the simple substitution of one kind of family metaphor for another. It was a prolonged experience in which accepted notions of domestic authority became contested and uncertain, much like the stability of the Old Regime.

What is more, even before the Age of Revolution, patriarchy was far from a stable system for those who lived within it. As Lynn Hunt has pointed out, the link between a father's authority in the home and monarchical power had always contained "its own internal ironies and contradictions."[19] Her comments underscore a key argument I have made for the case of colonial Lima. The Enlightenment and the Bourbon Reforms did bring about certain decisive transformations in how adult authority and child rearing were conceptualized, both legally and socially. Yet perhaps even more importantly, they revealed that, in a city where diverse adults possessed extralegal generational authority over children, patria potestad was a potentially unsteady ideological pillar to use to buttress the legitimacy of Spanish rule. Late colonial legal arguments—about a remarried widow's right to retain authority over her children, for instance—did not so much herald the demise of patriarchal domestic governance as announce openly that authority over children had, in practice, been vested in multiple adults for some time.

Viewing the end of Spanish colonialism as a period when paternal political legitimacy was swept away in favor of fraternal public spheres and cults of domesticity in countries such as Peru is also problematic for another reason. Family models of order and authority continued to underwrite modern national ideologies, even while they supported republican forms of political governance.[20] Importing concepts of patriarchy that emphasize the modern (liberal) variant of women's subordination to understand Latin America too easily glosses over the persistence of generational forms of patriarchy in postcolonial relations *among adult men*—a relationship of power that historians of the nineteenth and twentieth centuries often cast as "patronage" or "paternalism."

Peru's national lawmakers and liberal intellectuals never completely jettisoned the traditional Spanish paternalistic emphasis on attending to the "weak and needy" when they embraced equalizing concepts of citizenship.[21] By the early twentieth century, even liberal pedagogue José Antonio Encinas doubted the wisdom and justice of his nation's laws on Indians, which were now rooted in notions of equality and individual rights rather than minority and misery. In 1920 he proposed the reinfusion of Spanish colonial laws into Peruvian legislation and called for the reinstatement of minority status for Indians. He wrote, "The republican regime brought individualism, liberated the Indian from tutelage and from the social right (*acción*) that Spanish legislation had offered him, placing him on a terrain of manifest inequality without preparing him for the battle." Encinas proposed a resurrected "guardianship" of Indians as a means to both "protect" them and aid in their "development" to a stage of social and economic equality.[22] Perhaps nowhere was the long Spanish tradition of racial patriarchy so directly merged with the more recent legacy of Enlightenment notions of equality.

The words Víctor Raúl Haya de la Torre, founding father of the Alianza Popular Revolucionaria Americana, used to describe the relationships between party leaders and members suggest something more about the resilience of patriarchal ways in twentieth-century politics. "These ties are very strange," Haya explained, "because they come from the family." He continued by likening intraparty relations to the intimate, yet somehow distant, relationship between aristocratic families and their servants in Trujillo, the northern coastal city of his birth:

> I was nurtured in this aristocratic tradition. . . . One inherited this like a kind of code of conduct. . . . The families that lived in what were called the *casas grandes* followed this rule. That the children wait on the servants on their birthdays, that they do all sorts of things, be the godfather of their marriages, all this sort of thing. . . . And you have to go up to each one of the servants and kiss them. . . . It is a different spirit. And we who come from the North, for example, with the blacks, very affectionate, and everything. At the same time there was always something very cordial in the people. . . . We [the leaders] were educated in that school. . . . We were born of this stock. In a country which was not an industrial or bourgeois country, still a patriarchal country, these ties meant much.[23]

Haya's "strange ties" stretch back hundreds of years. The intimacy elite children and servants forged in the mansions of colonial Peru—and, ultimately, the social distance that this intimacy fostered—inspired late colonial ruminations about the "misunderstood love" between wet nurses and creole infants, just as it continues to inspire Peruvian writers today. In 1998, as I made my daily trips to Lima's archives while performing research for this book, I frequently encountered young street vendors busily hawking a popular new novel about the city's *pitucos*, or upper classes. Intrigued, I bought the book and discovered that the title of Jaime Bayly's *Yo amo a mi mami* [I love my mommy] refers to the protagonist's Indian nanny rather than his own mother.

In the late colonial period, the new politics of the child reconstituted fundamental features of colonial patriarchy and strained the ideological link between Father King and colony, but it did not dissolve paternal concepts of political power or reshape the private world of Peruvians. Nonetheless, even in conservative Lima, the politically charged notions of childhood that emerged in the late eighteenth century ultimately had dramatic implications for Spanish colonial rule. Bourbon social policies that drew, if even only in part, on philosophies that challenged traditional forms of domestic authority and modes of social reproduction produced a most unintended consequence for the inhabitants of the capital city.

It was almost just as don Francisco de Ormaza, the man who purchased an infant from Lima's foundling home in 1776, feared when he warned Peru's viceroy that the Bourbon crown was educating and raising at its bosom children who eventually would rip the Spanish empire asunder. However, those children were not, as he had predicted, Lima's castas or slaves but creole elites from other regions of Spanish America. Local elites may have resented the crown's emphasis on social inclusiveness for all of the king's children—ideas expressed, for instance, in the 1794 ruling on expósitos and in the 1789 royal instruction on slaves—when they were applied to children of lower status within the colonies. Yet notions of inclusiveness and equality became more appealing when some creoles considered them in terms of their own status within the larger empire.

No royal edict on foundlings or education, no legal petition challenging the prerogatives of a padre de familia or master in local courts, and no amount of flirting with potentially revolutionary ideas were in and of themselves enough to tear Lima from the paternal breast of Spain and from the social, racial, and gender hierarchies on which it had been nourished for three centuries. The city proved to be the last bastion of allegiance to the Father King in South America.[24] It would take invasions of a military rather than philosophical sort—the British invasion of Buenos Aires in 1806 and the entrance of Napoleon's troops into Iberia in 1808—to begin to shake colonial rule in Spanish America. Although a Peruvian deputy warned the Spanish Cortes during the Napoleonic crisis that "America is . . . no longer a child who, put to bed with promises, will forget them when he awakes," it was only a full decade later, after creole-led troops marched into Peru from the north and south of the continent, that many of Lima's elites finally began to view their own independence from Spain as inevitable.[25]

Leading the troops from the north was the rebellious Venezuelan boy who had been forced to return to his enlightened teacher. Arriving in Lima in 1823, Simón Bolívar, now forty-two years old, beheld a city of "gated mansions" and "interior fear."[26] The Liberator wondered at the peculiarity of Lima's elites, who preferred to retain the "tyranny of one," so as not to have to suffer the "tumultuous persecutions" of a revolution that would involve the lower classes and castes.[27] As Spanish colonial rule unraveled, Lima's creole upper classes, who had for so long sought to preserve patriarchal order amidst deep political turmoil in the metropole and just beyond the city's walls, paradoxically found that their Peru was no longer a favored son of the Father King. It had become what historian John Lynch could call "the problem child of the American rebellion."[28]

Appendix A
Sample of the Numeración of 1700

I conducted an analysis of a sample of 658 casas out of a total of 3,940 included in the Numeración of 1700. Thus my sample represents approximately 16.7 percent of the households counted in the census.

The sample casas were chosen through a process of arbitrary selection, and I recorded the information of every seventh entry. This method of selection ensured a broad sampling of entries and of individuals from different neighborhoods in the city. It also guaranteed that each enumerator who compiled statistics for the census would be represented. While it was clear that enumerators had different proclivities in how they recorded data, I have no reason to believe that any enumerator took down information with a systematic bias other than those noted in Chapter 2. Therefore, the difference between an arbitrary and a strictly random sample are, I believe, relatively inconsequential.

For simplicity, I analyzed casas by considering all members listed together, although in some cases, subheads of households were listed. I decided to use the primary entry for the casa as the basic unit in my sample, following scribes' marking of *c* to designate a household, rather than to analyze each entry. I did this for two reasons. First, enumerators seem to use very diverse criteria for making separate entries for subheads of household, making this too inconsistent a unit of analysis to use for statistical purposes. Second, I opted to use the casa entry after ascertaining that the average number of individuals per casa was roughly equivalent to, although slightly higher than, that found in households in Latin American and European cities during the same era.

Appendix B
Sample of Notary Contracts

To analyze the apprenticeship and guardianship contracts housed in the Sección Protocolos Notariales of the Archivo General de la Nación in Lima, I sampled notary records through an arbitrary selection process. I reviewed the records of notaries who worked in the city during seven five-year time blocks between 1645 and 1800. The time blocks reviewed are as follows: 1645–50, 1670–75, 1695–1700, 1720–25, 1745–50, 1775–80, and 1795–1800.

For each time block, the method of selecting records for review was relatively simple. Research assistants Claudia Valdivieso and Ilana Aragón and I reviewed records by selecting them alphabetically by notaries' last names, beginning with surnames starting with *A* and continuing until we had a sample drawn from between one-third to one-half of all of the scribes working in the city. This method produced 356 apprenticeship contracts and 213 guardianship contracts.

Just as with the sample of the Numeración of 1700, there is no reason to believe that there was a systematic bias in records related to notaries' last names, though certain notaries worked in certain neighborhoods or specialized in particular kinds of contracts, producing some variation in the results. Because I used a rule of thumb rather than a random sample in selecting notaries, the standard error for each mean number of contracts found in each block of time is different.

The projected total of the number of contracts contained in notary records based on my samples, along with projected totals that account for the upper and lower bounds of mean standard error for each time period, are represented in figures A.1 and A.2. Comparing lower and upper bounds demonstrates that the number of apprenticeship contracts diminished between the periods 1645–50

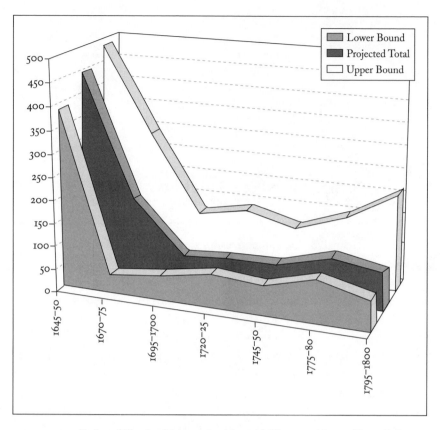

FIGURE A.1   Projected Totals of Apprenticeships with Upper and Lower Bounds for Mean Standard Error. Source: AGN, PN, Sample of Asientos de Aprendiz

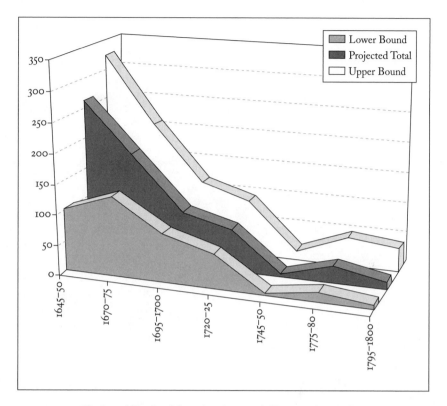

FIGURE A.2   Projected Totals of Guardianships with Upper and Lower Bounds for
Mean Standard Error. Source: AGN, PN, Sample of Tutelas and Curadurías

and 1670–75, while guardianships declined during the late seventeenth century
and again between the periods 1720–25 and 1745–50. Yet the upper and lower
bounds of each preceding and subsequent period make it uncertain whether
these declines reflected a consistent trend. For this reason, I have refrained
from analyzing change over time in the numbers of these contracts here.

Notes

ABBREVIATIONS

AAL	Archivo Arzobispal de Lima
ABPL	Archivo de la Beneficencia Pública de Lima
AGI	Archivo General de Indias, Seville
AGN	Archivo General de la Nación, Lima
AHE	Archivo Histórico de España, Madrid
BNP	Biblioteca Nacional del Perú, Lima
c.	cuaderno (file)
C. Civ.	Causas Civiles
C. Crim.	Causas Criminales
Cab.	Sección Colonial, Cabildo
EC	Sección Colonial, Asuntos Eclesiásticos
f., ff.	folio, folios
H-A	Huérfanos-Antecedentes
leg.	legajo (dossier)
NM	Nulidades de Matrimonios
P.	Protocolo
PN	Sección Colonial, Protocolos Notoriales
RA	Sección Colonial, Real Audiencia
SCA	Sección Colonial, Inquisición, Fundaciones, Santa Cruz de Atocha
TC	Tribunal de conventos y órdenes religiosos
Temporalidades	Sección Colonial, Real Junta de las Temporalidades

1 Ariès, *Centuries of Childhood*. Also see Hiner and Hawes, "Standing on Common Ground," 3; Wilson, "Myth of Motherhood," 181–90; Cox, *Shaping Childhood*; Cunningham, "Histories of Childhood."

2 Twinam, *Public Lives*, 159.

3 The essays in Hecht, *Minor Omissions*, are notable recent contributions.

4 Ingrid Brena Sesma dedicates only three pages of her history of Mexican state involvement in children's lives to the colonial period; see *Intervención del estado*, 33–46. None of the six articles in a 1998 special issue of the *Journal of Family History* (23, no. 3 [July 1998]) on the history of children in Latin America treated the era. Early studies of colonial children in Brazil and Mexico tellingly have taken the form of "research guides" for historians. See the essays by Asunción Lavrin and Elizabeth Kuznesof in Hiner and Hawes, *Children in Historical and Comparative Perspective*. For studies of custody that bridge the transition from colonial to republican rule, see Cicerchia, "Minors, Gender, and the Family," 341–47; Shumway, "Between Revolution, Power, and Liberty"; Lipsett-Rivera, "Marriage and Family Relations." On child custody battles in late nineteenth-century and early twentieth-century Argentina, see Guy, "Parents before the Tribunals." For welfare, see Blum, "Children without Parents." On labor and education, see Kuznesof, "Puzzling Contradictions"; Blum, "Public Welfare and Child Circulation."

5 Again, the *Journal of Family History* illustrates this historiographical point. Special issues dedicated to Latin America in 1978 (vol. 3, no. 4) and 1985 (vol. 10, no. 3) contained no articles on illegitimacy, whereas in 1991 (vol. 16, no. 3), four essays focused on aspects of abandonment and illegitimacy: Potthast-Jutkeit, "Ass of a Mare"; Kuznesof, "Sexual Politics"; Salinas Meza, "Orphans and Family Disintegration"; and Ramos, "Single and Married Women." Also see Gonzablo Aizpuru and Rabell, *Familia en el mundo iberoaméricano*. Important work on illegitimacy includes Mannarelli, *Pecados públicos*; Dueñas Vargas, *Hijos del pecado*; Twinam, *Public Lives*, 126–83; Nazarri, "Urgent Need to Conceal"; Milanich, "Historical Perspectives on Illegitimacy"; Lewin, *Surprise Heirs I* and *Surprise Heirs II*. For Spain, see Carrera Panchón, *Problema del niño expósito*; Sherwood, *Poverty in Eighteenth-Century Spain*; Vidal Galache and Vidal Galache, *Bordes y bastardos*.

6 Stearns, "Social History and History," 322.

7 Hiner and Hawes, "Standing on Common Ground," 1–2.

8 For reviews of feminist scholarship on social reproduction, see Scott, *Gender and the Politics of History*, 33–34; Orloff, "Gender and the Welfare State."

9 In this respect, my use of the concept owes much to Kathryn Burns's description of colonial Peruvian convents as sites of social reproduction, and specifically the role of these institutions in rearing mestiza girls; see *Colonial Habits*, 16–17.

10 Cutter, "Legal System," 57.

11 Gibson, *Aztecs*; Borah, *Justice by Insurance*; Stern, *Peru's Indian Peoples*; Seed, *Ceremonies of Possession*. On the legal system in late colonial Lima, see Flores Galindo, *Ciudad sumergida*, 21.

12 Age is increasingly taking up a fourth position in the former "holy trinity" of race, class, and gender in historical studies. See the special issue "Ages of Women: Age as a Category of Analysis in Women's History," *Journal of Women's History* 12, no. 4 (Winter 2001).

13 *Autos seguido por Caytana Cepeda, en calidad de madre de Vicente, contra doña Agustina Cepeda, sobre sevicia*, AGN, RA, C. Civ., leg. 325, c. 2935, f. 11, 1794.

14 Herrup, *House in Gross Disorder*, 8.

15 *Autos seguidos por María Josefa Delgado contra Polonia Peñaloza sobre la libertad de su hija María Lucía*, AGN, Cab., C. Civ., leg. 70, c. 1366, 1791.

16 For more on subjectivity in colonial Spanish American legal records, see Díaz, *The Virgin, the King, and the Royal Slaves*; Stern, *Secret History*, 38. On legal representation, law as language, and lawyers as translators, see the articles in "Legal Storytelling," special issue of *Michigan Law Review* 87 (1989).

17 Bruckener, *Manual of Roman Private Law*, 61–65; Nicholas, *Introduction to Roman Law*, 76–80.

18 This understanding is consistent with Steve Stern's four-part definition of patriarchy as a system of social relations based on male control of women's sexuality and labor, male superiority over women, elder/father authority, and political rule based on the family model; see *Secret History*, 21. However, by returning the concept of patriarchy to its critical historical legal context and by emphasizing the importance of age and law, rather than gender alone, in constructs of household and political governance, I also respond to recent criticism of the scholarly tendency to view patriarchy as the transhistorical, transcultural male subordination of women. For the criticism and debates, see Scott, *Gender and the Politics of History*; Bennett, "Feminism and History," 256, 258; Bennett, "Women's History," 173–82; Tilly, "Gender, Women's History, and Social History," 439–62; Hoff, "Gender as a Postmodern Category"; and the ensuing debate between Joan Hoff and other feminist historians in *Women's History Review* 5, no. 1 (1996). For colonial Spanish America, see Gauderman, *Women's Lives*. My thinking also has been influenced by Rich, *Of Woman Born*, 57; Gordon, *Heroes of Their Own Lives*, vi–vii; Hardwick, *Practice of Patriarchy*; Miller, *Transformations of Patriarchy*.

19 Lockhart and Schwartz, *Early Latin America*, 7; Besse, *Restructuring Patriarchy*; Seed, *To Love, Honor, and Obey*, 7; Cope, *Limits of Racial Domination*, 93, 163–64; Mallon, *Peasant and Nation*, 73.

20 Genovese, *Roll, Jordan, Roll*, 5. While historians have modified crucial tenets of Genovese's seminal interpretation of U.S. slavery, the primacy he assigns paternalism in master-slave relations remains uncontested. See Oakes, *Ruling Race*, xvii.

21 Elizabeth Fox-Genovese distinguishes between patriarchy and paternalism by arguing that the latter relies on a stark liberal distinction between the public (egalitarian, male) sphere and the private sphere; see *Within the Plantation Household*, 63–64. According to this definition, paternalism cannot exist where liberalism, modern constructions of the public sphere, and protocapitalism do not.

22 As Gordon states, "We need concepts of male supremacy that can explain the power

that women have managed to exert . . . [and] the compromises that men have often made" (*Heroes of Their Own Lives*, vi).

23 Scott, *Gender and the Politics of History*, 49.

24 This is not to say that conquest and colonization were not expressed through gendered as well as generational language and metaphors. See Lewis, "'Weakness'"; Vieira Powers, "Conquering Discourses." However, I have never encountered a reference from the period to the king as husband, while articulations of authority that cast the king as father abound.

25 See MacLachlan, *Spain's Empire*, xii, 1–19; Dore, "One Step Forward," 11.

26 Graham, *Independence in Latin America*, 6. Also see Ryan, "Assimilating New Worlds."

27 These are two key objections Gauderman raises to using the concept of patriarchy to understand gender in colonial Spanish America; see *Women's Lives*, esp. xx. In contrast to Gauderman, I believe "patriarchy" does not need to entail absolute male control over women or to be associated with an absolutist monarchy for it to be a useful term to explain the (Roman-based) ideal-typical model of male household governance that framed authority in colonial Spanish America. On Habsburg Spain, see Nader, *Liberty*; Mackay, *Limits*. It should also be remembered that even in a quintessentially absolutist regime like seventeenth-century France, absolutism was held together by competing pressures from elites and at least some tension with opposing, decentralized models of governance. See Beik, *Absolutism and Society*; Swann, *Provincial Power*.

28 Van Young, "Millennium," 407; Van Young, *Other Rebellion*, 17; Herzog, *Administración*, 306–7. Also see MacLachlan, *Spain's Empire*, xii, 1–19; Dore, "One Step Forward," 11; Graham, *Independence in Latin America*, 6; Ryan, "Assimilating New Worlds."

29 *Siete partidas*, 2:10:2, 2:13:14.

30 Taylor, *Drinking, Homicide, and Rebellion*, 168.

31 See Twinam, *Public Lives*, 27–29; Stern, *Secret History*, 99–104.

32 Amussen, *Ordered Society*; Burrows and Wallace, "American Revolution"; Fliegelman, *Prodigals and Pilgrims*; Yazawa, *From Colonies to Commonwealth*; Hunt, *Family Romance*; Merrick, "Fathers and Kings"; Shammas, *History of Household Government*.

33 Stoler, *Race and the Education of Desire*, 150.

34 On India, see Nandy, "Intimate Enemy," 11–18. On Africa, see Carton, *Blood from Your Children*; Kiernan, *Lords of Human Kind*, 243. For U.S. paternalism in Latin America, see Johnson, *Latin America in Caricature*, 80–95, 161–75.

35 Genovese, *Roll, Jordan, Roll*, 4.

36 Flores Galindo, *Ciudad sumergida*. For the founding of Lima and details about its cathedral, see Rodríguez Camilloni, "Utopia Realized."

37 "Race," as it is used here, does not connote biology as in twentieth-century conceptualizations. While in recent decades historians and ethnohistorians have interrogated the concept of race from multiple angles, I find Charles Wagley's concept of "social race" to continue to be a useful shorthand for describing how color, appearance, and genealogy combined (and still combine) to categorize individuals "racially" in Latin

America. Wagley emphasized that what we might refer to as "race," a categorization based on ancestry and phenotype, served as a fundamental social marker in the colonial period, but because of miscegenation, caste categories also "became entangled" with "social and cultural criteria (language, dress, education, wealth and other social and cultural characteristics)." See Wagley, "On the Concept of Social Race," and the modifications on the concept in Pitt-Rivers, "Race, Color, and Class." Also see Lewis, *Hall of Mirrors*; Cope, *Limits of Racial Domination*.

38 Mörner, *Race Mixture*; Mörner, *Estado, razas, y cambio social*.

39 For a summary discussion of Spanish American urban social and economic hierarchies, see Socolow, "Introduction," 7–9. For a description of the social hierarchy of Lima in the late colonial period, see Flores Galindo, *Ciudad sumergida*.

40 See Anna, "Spain and the Breakdown," 256; Elliot; *Spain and Its World*, 7–8; MacLachlan, *Spain's Empire*, 89.

41 See Burke, "New History," 11; Desan, "What's after Political Culture?," 193; Stoler, "Tense and Tender Ties."

42 Eric Van Young comments on Latin American historians' recent tendency to focus on the transition from colony to republic (ca. 1750–1850) and signals a need to examine what exactly changed in 1750; see his "Conclusion," 230–32.

43 In this way, this book contributes to recent scholarship, primarily of the Atlantic World, that argues for the existence of a colonial Enlightenment. The concept of a colonial Enlightenment is an inherent challenge to post-structuralist assertions about that "totalizing discourse" of Enlightenment universalism. On this point, see esp. Foucault, "What Is Enlightenment?" On colonial Enlightenment in Spanish America, see Cañizares-Esguerra, *How to Write the History of the New World*. On the Caribbean, see Ghachem, "Montesquieu in the Caribbean"; Desan, "What's after Political Culture?," 185–87; Dubois, *Colony of Citizens*; Fischer, *Modernity Disavowed*.

44 For psychological-historical analyses of the demise of the metaphor of the Father King as a "traumatic event" in Spanish America, see Goldwert, "Search for the Lost Father-Figure." For nineteenth-century paternalism, see Earle, "Rape and the Anxious Republic." For psychohistorical approaches to other historical contexts, see Burrows and Wallace, "American Revolution"; Hunt, *Family Romance*; Nandy, "Intimate Enemy."

CHAPTER 1

1 Causa seguida por Bernarda Calero contra José Bernabel por injuria sexual contra su hijo José Mariano de dos años de edad, AGN, RA, C. Crim., leg. 54, c. 631, f. 18, 1783.

2 Causa seguida por doña Alfonsa del Campo contra el menor Agustín de Castro por la muerte accidental ocasionada a su marido, AGN, RA, C. Crim., leg. 9, c. 75, f. 7, 1742.

3 Herzog, *Administración*, 304.

4 Quoted in van Kleffens, *Hispanic Law*, 1.

5 For the development of reliance on written law versus legal custom, see Herzog, *Administración*, 32–33.

6 Don Sebastián Covarrubias defines *derecho* as "alternately what is disposed or ordered

either by nature or a prince or a people (*pueblo*) or a nation (*gente*) or custom"; see "Derecho," in *Tesoro de la lengua castellana*, 406. Also see Cutter, *Legal Culture*, 34, 38.

7 Cutter, *Legal Culture*, 32.

8 Eugene Korthe and Della Flusche argue that, relative to the *Leyes de toro*, the *Siete partidas* gained "only partial and belated acceptance" in colonial Chile; see "Dowry and Inheritance," 396. In Lima, this is true only in terms of legal questions dealing with inheritance. Other codified laws, and the *Siete partidas* in particular, were more widely used in trials concerning issues such as guardianship, subjugation to paternal power, and legal capacity. For the importance of the *Partidas* on the northern frontier of New Spain, see Cutter, *Protector de Indios*, 8.

9 A law on orphans and guardians in the *Fuero juzgo* indicates that, upon turning twenty-five, an individual would reach majority; see *Fuero juzgo*, 4:3:4. On the other hand, the *Siete partidas*, 4:19:2, states, "He who has not completed twenty-five years of age is called a minor." While this discrepancy could create some confusion in Lima's court system, in general, anyone who claimed or was reported to be twenty-five years old (*tener veinticinco años*) was considered to have reached the age of majority.

10 *Siete partidas*, 1:6:27, 3:4:5, 7:1:9; *Canons and Decrees of the Council of Trent*, 24th sess., chaps. 1–9, and 25th sess., chap. 15. Also see Lavrin, "Mexico," 422.

11 The relationship between Spanish Christian organicism and patriarchal rule is discussed in Boyer, "Women," 254. Also see Arrom, *Women of Mexico City*, 77.

12 Bruckener, *Manual of Roman Private Law*, 61–65.

13 *Siete partidas*, 4:25:2, 4:17:3. Also see Arrom, *Women of Mexico City*, 73; Boyer, "Women," 254–55.

14 Díaz, *Female Citizens*, 65 n. 5.

15 "Menor," in Covarrubias, *Tesoro de la lengua castellana*, 749.

16 *Siete partidas*, 4:17. Roman law, and especially the sixth-century Justinian code *Corpus Juris Civilis*, had placed children under direct control of their paternal grandfather, particularly in terms of managing their own property after they married. However, subsequent medieval Castilian law, in part influenced by Germanic law, tended to blunt the authority of the grandfather. Canonist and jurist Juan Machado de Chávez y Mendoza, in *Perfeto confesor*, 2:618–19, argued that the power of the grandfather effectively ended with law 47 of the *Leyes de toro*.

17 *Siete partidas*, 4:13:1, 2; Arrom, *Women of Mexico City*, 54; Twinam, *Public Lives*, 218–20.

18 *Siete partidas*, 4:17:5, 6. Cases involving *peculio castrense* or *cuasi-castrense*, or property specifically obtained outside the control of the father through professional or military salaries or by royal donation, were exceptions.

19 *Siete partidas*, 4:17:11, 7:1:10; *Leyes de toro*, 55; Kagan, *Lawsuits and Litigants*, 10; Arrom, *Women of Mexico City*, 70–77.

20 Compare Arrom, *Women of Mexico City*, 78; Socolow, *Women of Colonial Latin America*, 9; Dore, "One Step Forward," 10–13.

21 Boyer, "Women," 252–53; Silverblatt, "'Universe Has Turned,'" 163.

22 Arrom aptly points out that the padre de familia's authority over his wife was "clearly

less" than his authority over slaves and minor children; see *Women of Mexico City*, 73. Also see Gauderman, *Women's Lives*.

23 Machado de Chávez y Mendoza, *Perfeto confesor*, 2:592.

24 This definition of patria potestad is consistent with the definition adopted by Catholic moralists after the collapse of the Roman republic, when stricter forms of patria potestas were cast aside. The tempered canonical concept of patria potestas was sustained throughout the Middle Ages, according to Sangmeister, *Force and Fear*, 23. He writes, "Primarily, the fulfillment of the duty [of patria potestas] rests with the father, although it affects also the mother as the associate of the father."

25 *Siete partidas*, 4:17:2.

26 Ibid., 4:19.

27 Ibid., 4:19:3.

28 Ibid., 4:19:5.

29 Ibid., 4:17:8.

30 Ibid., 4:18:2, 6.

31 "El fijo o fija casado e velado sea avido por hemancipado en todas las cosas para siempre," *Leyes de toro*, 47.

32 For a full treatment of colonial state paternalism toward the poor and marginalized in Spanish America, see Milton, "Many Meanings."

33 *Siete partidas*, 6:16:4. Also see "Madre," in Escriche y Martín, *Diccionario razonado*, 1228.

34 *Fuero juzgo*, 4:3:1. This definition of "orphan" was repeated, but less explicitly so, in the *Fuero real*, 3:7, which reads, "Huérfanos que sean sin edat fincaren sin padre et sin madre."

35 *Siete partidas*, 6:16:4, 5.

36 Ibid., 4:16:5, 6. Also see "Madre," in Escriche y Martín, *Diccionario razonado*, 1228. Note that Escriche y Martín, writing in the nineteenth century, stated that widows who remarried could continue to serve as tutors of their children if they purchased dispensation (*gracias al sacar*). The sale of these dispensations is discussed in Chapter 6.

37 *Siete partidas*, 6:16:5.

38 For the development of the role of guardians in medieval Spain and the history of increasing state regulation of guardians, see Merchán Alvarez, *Tutela de los menores*.

39 *Siete partidas*, 6:16:5.

40 Ibid., 6:18:1.

41 Ibid., 6:19:1.

42 Ibid., 4:18:18. Also see "sevicia," in Escriche y Martín, *Diccionario razonado*, 1462.

43 *Siete partidas*, 4:22:11.

44 Ibid., 4:18:11 and 12; 4:19:7.

45 Ibid., 3:5:4.

46 Ibid., 3:5:3.

47 Ibid., 3:2:8.

48 Ibid., 3:23:20, 3:18:41. Also see "caso de corte," in Escriche y Martín, *Diccionario razonado*, 425. Arlene Díaz finds few cases in late colonial Caracas in which widows

received caso de corte status; see *Female Citizens*, 61. However, Lima's court records reveal that it was common for widows to demand and receive this status throughout the eighteenth and early nineteenth centuries. See AGN, RA, Casos de Corte, 1707–1819.

49 Stern, *Peru's Indian Peoples*; Borah, *Justice by Insurance*. On the interconnections between law and state-building in Castile, see Kagan, *Lawsuits and Litigants*.

50 Pagden, *Fall of Natural Man*, esp. chap. 4.

51 Elliot, *Spain and Its World*, 49–50.

52 Quoted in Lewis, "'Weakness,'" 75.

53 Brading, *First America*, 83; Borah, *Justice by Insurance*, 91.

54 See Brading, *First America*, 100.

55 For the influence of Vitoria's argument, see Borah, *Justice by Insurance*, 43.

56 Trexler, "From the Mouths," 549–73; Clendinnen, "Disciplining the Indians," 27–48; Phelan, *Millennial Kingdom*, 66, 150.

57 Trexler, "From the Mouths," 549–50.

58 *Recopilación*, 2:6:1.

59 Ibid., 6:5:3.

60 Solórzano Pereira, *Política Indiana*, 122. For a detailed discussion of the rhetoric of Indians as miserables in the laws, see Borah, *Justice by Insurance*, 91–93.

61 Cutter, *Protector de Indios*, 14–16.

62 For the expansion of the number of lawyers in the colonies during the seventeenth and early eighteenth centuries, see Uribe-Uran, *Honorable Lives*, 20–21.

63 See Lowry, "Forging an Indian Nation," 163.

64 Examples of the intervention of the Protector of Natives of the Cercado in apprenticeships contracted during the 1690s can be found in AGN, PN, Marcelo Alvarez de Ron, P. 103, f. 911, and P. 104, ff. 172, 250, 294, 609, 822. Examples from the 1710s are found in PN, F. C. Arrendondo, P. 50, f. 582, 674, 684, 787. Also see Lowry, "Forging an Indian Nation," 163.

65 Peru's fifth viceroy, Francisco de Toledo, specially charged the Indian alcaldes with placing orphans of working age with artisans and with using community funds to pay for their care and upbringing. See the edicts in Levillier, *Gobernantes del Perú*, 8:326.

66 AGN, PN, Martín de Balcázar, P. 175, ff. 391–391v, 1645. In rare cases, the apprentice would be turned over by an *alcalde de crimen* acting as padre de menores, perhaps when placement in an apprenticeship post served a punishment. For instance, see AGN, PN, Thomás de Quesada, P. 1674, f. 674–674v., 1674.

67 Cutter, *Protector de Indios*, 7.

68 Arco, "Notable institución," 187–222.

69 Pérez de Herrera, "Discursos del amparo," 142.

70 The Seville office is referred to in Expediente de Confirmación del oficio de defensor y curador de menores en Lima, El Callao a Francisco Antonio de la Celda, 1695, AGI, Pleitos, Audiencia de Lima, 197, n. 18, but I have been unable to find details about its functions.

71 For examples of edicts on establishing local offices similar to the Defensor de Menores, see AGI, Pleitos, Audiencia de Quito, 211, leg. 12, f. 19, 1586; Confirmación de

oficio a Gonzalo Yáñez Dávila, Santa Fe, 157, n. 19, 1662; Confirmación de oficio de Padre de Menores a Miguel de Ynoriza, Santa Fe, 155, n. 31; and the adoption of the title "Padre general de menores," in Guanabacoa, Havana, Santo Espíritu, and Puerto Príncipe in the early nineteenth centuries. The post of padre de huérfanos was created for Chile in 1567, according to Dougnac Rodríguez, "Estatuto del huérfano," 52. The lack of a comprehensive code for the creation of the office has led modern historians to conclude incorrectly that the office was created sui generis in the nineteenth century. See "defensor de menores," in Mascareñas, *Nueva enciclopedia jurídica*, 4:343.

72 Marginalia in Confirmación del oficio de defensor y curador de menores en Lima, El Callao a Francisco Antonio de la Celda, 1695, AGI, Pleitos, Audiencia de Lima, 197, n. 18, f. 50.

73 See, for example, cases involving Defensor Domingo Gómez de Silva over the inventory and accounts of minors' inheritance, in AGN, Cab., C. Civ., leg. 3, c. 28, 1643; AGN, RA, C. Civ., leg. l. 147, c. 549, 1653.

74 Cédula dirigida a la Audiencia de Santo Domingo, que manda provea como en las haciendas de los menores haya buen recaudo y ninguno de ellos sea agraviado, 1525, in García-Gallo, *Cedulario indiano*, Tomo I, 10, no. 387; Ots de Capdequí, *Derecho de familia*, 72–73.

75 Real Cédula al presidente y oidores de la Audiencia del Perú mandándoles que tomen disposiciones para la buena administración y cuidado de la hacienda y bienes de los menores de edad del territorio de su jurisdicción, AGI, Indiferente General, 427, leg. 30, f. 28, 1543. The same royal order went out to the Audiencia of Hispañola and Los Confines.

76 Real Cédula al presidente y a los oidores de la Audiencia de Méjico mandándoles que se informen sobre los niños y niñas mestizos cuyo padre haya muerto, les designen tutores para que cuiden de sus personas y bienes y les proporcionen trabajo o les recoja en colegios, AGI, Indiferente General, 427, leg. 30, f. 73, 1555.

77 Don Manuel de Careceda Laya, vecino de la ciudad de Piura, que se le nombrase Protector de Naturales y Defensor de menores en la jurisdicción, AGN, Sección Colonial, Campesinado, Derecho indígena, leg. 20, c. 503, 1794.

78 *Recopilación*, 5:8:6. See also cases involving Defensor Domingo Gómez de Silva over the inventory and accounts of minors' inheritance, in AGN, Cab., C. Civ., leg. 3, c. 28, 1643, and AGN, RA, C. Civ., leg. l. 147, c. 549, 1653.

79 Gómez de Silva, *Instrucción General*. On Gómez de Silva's other charitable activities, see van Deusen, *Between the Sacred*, 110.

80 Gómez de Silva, *Instrucción General*, 11–12v. In fact, the Defensor de Menores might represent minors involved in litigation only as a second or third option. See, for example, the contract naming a curador ad litem to Francisco and Antonio del Cerro, AGN, PN, Bartolomé Fernández Salzedo, P. 521, ff. 310–12v, 1674.

81 For the sale of offices, see Burkholder and Chandler, *From Impotence to Authority*, 18–19.

82 AGN, PN, Bartolomé Fernández Salzedo, P. 519, ff. 254–56, 1673.

83 My discussion of Durán's candidacy for the office is derived from Expediente de

Confirmación, AGI, Pleitos, Audiencia de Lima, 197, n. 18, 1695. Note that his maternal surname is also sometimes spelled "Vicentelo."

84 Ibid., ff. 15, 16.

85 Informe que hace a SM Diego Antonio de Parada, arzobispo de Lima, sobre los méritos de don Domingo Larrión, Archivo Histórico de España, Madrid, Diversos-Documentos de Indias, 470, 1776; "Domingo Larrión," in Mendiburu, *Diccionario Histórico-Biográfico*, 4:386.

86 See Autos seguidos por el Defensor de Menores por lo que toca a doña Bernarda de la Parra Larrión contra María de Samudio, AGN, RA, C. Civ., leg. 21, c. 811, 1674, and Autos seguidos del Defensor de Menores por lo que toca a María Márquez contra Bartolomé de la Peña, AGN, RA, C. Civ., leg. 254, c. 952, 1686. The Defensor could also find himself on the defensive in Lima's courts. See Autos seguidos por don José de Villanueva en nombre de don Manuel de Ayesta, contra el Defensor de Menores, don Domingo Larrión, quien, representando a Juan José de Ayesta, hijo natural de don Baltazar, sobre que se le reconozca derecho a los bienes del extincto, AGN, RA, C. Civ., leg. 124, c. 1023, 1755.

87 For examples of cases involving the Defensor, see Expediente de los autos seguidos por Francisco Flores, en nombre de José Melchor Rodríguez, sobre la tutela de Josefa Frade, BNP, Z388, 1752 [*sic.*; 1792]; Autos seguidos por Tiburcia Arrosarena, parda libre, contra D. José Martín de Toledo sobre el procedimiento arbitrario contra su hijo Juan Bautista, esclavo de Fr. Silvestre Durán, AGN, Cab., C. Civ., leg. 22, c. 370, 1811; Autos seguidos por María del Rosario Hidalgo contra Manuel Saénz, sobre que venda sus dos hijos, AGN, Cab., C. Civ., leg. 31, c. 513, 1814; Autos seguidos por doña Paula de Silva sobre que su hija Gregoria Lobatón sea recluida en un convento, AGN, Cab., C. Civ., leg. 16, c. 236, 1809.

88 Autos seguidos por Simón Cayro, albacea de doña Unamunsaga, su muger . . . sobre el cumplimento de sus disposiciones testamentarias, AGN, Cab., C. Civ., leg. 33, c. 567, 1775, esp. ff. 16–16v.

89 Autos seguidos por Teresa Altolaguirre, madre de la menor Petita, esclava, sobre que haga retornar a la Capital a la mencionada y le ortogue boleta de venta en precio de tasación, AGN, Cab., C. Civ., leg. 34, c. 564, 1817.

90 Bermúdez, "La abogacia de pobres."

91 For examples of the variety of cases containing appeals based on *orfandad* and *minoridad*, see Causa seguida contra Luis Rubín por Fernando de Espinoza por el rapto y violación de su hija, Rosa, AGN, RA, C. Crim., leg. 24, c. 272, 1762; Autos seguidos por Juana María Ibáñez, zamba libre, contra doña María Josefa Negreiros, sobre que venda a su hija, AGN, RA, C. Crim., leg. 153, c. 1283, 1765; Autos seguidos por doña Teresa Alzamora y Ursino contra don Joaquín Navárez, sobre que le asigne una pensión alimenticia para el hijo natural habido entre ambos, AGN, RA, C. Civ., leg. 206, c. 1760, 1778; Autos criminales seguidos por don José Venegas, contra el soldado de número Manuel Caballero, por el rapto y estupro en agravio de su menor hija, AGN, RA, C. Crim., leg. 130, c. 1586, 1815.

92 Untitled, AGN, Cab., C. Civ., leg. 7, c. 15, 1784.

93 Autos seguidos por don Francisco Arias de Saavreda, tutor y curador de Grimanesa

de la Puente, contra el Marqués de Corpa, sobre la restitución e integración de su dote, AGN, RA, C. Civ., leg. 324, c. 2959, 1794, f. 33. This litigation between father and daughter was a notorious public affair, and some of Arias's arguments were, in fact, published; see *Discurso legal*.

CHAPTER 2

1 "Ley," in Covarrubias, *Tesorero de la lengua castellana*, 713.

2 Stoler, *Carnal Knowledge*, 10.

3 My argument here is inspired by Hardwick, *Practice of Patriarchy*.

4 Cook, "Introducción," iv–xi.

5 Mannarelli, *Pecados públicos*, 270.

6 Although the census places the total population at 37,259, this number was derived from an erroneous calculation of the totals for each neighborhood. Furthermore, the calculations for neighborhoods were sometimes erroneous as well. A figure of 34,724 was derived by Pérez Cantó and is based on a recalculation of the neighborhood totals provided by the enumerators, making it closer to the real number of individuals in the census but still not exact; see *Lima en el siglo XVIII*, 44.

7 Casas bear a close resemblance to what family historians characterize as households, or assemblages of individuals with or without kinship ties who occupied the same premises and shared relationships of cooperation, whether emotional or economic. See Laslett, "Introduction," 25, 39. Also see Cancian, Wolf Goodman, and Smith, "Introduction," 322.

8 The categories were, in order of appearance, priests; español males between the ages of sixteen and fifty capable of bearing arms; old or infirm español males unable to defend the city; española women; español males under the age of sixteen; española females twelve and younger; Indian men; Indian women; Indian children; free mulato males; free mulata females; free mulato children; free black males; free black females; free black children; mulato male slaves of all ages; mulata female slaves of all ages; black male slaves of all ages; black female slaves of all ages.

9 Frézier, "Bocetas de Lima."

10 See Harth-Terré and Márquez Abanto, *Historia de la casa*, 17; Bromley and Barbagelata, *Evolución de la ciudad*, 55; Durán Montero, *Lima en el siglo XVII*, 164–66.

11 "Quadra en contorno de mi Señora Sta. Ana," in Cook, *Numeración*, 85.

12 For similar findings on plebeian residential patterns and a discussion of race relations in colonial Mexico City, see Cope, *Limits of Racial Domination*, 57–67. Also see Cahill, "Colour by Numbers."

13 Pérez Cantó, *Lima en el siglo XVIII*, 76; cf. van Deusen, *Between the Sacred*, 11.

14 Pérez Cantó, *Lima en el siglo XVIII*, 79. My sample of the census roughly parallels this: 12.95 percent of the total population were classified as free and of African descent, while 21.45 percent were slaves. Put another way, 37.6 percent of individuals of African descent were free, and 62.4 percent were slaves.

15 *Recopilación*, 7:5:15; Bowser, *African Slave*, 149, 155–56.

16 Pérez Cantó, *Lima en el siglo XVIII*, 58. Michael Haitin points out that infant mor-

tality rates in eighteenth-century Lima seem comparable to those that have been calculated for other Spanish American cities; see "Late Colonial Lima," 201. Yet if slave children had been counted in a separate category and could be added to the total of the 1700 census, the city's population growth rate certainly would have been much lower still, since infant mortality generally was highest among slaves; see Bowser, *African Slave*, 95; Hünefeldt, *Paying the Price*, 49–50; Klein, *African Slavery*, 157–61. Note that Haitin concluded that his own attempt to compile infant mortality statistics based on sources such as the 1700 census was "pointless" and that data for mortality in Lima before the 1850s is not reliable; see "Late Colonial Lima," 245–46.

17 On high colonial elite birthrates and how the use of wet nurses might have also increased elite female fecundity, see Socolow, "Marriage, Birth, and Inheritance."

18 Sánchez de Albornoz, *Population of Latin America*, 81.

19 Contemporary descriptions of the earthquake of 1746 and its aftermath of epidemics and homelessness, especially among the city's poor, can be found in Conde de Superunda, *Relación de Gobierno*, 257–64; "Carta, o diario que escribe D. Joseph Eusebio de Llano y Zapata"; "Individual y Verdadera Relación."

20 Ariès, *Centuries of Childhood*, 39–44; Badinter, *Mother Love*. Cf. Pollack, *Forgotten Children*; Wilson, "Myth of Motherhood"; Cunningham, *Children and Childhood*. Also see Nancy Schepper-Hughes, *Death without Weeping*, 276–78.

21 Autos seguidos por Paulina Marchán contra doña María Marchando, sobre los alimentos que ha prestado a sus hijos, AGN, RA, C. Civ., leg. 358, c. 3260, 1797.

22 Autos seguidos por doña Rosa Guerrero, viuda, Albacea y tenedora de bienes, tutora y curadora de sus menores hijos habidos con don Juan Antonio Rivadeneyra, sobre el cumplimiento de su testamento, AGN, C. Civ., leg. 37, c. 664, 1777.

23 Autos seguidos por D. Gerónimo Muñoz Mudarra, padre de la menor María Francisca Mudarra y Cavero, AGN, RA, C. Civ., leg. 137, c. 1108, f. 43.

24 *Gazeta de Lima*, 18 July–8 August 1753. It is possible that this concern reflected a growing enlightened piety that would eventually dominate official Bourbon attitudes toward funerals and burials. See Voekel, *Alone before God*, and Casalino Sens, "Higiene pública."

25 Doña Manuela de Vera contra los bienes y herederos del l[icencia]do Lorenzo de Alarcón, canónigo desta cathedral, AGN, EC, leg. 51, 1670.

26 Ibid.; untitled, AGN, Cab., C. Crim., leg. 10, c. 21, 1797.

27 Autos que criminales sigue Dn. Franco. Venite contra don Tomas Loiaza y Quieroqua por el omicidio que executo en un negro su esclavo. Sr. Juez Dn. Josef. de la Cruz, AGN, Cab., C. Crim., leg. 1, c. 12, 1728.

28 Pérez Cantó, *Lima en el siglo XVIII*, 54.

29 Van Deusen, *Between the Sacred*, 11–12; Díaz, *Female Citizens*, 73; Kuznesof, "Role of the Female-Headed Household"; Arrom, *Women of Mexico City*, 130; Ramos, "Single and Married Women"; Dueñas Vargas, *Hijos del pecado*, 246–57.

30 Both residences are listed in Cook, *Numeración*, 250.

31 Autos seguidos por doña Agustina de Torres solicitando se le ortogue instrumento de donación, AGN, RA, C. Civ., leg. 51, c. 333, 1725.

32 For example, see Autos de don Diego de Esclante, Albaceas de Agustín de las Llanderas, sobre división y partición de bienes, AGN, RA, C. Civ., leg. 35, c. 217, 1718. Also see the case of an African-born woman who was accused of serving as midwife and then kidnapping the child of another slave, doña Lorenza de Salazar y Rojas contra María Josefa de casta Carabali, AAL, Causas de Negros, 1713.

33 Aguilar, *Sermones predicados.*

34 Carbón, *Libro del arte.* Also see Vives, *Instrucción de la mujer cristiana*, 37.

35 Gutiérrez de Godoy, *Tres discursos.*

36 Francisco Díaz de Tapia contra Alonso Martínez sobre que habiéndole vendido una Negra María por preñada en 555 ps. ensayados no lo estaba, BNP, A304, 1583.

37 Autos seguidos por doña Baltasara de Villegas contra los herederos de don Juan Villegas y Godoy, AGN, RA, C. Civ., leg. 267, c. 1006-A, 1690.

38 Average wages for slave women hired out as wet nurses and free women working for their own wages can be found in untitled, AGN, EC, TC, leg. 50, 1660–69; Autos seguidos por doña Isabel Dávil para que se le devuelva su esclava y cria que le tiene retenido en el dho monasterio, AAL, Monasterio de Santa Catalina, leg. 8, no. 84, 1695; Doña María Flores de Linares, tutora y curadora de doña Manuela Iglesias, su nieta, hija de don Franco de Iglesias, en los autos sobre el recogimiento de sus bienes, AGN, RA, C. Civ., leg. 18, c. 738, ff. 7, 19, 1739.

39 For the role of Spanish American wet nurses as accomplices to elite "private pregnancies," see Twinam, *Public Lives*, 161.

40 Autos seguidos por Rosa Fajardo contra doña María de Aarona, sobre la crianza de un esclavo mulatillo, AGN, RA, C. Civ., leg. 40, c. 254, 1721.

41 Twinam, *Public Lives*, 161–63.

42 Charney, "Negotiating Roots," 9–10.

43 Significantly, these works also primarily treat the seventeenth century. See Bowser, "Black Artisan," in *African Slave*; Lowry, "Forging an Indian Nation"; Charney, "Negotiating Roots," 7–10; Charney, "Indio urbano."

44 Bowser, *African Slave*, 143–44.

45 Macera D'Ossorio, "Noticias," 263.

46 See, for example, AGN, PN, Francisco de Acuña, P. 31, ff. 1045v–1047, and Pedro Bastante Cevallos, P. 186, ff. 25–25v, 1646.

47 See AGN, PN, Juan de Angulo y Estrada, P. 112, ff. 634, 679–680, 1672, 1675; AGN, PN, F. C. Arrendondo, P. 59, ff. 489, 543, 559, 583; AGN, PN, Francisco Fernández Pagán, P. 446, f. 181, 1724; AGN, PN, Nicolás García, P. 713, ff. 1196–1196v, 1670.

48 See the asientos de aprendiz in AGN, PN, Nicolás García, P. 1689.

49 The standard language, here taken from AGN, PN, Juan de Beltrán, P. 215, f. 416v–417, 1698, reads, "de no yr ni benir contra ella en manera alguna por Raçon de ser menor de hedad ni otra derecho tasito ni espresso alguno que le competa ni perdira absolucion ni rrelaxcion ni beneficio de rrestitucion y ni entrege."

50 Examples of the protector de indios of the Cercado intervening in apprenticeships contracted during the 1690s can be found in AGN, PN, Marcelo Alvarez de Ron, P. 103, f. 911, and P. 104, ff. 172, 250, 294, 609, 822. Examples from the 1710s are in AGN, PN, F. C. Arrendondo, P. 50, ff. 582, 674, 684, 787.

51 For the correlations between youth and Indian migration to Lima in the seventeenth century, see Lowry, "Forging an Indian Nation," 199.

52 See, for example, AGN, PN, Nicolás García, P. 173, f. 1196–1196v, 1670, and AGN, PN, F. C. Arrendondo, P. 50, f. 509, 1720.

53 AGN, PN, Pedro Joseph de Angulo, P. 47, ff. 110–11, 1779.

54 AGN, PN, Bartolomé Cívico, P. 365, ff. 1587–88, 1646.

55 Van Deusen, *Between the Sacred*, 93.

56 For similar arguments about the lack of social historical information on children in colonial ecclesiastical cases before the late colonial period in Mexico, see Lipsett-Rivera, "Marriage and Family Relations," 138. Also see Boyer, *Lives of the Bigamists*, 109–10.

57 Arrom, *Women of Mexico City*, 211. Also see van Deusen, *Between the Sacred*, chap. 4; Flores Galindo and Chocano, "Cargos del sacramento"; Cicerchia, "*Vida maridable*."

58 Martínez-Alier (Stolcke), *Marriage, Class*; Rípodas Ardanaz, *Matrimonio en Indias*; Gutiérrez, "Honor, Ideology"; Gutiérrez, *When Jesus Came*; Courturier, "Women and the Family"; McCaa, "Gustos de los padres"; Socolow, "Acceptable Partners."

59 Seed, *To Love, Honor, and Obey*.

60 This is not to say that parental dissent never occurred. See, for example, Baltasar de Chamora Ginojossa Presbitero, AAL, Litigios Matrimoniales, leg. 1, suelto, 1607; Da. Estefanía Rodríguez de la Gueva, AAL, NM, leg. 37, 1683. However, I found few such cases in the AAL or in the AGN until the end of the colonial period.

61 Burns, *Colonial Habits*.

62 Bernard Lavallé found that in Lima's 927 surviving divorce cases in the seventeenth century, a mere seven men who could be identified as españoles initiated proceedings, and only one of these was a member of the high elite of Lima's society; see *Amor y opresión*, 29–30. For the preponderantly female profile of those seeking divorce in colonial Latin America, also see Arrom, *Women of Mexico City*; Martín, *Daughters of the Conquistadores*, 141; van Deusen, *Between the Sacred*; Flores Galindo and Choque, "Cargos del sacramento"; Nizza da Silva, "Divorce in Colonial Brazil." In cases where men sued for marital annulment, they frequently mixed other claims—such as mistaken identity, "errors" in knowing the caste of their brides, or accusations against their wives themselves—with the excuse of elder force and referential fear. See, for example, Nulidad de matrimonio de Diego Herrera, AAL, NM, leg. 45, 1698; Nulidad de matrimonio de don Bartolomé del Beltrán, AAL, NM, leg. 42, 1692. In addition, men claimed to have been pressured by relatives of the bride rather than their own relatives. See Nulidad de matrimonio de Antonio González, AAL, NM, leg. 20, 1658.

63 Eighty-six petitions to annul vows of profession survive for the seventeenth century in the records of two of the major male monastic orders of the city, the Dominicans and the Franciscans, whereas I identified only nine cases involving nuns in Lima's archives.

64 Lavallé, *Amor y opresión*, 30.

65 For the evolution of canon law on force, see Sangmeister, *Force and Fear*; Chatam, *Force and Fear as Invalidating*; Brown, *Invalidating Effects*, 13–14. For Spain, note

renowned jurist Francisco Suárez's position on free will in Caput 8, "An ingressus religionis ex perfecta scentia et libertate fieri debeat," in *Opera Omni*. For colonial Spanish America and free will, see Lavrin, "Sexuality in Colonial Mexico," 54–56; Rípodas Ardanaz, *Matrimonio en Indias*, 97–101; Socolow, "Acceptable Partners," 23 n. 5. Cf. Seed, who in *To Love, Honor, and Obey*, 33, argues that Trent's decree on free will was primarily a response to the Reformation and writes that there was "nothing in Catholic tradition that made this position [on free will in marriage choice] inevitable."

66 See Brown, *Invalidating Effects*, 339–66; Sangmeister, *Force and Fear*, 7–9; Chatam, *Force and Fear as Invalidating*, 84.

67 Sangmeister, *Force and Fear*, 41–45, 62.

68 Ibid., 41–45.

69 Reform of Regular Orders, *Canons and Decrees of the Council of Trent*, 25th sess., chap. 16, 227.

70 Sánchez, *Disputaciones*; Rodríguez González, *Nulidad de matrimonio*, 76–80.

71 Nulidad de voto de Josef Torres de Picón, AAL, Convento de Santo Domingo, leg. 6, nos. 7, 9, and 13, 1671.

72 Nulidad de matrimonio de doña María de Arriaga, AAL, NM, leg. 37, f. 7, 1682.

73 Nulidad de matrimonio de doña María Francisca de Báldez, AAL, NM, leg. 37, 1683.

74 Nulidad de voto de Juan de Espinoza, AAL, NM, Convento de Santo Domingo, leg. 6, no. 5, 1672.

75 Nulidad de matrimonio de doña Barbara de Romero, AAL, NM, leg. 37, 1683. Also see Nulidad de matrimonio de doña Viviana de Córdova, AAL, NM, leg. 36, 1680. For other instances of financial collusion in arranged marriages, see Nulidad de matrimonio de Antonia de las Cuetas, AAL, NM, leg. 18, 1653; Nulidad de matrimonio de Inés de Rivera, AAL, NM, leg. 35, 1680; Nulidad de matrimonio de Gerónimo García, AAL, NM, leg. 49, 1713.

76 Nulidad de voto de Nicolás de Espinoza, AAL, NM, Convento de Santo Domingo, leg. 4, nos. 12 and 14, 1664, and leg. 4, no. 17, 1669. Also see Nulidad de voto de Juan de Loyaza, AAL, NM, Convento de Santo Domingo, leg. 4, no. 16, 1669; Nulidad de voto de Luís de Osorio, AAL, NM, Convento de Santo Domingo, leg. 4, nos. 6 and 16, 1662.

77 Nulidad de matrimonio de doña Aldosa Nuñes de Paredes AAL, NM, leg. 20, 1659.

78 Nulidad de matrimonio de doña Juana de Herencia, AAL, NM, legs. 35 and 36, ff. 1 and 19, 1711. Also see Nulidad de matrimonio de doña Melchora de Sambrano, AAL, NM, leg. 36, f. 20, 1681.

79 Nulidad de matrimonio de Josefa de Albarez, AAL, NM, leg. 37, f. 1, 1682.

80 See the case in which a mother's authority is described as "manly" (*varonil*), Nulidad de matrimonio de doña Ysabel de Miranda y Almeida, AAL, NM, leg. 18, 1653.

81 Nulidad de voto de Gerónimo de Solis, AAL, NM, Convento de Santo Domingo, leg. 6, no. 2, f. 8, 1671.

82 Nulidad de voto de Juan de Chavarre, AAL, NM, Convento de Santo Domingo, leg. 6, no. 19, f. 15, 1684.

83 Untitled, AGN, EC, TC, leg. 53, 1680.

84 Nulidad de matrimonio de doña María Teresa de Sáenz, AAL, NM, leg. 37, f. 19, 1682.

85 Seed, *To Love, Honor, and Obey*, 58, 81–83; Bennett, *Africans in Colonial Mexico*, esp. 128, 136, 139.

86 Nulidad de Gertrudis de Jesús negra, AAL, NM, leg. 48, no. 8, 1693.

87 Nulidad de matrimonio de doña Leonor de Arrebulo Ballesteros, AAL, NM, leg. 19, 1653. Also see Nulidad de matrimonio de doña María de Arriaga, AAL, NM, leg. 37, f. 7, 1682.

88 Nulidad de matrimonio de doña Ynés de Rivera, AAL, NM, leg. 35, f. 39, 1680.

89 Nulidad de voto de Francisco de Córdova, AAL, NM, Convento de Santo Domingo, leg. 6, no. 15, 1682.

90 Nulidad de doña María de Arriaga, AAL, NM, leg. 37, f. 9, 1682.

91 A copy of the brief is in Nulidad de voto de Miguel Adame de Sotomayor, AAL, Convento de Santo Domingo, leg. 5, no. 28, 1693. It cites two cases in which mothers inspired fear (*allegesset sibi a matre incussum metum*). Also see the statement issued specifically for the Franciscans contained in Nulidad de votos de Estevan Quiroz, AAL, NM, Convento de San Francisco, leg. 6, no. 24, 1701. For a description of the reform measures taken by Innocent XI to tighten control of the regular orders, see von Pastor, *History of the Popes*, vol. 32.

92 Nulidad de voto de Diego de Torres, AAL, NM, Convento de San Francisco, leg. 6, c. 11, 1698.

93 Lavallé, *Amor y opresión*, 24.

94 Also note the caution with which the prosecution made its case in the annulment case published as "Breve apunte." For the circumstances of successful annulments based on reverential fear after 1750, see Juana Rivaneyra Negra de casta Terranova esclava contra Josef Yonofro, AAL, NM, leg. 55, 1775; Nulidad de Da. Ysabel María de Roxas, AAL, NM, leg. 55, 1773; Nulidad de Da. Gerónima Fernández, AAL, NM, leg. 53, 1747.

95 On the eighteenth-century church "retreat" in marriage cases, see Lavallé, *Amor y opresión*, 24; Seed, *To Love, Honor, and Obey*, 192; Rípodas Ardanaz, *Matrimonio en Indias*, 392.

96 AGN, PN, Francisco de Acuña, P. 26, ff. 43–45v, 1647. Also see AGN, PN, Bartolomé de Cívico, P. 364, ff. 2264–2269v, 1645.

97 One was a grandmother; see AGN, PN, Bartolomé Fernández de Salzedo, P. 513, ff. 51–64, 1670. Another was an aunt; see AGN, PN, Manuel de Echeverez, P. 219, ff. 695–96, 1747. The final, and most unusual, case is discussed later.

98 See, for example, AGN, PN, Pedro de Espino Alvarado, P. 269, ff. 802–5, 1725.

99 *Siete partidas*, 4:16:16, 19; Machado de Chávez y Mendoza, *Perfeto confesor*, 2:660.

100 AGN, PN, Francisco de Acuña, P. 26, ff. 69–71v, 1647.

101 AGN, PN, Bartolomé Fernández de Salzedo, P. 520, ff. 1170–76, 1673.

102 For statistical analysis of civil cases over minors of age during this period, see Chapter 6, n. 6.

103 Mannarelli, *Pecados públicos*, 194.

104 Autos seguidos por don Alonso Ruiz Calderón, tutor y curador de Martín y Luisa

[*sic*] Melgarejo contra los bienes, albacea y herederos de don Juan Martel Melgarejo sobre que se declaren ser hijos naturals, AGN, RA, C. Civ., leg. 212, c. 801, 1673.

105 For a summary study of illegitimacy in Latin American history, see Milanich, "Historical Perspectives on Illegitimacy."

106 Lewin, *Surprise Heirs I*, advances a similar argument about the commonplace acceptance of natural children as successors to inheritance in colonial Brazil.

107 See, for example, Autos seguidos por doña Baltasara de Villegas contra los herederos de don Juan de Villegas y Godoy sobre su filiación y declarada hija natural de éste, AGN, RA, C. Civ., leg. 267, c. 10006-A, 1690.

108 Autos seguidos por don José de Villanueva, en nombre de don Manuel de Ayesta, con el Defensor de Menores, D. Domingo Larrión, quien representando a D. Juan José de Ayesta, hijo natural de D. Baltazar, sobre que se le reconozca derecho a los bienes del extincto, AGN, RA, C. Civ., leg. 124, c. 1023, 1755. Also see Autos seguidos por doña María Francisca de Cosar Bueno, AGN, RA, C. Civ., leg. 239, c. 898, 1682.

109 Mannarelli, *Pecados públicos*, 184–203; Twinam, *Public Lives*, 216–22.

110 Autos seguidos por don Juan Rodrigues de Pelaustán, curador de los hijos de doña Josefa de la Cruz, AGN, Cab., C. Civ., leg. 81, c. 1535, f. 21, 1796 [*sic*; 1696], f. 21.

111 On informal, extralegal inheritance practices among colonial Brazilian peasants, see Metcalf, *Family and Frontier*.

112 Mannarelli, *Pecados públicos*, 181–83, 193–94.

113 Autos seguidos por Juan López solicitado la tutoría de los hijos de su hermana, María Rosa, muerta ab-intestato, AGN, Cab., C. Civ., leg. 1, c. 4, 1700.

114 For cases in which litigants referred to women holding children in custody while men held the title of guardian, see Autos seguidos por Fernando Cuadrado, tutor y curador del menor José de Ribera, hijo natural de don Juan de Ribera contra el Alférez Fernando de Arco, AGN, RA, C. Civ, leg. 165, c. 618, 1659; Autos seguidos por doña Baltazar de Villegas, AGN, RA, C. Civ., leg. 267, c. 1006-A, 1690; Autos seguidos por don Salvador Apello, curador ad litem de los menores hijos de doña Ana Camino Lis de Vergara, contra don Gaspar de Mariacas, tutor de los mismos, AGN, RA, C. Civ., leg. 205, c. 778, 1671; Autos seguidos por el Capitan Don Pedro de Urrutía albacea y tenedor de bienes de don Pedro de Aspiunza, y tutor de sus menores hijos, sobre el recogimiento de sus bienes y división y partición de éstos, AGN, Cab., C. Civ., leg. 11, c. 142, 1692.

115 *Siete partidas*, 6:16:14.

116 Autos seguidos por doña Guillerma Vargas contra Francisco Sánchez, sobre le asigne una pensión alimenticia a su hija, María Josefa, AGN, RA, C. Civ., leg. 63, c. 461, 1729. The only other case of this type I identified during the period was Autos seguidos por doña Ysidora de Ibarra contra don Isidro Jaime de los Ríos sobre la remoción de tutela, AGN, Cab., C. Civ., leg. 12, c. 148, 1693. Far more frequent were cases in which men represented women who clearly were the primary interested adult parties. I found one other case in which a woman litigated to access more of children's inheritance even though a man acted as their official guardian; see Petición de doña María Fernández de Córdova para que se señale cantidades distinctas a sus hijos en razón de su edad, AGN, RA, C. Civ., leg. 203, c. 773, 1670.

117 See, for example, the calculations of crianza deducted from seven-year-old Micaela Sánchez's property, in which her clothing and medical needs amounted to only 40 of 235 pesos spent: Autos seguidos por doña Isidora de Ibarra, AGN, Cab., C. Civ., leg. 12, c. 148, ff. 16–18, 1693. Also see Petición de doña María Fernández de Córdova, AGN, RA, C. Civ., leg. 203, c. 773, 1670; Autos seguidos por don Pedro Llaguno Gomes, curador ad litem de don Pedro Moreda contra don Francisco Martínez de Saavreda, tutor de éste, sobre cantidad de pesos, AGN, Cab., C. Civ., leg. 14, c. 162, 1697.

CHAPTER 3

1 *Siete partidas*, 4:19:1.
2 Martín, *Daughters of the Conquistadores*, 174.
3 Van Deusen, *Between the Sacred*; Martín, *Daughters of the Conquistadores*, 163–70.
4 Carta de la abadesa doña María de Vera dirigida al Arzobispo informándole haber recibido su orden de que no sean porteras del monasterio las recién profesas sino las monjas de más edad, AAL, Monasterio de Santa Clara, leg. 25, no. 75, n.d. [1730s?].
5 Información de la madre priora sobre el ingreso forzoso de varones, AAL, Monasterio del Prado, leg. 6, no. 41A, 1758. Also see Autos criminales seguidos por Lucía de la Santísima Trinidad, abadesa, contra Juan Sánchez, regidor de la ciudad p[o]r haber entrado violentamente y sacado a fuerza a la seglar Beatriz Osorio, AAL, Monasterio de Santa Catalina, leg. 2, no. 17, 1642; El promotor fiscal contra Juan José Prieto para que se le castigue duramente por haber violentado el claustro con el fin de sacar la seglar, doña Lorenza Saniestevan, AAL, Monasterio de Santa Clara, leg. 18, no. 58, 1686.
6 Burns, *Colonial Habits*.
7 Martín, *Daughters of the Conquistadores*, 179.
8 For the development of these distinctions in colonial Cuzco, see Burns, *Colonial Habits*, 32–33.
9 Nulidad de profesión de Fran[cisc]o de Córdova, AAL, Convento de Santo Domingo, leg. 6, no. 15, 1682.
10 Martín, *Daughters of the Conquistadores*, 75–92.
11 Cook, *Numeración*, 357; Martín, *Daughters of the Conquistadores*, 176–78; Reform of Regular Orders, *Canons and Decrees of the Council of Trent*, 25th sess., chap. 15.
12 Martín, *Daughters of the Conquistadores*, 192–200.
13 See, among many examples, AAL, Monasterio de Santa Catalina, leg. 5, no. 44, 1678, and Monasterio de Santa Clara, leg. 11, no. 7, 1663. Also see Burns, *Colonial Habits*, 113–14; Martín, *Daughters of the Conquistadores*, 192–200.
14 Auto de ingreso de Petronila de la Santísima Trinidad y dela Cueva, AAL, Monasterio de Santa Clara, leg. 8, no. 108, 1699; Auto de ingreso de Rafaela Tornero, AAL, Monasterio de Santa Catalina, leg. 9, no. 28, 1703; Auto de ingreso de Tomasa Quino, AGN, EC, TC, Santa Catalina, leg. 28, suelto, 1735.
15 Santa Clara's autos de ingreso for the second half of the seventeenth century can be found in AAL, Monasterio de Santa Clara, legs. 9–14.

16 Martín and Pettus, *Scholars and Schools*; Valcárcel, *Historia de la educación*; Macera D'Ossorio, "Noticias," 215–316; "Historia de la Hermandad, y Hospital de la Caridad," *Mercurio Peruano*, 6 January 1791.

17 *Canons and Decrees of the Council of Trent*, 25th sess., chap. 15.

18 AGN, EC, TC, Santa Catalina, leg. 28, suelto, 1628. Note that donadas entering during this period usually were not asked to express their consent and free will.

19 Autos de oficio del monasterio de Santa Catalina de Sena, AAL, Monasterio de Santa Catalina, leg. 8, no. 87, 1695.

20 Testimonios de algunas religiosas en los autos para averiguar si existe dentro del claustro una ama de leche criando un esclavo recién nacido, AAL, Monasterio de Santa Clara, leg. 21, no. 10, 1695.

21 Ibid.

22 AGN, EC, TC, Santa Catalina, leg. 28, suelto, 1718.

23 AGN, PN, Pedro de Arias, P. 163, no. 1, f. 146, 1669.

24 Mannarelli, *Pecados públicos*, 273–75; Twinam, *Public Lives*, 133–35.

25 AGN, EC, TC, Santa Catalina, leg. 58, suelto, 1736.

26 See the autos de ingreso in AAL, Monasterio de Santa Catalina, leg. 9, nos. 31, 32, 34, and 35, 1703.

27 AGN, EC, TC, Santa Catalina, leg. 28, suelto, 1705.

28 AGN, EC, TC, Santa Catalina, leg. 28, suelto, 1668.

29 AGN, EC, TC, Santa Catalina, leg. 58, suelto, 1708.

30 Cuadernos de autos por Fernando Arias de Ugarte que tratan acerca de las muchas niñas que hay en los conventos, AAL, Papeles Importantes, leg. 24, no. 8, 1680. Originally cited and translated in Martín, *Daughters of the Conquistadores*, 84.

31 Auto arzobispal que prohibe la entrada de niños a los monasterios de clausura, AAL, Papeles Importantes, leg. 24, no. 16, 1678.

32 Ibid.

33 Autos de oficio del monasterio de Santa Catalina de Sena, AAL, Monasterio de Santa Catalina, leg. 8, no. 87, 1695; Testimonio de algunas religiosas, AAL, Monasterio de Santa Clara, leg. 21, no. 10, 1695.

34 See Lavrin, "Ecclesiastical Reform," 184.

35 AAL, Monasterio de Santa Clara, leg. 27, no. 65, 1755.

36 Martín, *Daughters of the Conquistadores*, 83.

37 Autos seguidos por Beatríz Francisco de León en nombre de Juan Rosado, su yerno, solicitando a la madre abadesa del monasterio de Santa Catalina expulse a la novicia Catalina Rosada, su nieta, AAL, Monasterio de Santa Catalina, leg. 2, no. 13, 1642.

38 Autos seguidos por María de Vargas . . . contra la abadesa del monasterio de Santa Catalina, para que se expulse de dicho monasterio y se le entregue a doña Francisca Arias, su entendada, AAL, Monasterio de Santa Catalina, leg. 2, no. 45, 1649. The age of the novice was never discussed in the case, but she had been in the convent for at least ten years.

39 Autos que sigue doña Magdalena de Haro y Sotomayor contra doña Helena de la Cueba, monja del monasterio de Santa Clara, para que le devuelva una sobrina suya

llamada Petronila, que le dió para que le sirviera en la clausura, por el maltrato de que es objeto, AAL, Monasterio de Santa Clara, leg. 14, no. 14, 1672.

40 On Peruvian patterns of conditional liberty, see Bowser, *African Slave*, 275–78. On religion and emancipation, see Lane, "Captivity and Redemption," 228.

41 Autos seguidos por Ana de la O contra doña Beatríz de Velasco, monja, para que no moleste más su hija, María Velazco, cuarterona, tratándole como esclava, AAL, Monasterio de Santa Clara, leg. 8, no. 64, 1686.

42 Autos seguidos por Feliciana de Salinas, contra doña María de Salinas, monja del monasterio de Santa Clara, para que se le reconozca como persona libre, AAL, Monasterio de Santa Clara, leg. 11, no. 71, 1663.

43 Martín, *Daughters of the Conquistadores*, 171. For redefinitions of family and gender in convents, see Burns, *Colonial Habits*, 114.

44 Trexler, "From the Mouths," 549.

45 Kobayashi, *Educación como conquista*. Also see Clendinnen, "Disciplining the Indians"; Gutiérrez, *When Jesus Came*.

46 Van Deusen, *Between the Sacred*; Burns, *Colonial Habits*.

47 Real Cédula al presidente y a los oidores de la Audiencia de México mandándoles que se informen sobre los niños y niñas mestizos, AGI, Indiferente General, 42, leg. 30, f. 28, 1555.

48 See the compilation of the three laws on this subject in *Recopilación*, 6:3:4.

49 Real Cédula al Presidente y oidores de la Audiencia de Quito para que impidan que los niños indios sean quitados de sus familias y empleados en servicios con la excusa de educarlos mejor, AGI, Pleitos, Audiencia de Quito, 211, leg. 1, f. 217. On *policía*, see Martínez, "Space, Order," 20–21.

50 Spalding, *Huarochirí*, 246–48; Stern; *Peru's Indian Peoples*, 51–76; MacCormack, *Religion in the Andes*, 383–484; Mills, *Idolatry and Its Enemies*.

51 Documentos sobre la Fundación del Colegio de Príncipe, AGN, Temporalidades, Colegios, leg. 171, no. 1, f. 22, 1618; Cárdenas Ayaipoma, "Colegio de Caciques," 6–7.

52 Documentos sobre la Fundación del Colegio de Príncipe, AGN, Temporalidades, Colegios, leg. 171, no. 1, ff. 1–2, 1618.

53 For the church-state struggle over the settlement of Lima's Indians in the Cercado in 1590, see Lowry, "Forging an Indian Nation," 44–50.

54 Constituciones del colegio de los caciques q[u]e p[o]r órden de S[u] Mag[esta]d ha fundado en el cercado de Santiago desta ciudad [1620], AGN, Temporalidades, Colegios, leg. 171, no. 3.

55 Quoted in Valcárcel, *Historia de la educación colonial*, 95.

56 For a discussion of the financing of the colegios in both Lima and Cuzco, see Valcárcel, *Historia de la educación colonial*, 93–95; Cárdenas Ayaipoma, "Colegio de Caciques," 11.

57 Item 10, Constituciones del colegio de los caciques q[u]e p[o]r órden de S[u] Mag[esta]d ha fundado en el cercado de Santiago desta ciudad [1620], AGN, Temporalidades, Colegios, leg. 171, no. 3.

58 Item 12, ibid.

59 See Galdo Gutiérrez, *Educación de los curacas*, 55.

60 Cárdenas Ayaipoma, "Colegio de Caciques," 10.

61 Ibid., 16.

62 Some of the colegio's landholdings are listed in Memoria del estado en que esta el colegio del cercado y su hacienda Vilcahuara, el año 1679, BNP, 322, 1699. Also see AGN, Temporalidades, Colegios, Leg. 155.

63 Satisfacción de la real renta . . . para la manutención y enseñanza de hijos de caciques en el Cercado, BNP, C11667, 1762.

64 Información hecha por el Licenciado Boan, Oidor de la Audiencia de los Reyes, acerca de la petición del Hermano Luis Pecador solicitando licencia para fundar la casa de niños expósitos, ABPL, H-A, tomo 1, no. 1, 1602–3.

65 Ibid.; Breve Apostólico expedido por la Santidad Paulo V en 21 de marzo de 1605, a favor de la Casa y Hóspital de los Niños Expósitos de N[ue]s[t]ra Señora de Atocha, ABLP, H-A, tomo 1, no. 2, 1605; Hesperiofilo [José Rossi y Rubi], "Noticia Histórica de la Real Casa de Niños Expósitos," Mercurio Peruano, 21 August 1791.

66 Boswell, *Kindness of Strangers*, 25. For a critical appraisal of Boswell's contention that abandonment was a benevolent practice that did not expose children to risk, see Tilly et al., "Child Abandonment."

67 Boswell, *Kindness of Strangers*, 25.

68 *Siete partidas*, 4:4.

69 Machado de Chávez y Mendoza, *Perfeto confesor*, 2:621.

70 Perry, *Gender and Disorder*, 162.

71 Brochero, *Discurso breve*.

72 Ibid., 49–51.

73 The description appears in Martín, *Daughters of the Conquistadores*, 92; Fildes, *Wet Nursing*, 127; Mendieta Ocampo, *Hospitales de Lima*, 82–83; Mannarelli, *Pecados públicos*, 279–80.

74 Brochero, *Discurso breve*, 30–35.

75 González, "Down and Out," 102; Moreno, "Casa de Niños," 23.

76 The classic arguments about "abusive" parents prior to the modern era can be found in Ariès, *Centuries of Childhood*; Badinter, *Mother Love*; Stone, *Family, Sex, and Marriage*; De Mause, *History of Childhood*, 1–74. Also see Clément, "Enfants exposés." Cf. Wilson, "Myth of Motherhood"; Fuchs, *Abandoned Children*, 62–116.

77 Breve apostólico, ABLP, H-A, tomo 1, no. 2, 1605.

78 Curas beneficiarios contra el procurador de la hermandad de los Niños Huérfanos sobre la poseción que tienen los referidos de administrar sacramentos, AAL, Hospitales, leg. 2, no. 11, 1627.

79 Mendieta Ocampo, *Hospitales de Lima*, 84–86.

80 Extracto de varios documentos oficiales despachados a favor de la Real Casa de Niños Expósitos, ABPL, H-A, tomo 1, no. 4, 1672–1718.

81 Expediente seguido por don Antonio de Llano, Mayordomo de la Real Casa de Niños Expósitos, solicitando amparo y protección para la d[ic]ha casa, Superior Gobierno, ABPL, H-A, tomo 1, no. 7, 1712.

82 Ibid., f. 18. Also note that, in 1755, the crown reached deeper into the royal coffers to support the casa, increasing the annual contribution by 4,000 pesos, which was drawn

from the income from purchases of ecclesiastical posts. See Real Cédula expedida en Buen Retiro a 2 de marzo de 1755 para que el Arzobispo de Lima informe sobre el estado de la Real Casa de Niños Expósitos, APBL, H-A, tomo 1, no. 19.

83 Twinam, *Public Lives*, 133–39. For the correlation between "whiteness" and abandonment in other areas of colonial Latin America, see Salinas Meza, "Orphans and Family Disintegration," 318; Nazarri, "Urgent Need to Conceal," 111.

84 Mannarelli, *Pecados públicos*, 271. Data for Mexico and Colombia are comparable. See Avila Espinosa, "Niños abandonados," 272; Cramaussel, "Ilégitimos y abandonados," 428; Dueñas Vargas, *Hijos del pecado*, 196.

85 Malvido, "Abandono de los hijos." Also see the comments on poverty and exposure in Sherwood, *Poverty in Eighteenth-Century Spain*, 99.

86 The number of children being nursed and cared for in the homes of amas de leche always seemed to be greater than the number in the casa itself. See Información hecha por el Licenciado Boan, ABPL, H-A, tomo 1, no. 1, 1602–3.

87 *Constituciones del Colegio de Niñas Expósitas de Santa Cruz de Atocha*, BNP, B237, 659; Martín, *Daughters of the Conquistadores*, 94.

88 Petición de María de la Merced, AGN, SCA, leg. 2, no. 37, 1784; Petición de Paula de Atocha, AGN, SCA, leg. 2, no. 38, 1783; Petición de María Dolores de Atocha y Coronel, AGN, SCA, leg. 2, no. 60, 1772.

89 Petición de Sebastiana de Atocha y Soría, AGN, SCA, leg. 2, no. 50, 1776; Petición de María de Asención, AGN, SCA, leg. 2, no. 35, 1766. Also see Mannarelli, *Pecados públicos*, 289.

90 Petición de María Liberata, AGN, SCA, leg. 2, no. 26, 1753.

91 Petición de Paula de Atocha Ynclán, AGN, SCA, leg. 2, no. 45, 1781.

92 Unfortunately, no rates of mortality are available for the expósitos of Lima. In Spanish America, the mortality rates at foundling homes figured between 40 and 70 percent. See Dueñas Vargas, *Hijos del pecado*, 199; González, "Down and Out," 103; Salinas Meza, "Orphans and Family Disintegration," 323–25. Clément places the death rate in similar institutions in Europe around 46.5 percent by the age of ten; see "Les enfants exposés," 2. For European rates, also see Fildes, *Wet Nursing*, 160–61; Andrés-Gallego, *Historia general*, 17–18.

93 For one of the thirteen cases I identified in which the death of a wet nurse started a chain of child circulation, see Petición de Rufina de Atocha y Pacheco, AGN, SCA, leg. 2, no. 55, 1767. The others are in AGN, SCA, leg. 2, nos. 15, 16, 37, 48, 53, 55, 57, 64, 65, 71, and 72.

94 Petición de Vicenta de las Mercedes Atocha, AGN, SCA, leg. 2, no. 15, 1750; Petición de María del Carmen," AGN, SCA, leg. 2, no. 31, 1761; Petición de María Josefa de Atocha y Granados, AGN, SCA, leg. 2, no. 57, 1774; Petición de Tomasa de Atocha y Pérez Buelta, AGN, SCA, leg. 2, no. 69, 1765; Petición de María Juana de Atocha, AGN, SCA, leg. 2, no. 67, 1765.

95 Twinam, *Public Lives*, 133–39; Twinam, "Honor, Sexuality, and Illegitimacy," 131.

96 Petición de María Antonia de Atocha, AGN, SCA, leg. 2, no. 61, 1772.

97 Petición de María de la Asención, AGN, SCA, leg. 2, no. 46, 1781.

98 Ibid. Also see Petición de Josefa Petronila, AGN, SCA, leg. 2, no. 33, 1767; Petición de Thomasa de Atocha y Salazar, AGN, SCA, leg. 2, no. 64, 1770; Petición de Petronila de Atocha, AGN, SCA, leg. 3, no. 7, 1787; Doña Manuela de Vera contra los bienes y herederos del l[icencia]do Lorenzo de Alarcón, canónigo desta cathe-dral, AGN, EC, Tribunal eclesiástico, leg. 51, 1670; Autos que criminales sigue Dn. Franco. Venite contra don Tomas Loiaza y Quieroqua por el omicidio que executo en un negro su esclavo. Sr. Juez Dn. Josef de la Cruz, AGN, Cab., C. Crim., leg. 1, c. 12, 1728; untitled AGN, Cab., C. Crim., leg. 10, c. 21, 1797.

99 See, for example, Petición de Josefa Petronila, AGN, SCA, leg. 2, no. 33, 1767; Petición de Thomasa de Atocha y Salazar, AGN, SCA, leg. 2, no. 64, 1770; Petición de Petronila de Atocha, AGN, SCA, leg. 3, no. 7, 1787. Amas de leche normally reported that the umbilical cords fell off three to four days after birth.

100 While Spanish law forbade the legal adoption of children under the age of seven, it recognized a similar process that subsumed the transference of parental authority into guardianship. See *Siete partidas*, 4:16:4; Machado de Chávez y Mendoza, *Perfeto confesor*, 1:620–25.

101 Petición de María Josefa del Sacramento, AGN, SCA, leg. 2, no. 68, 1769.

102 Petición de María Liberata, AGN, SCA, leg. 2, no. 27, 1753; Petición de María Ambrosia de Atocha, AGN, SCA, leg. 2, no. 52, 1774.

103 See, for example, Petición de María Pasquala de Atocha, AGN, SCA, leg. 2, no. 29, 1758. Also see Mannarelli, *Pecados públicos*, 286.

104 Petición de Paula de Atocha y Molina, AGN, SCA, leg. 2, no. 59, 1773.

105 Petición de Severina de Atocha y Echenique, AGN, SCA, leg. 2, no. 47, 1781.

106 Petición de María del Carmen, AGN, SCA, leg. 2, no. 40, 1777.

CHAPTER 4

1 For this view, see Röggenbuck, "Historia social."

2 Flores Galindo, *Ciudad sumergida*, 138.

3 Autos criminales de oficio de la R[ea]l J[ustici]a que se sigue contra Joséf Tunco y otros sobre hurto de doblones, AGN, Cab., C. Crim., leg. 7, c. 4, 1782. "Sala de Crimen" often referred to high court judges who heard criminal cases. In Lima, the "sala" also referred to a room where interrogations were conducted and scribes took statements. See MacLachlan, *Criminal Justice*, 21–22; Cutter, *Legal Culture*, 109; Scardaville, "(Hapsburg) Law."

4 A note on sources and chronology is in order. The AGN houses 1,104 criminal cases heard by the Audiencia in the eighteenth century and a staggering 1,784 cases for the first twenty years of the 1800s. While these cases are cataloged by description, it is often impossible to determine the regional origin of cases or ages of individuals by description alone, since the Audiencia served as a court of appeals as well as a first-instance court for some of Lima's cases, and because the descriptions do not always (or even normally) indicate whether minors of age were involved in cases. The Cabildo series, on the other hand, while not cataloged, contains a more manageable

run of criminal cases, spanning the years 1714 to 1813. I opted to analyze all of the 334 cases in the Cabildo series and to sample cases from the Real Audiencia, focusing the better part of my analysis on the 54 cases I identified that involved minors.

5 Machado de Chávez y Mendoza here uses *los padres*, a term that in Spanish means both "parents" and "fathers"; see *Perfeto confesor*, 2:621. The use of the term *padres* presents a continual problem of translation, since it is unclear at times whether authors refer to both parents or to fathers. Normally, if the plural is used (as opposed to *el padre*), I translate it as "parents." I translate the word as "fathers" here because of the context in which Machado de Chávez uses it.

6 Machado de Chávez y Mendoza, *Perfeto confesor*, 2:621. The archbishop argued the same of husbands' punishment of wives (ibid., 610).

7 *Siete partidas*, 2:10:2, 3.

8 Ibid., 7:31:8. Note that judgment by *albedrio* was a medieval practice that allowed magistrates to render decisions not based on law but on their own determination of "what was right and proper"; see Kagan, *Lawsuits and Litigants*, 22.

9 "Quia no haver [*sic*] animu, intellecu, nec iudiciu rrationis, ut possi ille dolus, vel culpa imputari" (Machado de Chávez y Mendoza, *Perfeto confesor*, 1:808).

10 "Menor," in Escriche y Martín, *Diccionario razonado*, 586.

11 *Siete partidas*, 7:31:8.

12 Ibid., 7:31.

13 For example, royal mandates repeated the order that the imprisonment of an individual should be in accordance with his or her "quality." See the three royal edicts on this point in the *Recopilación*, 7:6.

14 This, of course, does not mean that youths actually committed more crimes during the period. See the essays in Cox and Shore, *Becoming Delinquent*; King, "Rise of Juvenile Delinquency"; Cunningham, *Children and Childhood*, 149. For considerations of criminality in nineteenth-century Lima, see Aguirre, "Lima Penitentiary."

15 Witnesses in criminal cases were supposed to be twenty years old; in civil cases, at least fourteen years old, although the testimony of the latter was to be considered "presumption." Nonetheless, even younger witnesses were routinely used in criminal trials as long as they could answer basic questions about Christian doctrine. See Autos Criminales que de oficio de la R[ea]l Justicia se siguen contra Miguel Roxas y Ore Nicolas Romera y Damiana Vicara, sobre barios hurtos, AGN, Cab., C. Crim., leg. 7, c. 7, 1783; Causa seguida por Bernarda Calero contra José Bernabe por injuria sexual contra su hijo José Mariano de dos años de edad, AGN, RA, C. Crim., leg. 54, c. 631, 1784. In addition, victims as young as five and six years old were called upon to give testimony. See Causa seguida por María Evarista de Liñán contra José Antonio de los Ríos y un esclavo suyo nombrado Pedro de los Ríos por el estupro cometido en perjuicio de su hija, María Josepha de ocho años, AGN, RA, C. Crim., leg. 18, c. 209, 1756; Autos criminales seguidos de oficio p[o]r la R[ea]l Just[ici]a contra Bartolomé Aliento [*sic*] p[o]r haver estrupado a una menor de seis años, AGN, RA, C. Crim., leg. 116, c. 1405, 1809.

16 Cutter cites an instance where Spanish officials were instructed to solve "petty" conflicts between parties extrajudicially; see *Legal Culture*, 9.

17 *Recopilación*, 7:6:2. The first decree was in 1595, D. Felipe II en la Instrucción de Virreyes de 1595. Similar decrees were issued against españoles, mestizos, and orphans in 1558 and 1609.

18 *Recopilación*, 7:6:4; Sobre el Hóspital de los Pobres en el antiguo Colegio del Cercado, AGN, Sección Colonial, Campesinado, Derecho indígena, Fáctica del Corregidor o Subdelegato de Indios del Cercado, leg. 1, suelto, 1769; van Deusen, *Between the Sacred*.

19 Cope, *Limits of Racial Domination*, 103–4; Scardaville, "(Hapsburg) Law." Also see Lowry, "Forging an Indian Nation," 163–65.

20 Division de Quarteles y Barrios e Instrucción para el establecimiento de Alcaldes de Barrio en la Capital de Lima, BNP, X362 L73, 1785. For Bourbon policies to round up the destitute in Mexico City, see Arrom, *Containing the Poor*.

21 AGN, PN, Lucas de Bonilla, P. 145, ff. 274–75, 1796.

22 For the creative use of institutions as reformatories in Spain, see Tikoff, "Before the Reformatory."

23 Autos criminales que sigue: don Martin Luna Victoria contra Marselo Matunano, s[ob]re un robo q[u]e este le hizo de 1060 p[eso]s en dinero, AGN, Cab., C. Crim., leg. 5, c. 18, 1774; also see Autos . . . contra Joséf Tunco, AGN, Cab., C. Crim., leg. 7, c. 4, 1782.

24 The accusations against an elite español student also reveal how parents of "incorrigible" español youths continued to use monasteries as reformatories. See Autos criminales que sigue Dn. Eustaquio Núñez contra José Maria Tapia por hurto de cantidad de pesos, AGN, Cab., C. Crim., leg. 11, c. 17, 1806.

25 Juan y Colom, *Instrucción de Escribanos*, 207–11.

26 The *agente fiscal* also might attempt to overcalculate the ages of very young suspects to guarantee that they would stand trial, as the case of Josef Tunco demonstrates. See Autos . . . contra Joséf Tunco, AGN, Cab., C. Crim., leg. 7, c. 4, 1782, and compare f. 1 with f. 11v. Also see Autos criminales que de ofisio de la Real Justicia se siguen contra Simona Laredo Negra Esclava de Da. Franca. Laredo por la heridad que dio a Joséf. Zeballos Moreno libre, AGN, Cab., C. Crim., leg. 5, c. 9. 1773.

27 Examples abound. A few, listed here without titles for the sake of space, can be found in AGN, Cab., C. Crim., leg. 1, c. 5, 1717; leg. 4, c. 14, 1768; leg. 4, c. 11, 1784; leg. 13, c. 10, 1813; and several of the accusations in leg. 13, c. 17, 1813. One of the suspects in AGN, Cab., C. Crim., leg. 7, C.4, 1782, who was assigned the age of "twenty-four to twenty-five years old," did not receive a court-appointed attorney.

28 Quaderno segundo: Autos que de oficio se siguen contra Patricio Dillon de nación Irlandes, Manuel Perfecto de Salaza y consortes sobre Varios hurtos que han cometido, AGN, Cab., C. Crim., leg. 5, c. 1, f. 43v., 1772. Lawyers representing minors could be complicit in lowering the ages of their clients. See Autos . . . contra Simona Laredo, AGN, Cab., C. Crim., leg. 5, c. 9, 1773. For a case outside Lima of an Indian who admitted to robbing and killing a five-year-old boy, and the ensuing dispute over the age of the prisoner, see Autos seguidos contra Gregorio Choque, indio del Pueblo de San Pablo Cacha por el homicidio del niño Angel Borda, AGN, RA, C. Crim., leg. 4, c. 269, 1762.

29 Autos que criminales sigue Dn. Franc[isc]o. Venite contra Dn. Tomas Loiaza

y Quieroqua por el omicidio que executo en un negro su esclavo, AGN, Cab., C. Crim., leg. 1, c. 12, 1728. Also see Causa seguida por D. Manuel Fernández contra Francisco Morel, por el rapto y estupro de su hija Joséfa, AGN, RA, C. Crim., leg. 84, c. 1032, 1797.

30 Autos criminales que de oficio se siguen contra Joséph Medizabal, Joséph Arostegui, y consortes sobre varios hurtos que ha [*sic*] cometido, AGN, Cab., C. Crim., leg. 5, c. 11, 1773.

31 The majority of rape cases identified brought before secular courts were heard before the Real Audiencia in the first instance. The Real Audiencia held first-instance jurisdiction over such cases, according to *Siete partidas*, 3:3:5.

32 Castañeda, *Violación*, 47; Lipsett-Rivera, "Intersection of Rape and Marriage," 570. Under Spanish law, special punishment had, in fact, always been reserved for those who raped virgins. See *Fuero juzgo*, 3:3:1. However, no law specifically stated that the age of the victim would be a consideration, only her prior sexual experience.

33 *Siete partidas*, 7:19, cf. 7:20. Canonists and legal scholars such as Gracian and Tomás Sánchez debated the meaning of *estupro* and the degree to which seduction should mitigate the culpability of the rapist. Such debates took on greater importance in the sixteenth century following the Tridentine emphasis on free will in marriage choice. See Machado de Chávez y Mendoza's commentary in *Perfeto confesor*, 1:409–11. Also see Arrom, *Women of Mexico City*, 63.

34 See Castañeda, *Violación*; Lipsett-Rivera, "Intersection of Rape and Marriage"; Seed, *To Love, Honor, and Obey*; Lavrin, "Sexuality in Colonial Mexico," 70–71; Lavrin, "*Lo femenino*," 160–61.

35 Autos . . . contra Bartolomé Aliento, AGN, RA, C. Crim, leg. 116, c. 1405, 1809.

36 Causa seguida por María Evarista de Liñán contra José Antonio de los Ríos y un esclavo suyo nombrado Pedro de los Ríos por el estupro cometido en perjuicio de su hija, AGN, RA, C. Crim., leg. 18, c. 209, 1756. De los Ríos called in a surgeon of his own to examine his eleven year-old son and to testify that the boy had earlier suffered from the malady *tiphovoses* (perhaps typhus), which had affected his reproductive organs and left him incapable of sexual intercourse.

37 Autos seguidos por Evarista Liñán, AGN, RA, C. Crim., leg. 18, c. 209, 1756, cf. ff. 59 and 72.

38 See, for example, untitled, AGN, Cab., C. Crim., leg. 10, c. 21, f. 42, 1797. Note in this case that a sixteen-year-old slave criminal was referred to by his lawyer as fifteen years old but was determined to be eighteen years of age by an *asesor* hired to establish the youth's selling price.

39 Causa seguida contral Justo Manrique, mulato libre por la violación de una menor de cinco años, AGN, RA, C. Crim., leg. 28, c. 344 and 345, 1768.

40 Autos contra Bartolomé Aliento, AGN, C. Crim., leg. 116, c. 1405, f. 54v, 1809.

41 Here it should be underscored that the following figures are based on cases where both sex and race were registered. There were other cases where women who can be presumed to be white were accused of crimes, and many of these women were charged with sevicia, or the "excessive" punishment of slaves, which was often treated as a civil offense and usually did not result in imprisonment.

42 Autos criminales que sigue Pedro Seballos contra Franc. Pina y su Muger, AGN, Cab., C. Crim., leg. 5, c. 14, 1773.

43 Autos criminales de oficio de la Rl Justicia se siguen contra Diego Cruces por Regaton antiguo, AGN, Cab., C. Crim., leg. 9, c. 18, 1792.

44 Only one criminal case from the AGN Fáctica del Corregidor o Subdelegato de Indios del Cercado involved a minor. The series, in fact, contains a surprisingly low number of criminal cases in general.

45 AGN, Sección Colonial, Campesinado, Derecho indígena, Fáctica del Corregidor o Subdelegato de Indios del Cercado, leg. 1, c. 16, f. 29, 1800.

46 Certainly, illegitimacy did not always mean paternal abandonment, referring as it did to all manner of consensual unions not sanctioned by the Catholic Church and to the offspring of such unions. A number of Lima's youths were probably children of long-term consensual unions. However, Mannarelli shows that there was, in fact, a correlation between illegitimate status and fatherlessness, with far more children born of "unknown fathers" than "unknown mothers" or "unknown parents"; see *Pecados públicos*, 172.

47 Autos criminales que se sigue por don Antonio Lopes con Asencia Samudio sobre el robo de unas onzas de oro hecho por José Lopes, AGN, Cab., C. Crim., leg. 9, c. 2, f. 106, 1789.

48 Carmen Castañeda found similar patterns of weak patriarchal families among girls who were raped in the Audiencia of Guadalajara, Mexico; see "Memoria y las niñas violadas," 110. Also see Díaz, *Female Citizens*, 61–62.

49 Causa seguida por Hipólita Pérez contra Tomás Calderón y su cómplice en el estupro de una niña de once años llamada Tomasa, AGN, RA, C. Crim., leg. 37, c. 441, 1777.

50 Causa seguida por María Evarista de Liñán, AGN, RA, C. Crim., leg. 18, c. 209, f. 41v., 1756.

51 See, for example, Causa seguida por María del Carmen Ibáñez contra José Loarte por el rapto y estupro de su hija María Concepción, AGN, RA, C. Crim., leg. 42, c. 495, 1779; Causa seguida contra D. Luis de Landavere por el rapto y estupro de Da. Manuela Quiroz, AGN, RA, C. Crim., leg. 84, c. 1034, 1797; Causa seguida por D. Manuel Fernández contra Francisco Morel, por el rapto y estupro de su hija Joséfa, AGN, RA, C. Crim., leg. 84, c. 1302, 1797; Causa seguida contra José Rivera por rapto y estupro de Juana Solano AGN, RA, C. Crim., leg. 84, c. 1051, 1797; Causa seguida por José Mariano Toro contra Fernando Duran por rapto y violación de dos hijas menores del demandante, AGN, RA, C. Crim., leg. 102, c. 1244, 1804.

52 Causa seguida pr Francisco de los Ríos contra Isidrio Pérez por el estupro cometido contra María Joséfa, su hija, con la promesa de casarse con ella, AGN, RA, C. Crim., leg. 19, c. 217, 1757; Causa seguida por Melchor Navajas contra José Alvarado Perales por violación de su hija Margarita, AGN, RA, C. Crim., leg. 34, c. 410, 1775; Causa seguida por José Rivera, AGN, RA, C. Crim., leg. 80, c. 1051, 1797; Causa seguida por José Mariano Toro contra Fernando Duran, AGN, RA, C. Crim., leg. 102, c. 1244, 1804.

53 Causa seguida por Melchor Navajas, AGN, RA, C. Crim., leg. 34, c. 410, 1775.

54 Causa seguida por Da. Ana Rivera contra Sebastián Espindola por el estupro come-

tido en perjuicio de María Dolores, pupila de la demandante, AGN, RA, C. Crim., leg. 34, c. 410, f. 3, 1775.

55 Causa seguida contra Luís Rubin por Fernando de Espinoza por el rapto y violación de su hija Rosa, AGN, RA, C. Crim., leg. 24, c. 272, 1762. See also Causa seguida por D. Manuel de la Torre y Castaño contra Francisco de las Llagas, pardo libre por el rapto de su hija doncella, AGN, RA, C. Crim., leg. 15, c. 161, 1752.

56 Socolow, "Women and Crime," 46.

57 See Lavrin, "Sexuality in Colonial Mexico," 64.

58 In the Cabildo series, there are a total of 242 legajos, or dossiers, 74 of which included prosecutions involving minors of age. Several individuals arrested for the same crime would appear in the same criminal dossier. The charts in Fig. 4.2 are based on the total number of cases, rather than individuals, prosecuted before the Cabildo.

59 Several recent works deepened our understanding of the multiple types of honor that were articulated among various classes and castes in colonial Latin America. See Stern, *Secret History*; the essays in Johnson and Lipsett-Rivera, *Faces of Honor*; Chambers, *From Subjects to Citizens*; Twinam, *Public Lives*.

60 Causa seguida por doña Alfonsa del Campo, AGN, RA, C. Crim., leg. 9, c. 75, 1742.

61 See, for example, Tutino, "Power, Class, and Family." Also see Stern, *Secret History*, 21, 198.

62 Autos criminales que sigue Dn. Antonio Subiaga contra Francisco Risco sobre ynjurias, AGN, Cab., C. Crim., leg. 8, c. 5, 1785.

63 Chambers, *From Subjects to Citizens*, 162–80; Johnson and Lipsett-Rivera, introduction to *Faces of Honor*.

64 Joséph Alcoser contra Luis de Ciudad, aprendiz, por hurto, AGN, Cab., C. Crim., leg. 6, c. 6, 1775.

65 Autos criminales que de oficio de la Rl. Justicia se sigue contra Mariano Oyague Negro esclavo de Da. Jacoba Oyague pr. hacerse entrado de la casa de Nodriza, AGN, Cab., C. Crim., leg. 6, c. 25, 1775.

66 Autos . . . contra Simona Laredo, AGN, Cab., C. Crim., leg. 5, c. 9. 1773.

67 See Johnson, "Dangerous Words"; Lavrin, "*Lo femenino*," 162. Sonya Lipsett-Rivera argues that elite women in Mexico resorted to violence to uphold honor, but her examples are mostly of nonwhite women engaging in physical attacks; see "Slap in the Face," 185–87. In my investigations of the Cabildo records of Lima, I have not encountered elite white women in court over physical attacks, although there are a healthy number of white female plebeians involved in such cases. Elite women would engage in altercations by exchanging verbal insults, however. For examples, see AGN, Cab., C. Crim., leg. 10, c. 16, 1796, and leg. 5, c. 4, 1809.

68 Autos . . . contra Simona Laredo, AGN, Cab., C. Crim., leg. 5, c. 9, f. 20v, 1773.

69 Autos criminales que de oficio de la Real Justa. Se sigue contra Franco. Cardenas que el la causa agregada dijo nombrar Joséph Manuel Mora, AGN, Cab., C. Crim., leg. 10, c. 9, f. 21, 1798.

70 Lanuzo y Sotelo, *Viaje ilustrada*.

71 "Plan demostrativo de la población comprendida en el recinto de la ciudad," *Mercurio Peruano*, 3 February 1791; Cook, *Numeración*; Pérez Cantó, *Lima en el siglo XVIII*, 52.

72 For elite concerns with the blurring of color distinctions and Bourbon attempts at racial classification by nomenclature as a means of social control, see Mörner, *Race Mixture*; Mörner, *Estado, razas, y cambio social*; Sánchez de Albornoz, *Population of Latin America*, 130; Flores Galindo, *Ciudad sumergida*. For discussions of the late colonial tightening on family relations as related to perceived racial disorder, see Stern, *Secret History*, 23, 25, 86; Twinam, *Public Lives*, 18–20; Chambers, *From Subjects to Citizens*, chap. 5.

73 Domínguez Ortiz, *Carlos III*, 106–7; Reyes Leoz, "Padre."

74 Flores Galindo, *Ciudad sumergida*, 122. Documents concerning the police force and the serenazgo are found in AGN, RA, Cabildo, 1779–1818. The title of the police official can be found in Autos criminales . . . que sigue contra Franco. Cardenas, AGN, Cab., C. Crim., leg. 10, c. 19, 1798. Connections between youth and vagrancy are clear in an addendum to the *Recopilación* in Sylvestre, *Librería de jueces*, esp. libro 8, nota 3.

75 Flores Galindo, *Ciudad sumergida*, 128.

76 Autos . . . contra Patricio Dillon, AGN, Cab., C. Crim., leg. 5, c. 1, f. 103v, 1772.

77 Autos criminales que de oficio de la Real Justa. Se sigue contra Franco. Cardenas que el la causa agregada dijo nombrar Joséph Manuel Mora, AGN, Cab., C. Crim., leg. 10, c. 9, f. 21, 1798. Chambers provides evidence of similar arguments and several sentences aimed at reforming youths and adults in early republican Arequipa; see *From Subjects to Citizens*, 195–96. This may suggest an increasing tendency for the court to accept its role as rehabilitator after independence.

78 "Carta al Editor," *Diario*, 15 November 1790.

79 Anónimo, "Historia Moral Extraida de Algunos Papeles Extranjeros, Para escarmiento de los jóvenes demasiado acesibles al mal exemplo," *Mercurio Peruano*, 26 June 1791.

80 "Plan de educación," *El Investigador*, 22 August 1813.

81 Anónimo, "Instrucciones sobre las costumbres," *Diario de Lima*, 10–14 October 1790.

82 It appears, based on extant criminal cases, that more individuals were arrested and the courts processed more crimes beginning in the 1770s. But my examination of the average age of suspected criminals from the Cabildo series over the period 1714–1813 produced inconclusive results: the average ages swing from twenty-two to thirty-five years at random. Likewise, the overall rate at which minors were arrested relative to nonminors varied widely from 18 to 50 percent without discernible patterns.

83 See Estensorro Fuchs's delightful discussion of fears of popular (African) dances among elite español parents in "Plebe ilustrada," 52–54. For Mexico, see Viqueira Albán, *Propriety and Permissiveness*; Voekel, "Peeing on the Palace."

84 Autos criminales que sigue D. Tadeo Sandoval contra Blas Changay sobre un hurto, AGN, Cab., C. Crim., leg. 8, c. 6, ff. 1 and 10, 1785.

85 Details of the case and description of the executions can be found in Valero, "Relación del exemplar."

86 Autos . . . contra Patricio Dillon, AGN, Cab., C. Crim., leg. 5, c. 1, 1772.

87 Autos contra Joséf Tunco, AGN, Cab., C. Crim., leg. 7, c. 4, f. 20, 1782.

88 Autos . . . contra Simona Laredo, AGN, Cab., C. Crim., leg. 5, c. 9, f. 21, 1773.

89 Autos Criminales qe. sigue Pedro Seballos, AGN, Cab., C. Crim., leg. 5, c. 14, 1773.

90 Chambers, *From Subjects to Citizens*, 161, 170.

91 Autos criminales que de oficio de la Real Justa. Se sigue contra Franco. Cardenas que el la causa agregada dijo nombrar Joséph Manuel Mora, AGN, Cab., C. Crim., leg. 10, c. 9, f. 21, 1798. This was the maximum sentence according to the *Recopilación*, 6:13:6.

92 Autos criminales seguidos de oficio contra Balentín Cadenas por urto, AGN, Cab., C. Crim., leg. 13, c. 11, f. 14, 1813.

93 Autos criminales que sigue Pedro Seballos, AGN, Cab., C. Crim., leg. 5, c. 14, 1773.

94 Autos criminales que se sigue por don Antonio Lopes con Asencia Samudio, AGN, Cab., C. Crim., leg. 9, C.2, f. 106, 1789.

95 See Stern, *Secret History*, 17–19, 38–40.

96 See Herzog, *Administración*, 269–78, 304–5.

CHAPTER 5

1 "Relación de algunos puntos."

2 Viscardo y Guzmán, *Letter to the Spanish Americans*, 81–82, 85.

3 Filómates [Demetrio Guasque?], "Educación, O Carta escrita a la Sociedad sobre el abuso de los hijos tuteen a sus padres," *Mercurio Peruano*, 16 January 1791; "Amas de leche. Segunda carta de Filómates sobre la educación," *Mercurio Peruano*, 27 January 1791.

4 This phrase is from Uztáriz, in *Theory and Practice of Commerce*, who urged the Spanish monarchy to adopt the *nueva política*, or new commercial policies, of other European absolutist states. Also see Brading, *First America*, 469.

5 See, for example, Lynch, *Spanish American Revolutions*, 7; Lynch, *Bourbon Spain*, 254; Rodríguez, *Independence of Spanish America*, 35.

6 Rodríguez, *Independence of Spanish America*, 35; Lynch, *Bourbon Spain*, 254; Stein and Stein, *Apogee of Empire*.

7 For variants on this argument, see Brading, "Bourbon Spain," 409; Coatsworth, "Limits of Colonial Absolutism," 36; MacLachlan, *Spain's Empire*, 127–30; Stein, "Bureaucracy and Business," 7; Walker and Guardino, "State, Society, and Politics"; Stein and Stein, *Apogee of Empire*.

8 On the Bourbon Reforms and race, see Twinam's overview in *Public Lives*, 18. On patriarchy and race in Bourbon marriage legislation, compare Seed, *To Love, Honor, and Obey*; Gutiérrez, *When Jesus Came*, 298–336; Stern, *Secret History*, 384–85 n. 13.

9 O'Phelan Godoy, "Introducción," 8; O'Phelan Godoy, "Algunas reflexiones," 309–10.

10 Gordon, "Introduction," 1–6.

11 See the essays in Scott, *Enlightened Absolutism*.

12 This point is also made in Whitaker, "Dual Role," 5–6.

13 On the relationship between the Enlightenment and social reforms in Spain, see Domínguez Ortiz, *Sociedad y Estado*, 488–89; Equipo Madrid de Estudios Históricos, *Carlos III*; Pérez Estévez, *España de la ilustración*, 96. On the tightrope walk

between the Enlightenment and reforms for the colonies, see Domínguez Ortiz, *Carlos III*, 211–23; several essays in Whitaker, *Latin America and the Enlightenment*.

14 See Burkholder and Chandler, *From Impotence to Authority*; Flores Galindo, *Ciudad sumergida*, 47–69.

15 Fisher, *Government and Society*, 158; Brading, "Bourbon Spain," 112–62; Lynch, *Bourbon Spain*.

16 Historians debate whether the Bourbon Reforms were an economic stimulus or caused recession in Peru; see Haitin, "Late Colonial Lima," 100–26; Fisher, *Bourbon Peru*. For period commentary on the positive economic effects of the reforms, see Hesperióphylo [J. Rossi y Rubi], "Reflexiones históricas y políticas sobre el estado de la población de ésta ciudad," *Mercurio Peruano*, 3 February 1791; Cephalio [José Baquíjano y Carrillo], "Disertación histórica-política sobre el comercio del Perú," *Mercurio Peruano*, 20 March–17 April 1791.

17 For discussions of the relationship between the Bourbon Reforms and the uprisings, see O'Phelan Godoy, *Siglo de rebeliones*; Walker, *Smoldering Ashes*, 18–26. Also see Fisher, Kuethe, and McFarlane, *Reform and Insurrection*.

18 See Griffin, "Enlightenment," 136. For a discussion of reporting on the French Revolution in other South American periodicals, see Silva, "Revolución Francesa."

19 For a study that considers enlightened absolutism in a time frame longer than that of traditional scholarship on the Bourbon Reforms, see Walker, "Upper Classes."

20 It should be stressed that the Jesuits had been staunch proponents of creoles and the New World in general against some of the most critical Enlightenment ideas about colonial Americans. See Brading, *First America*, 464.

21 Quoted in Eugía Ruiz, "Staggering Blow," 178.

22 See Ramón, "Urbe y orden"; Walker, "Upper Classes."

23 Expediente sobre que se le aumente el sueldo a Dn. Juan de Loayza como a maestro de Latinidad en la tercera aula de estudios públicos, reestablecidos por la expulsión de los jesuitas en el Logicado del Colegio Máximo de San Pablo, BNP, C955, 1771; Sobre el Hospicio de Pobres, AGN, Sección Colonial, Campesinado, Derecho indígena, Fáctica del Corregidor o Subdelegato de Indios del Cercado, Leg. 1, suelto, 1770.

24 Expediente sobre que se le aumente el sueldo a Dn. Juan de Loayza . . . , BNP, C955, 1771; also see Cárdenas Ayaipoma, "Colegio de Caciques," 16.

25 Cárdenas Ayaipoma, "Colegio de Caciques," 17.

26 For late colonial changes in San Carlos, see Grover, "Reforma de la educación," 230–31.

27 Expediente promovido por los Alumnos del R[ea]l Colegio del Príncipe sobre q[ue] les hagan uniformes o vecas, AGN, Temporalidades, Colegios, leg. 171, c. 14, 1803.

28 Outside Lima—and throughout Spanish America—Bourbon officials established a sizable number of Indian schools of primeras letras in the late eighteenth and early nineteenth centuries. See Macera D'Ossorio, "Noticias"; Sobre fundación de escuelas de primeras letras de orden de S.E. el Virrey del Reyno, BNP, D5889, 1811. Also see Tanck de Estrada, *Pueblos de indios*.

29 See Cunningham, *Children and Childhood*, 64–68.

30 Rousseau, *Émile*. Historians have pointed out that Rousseau's ideas about child rearing were far from original, although he did popularize emerging pedagogies; see Cunningham, *Children and Childhood*, 68; Sussman, *Selling Mother's Milk*, 27–28.

31 Lynch, *Bourbon Spain*, 257.

32 Jovellanos, "Memória," 83.

33 Ibid., 89–90. The meanings of the verb *criar*, as well its relationship to the terms "education" (*educación*) and "teaching" (*enseñanza*), have proven difficult for modern scholars to pin down. For example, Rafael Crevea y Altamira attempted to differentiate "education" and "teaching" in his juridical dictionary of colonial Spanish law and constantly was forced to contend with the appearance of *crianza* as a link between the two, which he regarded as a tautology; see *Diccionario castellano*, 118–19. I propose that the key to solving this linguistic puzzle is that the meaning of *crianza* underwent significant change during the Spanish Enlightenment.

34 The rise of notions of *crianza* corresponds to some aspects of Norbert Elias's classic argument concerning the Enlightenment's promotion of internal restraint; see *Civilizing Process*.

35 See MacLachlan, *Spain's Empire*, 80.

36 For the inherent "equality" of children with adults in Rousseau's thought, see Badinter, *Mother Love*, 132–43.

37 Jovellanos, "Memória," 94–95.

38 "Real Cédula por la qual su magestad funda un colegio de Nobles Americanos en la ciudad de Granada," *Mercurio Peruano*, 26 August 1792.

39 Orellana, *Introducción de la Lengua Latina*. Also see Macera D'Ossorio, "Noticias," 269–75.

40 Permiso ortogado por el Superior Gobierno a la Real Casa de Niños Expósitos, para imprimir el catecismo del Padre Pouget, ABPL, H-A, tomo 2, no. 11, 1801.

41 "Examen histórico-crítico de la fundación, progresos, y actual estado de la Real Casa ó Recogimiento de las Amparadas de la Concepción," *Mercurio Peruano*, 5, 8, 12 April 1792.

42 Ibid., 254–55.

43 Reglamiento de la Casa de Amparadas, Archivo del Convento de San Francisco de Lima, Grupo Diversos. My thanks to Dr. José Rabí for generously sharing this document with me. Also see "Examen histórico-crítico de la fundación, progresos, y actual estado de la Real Casa ó Recogimiento de las Amparadas de la Concepción," *Mercurio Peruano*, 5, 8, 12 April 1792.

44 Macera D'Ossorio, "Noticias," 275.

45 Visitas realizadas por los Señores Patrones al Colegio de Santa Cruz de la ciudad de Lima, 1674–1820, AGN, Sección Colonial, Inquisición, Fundaciones, Mateo Pastor, leg. 17.

46 Untitled, AGN, Sección Colonial, Inquisición, Fundaciones, Santa Cruz de Atocha, leg. 3, c. 102, 1799. For an illuminating discipline problem in 1772 involving a nonwhite student in the school that demonstrates increased upper-class exclusivity in terms of race, see Autos criminales de don Juan Ignacio de Obiaga, Inquisidor y Juez superintendente del colegio de Santa Cruz, contra Mariana de Atocha y Zumarán, por

arañar a la Madre vice-rectora, AGN, Sección Colonial, Inquisición, Fundaciones, Santa Cruz de Atocha, leg. 2, c. 72, 1771; Mannarelli, *Pecados públicos*, 306–7; Martín, *Daughters of the Conquistadores*, 99–100.

47 Memorial presentado por los Colegiales de San Carlos, contra la conducta de su Rector [1770s?], uncataloged compendium of manuscripts from Lima, no. 20, John Carter Brown Library, Brown University.

48 Untitled, AGN, Temporalidades, Colegios, leg. 171, c. 8, 1793.

49 Expediente inciado por los padres de los niños de la Escuela de los Desamparados para que se les de a estos debalde de papel, tinta y plumas por haber renta determinada y corriente para este destino, etc., BNP, D9947, 1806.

50 *El Investigador*, 23 November 1813.

51 Burkholder, *Politics of a Colonial Career*, 87.

52 See *Diario de Lima*, 15 May 1791. For a discussion of *Mercurio Peruano*'s readership, see Clément, *Mercurio Peruano*, vol. 1, chap. 3, "Lectores y suscriptores."

53 "Disertación en la que se proponen las reglas que deben observar las mujeres en el tiempo de preñez," *Mercurio Peruano*, 5 June 1791; *Diario de Lima*, 12 June 1791. Note that, in part, the advice on birthing was intended as a corrective to the "deplorable" practices of midwives of the "humble sphere" who normally aided in childbirth. See Clément, *Mercurio Peruano*, 1:122.

54 "Inconvenientes que resultan de encerrar las Señoritas en los conventos quando están próximas a la pubertad," *Diario de Lima*, 11 January 1791. Also see the poem "La crianza mugeríl al uso," *Diario de Lima*, 10 January 1791; Rosas Lauro, "Jaque a la Dama," 152.

55 Claudia Rosas Lauro argues that women, and particularly mothers, were the prime audience of the *Semanario Crítico*; see "Educando al bello sexo," 372. Also see her "Jaque a la Dama," 146. My reading of the *Diario*'s articles on child rearing indicates the same.

56 *Diario de Lima*, 14 October 1790.

57 Ibid., 13 October 1790.

58 See the reference to using Samaniego's works in the proposed "Plan de educación," *El Investigador*, 22 August 1813.

59 Samaniego, *Fábulas en verso castellano*.

60 Phelan, *People and the King*, 3.

61 Libro de Reales Ordenes y Actas concernientes a la Expedición Filatrópica de la vacuna . . . 1802–1820, BNP, D13105; Sobre establecimiento del hospital de pobres en el antiguo colegio del Cercado, AGN, Sección Colonial, Campesinado, Derecho indígena, Fáctica del Corregidor o Subdelegado de Indios del Cercado, leg. 1, 1770; *Minerva Peruana*, 19 November 1805, 367.

62 Unánue, *Actuaciones literarias*.

63 Cited in Arrom, *Containing the Poor*, 45.

64 Ladrón de Guevara, in *Memorial en que el Dean*.

65 Entry on 28 March 1758, Libros de Cabildo, Archivo de la Municipalidad de Lima; "Don Diego Ladrón de Guevara," in Mendiburu, *Diccionario Histórico-Biográfico*, 2:373–75.

66 Sobre el hospicio, AGN, Sección Colonial, Campesinado, Derecho indígena, Fáctica del Corregidor o Subdelegato de Indios del Cercado, leg. 1, 1770.

67 *Proyecto Instructivo*. Two of the six members of the Sociedad de Beneficencia were Antonio and Josef Mathias de Elizade, who were Basque emigrants. Also see Expediente promovido ante el Superior Gobierno por el Marqués de Zelada de la Fuente . . . y otros solictando licencia para el establecimiento de unas casas escuelas . . . y la adjucicación de la casa habitación con el nombre de la Casa de los Pobres del Cercado, 1799–1803, AGN, Sección Colonial, Superior Gobierno, Expedientes Contensioso, leg. 30, c. 940. It should be noted that, during these decades, the crown also instituted policies in other areas intended to promote female occupational training and to remove work restrictions, an effort in part influenced by the work of Campomanes. See Arrom, *Women of Mexico City*, 26–29; Deans-Smith, "Working Poor."

68 *Proyecto Instructivo*.

69 El Maiordomo del Hospicio de Pobres del Cercado pide se le entreguen vajo de fianza . . . los Reditos de la Obrapía, 191, BNP, C3466; Meligario, "Disertación histórico-ética sobre el Real Hospicio general de pobres de esta ciudad, y la necesidad de sus socorros," *Mercurio Peruano*, 23 February 1792.

70 Meligario, "Disertación histórica-ética sobre el Real Hospicio general de pobres de esta ciudad, y la necesidad de sus socorros," *Mercurio Peruano*, 23 February 1792. Clément, in *Mercurio Peruano*, 2:293, identifies the author as Fr. Jerónimo Calatayud.

71 "Real Cédula declarando que los jueces eclesiásticos sólo deben entender en la causas de divoricios, sin mezclarse en las temporales y profanas sobre alimentos, litisexpensas o restitución de dotes, 22 de Marzo, 1787," in *Cedulario de la Real Audiencia*. Unfortunately, I have not been able to locate the local hearings of the case in Lima's ecclesiastical archives.

72 *Real Cédula de 10 de agosto de 1788*.

73 Sanción Prágmatica para evitar el abuso de contraer matrimonios disiguales, in Konetzke, *Colección de documentos*, 3:404. The law states that minors of age should obtain the "advice and consent of the father, and in [case of] his defect, of the mother, and in absence of both, of their grandparents on both sides."

74 Some have argued that the edict was issued in response to a conflict over the marriage choice of the king's brother, but this is doubtful. See Seed, *To Love, Honor, and Obey*, 201; Rípodas Ardanaz, *Matrimonio en Indias*, 289–300.

75 As argued in Chapter 2, local Spanish statutes and canon law traditionally had prohibited superiors from forcing minors into marriage, but whether children had to seek elder consent to marry was another matter. Patricia Seed claims that the Council of Trent specifically stated that parental consent was not necessary for marriage, but a closer look at the first chapter of Trent's reform of matrimony shows that its language was more nebulous than this might suggest. The council did not precisely state that children could or should marry without parental permission, only that marriages contracted against the will of the parents were not ipso facto invalid. Cf. Seed, *To Love, Honor, and Obey*, 34, and *Canons and Decrees of the Council of Trent*, 183. Therefore, Charles III was drawing an important distinction between forced mar-

riages and elder consent as he tried to steer clear of violating a major tenet of Catholic doctrine on marriage.

76 Disensos based on racial inequality include Causa seguida por D. Agustín Salazar contra José de los Santos Vitaliano por el estupro perpetrado contra su hija Isabel, AGN, RA, C. Civ., leg. 80, c. 980, 1795; don José Jiménez contra Manuel Salinas, AGN, Cab., C. Civ., leg. 25, c. 417, 1813. Age-related cases include Autos seguidos por doña Paula de Silva . . . para impedirle contraiga matrimonio con persona inadecuada, AGN, Cab., C. Civ., leg. 16, c. 236, 1809; Autos seguidos por don Alejandro Aldón contra don Manuel Aldón, su hermano, sobre . . . matrimonio con la mulata Manuela Villalta, tanto por la disigualdad de su condición social, cuanto por ser menor de edad sin recursos económicos, AGN, RA, C. Civ., leg. 331, c. 3010, 1794. Cases argued on the basis of a fiancé's lack of occupation include Autos seguidos por doña Petronila Fernández García contra don Luis Manrique sobre el rapto de su hija, doña Francisca Argumaniz, AGN, RA, C. Civ., leg. 310, c. 2807-A, 1792; Autos seguidos por don José Ramírez su curador sobre que le conceda licencia para casarse, AGN, RA, C. Civ., leg. 83, c. 862, 1808. As is obvious from the titles of some of these cases, elders often had more than one basis for objecting to marriages, and race formed only one of a composite of justifications. Seed, *To Love, Honor and Obey*, 215, finds the same for post-1778 Mexico.

77 Causa seguida por D. Manuel Fernández contra Francisco Morel, por el rapto y estupro de su hija Josefa, AGN, RA, C. Crim., leg. 84, c. 1032, 1797.

78 There are several studies of patterns of dissent cases in colonial Spanish America following the Pragmatic Sanction. See Martínez-Alier (Stolcke), *Marriage, Class*; Rípodas Ardanaz, *Matrimonio en Indias;* Gutiérrez, "Honor, Ideology"; Gutiérrez, *When Jesus Came*; Seed, *To Love, Honor, and Obey*; Socolow, "Acceptable Partners"; McCaa, "Gustos de los padres."

79 Seed, *To Love, Honor, and Obey*, 205. This interpretation is often repeated in more recent scholarship. See Chaves, "Slave Women's Strategies," 119; Stoler, "Tense and Tender Ties," 7; Gauderman, *Women's Lives*, 24. On race, see Socolow, "Acceptable Partners"; Rípodas Ardanaz, *Matrimonio en Indias*. Also see Twinam, *Public Lives*, 18–20, 309–14.

80 Cases containing verdicts from Lima demonstrate that judges did not always rule in elders' favor, often because the children were older than the age of majority established in the Pragmatic Sanction. For other examples on the varied verdicts in disenso cases, see Díaz, *Female Citizens*, 99; Socolow, "Acceptable Partners," 234.

81 Saether, "Bourbon Absolutism." Also see Seed, *To Love, Honor, and Obey*, 206 n. 4; Martínez-Alier (Stolcke), *Marriage, Class*; Twinam, *Public Lives*, 309.

82 Real Cédula declarando la forma en que se ha de guardar y cumplir en las indias la Pragmática Sanción, de 23 de Marzo de 1776 sobre contraer matrimonios, 23 March 1778, in Konetzke, *Colección de documentos*, 3:438–42. The sanction also provided an exception to the exceptions. Minors of age who were black and mixed-race militiamen—those "who distinguish themselves from the rest by reputation, good conduct, and service"—were to obtain consent to marry from military superiors.

83 Rípodas Ardanaz, *Matrimonio en Indias*, 286.

84 Consulta del Consejo de Indias sobre las dificutaldes que se promueven en cumplir la Real Prágmatica sobre Matrimonios, 17 February 1798, in Konetzke, *Colección de documentos* 3:759–66. Saether, "Bourbon Absolutism," explores an outpouring of colonial objections and demands for more specificity found in the Archivo de Indias.

85 Konetzke, *Colección de documentos*, 3:794–96; also see Rípodas Ardanaz, *Matrimonio en Indias*, 273.

86 The age of minority for elder consent to marry was lowered from twenty-five to twenty-one for women and twenty-three for men; it fell by a year if the elder objecting was a mother, by another year if the elder was a grandfather, and even lower if the elder was a guardian.

87 Saether, "Bourbon Absolutism," 507–8.

88 "Consulta del Consejo sobre la habilitación de pardos para empleos y matrimonios," in Konetzke, *Colección de documentos*, 3:826. Note that, in his petition, the archbishop connected marriage legislation to controlling people of African descent, especially in light of the Túpac Amaru II rebellion, which, he stated, was instigated by blacks "improperly titled mestizos" (827).

89 Saether, "Bourbon Absolutism," 508; Lewis, *Hall of Mirrors*, 180.

90 For the rise of romantic love in England, see Stone, *Family, Sex, and Marriage*, 189–91. For the rise of an ideology of romantic love in late eighteenth- and early nineteenth-century Spanish America, see Gutiérrez, "Honor, Ideology"; Shumway, "Between Revolution, Power, and Liberty." Cf. Seed, *To Love, Honor, and Obey*, 230–31.

91 See the columns in *Diario de Lima*, 19, 25 January 1791.

92 Autos que siguió don Francisco de Ormaza y Coronel, sobre un mulatillo que le vendió en usufructo al Mayordomo de la Real Casa de Niños Expósitos, ABPL, H-A, tomo 1, no. 26, 1777. The director's portion of the bill of sale reads, "rendo y doy captivo sujeto de servidumbre."

93 The proportion of slaves in the city held fast at one-fifth between 1700 and 1790, indicating that proportionally fewer of Lima's inhabitants of African descent were enslaved. By my calculations from the sample of the 1700 census, slaves made up 34.5 percent of the total population of African descent in 1790, the inverse of almost a century earlier, when 62.4 percent of the population of African descent was enslaved and 37.6 percent was free. See Cook, *Numeración*; "Plan demostrativo de la población comprendida en el recinto de la ciudad de Lima," *Mercurio Peruano*, 3 February 1791. For longer-term changes in the racial composition of Lima, see Haitin, "Late Colonial Lima."

94 See Twinam, *Public Lives*, 336. Also see Dueñas Vargas, *Hijos del pecado*; Mörner, *Race Mixture*.

95 "Disertación histórico-ética sobre el real hospicio general de Pobres de esta Ciudad, y la necesidad de sus socorros," *Mercurio Peruano*, 1 March 1792.

96 "Autos que siguió Don Francisco de Ormaza y Coronel," ABPL, H-A, tomo 1, no. 26, 1777.

97   Ibid. Ormaza did argue that rearing children was a legitimate economic activity if not undertaken for commerce or profit.

98   AGN, PN, Alejandro de Cueto, P. 201, no. 58, 1779.

99   Beginning in the 1750s, various governing bodies in both Spain and the Americas made similar decisions that erased the presumption of illegitimacy. See Twinam, *Public Lives*, 301.

100   Real cédula expedida en Aranjuez, a 20 de enero de 1794, por la cual S. Magestad legitima a los niños expósitos, y les acuerde privilegios, ABPL, H-A, tomo 2, no. 5. The edict is also found in Para que se observe lo resuelto en fabor de los Niños Expósitos, 19 February 1794, AGI, Indiferente General, leg. 1543, no. 179.

101   Sussman, *Selling Mother's Milk*, 26–27; Cunningham, *Children and Childhood*, 61.

102   Clément, "Enfants exposés," 174; Sussman, *Selling Mother's Milk*, 19–20.

103   Sherwood, *Poverty in Eighteenth-Century Spain*, 101.

104   Instrucción para el cuidado de los expósitos a cargo de los obispos, 3 mayo de 1797, Real Academia de la Historia, Madrid, Sección Mata Linares, leg. 118, ff. 351–61.

105   Autos promovidos por D. Juan José Cavero, Mayordomo de la Real Casa de Niños Expósitos, a fin de que éstos pudiesen en su oportunidad ser admitidos al estudio de la Náutica en la Escuela de Pilotos de Callao, ABPL, H-A, tomo 2, no. 10, 1801.

106   Ibid.

107   Autos que promovió el Dr. Don Juan de Bordanave, Rector del Colegio del Príncipe, sobre que a los alumnos del d[ic]ho colegio se les señalase sitio en la plaza mayor, para ver los toros y demás fiestas reales, ABPL, H-A, tomo 2, no. 2, 1788–91.

108   Cavero, *Dictamenes Teológico-legales*.

109   Milton, "Many Meanings," 315–24.

110   Twinam, *Public Lives*, 303.

111   "Dictamen del fiscal del Consejo de las Indias sobre admission de un expósito al exámen de abogado," 26 December 1805, in Konetzke, *Colección de documentos*, 3:816–18.

112   Hunt, *Family Romance*, 114. Also see n. 44 in the Introduction to this book.

113   Rousseau, "Social Contract," 1821; Badinter, *Mother Love*, 132–43. Also see Hobbes, *Leviathan*, chap. 20, "Of Dominion Paternal and Despotical."

114   "Viva Fernando VII," *Minerva Peruana*, 9 September 1809, 553.

115   Untitled letter to the editor, *Minerva Peruana*, 10 November 1809, 693.

116   Brading, *First America*, 429–30; Eze, *Race and the Enlightenment*.

117   Guillaume-Thomas Raynal quoted in Rodríguez, *Independence of Spanish America*, 15.

118   Anonymous, "Descripción de la Ciudad de Lima Capital del Reyno del Perú, su tempermento, opulencia, carácter de sus Naturales, y comercio . . ." [1774?], in Theiercelin, *Cultures et sociétés*, 287. My thanks to Chuck Walker for calling this piece to my attention and sharing a copy with me.

119   Gerbi, *Dispute of the New World*, 183.

120   "J. P. Viscardo propone a John Udny [*sic*], que el gobierno británico ayude a Túpac Amaru desde el Río de la Plata . . . Massacarrara, 30 septiembre 1781," in Batllori,

Abate Viscardo, 206. Also see Rosas Lauro, "Jaque a la Dama," 151; Lavallé, *Promesas ambiguas*, 42.

121   Anderson, *Imagined Communities*, 60.

122   Foucault, *History of Sexuality*.

123   Locke, *Some Thoughts Concerning Education*, 47. Also see Stoler, *Race and the Education of Desire*, 153.

124   The deprecation of wet nurses ran through the 1797 cédula on foundlings, Real cédula expedida en Aranjuez, a 20 de enero de 1794, por la cual S. Magestad legitima a los niños expósitos, y les acuerde privilegios, ABPL, H-A, tomo 2, no. 5. Rousseau was among the most vocal critics of wet nursing; see *Émile*, 13. Also see Sussman, *Selling Mothers' Milk*, 19–29; Webre, "Wet Nurses."

125   Juan Antonio de Olavarrieta, "Práctica general de la Educación, y defectos que abraza," *Semanario Crítico* 6 (1790).

126   Olavarrieta, "Práctica general," *Semanario Crítico* 2 (1791).

127   "Justificación de la Sociedad, y del Perú," *Mercurio Peruano*, 19 June 1791.

128   See Olavarrieta, "Justa repulsa contra inicuas acusaciones . . . de la Real Sociedad Académica," *Semanario Crítico* 5 (1791).

129   Terralla y Landa, *Lima por dentro*, 58.

130   Palma, "Poeta de las adivinanzas," 712.

131   Eustaquio Filómates [Demetrio Guasque?], "Educación: Carta sobre el abuso de los hijos que tuteen a sus padres," *Mercurio Peruano*, 23 January 1791.

132   Ibid.

133   For a discussion of Richardson's *Clarissa*, see Fliegelman, *Prodigals and Pilgrims*, 28. On *La nouvelle Clarise* as female response to Richardson, see Johns, "Reproducing Utopia."

134   Filómates, "Amas de leche," *Mercurio Peruano*, 27 January 1791.

135   Clément, *Mercurio Peruano*, 2:43.

136   Greer Johnson, *Satire in Colonial Spanish America*, 5.

137   Filaletes, "Carta sobre los maricones," *Mercurio Peruano*, 27 November 1791.

138   Also see Olavarrieta's comments on Lima's "malign climate," in "Práctica general del la educación, y defectos que abraza," *Semanario Crítico* 2 (1791). The scientific strain of thought that attributed customs or cultural characteristics to the climate of a region was reaching its apogee during the period. For a careful, and favorable, study of Lima's climate by a contemporary ilustrado, see Unánue, *Observaciones sobre el clima*.

139   Teagnes [Fray Tomás de Méndez y Lachica], "Carta remitida a la *Sociedad* haciendo algunas reflexiones sobre la que se contiene en el *Mercurio* núm 94. en que se pinta a los *maricones*," *Mercurio Peruano*, 19 February 1792. The phrasing in Spanish is somewhat nebulous: "Niño abandonado a los manos de su nutriz, o sea de su propia madre . . . ."

140   Ibid. The author said separation of children from mothers was practiced on the island of Celebes, in eastern Indonesia.

141   Descriptions of the painting can be found in Kubler and Soria, *Art and Architecture*, plate 179(b); Mills and Taylor, *Colonial Spanish America*, 339–40.

142   Vieira Powers, "Conquering Discourses"; Montrose, "Work of Gender."

143 See Dean, "Sketches of Childhood."

144 For this model, see Phelan, *People and the King*, 239.

145 See Rodríguez, *Independence of Spanish America*, 36–37; Whitaker, "Changing and Unchanging Interpretations"; Phelan, *People and the King*, xvii.

146 Twinam, *Public Lives*, 298–314.

CHAPTER 6

1 I have traced this case from Lima's Cabildo to the Council of the Indies. See Autos seguidos por don Gerónimo Muñoz Mudarra, padre de la menor María Francisca Mudarra y Cavero, sobre la entrega de ésta y de los bienes dejados por su difunta mujer, AGN, RA, C. Civ., leg. 136, c. 1101, and Leg. 137, C. 1108, 1759; Autos seguidos por doña Rosa de la Mercedes Daga contra don Gerónimo Mudarra, sobre asignación de pensión alimenticia para su sobrina, AGN, Cab., C. Civ., leg. 25, c. 442, 1771; don Gerónimo Muñoz Mudarra vezno. de la Ciudad de Lima con El Marqués de Casaboza vezino de ella sobre la entrega de diferentes vienes y alaxas que quedaron en su cassa con motivo de la muerte repentina acahecida en ella de don Franca. Cavero y Mendoza su Muger, AHE, Consejos. Leg. 20290, Exp. 5, 1765.

2 See, for example, van Deusen, *Between the Sacred*; Stern, *Secret History*; Chambers, *From Subjects to Citizens*, 101–9; Boyer, "Women"; Nizza da Silva, "Divorce in Colonial Brazil."

3 Stern, *Secret History*.

4 The term "privilege" was often invoked in contradistinction to "right." The difference between privileges and rights may be conceived of along the lines of Weber's distinction between "power," which is the "probability that an individual can exert his or her will over another individual," and "authority," which is the belief that the exercise of power is legitimate and, in modern societies, lawful. See Weber, *Theory of Social and Economic Organization*, 152.

5 The rate of population change is derived from comparing the *Numeración* with "Plan demostrativo de la población comprehendida en el recinto de la Ciudad de Lima," *Mercurio Peruano*, 30 January 1791. Also see Haitin, "Late Colonial Lima," 192–202. Note that many historians describe a striking eighteenth-century increase in other kinds of court cases as well. For example, Stern finds the number of domestic violence prosecutions in the Mexican archives increased at the end of the 1700s for each of the three regions he studied—a "remarkable" number of "interregional consistencies" (Stern, *Secret History*, 421 n. 9). Though he dismisses the impact of the Bourbon Reforms on these cases because the regions experienced highly variable integration into broader Spanish political and economic control, the inter-viceroyalty consistency between Peru and Mexico is also remarkable and begs the question of how the expansion of Bourbon bureaucracy through the court system might have affected contests over gender rights.

6 It is impossible to perform a rigid statistical analysis of all formal cases involving Lima's minors due to the manner in which cases are cataloged in the AGN, but an analysis of the 176 cases I reviewed from the Real Audiencia civil case series provides a

good measure of the kind of change in court cases to which I refer. During the period 1650–1750, Audiencia cases over the recognition and inheritance of illegitimates who were minors of age comprised more than half of all cases that I could identify as centering on children (54.8 percent). This percentage is probably low, since many case descriptions do not indicate whether natural children were minors of age at the time of trial and therefore escaped detection. Cases that dealt primary with slave children comprised a small number (around 6.5 percent) of suits over children during the period. Cases over child custody and support, when they occurred, were distributed among the inheritance cases and a small number of guardianship cases (9.7 percent). In the second half of the eighteenth century, in contrast, simple custody and child support cases not involving inheritance took up a much greater share of the cases I examined (around 40 percent), as did cases involving slave children (28 percent).

7 Guerra, "Forms of Communication," 10–13.

8 See, for example, the collection of legal briefs in Bravo de Lagunas y Castilla, *Colección legal de Cartas*; Arias de Saavedra, *Discurso legal*.

9 Quoted in Kagan, *Lawsuits and Litigants*, 1.

10 Don Gerónimo Muñoz Mudarra vez[i]no. de la Ciudad de Lima con El Marqués de Casaboza, AHE, Consejos. Leg. 20290, Exp. 5, 1765.

11 El Dr. Dn. Blas de Quiros Vez[i]no de la Ciudad de los Reyes contra Da. Casimira Rodríguez de estado soltera doncella sobre esponsales, d[ote]s(?) y otras cosas AHE, Consejos, 20298, Leg. 129, Ex. 1–23, 1774; also see Causa de don Blas Quiroz in Residencia del Exmo. Señor don Manuel Amat y Juniet, AHE, Consejos, 20341, Exp. 1. For examples of cases in which the Quiroz case was cited as precedent, see Causa que sigue Da. Josefa Peres Muchotrigo contra Josef Falcón Chino Libre por raptor, AAL, Causas Criminales de Matrimonios, leg. 7, 1776; Autos criminales seguidos por doña María Arnao viuda de Bernabé Sáenz, contra Pedro Celestino López, por el delito de estupro en agravio de su hija llamada Escolástica Sáenz, AGN, RA, C. Crim., leg. 116, c. 1401, 1809 [*sic*; 1802].

12 "Real Cédula declarando que los juices eclesiásticos sólo deben entender en las causas de divorcios," *Cedulario de la Real Audiencia*.

13 Cicerchia, "*Vida maridable*," 88. Note that not until 1821, after independence, was a detailed outline of the role of the Argentine Defensor put into law.

14 Pérez y López, *Teatro de la Legislación*, 155–73.

15 A review of the inventory of late eighteenth-century Lima's gracias requests in AGI, Pleitos, Audiencia de Lima, 982, failed to turn up specific requests for widows' dispensations. However, widows in late nineteenth-century Cuba requested dispensations in AHE, Ultramar, 2095, exs. 16 and 20; 2063, ex. 22, and 2083, ex. 20. For a history of gracias al sacar and legitimation, see Twinam, *Public Lives*. My thanks to Ann for sharing her expertise on the topic and directing me toward widows' dispensations.

16 Escriche y Martín, *Diccionario razonado*, 1228. Also see Díaz, *Female Citizens*, 74.

17 Autos seguidos por don Gerónimo Muñoz Mudarra, AGN, RA, C. Civ., leg. 136, c. 1101, f. 7, 1759.

18 Stone, *Family, Sex, and Marriage*, 149. Badinter claims that women were particularly susceptible to accepting the new emphasis on sentiment for children because it

offered some hope of equality with men; see *Mother Love*, 119. Here my argument stands in contrast to Patricia Seed's contention that discourses of love were replaced by economic interests in family battles between parents and children in Mexico; see *To Love, Honor, and Obey*, esp. chaps. 9 and 10. My research on Lima indicates that, while new mercantile economic ideas became particularly pronounced during the eighteenth century, especially in terms of economically investing in child rearing, there is little evidence that these discourses supplanted ideas about affection and free will, whether between children who wished to marry or between parents and children. In fact, in the case of child rearing, ideas about love and will worked together with newer mercantile ideas about economics and investment.

19 Curaduría of José and Buenaventura Marín, AGN, PN, Ignacio Ayllón Salazar, P. 92, ff. 622–24, 1799.

20 Autos seguidos por don Manuel Toribio Vásquez de la Riva contra don Pedro Antonio Molina, sobre la curatela de la menor, doña María Mercedes Vásquez de Vásquez, AGN, RA, C. Civ., leg. 112, c. 1183, 1813. Also see the petition of doña María Mercedes Blanco y Raez to name her stepfather as her guardian based on his "good conduct and the love with which he treats me," AGN, PN, Gervasio de Figuerola, P. 453, 1780.

21 See the guardianship contract in which a widow provides an unsolicited exposition on the difference between Roman law on guardianship, which favored male relatives (agnation), and Spanish law and custom, which granted widows guardianship with preference: Tutela of Narcisa de Bustamante, AGN, PN, Gervasio de Figueroa, P. 451, f. 219, 1777.

22 *Siete partidas*, 6:16:4, 5:1:19.

23 Tutela of Josef Antonio de Zeballos y Calderón et al., AGN, PN, Phelipe Joseph Jarava, P. 559, ff. 123–26, 1776. For an unusual instance when the alcalde of Lima permitted a widow who remarried to retain guardianship of her children but required her to officially reaffirm her commitment to her children, see Discernamiento of tutela of children of doña Francisca Bravo de Sotronca, AGN, PN, Juan Nuñez de Porras, P. 807, ff. 910–12, 1724.

24 Autos seguidos por doña Paula de Silva sobre que su hija Gregoria Lobatón sea recluida en un convento, AGN, Cab., C. Civ., leg. 16, c. 236, 1809.

25 Autos seguidos por doña Josefa Escudero de Sicilia y Ugarte, madre del menor Antonio Arburúa, sobre su tutoría vacante, AGN, RA, C. Civ., leg. 36, c. 381, 1804.

26 In 1821 the Defensor de Menores issued a decision that reflected a growing belief that retaining mothers in positions of guardianship was best and would most assuredly "not prejudice minors." See Autos seguidos por Manuela Santiago y Martínez sobre la tutela de sus menores hijos y el albaceazgo de los bienes de su difunto marido, AGN, Cab., C. Civ., leg. 43, c. 682, 1821.

27 Stone, *Family, Sex, and Marriage*, 162–65. Also see Fliegleman's comments on the basic philosophical agreement between the Lockean tradition of reason and other Enlightenment (Scottish) philosophies focused on natural sentiment, in *Prodigals and Pilgrims*, 23–26.

28 The historiography of European, and particularly French, Enlightenment views

on women and nature is expansive. Important works published in English include Tomaselli, "Enlightenment Debate"; Landes, *Women and the Public Sphere*; Melzer and Rabine, *Rebel Daughters*; Goodman, *Republic of Letters*; Stienbrügge, *Moral Sex*. Also see Desan, *Family on Trial*, 120.

29 See Bolufer Peruga and Morant Duesa, "On Women's Reason"; Badinter, *Mother Love*, esp. chap. 5.

30 Litigants and lawyers often discussed how the application of the law would have irrational results. See Autos seguidos por doña Josefa Miranda contra don José Tamarria, sobre le asigne una pensión alimenticia para su hija, AGN, RA, C. Civ., leg. 336, c. 3058, 1795; Autos seguidos por doña Gertrudis Carrillo contra don José Gabriel Torres sobre reconocimiento del hijo natural habido entre ambos, AGN, Cab., C. Civ., leg. 33, c. 549, 1816.

31 *Siete partidas*, 4:19.

32 Autos seguidos por doña Antonia Hernández contra Teodoro Martínez, por alimentos, AGN, Cab., C. Civ., leg. 11, c. 130, 1806. Note that Teodoro was under age twenty-five and attempted to use his minority status to mitigate his culpability for having had sexual relations with Antonia.

33 Autos seguidos por doña María Ignacia del Castillo contra don Manuel García Quandía, su marido, sobre alimentos, AGN, Cab., C. Civ., leg. 11, c. 138, 1806. Also see Autos seguidos por doña Cipriana de la Cerda contra don Miguel Echeandía, sobre alimentos para sus cuatro menores hijos, AGN, RA, C. Civ., leg. 79, c. 810, 1808.

34 Autos seguidos por Flora Guerrero contra don José Antonio Cueto, sobre asignación de pensión alimenticia para su hijo natural, AGN, Cab., C. Civ., leg. 70, c. 1349, 1791.

35 Autos seguidos por doña Teresa Alzamora y Ursino contra don Joaquín Navárez, sobre que asigne una pensión alimenticia para el hijo natural habido entre ambos, AGN, RA, C. Civ., leg. 206, c. 1760, 1778.

36 Causa seguida por D. Manuel de la Torre y Castaño contra Francisco de las Llagas, pardo libre por el rapto de su hija doncella, AGN, RA, C. Crim., leg. 15, c. 161, 1752; Causa seguido contra Luis Rubin por Fernando de Espinoza por rapto y violación de su hija, Rosa, AGN, RA, C. Civ., leg. 24, c. 272, 1762; Juan de Aguilar Curador de María Carrasco contra Gregorio Bernal sobre el estupro, AAL, Causas Criminales de Matrimonios, leg. 7, 1783; Causa seguida por doña María Mercedes de Aguilar contra Christobal Carrasco, por rapto de su hija Petronila Luza, AGN, RA, C. Crim., leg. 57, c. 665, 1785; Causa seguida por Lorezo Cerver contra Melchor de Zúñiga por el estupro perpetrado contra su hija Juana, AGN, RA, C. Crim., leg. 64, c. 758, 1789.

37 Cited in Arrom, *Women of Mexico City*, 237. Fernández de Lizardi's views on abusive patriarchs had Enlightenment roots stretching back to Montesquieu and Condorcet. See Tomaselli, "Enlightenment Debate," 107–15.

38 "Relación de algunos puntos."

39 Autos seguidos por doña[s] Manuela, Francisca y Evarista de Lara, contra su hermano don José de Lara, sobre se le corrija por "vago y mal entretenido," AGN, RA, C. Civ., leg. 318, c. 2896, 1793.

40 Expediente promovido ante el Superior Gobierno por Dn. Manuel Placios, Maestro

zapatero, solicitando licencia, para enviar a los Reynos de España a su hijo natural nombrado José Palacios por su mala conducta y la mala condición de los sujetos con quienes se junta, solicitó se le pusiese preso en la Panadería de las Mantas . . . , AGN, Sección Colonial, Superior Gobierno, Expedientes Contenciosos, leg. 34, c. IIII, 1811.

41 Autos seguidos por don Diego Robledo contra doña Rufina Robledo, su hija, sobre la fuga de otra de sus hijas, doña Felipa Robledo, hecho que imputa a la demandada, AGN, Cab., C. Civ., leg. 14, c. 209, 1808.

42 Autos seguidos por Fr. José Rivera contra d Pedro Rivera, su padre, sobre que contribuya a su sostenimiento, AGN, Cab., C. Civ., leg. 82, c. 1543, 1797.

43 In my review of all cases in the criminal series throughout the Audiencia district, I found fifteen accusations against adults for committing violence against children (including rape but not seduction cases). All but one date from the 1760s onward. Within this group, in only four cases were the children cared for by both parents. Three cases involved accusations against a parent: one charge of filicide against an indigenous father from Cuzco and two charges of child abuse leveled against mothers.

44 Autos criminales de oficio ante el Alcalde de barrio quinto Cuartel cuatro contra María Díaz (alias "china libre"), por intento de filicidio en su hijo de 5 a 6 años, AGN, RA, C. Crim., leg. 136, c. 1656, 1817.

45 Autos criminales seguidos de oficio por la Real Justicia contra Manuela Aseves por haber dado muerte a una criatura, AGN, RA, C. Crim., leg. 131, c. 1595, 1815.

46 Machado de Chávez y Mendoza, *Perfeto confesor*, 2:621.

47 Autos seguidos por doña María Luisa de Armas contra el Albacea de los bienes de don Toribio Boza . . . sobre alimentos de sus hijos, AGN, RA, C. Civ., leg. 353, c. 3210 and 3211, 1793.

48 For a case in which a woman's honor was proved through education, see Autos seguidos por doña Michaela Portocarrero contra don Luis Bueno, padre natural de dos hijos entre ambos, sobre alimentos, AGN, RA, C. Civ., leg. 366, c. 3354, 1798. For motherly love equated with education, see Causa seguida contra D. Luis de Landavere por el rapto y estupro de Da. Manuela Quiroga, AGN, RA, C. Crim., leg. 84, c. 1034, 1797.

49 Autos seguidos por doña Baltazara de Alva y Vélez contra don Pedro Prieto, sobre filiación de un hijo habido de sus relaciones extraconjugles, asignación de una dote por alimentos y donación de una esclava, AGN, RA, C. Civ., leg. 237, c. 2028, 1789.

50 Also see Autos seguidos por Fray Manuel Antonio Aramburú contra doña Josefa Flores sobre la entrega de su sobrina, AGN, Cab., C. Civ., leg. 8, c. 87, 1804; Autos seguidos por doña María Miranda, viuda . . . contra don Tomas Lovera, curador de su hijo, AGN, RA C. Civ., leg. 220, c. 1877, 1780.

51 Autos seguidos por doña Petronila Gómez contra don José Antonio Pro, sobre asignación de pensión alimenticia, AGN, Cab., C. Civ., leg. 68, c. 1317, 1791. For a similar case, see Autos seguidos por Fray Manuel Antonio Aramburú contra doña Josefa Flores sobre la entrega de su sobrina, AGN, Cab., C. Civ., leg. 8, c. 87, 1804.

52 Autos seguidos por don Pedro Llaguno Gómez, curador ad litem de don Pedro Moreda, contra don Francisco Martínez de Saavedra, tutor de éste, sobre cantidad de

pesos, AGN, Cab., C. Civ., leg. 14, c. 162, 1697. Also see Autos seguidos por el Dr. Don Mariano de Salazar y Robles sobre que se le concede la venia de edad . . . , AGN, Cab., C. Civ., leg. 22, c. 371, 1768.

53 Autos seguidos por don Manuel Toribio Vásquez de la Riva contra don Pedro Antonio Molina, AGN, RA, C. Civ., leg. 112, c. 1183, 1813.

54 Autos seguidos por doña María Ignacia de la Fuente y Loayza, sobre su curatela, AGN, RA, C. Civ., leg. 213, c. 1818, 1779.

55 Tutela of Petronila Dávila y Castillo, AGN, PN, Phelipe Joseph Jarava, P. 561, ff. 142–44, 1780.

56 Autos seguidos por don [*sic*] José Santos Castro contra don [*sic*] José Bracadeli, que indebidamente pretende ejercer su tutela, AGN, Cab., C. Civ., leg. 11, c. 145, 1806. The "dons" appear in the archive's case titles but not in the original scribes' titles for the cases.

57 Autos seguidos por Flora Guerrero contra don José Antonio Cueto, AGN, Cab., C. Civ., leg. 70, c. 1349, 1791.

58 Autos seguidos por doña Teresa Alzamora y Ursino contra don Joaquín Navárez, sobre que asigne una pensión alimenticia para el hijo natural habido entre ambos, AGN, RA, C. Civ., leg. 206, c. 1760, 1778.

59 Autos seguidos por Fray Manuel Antonio Aramburú, AGN, Cab., C. Civ., leg. 8, c. 87, 1804.

60 Autos seguidos por doña Petronila Gómez contra don José Antonio Pro, AGN, Cab., C. Civ., leg. 68, c. 1317, 1791.

61 Autos seguidos por Sebastiana Avila contra Tomasa Vergara [*sic*; Agustian Coca] por el rapto de un niño, AGN, Cab., C. Civ., leg. 25, c. 435, 1771.

62 Autos seguidos por doña Josefa Varela contra el Mayordomo de la Casa de Expósitos sobre la entrega de su hija, Feliciana . . . , AGN, RA, C. Civ., leg. 308, c. 2793, 1792.

63 Autos seguidos por Josefa Orué contra Juan Escurra por cantidad de pesos de la lactancia de su hijo, AGN, Cab., C. Civ., leg. 11, c. 153, 1806.

64 *Siete partidas*, 4:19:3.

65 Autos seguidos por María del Carmen Campos contra Antonio Vergara, sobre alimentos para la hija natural habida entre ambos, AGN, RA, C. Civ., leg. 17, c. 194, 1802.

66 Autos seguidos por doña Ancieta Montero contra don Mariano Baldeón, su marido, sobre alimentos, AGN, Cab., C. Civ., leg. 9, c. 95, 1804. Also see Autos seguidos por doña Antonia Bocarando contra don Gabriel Barbadillo, sobre alimentos para sus hijos, AGN, RA, C. Civ., leg. 324, c. 2955, 1794.

67 Autos seguidos por doña Gertrudis Carrillo contra don José Gabriel, AGN, Cab., C. Civ., leg. 33, c. 549, 1816.

68 Autos seguidos por doña Baltazara de Alva y Vélez contra don Pedro Prieto . . . , AGN, RA, C. Civ., leg. 237, c. 2028, 1789.

69 Autos seguido por don Mariano de Espinoza solicitando se le entregue a su hija Inés de Espinoza que se encuentra en el Monasterio de Santa Catalina bajo tutela de María Trinidad, AAL, Monasterio de Santa Catalina, leg. 8, no. 49, 1790.

70 Examples include Boyer, "Women"; van Deusen, *Between the Sacred*.

71 Stern, *Secret History*, 313.

72 Cf. ibid., 22, 24–36.

CHAPTER 7

1 For the use of diminutives, see Bowser, *African Slave*, 224.

2 Eugene Genovese defines paternalism within New World slavery, both in North America and Latin America, as "a sense of reciprocal rights and duties between masters and slaves"; see *From Rebellion to Revolution*, 6. Genovese, however, viewed paternalism not as an intrinsic aspect of African bondage but as a specific social response to the closing of the slave trade and owners' rising incentive to naturally reproduce the slave population (5).

3 Hünefeldt, *Paying the Price*, 118, 7.

4 *Siete partidas*, 4:22.

5 Ibid., 4:21:2.

6 Ibid., 4:24:3.

7 Ibid., 4:20:3, 8. For slaves, the natural debt was particularly binding if they were freed by their masters; see ibid., 4:24:2.

8 Trazegnies, *Ciraco de Urtecho*; Townsend, "'Half My Body Free,'" 108; Chaves, "Slave Women's Strategies," 119.

9 Aguirre, *Agentes de su propia libertad*, 184.

10 See Chapter 6, n. 6.

11 Stern, *Peru's Indian Peoples*, 115.

12 Autos seguidos por María del Carmen Ansieta, en nombre propio y de sus hijos contra la testamentaria de doña Mariana Ansieta, su ama, sobre la libertad a todos ellos se les concedió, AGN, Cab., C. Civ., leg. 72, c. 1403, 1792. Also see the importance of superior decree preventing a master from seizing control of a slave in Autos seguidos por María Tomas Vásquez contra doña Juana de la Viña. Sobre que venda a la esclava Juana, hija de la demandante, AGN, Cab., C. Civ., leg. 28, c. 482, 1773.

13 The code is printed as "Instrucción sobre la educación, trato y ocupación de los esclavos," in Konetzke, *Colección de Documentos*, 3:643–52, and as "Real Cédula insertando la Instrucción acerca de la educación, trato, ocupación, derechos, deberers, garatías, etc. de los esclavos que debe observarse en los dominios de Indias e Islas Filipinas sin perjuicio de las leyes existentes," *Cedulario de la Real Audiencia*, 299–306. Also see Watson, *Slave Law*, 49–50.

14 *Siete partidas*, 4:21:6.

15 Ibid. and 3:5:4. The second law only allowed family members to litigate over wrongful enslavement, not the purchase of family members (*coartación*). Coartación was a controversial part of customary law rather than a matter of codified law and will be discussed later in this chapter. See Watson, *Slave Law*, 50–54.

16 Lucena Salmoral, *Códigos negros*, 21, 112–23.

17 Quoted in ibid., 119.

18 Hünefeldt, *Paying the Price*, 80.

19 According to my sample of the 1700 census, free women of African descent outnum-

bered men by almost 2:1. Also see Hünefeldt, *Paying the Price*, 205–6. For gendered patterns of manumission, in which female slaves were freed or purchased freedom in greater numbers than men throughout Latin America, see Schwartz, "Manumission of Slaves," esp. 611; Johnson, "Manumission in Colonial Buenos Aires," 266; Chandler, "Family Bonds"; Klein, *African Slavery*, 227; Ingersoll, "Free Blacks"; Lane, "Captivity and Redemption."

20 The possibility that there is a connection between manumission patterns and litigation patterns in late colonial Spanish America deserves more scholarly attention. It appears that manumission rates were correlated not only to slave gender but also to master gender, as well as to circumstances of the slave's birth, meaning whether or not a slave was born in the house or "power" of a particular master. See chap. 5 in Proctor, "Slavery, Identity, and Culture." Another possible cause for high rates of litigation against female owners might be that women more often resorted to violence to punish their slaves. See Karasch, "Anastácia and the Slave Women," 83; Brana-Shute, "Slave Manumission."

21 Schwartz, "Manumission of Slaves," 622. On religion, manumission, and gender, see Lane, "Captivity and Redemption," 228–29; Lauderdale Graham, *House and Street*, 96–99.

22 AGN, PN, Juan del Corro, P. 409, f. 99, 1695.

23 Autos seguidos por Julián Cabeduzo en nombre de su hermana Victoria y su menor hijo sobre la libertad de ambos, ortogado por su anterior ama, María Antonia Collasos, AGN, RA, C. Civ., leg. 57, c. 582, 1805.

24 Autos seguidos por Juan Manuel Belsunce contra doña Petronila Vásquez, sobre que venda su sobrina, María Antonia, AGN, RA, C. Civ., leg. 323, c. 2938, 1794.

25 Autos seguidos por Mónica Foronda contra el Dr. D. Gaspar de la Puente Ibáñez sobre que ortogue carta de venta a su hijo, Faustino, esclavo, AGN, Cab., C. Civ., leg. 33, c. 1772, 1775.

26 This expression is from Genovese, *Roll, Jordan, Roll*, 4, who is quoting Imamu Amiri Baraka.

27 Autos seguidos por Juan Manuel Belsunce, AGN, RA, C. Civ., leg. 323, c. 2938, ff. 24–24v, 1794.

28 Stern, *Secret History*.

29 Autos seguidos por Francisca Suazo, morena liberta, contra don Juan José Alzamora, sobre la libertad de su hija Jacinta, AGN, RA, C. Civ., leg. 70, c. 720, 1807. Also see Autos seguidos por Juana Negrón contra doña Manuela de los Ríos sobre su libertad y la de su hija, AGN, RA, C. Civ., leg. 373, c. 3433, 1798; Autos seguidos por Mónica Foronda, AGN, Cab., C. Civ., leg. 33, c. 1772, 1775; Autos seguidos por María Josefa Delgado contra Polonia Peñaloza sobre la libertad de su hijo María Lucía, AGN, Cab. C. Civ., leg. 70, c. 1366, 1791.

30 Autos seguidos por Petronila Sánchez, samba libre, contra doña Lugarda Márquez, sobre la libertad de su hijo, José Andrés, AGN, RA, C. Civ., leg. 32, c. 352, 1803.

31 Autos seguidos por Tiburcia Arrosarena, parda libre, contra D. José Martín de Toledo sobre procedimiento arbitrario contra su hijo Juan Bautista, esclavo de Fr. Silvestre Durán, AGN, Cab., C. Civ., leg. 22, c. 370, 1811.

32 Autos seguidos por Manuela Olaza contra su ama doña Juana Hurtado y Sandoval sobre alimentos para sus hijos, AGN, RA, C. Civ., leg. 304, c. 2736, 1792.

33 See Watson, *Slave Law*, 44. For a discussion of Spanish thought on natural laws and slavery in the context of the conquest and colonization of the Indians of the Americas, see Pagden, *Fall of Natural Man.*

34 See Davis, *Problem of Slavery*, esp. the discussion of philosophes in the Caribbean in chap. 4, "The Boundaries of Idealism." For Montesquieu's struggle with "political slavery" and African bondage in the Caribbean, see Ghachem, "Montesquieu in the Caribbean," 13–14; Dubois, *Colony of Citizens.* For Latin America, see Soulodre-La France, "Socially Not So Dead!"; Klein, *African Slavery*, 243–44.

35 See, for example, Autos que sigue Thoribio de Sosa contra su Amo Dn. Juan de Sosa sobre sebicia, AGN, Cab., C. Crim., leg. 6, c. 9, 1776.

36 *Siete partidas*, 4:22.

37 Autos seguidos por Josefa Arriaga y Córonel, morena libre, contra doña Juana María Rondón, sobre la libertad de su hijo, José María, AGN, RA, C. Civ., leg. 315, c. 2865, 1793.

38 Autos seguidos por Julián Cabeduzo . . . , AGN, RA, C. Civ., leg. 57, c. 582, f. 8, 1805. In another case, a female master used similar language to resist returning a portion of the money a mother had paid toward her child's freedom; see Autos seguidos por Mercedes Villaverde, madre de Manuela Bernal, esclava de Da. Josefa Bernal, sobre la subsistencia del compromiso de venta de su hija, AGN, Cab., C. Civ., leg. 29, c. 476, 1814.

39 Autos seguidos por Tiburcia Arrosarena, parda libre, contra D. José Martín de Toledo sobre procedimiento arbitrario contra su hijo Juan Bautista, esclavo de Fr. Silvestre Durán, AGN, Cab., C. Civ., leg. 22, c. 370, 1811.

40 Autos seguidos por Norberta Nuñez, esclava de don Cipriano Domínguez, Alcalde de Naturales del Cercado, sobre que se le ortogue boleta de venta y se declare la libertad de su hija Manuela, AGN, RA, C. Civ., leg. 131, c. 1343, 1815.

41 Autos seguidos por María Josefa Oyague contra D. Manuel Domínguez, sobre su libertad y la de su hija, Petronila, AGN, RA, C. Civ., leg. 57, c. 586, ff. 19 and 1, 1805. For a case in which a lawyer argued that African slaves, particularly bozales, lacked the faculty of "rational consideration" because of their "rusticity and dimness," see Autos seguidos por Marta del Carmen Breña contra don Francisco Iturrino, sobre se le ortogue el instrumento de libertad y se le permita lactar a su hija en su propia casa, AGN, RA, C. Civ., leg. 132, c. 1345, f. 14, 1815.

42 On "derecho vulgo" in Spanish law, see Cutter, *Legal Culture*, 34, 38.

43 Autos seguidos por Petronila Sánchez, AGN, RA, C. Civ., leg. 32, c. 352, 1803. A similar argument can be found in Autos seguidos por Juan de Mata, negro libre, contra María Antonia Guerrero, AGN, RA, C. Civ., leg. 258, c. 2276, 1787. For a slave owner's interpretation of a "vulgarity" that had developed around the practice of coartación, see Autos seguidos por Mónica Foronda, AGN, Cab., C. Civ., leg. 33, c. 1772, 1775.

44 Lavallé, *Amor y opresión*, 236.

45 On church doctrine in Lima, see Bowser, *African Slave*, 254–55; Hünefeldt, *Paying the Price*, 119–20.

46 Autos seguidos por don Raymundo Meza, Albacea de D. Juan de Chávez, sobre el cumplimiento de su testamento en los que incide la presentación de la esclava Juana Medina sobre la libertad de su hija Teresa, AGN, Cab., C. Civ., leg. 7, c. 75, 1803.

47 Autos seguidos por María del Rosario Hidalgo contra Manuel Saénz, sobre que venda a sus dos hijos, AGN, Cab., C. Civ., leg. 31, c. 513, 1814.

48 Autos seguidos por José Llanos, padre de María del Carmen Marín, esclava de doña María de la Daga, sobre que no la venda, AGN, Cab., C. Civ., leg. 16, c. 242, 1809.

49 The law reads, "Some españoles have children with black women, and want to buy them to give them liberty: We order that, if they are to be sold, the fathers who wish to purchase them shall be preferred" (*Recopilación*, 7:5:6).

50 Autos seguidos por Francisco Pimentel, padre de Matías Pimentel, contra Juana Zagal, sobre la libertad de su hijo, AGN, Cab., C. Civ., leg. 57, c. 1172, 1786.

51 Several recent studies have explained how slaves and plebeians in colonial Spanish America followed codes of honor that paralleled those of elite society, but we need more studies of the culture and meanings of parental legitimacy. See Mannarelli, *Pecados públicos*. For slaves and honor, see Hünefeldt, *Paying the Price*, esp. chap. 5; Chaves, "Slave Women's Strategies," 110–11; Lauderdale Graham, "Honor among Slaves."

52 Autos seguidos por María Josefa de Musarreta contra doña Paula de Musarreta, sobre el cumplimiento de disposiciones testamentarias de da. Andrea, AGN, RA, C. Civ., leg. 80, c. 664, 1736; Autos seguidos por María Josefa Oyague contra D. Manuel Domínguez, AGN, RA, C. Civ., leg. 57, c. 586, ff. 19 and 1, 1805.

53 Autos criminales que de ofisio de la Real Justicia se siguen contra Simona Laredo, AGN, Cab., C. Crim., leg. 5, c. 9, 1773; Autos seguidos por Tiburcia Arrosarena, parda libre, contra D. José Martín de Toledo sobre procedimiento arbitrario contra su hijo Juan Bautista, esclavo de Fr. Silvestre Durán, AGN, Cab., C. Civ., leg. 22, c. 370, 1811; Autos seguidos por don Raymundo Meza, Albacea de D. Juan de Chávez, sobre el cumplimiento de su testamento, AGN, Cab., C. Civ., leg. 7, c. 75, 1803; Autos seguidos por doña María Pontaza, contra don Mariano Tramarría, Albacea de Manuela Aguilar, sobre alimentos para la liberta Fidela Aguilar, AGN, RA, C. Civ., leg. 169, c. 1742, 1821.

54 Autos seguidos por Francisco Pimentel, padre de Matías Pimentel, contra Juana Zagal, sobre la libertad de su hijo, AGN, Cab., C. Civ., leg. 57, c. 1172, 1786; Autos seguidos por José Llanos, AGN, Cab., C. Civ., leg. 16, c. 242, 1809.

55 Autos seguidos por Catalina del Castillo contra el Padre Juan de la Reynaga, amo de su hijo, Juan Pablo, sobre se le extienda la boleta de venta, AGN, RA, C. Civ., leg. 41, c. 733, 1779.

56 Autos seguidos por Cayetana Cepeda, en calidad de madre de Vicente, contra doña Agustina Cepeda, sobre sevicia, AGN, RA, C. Civ., leg. 325, c. 2965, 1794. Also see, among many examples, Autos seguidos por María Antonia Oyague contra da. Agustina Sotomayor sobre sevicia que practica conra la esclava María Ignacia, hija de la demandante, AGN, RA, C. Civ., leg. 36, c. 3366, f. 6, 1798; Autos seguidos por Juan de Mata, negro libre, contra María Antonia de Guerrero, sobre que le extienda boleta de venta de su hijo, Francisco Guerrero, AGN, RA, C. Civ., leg. 258, c. 2276, f. 3v., 1787.

57 Autos seguidos por María Antonia Oyague contra doña Agustina Sotomayor, AGN, RA, C. Civ., leg. 36, c. 3366, f. 6, 1798.

58 Autos seguidos por Josefa Cavero, madre de José Tereso contra D. Domingo Casas de Novoa, amo de Tereso, sobre que lo venda, AGN, Cab., C. Civ., leg. 65, c. 1274, 1790.

59 See Autos seguidos por Catalina Castillo and Autos seguidos por Juan Manuel Belsunce, AGN, RA, C. Civ., leg. 323, c. 2938, 1794; Autos seguidos por María Tomas Vásquez contra doña Juana de la Viña sobre que venda a la esclava Juana, hija de la demandante, AGN, Cab., C. Civ., leg. 28, c. 482, 1773; Autos seguidos por Josefa Arriaga y Córonel, morena libre, contra doña Juana María Rondón, sobre la libertad de su hijo, José María, AGN, RA, C. Civ., leg. 315, c. 2865, 1793; Autos seguidos por Francisco Pimentel, AGN, Cab., C. Civ., leg. 57, c. 1172, 1786.

60 Autos seguidos por Petronila Sánchez, AGN, RA, C. Civ., leg. 32, c. 352, 1803.

61 *Siete partidas*, 7:31:1.

62 Autos seguidos por María Teresa Llanos, madre de María Natividad Llanos, esclava de doña María Rosa de Llano y Váldez, sobre que la venda, AGN, Cab., C. Civ., leg. 54, c. 1021, 1785.

63 Autos seguidos por Mónica Muñoz, como madre de José de Rivas contra don José Gamarra, sobre se ortogue carta de venta a su hijo, AGN, Cab., C. Civ., leg. 71, c. 1388, 1792.

64 Autos seguidos por María Josefa Oyague contra D. Manuel Domínguez, AGN, RA, C. Civ., leg. 57, c. 586, f. 44, 1805.

65 Autos seguidos por Catalina del Castillo contra el Padre Juan de la Reynaga, amo de su hijo, Juan Pablo, sobre se le extienda la boleta de venta, AGN, Cab., C. Civ., leg. 41, c. 733, 1779.

66 Autos seguidos por Petronila Sánchez, AGN, RA, C. Civ., leg. 32, c. 352, 1803.

67 Autos seguidos por María Antonia Oyague contra da. Agustina Sotomayor, AGN, RA, C. Civ., leg. 36, c. 3366, f. 9, 1798.

68 Autos seguidos por Mónica Foronda, AGN, Cab., C. Civ., leg. 33, c. 1772, 1775.

69 In a coincidence that further underscores how a constellation of matters concerning children and minority connected the social universe of colonial Lima, the lawyer here may have been referring to Domingo Larrión, the Defensor de Menores.

70 Autos seguidos por Mónica Foronda, AGN, Cab., C. Civ., leg. 33, c. 1772, f. 27, 1775.

71 Autos seguidos por Juan Manuel Belsunce, AGN, RA, C. Civ., leg. 323, c. 2938, f. 3, 1794.

72 Autos seguidos por Mónica Foronda, AGN, Cab., C. Civ., leg. 33, c. 1772, 1775.

73 See Rama, *Lettered City*, 41–42.

74 Autos seguidos por doña María Luisa de Armas contra el Albacea de los bienes de don Toribio Boza . . . sobre alimentos de sus hijos, AGN, RA, C. Civ., leg. 353, c. 3210 and 3211, 1793.

75 See capítulo 3 of "Instrucción sobre la educación, trato y ocupación de los esclavos," in Konetzke, *Colección de Documentos*.

76 Autos seguidos por María Antonia Oyague contra da. Agustina Sotomayor, AGN, RA, C. Civ., leg. 36, c. 3366, ff. 1 and 8, 1798.

77 Rafaela Araujo, esclava de Florentina López, contra don Juan José Castro, amo de su

hija menor, sobre se le extiende boleta de venta teniendo en quanta que por falta de atención pudiera prostituirla, AGN, RA, C. Civ., leg. 107, c. 1139, 1812.

78 Hünefeldt, *Paying the Price*, 123.

79 Autos seguidos por Marta del Carmen Breña contra don Francisco Iturrino, AGN, RA, C. Civ., leg. 132, c. 1345, f. 14, 1815; also see Hünefeldt, *Paying the Price*, 119.

80 Hünefeldt, *Paying the Price*, 64–65; Bowser, *African Slave*, 103.

81 Autos seguidos por Manuela Olaza contra su ama doña Juana Hurtado y Sandoval sobre alimentos para sus hijos, AGN, RA, C. Civ., leg. 304, c. 2736, 1792.

82 Autos seguidos por Paula Marchan contra doña María Marchando, sobre los alimentos que ha prestado a su hijos, AGN, RA, C. Civ., leg. 358, c. 3260, 1797.

83 For this argument, see Autos seguidos por Francisca Suazo, morena liberta, contra don Juan José Alzamora, sobre la libertad de su hija Jacinta, AGN, RA, C. Civ., leg. 70, c. 720, 1807; Autos seguidos por Juana María Ibáñez, samba libre, contra da. María Josefa Negreiros, sobre que venda a su hija, María Natividad . . . víctima de tratos inhumanos, AGN, RA, C. Civ., leg. 153, c. 1283, 1785 [*sic*; 1765].

84 Doña María Echenique contra negra Antonia Barrera, su esclava, sobre la esclavitud de los hijos de ésta última, AGN, RA, C. Civ., leg. 159, c. 1645, 1819.

85 Reference to the decree is found in Expediente seguido por el Abogado Defensor G[ene]r[a]l de Menores contra doña Rosa Moreno sobre la libertad del liberto, Rafael, AGN, Sección Republicano, Poder Judicial, Corte Superior de Justicia, C. Civ., leg. 278, c. 16, 1841.

86 Hünefeldt, *Paying the Price*, 124.

87 Aguirre, *Agentes de su propia libertad*, 205.

88 Blanchard, *Slavery and Abolition*, 41–42; Aguirre, *Agentes de su propia libertad*, 206–7; Hünefeldt, *Paying the Price*, 65. For a summary discussion of early republican laws on slavery in South America, see Davis, *Problem of Slavery*, 90–91.

89 Flores Galindo, *Ciudad sumergida*, 105.

90 The analogy is obvious in *Siete partidas*, 4:25:2.

91 Aguirre, *Agentes de su propia libertad*, 207.

CONCLUSION

1 *Litigio Ventilado*. This story is also repeated in Ruíz, *Educación*, 50–57, and in Villasmil, *Parentela*, 50–53.

2 Brading, *First America*, 609. Also see Masur, *Simón Bolívar*, 34–37.

3 For custody disputes in the late colonial and early republican period, see Cicerchia, "Minors, Gender, and the Family"; Shumay, "Between Revolution, Power, and Liberty," esp. 77–85; Dueñas Vargas, *Hijos del pecado*, 267–71; Lipsett-Rivera, "Marriage and Family Relations."

4 See Barreda Laos, *Vida intellectual*; Whitaker, *Latin America and the Enlightenment*. For more recent historical scholarship on the Enlightenment in Latin America, see Burkholder, *Politics of a Colonial Career*; Clément, *Mercurio Peruano*, vol. 1; several of the essays in O'Phelan Godoy, *Perú en el siglo XVIII*; Cañizares-Esguerra, *How to Write the History of the New World*.

5 For Lima, see Estensorro Fuchs, "Plebe ilustrada." For Mexico, see Voekel, "Peeing on the Palace"; Viqueira Albán, *Propriety and Permissiveness*.

6 Flores Galindo, *Ciudad sumergida*, 123.

7 Lanning, "Reception," 72.

8 While postcolonial convents eventually lost their educative function, the Catholic Church continued to play a central role in elite female primary education in Peru. See Miller, *Latin American Women*, 64–65; Burns, *Colonial Habits*, 193–94. In 1819, control of the city's foundling home was shifted to a crown agency, the Junta de Beneficencia, as part of yet another plan to create a poorhouse. In 1826, the republican government converted the Junta into the Sociedad de Beneficencia Pública. The Hospital of Orphans (note, no longer "expósitos") continued functioning into the twentieth century. See Sociedad de Beneficencia, *Album Fotográfico*.

9 On the endurance of Latin American patriarchy in modern forms of political legitimacy, see Stern, *Secret History*, 320, 324–26; Mallon, *Peasant and Nation*, 73–88.

10 Pateman, *Sexual Contract*. For comments on Pateman's arguments, see Hunt, *Family Romance*, 201; Desan, *Family on Trial*, 392–93 n. 86.

11 Chambers, *From Subjects to Citizens*, 200–215.

12 Arrom, *Women of Mexico City*, 85–90.

13 Quoted in Arrom, *Women of Mexico City*, 89.

14 This is a concept with which many philosophes would have agreed, for Rousseau wrote that a mother was given to "a cruel kindness" and the tendency to "lavish excess care on her child," an argument that was repeated in Lima's late colonial periodicals; see *Émile*, 16. Also see Kerber, *Women of the Early Republic*, 25–27.

15 Hünefeldt, *Liberalism in the Bedroom*, 346 n. 39.

16 Chambers, *From Subjects to Citizens*, 164–67; Lipsett-Rivera, "Gender and Family Relations"; Díaz, *Female Citizens*, 196–97. For the late nineteenth-century growth of liberal judicial power over both parents, see Guy, "Parents before the Tribunals." Also see Milanich, "Historical Perspectives on Illegitimacy," 85–87.

17 Desan, *Family on Trial*, 11–12.

18 See Mallon, *Peasant and Nation*; Dubois, *Colony of Citizens*; Mehta, *Liberalism and Empire*; Fischer, *Modernity Disavowed*.

19 Hunt, *Family Romance*, 202.

20 Anne McClintock, in "'No Longer,'" 262, argues that all modern nations have a "domestic genealogy" and are understood through a "family trope." For a criticism of feminist theories that stress the continuity of patriarchy in the form of "state control" of women without attention to deep historical changes in political models and in the domestic realm, see Gordon, *Women, the State, and Welfare*, 22.

21 For this phrasing used to justify denying citizenship to women in Mexico, see Arrom, *Women of Mexico City*, 84. For the denial of citizenship to slaves and Indians in early republican Arequipa, see Chambers, *From Subjects to Citizens*, 214.

22 Encinas, *Legislación tutelar*, 12, 113.

23 Quoted in Stein, "Paths to Populism," 105.

24 A discussion of the position of Lima's elites vis-à-vis San Martín's plans for constitu-

tional monarchy and subsequent provincial declarations of political autonomy in Peru is found in Rodríguez, *Independence of Spanish America*, 213–17.

25 Quoted in Anna, "Spain and the Breakdown," 260.

26 Flores Galindo, *Ciudad sumergida*, 181. An excellent summary description of the protracted independence struggles in Peru that integrates a discussion of recent historiography can be found in Klarén, *Peru*, 124–33. For Bolívar's changing political philosophy, see Brading, *First America*, 603–20.

27 Quoted in Flores Galindo, *Ciudad sumergida*, 181.

28 Lynch, *Spanish American Revolutions*, 267.

Bibliography

ARCHIVAL MANUSCRIPTS

Durham, N.C.
Duke University, Special Collections Library

Lima, Peru
Archivo Arzobispal de Lima
    Causas Criminales de Matrimonios
    Causas de Negros
    Conventos
        San Francisco
        Santo Domingo
    Divorcios
    Hospitales
    Litigios Matrimoniales
    Monasterios
        de la Encarnación
        del Prado
        Santa Catalina
        Santa Clara
    Nulidades de Matrimonios
    Papeles Importantes
Archivo de la Beneficencia Pública de Lima
    Huérfanos-Antecedentes
Archivo de la Municipalidad de Lima
    Libros de Cabildos de Lima
Archivo Franciscano
Archivo General de la Nación
    Sección Colonial
        Asuntos Eclesiásticos
            Tribunal de conventos y órdenes religiosos
                San Juan de Diós
                Santa Catalina
                Santísima Trinidad
            Tribunal eclesiástico
        Cabildo

Justicia Ordinaria
    Causas Civiles
    Causas Criminales
    Corte de Superior Justicia
Campesinado
    Derecho indígena
        Fáctica del Corregidor o Subdelegato de Indios del Cercado
Compañía de Jesús
    Colegios
    Sermones
Inquisición
    Fundaciones
        Santa Cruz de Atocha
Protocolos Notoriales
Real Audiencia
    Casos de Corte
    Causas Civiles
    Causas Criminales
    Sentencias
Real Junta de las Temporalidades
    Colegios
    Cuenta de Colegios
    Varios
Superior Gobierno
    Cabildo
    Expedientes Contenciosos
Sección Repúblicano
    Poder Judicial
        Corte Superior de Justicia
Biblioteca Nacional del Perú
    Colección de Raul Porras Barranchea
    Colección Zegarra

Madrid, Spain
Archivo Histórico de España
    Cleros
    Consejos Suprimidos
        Pleitos, residencias, comisiones y visitas del Virreinato de Lima
        Sala de Justicia-Escribanía de Cámara
    Diversos-Documentos de Indias
    Estados
    Inquisición
        Causas de fé

Biblioteca Nacional
    Manuscritos de América
Real Academia de Historia
    Sección Mata Linares
        Papeles varios sobre América

Providence, R.I.
Brown University
    John Carter Brown Library
    John Hay Library, Microfilm Collection

Seville, Spain
Archivo General de Indias
    Contratación
    Escribanía
    Expedientes
    Indiferente General
    Informaciones
    Mapas y Planos
    Pleitos
        Audiencia de Lima
        Audiencia de México
        Audiencia de Quito

Washington, D.C.
Catholic University, Canon Law Series

NEWSPAPERS AND PAMPHLETS

Diario de Lima
Gazeta de Lima
El Investigador
Mercurio Peruano
Semanario Crítico

PUBLISHED PRIMARY SOURCES

Aguilar, Joseph de. *Sermones predicados en la ciudad de Lima, corte de los reynos del Perú.* Bruselas: Francisco Tsestevens, 1684.

Arias de Saavedra, Francisco. *Discurso legal que en defenza de la menor doña Grimaneza de la Puente, hija legítima, y absoluta heredera del Señor Marque de la Puente.* Lima: 1792. Microfilm Collection, John Hay Library, Brown University.

Bravo de Lagunas y Castilla, Pedro, ed. *Colección legal de cartas, dictamenes y otros papeles en derecho*. Lima: Casa de Niños Huérfanos, 1761.

"Breve apunte en el derecho sobre la causa de nulidad de matrimonio de Doña María Belzunze con el Conde de Casa Dávalos." In *Colección legal de cartas, dictamenes y otros papeles en derecho*, edited by Pedro Bravo de Lagunas y Castilla. Lima: Casa de Niños Huérfanos, 1761. Special Collections Library, Duke University.

Brochero, Luis. *Discurso breve del uso de exponer los niños*. Seville, 1626.

Canons and Decrees of the Council of Trent. Translated by Rev. H. J Schroeder, O.P. St. Louis: B. Herder, 1941.

Carbón, Damian. *Libro del arte de las comadres o madrinas*. 1541. Transcribed by Francisco Susarte. Alicante: Universidad de Alicante, 1995.

"Carta, o diario que escribe D. Joseph Eusebio de Llano y Zapata . . . en que la mayor verdad, y crítica mas segura le dá cuenta de todo lo acaecido en esta Capital del Perú, desde el Viernes 28 de Octubre de 1746." In *Noticias del Perú*, 714. John Carter Brown Library, Brown University.

Cavero, Juan José de. *Dictamenes teológico-legales acerca de la obligación que tienen los padres pudientes de costear los alimentos y educación de sus hijos expuestos*. Lima: Imprenta Real de Niños Expósitos, 1811.

Cedulario de la Real Audiencia de Buenos Aires. La Plata: Archivo Histórico de la Provincia de Buenos Aires, 1929–38.

Cobo, Father Bernabé. *Inca Religion and Customs*. Translated by Roland Hamilton. Austin: University of Texas, 1990.

Conde de Superunda. *Relación de Gobierno, Perú (1745–1761)*. Edited by Alfredo Moreno. Madrid: Consejo Superior de Investigaciones Científicas, 1983.

Constituciones del Colegio de Niñas Expósitas de Santa Cruz de Atocha. Lima, 1659.

Cook, Noble David. "Introducción." In *Numeración general de todas las personas de ambos sexos, edades y calidades q[ue] se ha [h]echo en esta Ciudad de Lima, año de 1700*, compiled by Noble David Cook. Facsimile ed. Lima: COFIDE, 1985.

———, comp. *Numeración general de todas las personas de ambos sexos, edades y calidades q[ue] se ha [h]echo en esta Ciudad de Lima, año de 1700*. Facsimile ed. Lima: COFIDE, 1985.

Covarrubias Orozco, Sebastián de. *Tesoro de la lengua castellana o española*. 1611. Edited by Felipe C. R. Maldonado. Revised by Manuel Camarero. Madrid: Ediciones Castalia, 1995.

Encinas, José Antonio. *Una legislación tutelar indígena*. Lima: Facultad de Jurisprudencia de la Universidad Mayor de San Marcos de Lima, 1920.

Escriche y Martín, Joaquín. *Diccionario razonado de legislación y jurisprudencia*. Paris: Librería de Rósa, Bouret y Cia., 1851.

Frézier, Amedée François. "Bocetos de Lima." In *El Perú visto por viajeros*. Edited by José Muñoz Rodríguez, Lima: Ediciones Peisa, 1973.

Fuero juzgo o libro de los juices. 7th century. Barcelona: Editoriales Zeus, 1968.

García-Gallo, Alfonso, ed. *Cedulario indiano, recopilado por Diego de Encinas*. Madrid: Ediciones Cultura Hispánica, 1945–46.

Gómez de Silva, Domingo. *Instrucción general, y práctica para la buena adminstración de los bienes de los menores destos reynos del Pirú.* Lima: Pedro Cabrera, 1640. Microfilm Collection, John Hay Library, Brown University.

Gutiérrez de Godoy, Dr. Juan. *Tres discursos para provar que estan obligadas a criar sus hiios a sus pechos todas las madres . . . .* Jaen: Pedro de la Cuesta, 1629.

Hobbes, Thomas. *Leviathan.* Pts. 1 and 2 [1651]. New York: MacMillan, 1985.

"Individual y Verdadera Relación de la extrema ruyna que padeció la Ciudad de los Reyes Lima." In *Noticias del Perú,* 714. John Carter Brown Library, Brown University.

Jovellanos, Gaspar Melchor de. "Memória sobre educación pública." 1792. In *La reforma ilustrada: Propuestas democráticas en la España borbónica,* edited by Franco Cerutti. San José, Costa Rica: Libro Libre, 1987.

Juan y Colóm, Joseph. *Instrucción de escribanos, en orden a lo judicial utilíssima también para procuradores, y litigantes, donde sucintamente se explican lo ritual, y forma de proceder en las causas civiles, y criminales, assí en la theoría, como en la práctica.* 5th ed. Madrid: Imprenta de Antonio Marín, 1761.

Konetzke, Richard, ed. *Colección de documentos para la historia de la formación social de Hispanoamérica, 1493–1810.* 4 vols. Madrid: Consejo Superior de Investigaciones Científicas, 1962.

Ladrón de Guevara, Diego. Untitled. In *Memorial en que el Dean, y Cabildo de esta Santa Iglesia Metropolitana de los Reyes propone, y representa los derechos que tiene para pedir reform de los Autos promovidos en visita.* Lima, 1754. John Carter Brown Library, Brown University.

Lanuzo y Sotelo, Eugenio. *Viaje ilustrada a los reinos de Perú.* 1738. Lima: Pontificia Universidad Católica del Perú, 1995.

Levillier, Roberto, ed. *Gobernantes del Perú, cartas y papeles, siglo XVI, documentos del Archivo de Indias.* 14 vols. Madrid, 1921–26.

Leyes de toro. 1505. Madrid: Ministerio de Educación y Ciencia, 1977.

Libro de Reales Ordenes y Actas concernientes a la Expedición Filantrópica de la vacuna; y la mejor conservación y propagación del fluido. Vice-Presidente el S. Oidor de esta Rl. Audiencia Dn. Manuel García Plata. 1802–20.

Litigio ventilado ante la Real Audiencia de Caracas sobre domicilio tutelar y educación del menor Simón Bolívar, año 1795. Caracas: Imprenta Nacional, 1955.

Locke, John. *Some Thoughts Concerning Education.* 1693. Menston, England: Scolar Press, 1970. Quoted in Ann Laura Stoler, *Race and the Education of Desire: Foucault's History of Sexuality and the Colonial Order of Things,* 153. Durham: Duke University Press, 1997.

Machado de Chávez y Mendoza, Juan. *El perfeto [sic] confesor y cura de almas.* 2 vols. Madrid: Pedro de Cavalleria, 1646.

Memorial en que el Dean, y Cabildo de esta Santa Iglesia Metropolitana de los Reyes propone, y representa los derechos que tiene para pedir reform de los Autos promovidos en visita (Lima: n.p., 1754). John Carter Brown Library, Brown University.

Orellana, Esteban de. *Introducción de la Lengua Latina . . . .* Lima, 1759.

Pérez de Herrera, Cristóbal. "Discursos del amparo de los legítimos pobre, y reducción de los fingidos." In *Fuentes para la historia de Madrid y su provincia,* compiled by José Simón Díaz. Madrid, Instituto de Estudios Madrileños, n.d. [16th century].

Pérez y López, Antonio Javier. *Teatro de la Legislación, universal de España e indias.* Madrid: M. González, 1791–98.

Proyecto instructivo, patriótico y político sobre el establecimiento de escuelas de hilar y texar el algodan, lino y camaño, para fomentar la industria entre las gentes pobres de ambos sexos de la capital de Lima. Lima: Los Huérfanos, 1799. Microfilm Collection, John Hay Library, Brown University. FHA 241.8.

Real Cédula de 10 de agosto de 1788, por la qual se ha servido S.M. declarar a quién toca y pertenece el conocimiento de el delito de poligamía . . . . Lima: Imprenta Real de los Niños Huérfanos, 1789. Microfilm Collection, John Hay Library, Brown University. HA-M216.

Recopilación de leyes de los reynos de las Indias. 1681. Madrid: Viuda de Joaquín Ibarra, 1791. Facsimile reprint. Madrid, 1941.

"Relación de algunos puntos de consultas de Indias." In *Colección de todas las pragmáticas, cédulas, provisiones, circulares, autos acordados, vandos y otras providencias publicadas en el actual reynados del Señor Don Carlos IV . . . ,* edited by Santos Sánchez. Vol. 1. Madrid: Viuda e Hijo de Marím, 1794.

Rousseau, Jean-Jacques. *Émile.* 1762. Edited by P. D. Jimack. Translated by Barbara Foxley. Rutland, Vt.: Everyman/Charles E. Tuttle, 2000.

——. "The Social Contract or Principles of Political Right." 1762. In *The Social Contract and Discourses.* 1973. Reprint, London: Everyman, 1990.

Samaniego, Don Félix María. *Fábulas en verso castellano.* Paris: Librería de Garnier, 1859.

Sánchez, Santos. *Colección de todas las pragmáticas, cédulas, provisiones, circulares, autos acordados, vandos y otras providencias publicadas en el actual reynados del Señor Don Carlos IV . . . .* Vol. 1. Madrid: Viuda e Hijo de Marím, 1794.

Sánchez, Tomás. *Disputaciones de sacro matrimonium sacramentum.* 3 vols. Madrid, 1602–3.

Las siete partidas del sabio rey Alfonso el X, glosados por el Lic. Gregorio López. 12th century. Valencia: Imprenta de Benito Momfort, 1767.

Solórzano Pereira, Juan de. *Política Indiana.* 1647. Reprint, Amberes: Henrico y Cornelio Verdussen, 1703.

Suárez, Francisco. *Opera omni.* 16th century. Edited by Carolo Berton. Reprint, Paris, 1859.

Sylvestre, Don Manuel. *Librería de jueces, ultilísima, y universal para toda clase de personas.* Madrid: Imprenta de la Viuda de Eliseo Sánchez, 1765.

Terralla y Landa, Esteban. *Lima por dentro y fuera.* 1790. Edited by Alan Soons. Exeter: University of Exeter, 1978.

Unánue, José Hípolito. *Actuaciones literarias de la vacuna en la Real Universidad de San Marcos de Lima.* Lima: Casa de Niños Huérfanos, 1807.

——. *Observaciones sobre el clima de la ciudad de Lima, y sus influencias en los seres organizados, en especial el hombre.* Lima: Imprenta Real de los Niños Huérfanos, 1806.

Uztáriz, Jerónimo de. *The Theory and Practice of Commerce and Maritime Affairs.* 2 vols. 1724. London: John and James Rippington, 1751.

Valero, Juan Bernardo. "Relación del exemplar castigo que acaba de executarse en esta Ciudad de los Reyes en una Quadrilla de Ladrones el día de 13 de agosto de este año

de 1772 de órden del Exmo. Señor Virey D. Manuel de Amat y Juniet." John Carter
Brown Library, Brown University. D 772 v165r.

Viscardo y Guzmán, Juan Pablo. *Letter to the Spanish Americans.* 1810. Edited by D. A.
Brading. Facsimile reprint. Providence: John Carter Brown Library, 2002.

Vives, Juan Luis. *Instrucción de la mujer cristiana.* 1523. Salamanca: Universidad Pontificia
de Salamanca, 1995.

SECONDARY WORKS

Aguirre, Carlos. *Agentes de su propia libertad: Los esclavos de Lima y la desintegración de la
esclavitud, 1821–1854.* Lima: Pontificia Universidad Católica del Perú, 1993.

——. "The Lima Penitentiary and the Modernization of Criminal Justice in Nineteenth-
Century Peru." In *The Birth of the Penitentiary in Latin America: Essays on
Criminology, Prison Reform, and Social Control, 1830–1940,* edited by Carlos Aguirre
and Ricardo Salvatore, 44–77. Austin: University of Texas Press, 1996.

Alarcón, Walter. *Ser niño: Una nueva mirada de la infancia en el Perú.* Lima: Instituto de
Estudios Peruanos/UNICEF, 1994.

Amussen, Susan Dwyer. *An Ordered Society: Gender and Class in Early Modern England.*
New York: Columbia University Press, 1988.

Anderson, Benedict. *Imagined Communities: Reflections on the Origins and Spread of
Nationalism.* 1983. Reprint, New York: Verso, 1991.

Andrés-Gallego, José. *Historia general de la gente poco importante (América y Europa hacía
1789).* Madrid: Gredos, 1991.

Anna, Timothy. "Spain and the Breakdown of the Imperial Ethos: The Problem of
Equality." *Hispanic American Historical Review* 62, no. 2 (1982): 254–72.

Arco, Ricardo del. "Una notable institución social: El padre de huérfanos." In *Estudios de
historia social de España.* Vol. 3. Madrid: Consejo Superior de Investigaciones
Científicas, 1955.

Ariès, Philippe. *Centuries of Childhood: The Social History of Family Life.* Translated by
Robert Baldick. New York: Vintage, 1962.

Arrom, Silvia Marina. *Containing the Poor: The Mexico City Poor House, 1774–1871.*
Durham: Duke University Press, 2001.

——. *The Women of Mexico City, 1790–1857.* Stanford: Stanford University Press, 1985.

Avila Espinosa, Felipe Arturo. "Los niños abandonados a la Casa de Niños Expósitos,
1767–1821." In *La familia en el mundo iberoaméricano,* edited by Pilar Gonzablo
Aizpuru and Cecilia Rabell, 265–311. Mexico City: Instituto de Investigaciones
Sociales, Universidad Nacional Autónoma de México, 1994.

Badinter, Elisabeth. *Mother Love, Myth and Reality: Motherhood in Modern History.* New
York: Macmillan, 1981.

Barreda Laos, Felipe. *Vida intellectual del virreinato del Perú.* Buenos Aires: Talleres
gráficos Argentinos L. J. Rosso, 1937.

Batllori, Miguel, ed. *El abate Viscardo: Historia y mito de la intervención de los jesuítas en la
independencia de Hispanoamérica.* Caracas: Instituto Panamericano de Geografía e
Historia, 1953.

Beik, William. *Absolutism and Society in Seventeenth-Century France: State Power and Provincial Aristocracy in Languedoc*. Cambridge: Cambridge University Press, 1985.

Bennett, Herman L. *Africans in Colonial Mexico: Absolutism, Christianity, and Afro-Creole Consciousness, 1570–1640*. Bloomington: Indiana University Press, 2003.

Bennett, Judith. "Feminism and History." *Gender and History* 1, no. 2 (Autumn 1989): 251–72.

——. "Women's History: A Study in Continuity and Change." *Women's History Review* 2, no. 2 (1993): 173–82.

Bennett, Ralph, ed. *Settlements in the Americas: Cross Cultural Perspectives*. Newark: University of Delaware Press, 1993.

Bermúdez, Agustín. "La abogacia de pobres en Indias." *Anuario de Historia del Derecho Español* 50 (1980): 1039–54.

Besse, Susan K. *Restructuring Patriarchy: The Modernization of Gender Inequality in Brazil, 1914–1940*. Chapel Hill: University of North Carolina Press, 1996.

Blanchard, Peter. *Slavery and Abolition in Early Republican Peru*. Wilmington, Del.: Scholarly Resources, 1992.

Blum, Ann Shelby. "Children without Parents: Law, Charity, and Social Practice, Mexico City, 1867–1940." Ph.D. diss., University of California, Berkeley, 1998.

——. "Public Welfare and Child Circulation, Mexico City." *Journal of Family History* 23, no. 3 (1998): 240–71.

Bolton, Ralph, and Enrique Meyer, eds. *Andean Kinship and Marriage*. Washington, D.C.: American Anthropological Association, 1977.

Bolufer Peruga, Mónica, and Isabel Morant Duesa. "On Women's Reason, Education, and Love: Women and Men of the Enlightenment in Spain and France." *Gender and History* 10, no. 2 (August 1998): 183–216.

Borah, Woodrow. *Justice by Insurance: The General Indian Court of Colonial Mexico*. Berkeley: University of California Press, 1983.

Boswell, John. *The Kindness of Strangers: The Abandonment of Children in Western Europe from Late Antiquity to the Renaissance*. 1988. Reprint, Chicago: University of Chicago Press, 1998.

Bowser, Frederick. *The African Slave in Colonial Peru, 1524–1650*. Stanford: Stanford University Press, 1974.

Boyer, Richard. *Lives of the Bigamists: Marriage, Family, and Community in Colonial Mexico*. Albuquerque: University of New Mexico Press, 1995.

——. "Women, *La Mala Vida*, and the Politics of Marriage." In *Sexuality and Marriage in Colonial Latin America*, edited by Asunción Lavrin, 252–86. Lincoln: University of Nebraska Press, 1989.

Brading, David. "Bourbon Spain and Its American Empire." In *Colonial Latin America*. Vol. 1 of *The Cambridge History of Latin America*, edited by Leslie Bethell, 112–62. Cambridge: Cambridge University Press, 1987.

——. *The First America: The Spanish Monarchy, Creole Patriots, and the Liberal State*. New York: Cambridge University Press, 1991.

Bran-Shute, Rosemary. "Slave Manumission in Suriname, 1760–1828." *Slavery and Abolition* 10, no. 3 (1989): 40–63.

Brena Sesma, Ingrid. *Intervención del estado en la tutela de menores*. Mexico: Universidad Autónomo de México, 1994.

Bromley, Juan, and José Barbagelata. *Evolución de la ciudad de Lima*. Lima: Consejo Provincial de Lima, 1945.

Brown, James Victor. *The Invalidating Effects of Force, Fear, and Fraud on the Canonical Noviciate*. Catholic University of America Canon Law Series, no. 331. Washington D.C.: Catholic University of America Press, 1951.

Bruckener, W. W. *A Manual of Roman Private Law*. Cambridge: Cambridge University Press, 1939.

Burke, Peter. "The New History: Its Past and Future." In *New Perspectives on Historical Writing*, edited by Peter Burke, 1–24. 1992. Reprint, University Park: Pennsylvania State University Press, 2001.

Burkholder, Mark A. *Politics of a Colonial Career: José Baquíjano and the Audiencia of Lima*. 1980. Reprint, Wilmington, Del.: Scholarly Resources, 1990.

Burkholder, Mark, and D. S. Chandler. *From Impotence to Authority: The Spanish Crown and the American Audiencias, 1687–1808*. Columbia: University of Missouri Press, 1977.

Burns, Kathryn. *Colonial Habits: Convents and the Spiritual Economy of Cuzco, Peru*. Durham: Duke University Press, 1999.

Burrows, Edwin, and Michael Wallace. "The American Revolution: The Ideology and Psychology of National Liberation." In *Perspectives in American History*, edited by Donald Fleming and Bernard Bailyn, 4:167–302. Cambridge, Mass.: Charles Warren Center for Studies in American History, Harvard University Press, 1972.

Cahill, David. "Colour by Numbers: Racial and Ethnic Categories in the Viceroyalty of Peru, 1532–1824." *Journal of Latin American Studies* 26, no. 2 (May 1994): 325–47.

Cancian, Francesca M., Luis Wolf Goodman, and Peter H. Smith. "Introduction." *Journal of Family History* 3, no. 4 (1978): 314–22.

Cañizares-Esguerra, Jorge. *How to Write the History of the New World: Histories, Epistemologies, and Identities in the Eighteenth-Century Atlantic World*. Stanford: Stanford University Press, 2001.

Canning, Kathleen. "Feminist History after the Linguistic Turn: Historicizing Discourse and Experience." *Signs* 19, no. 2 (1994): 368–404.

Cárdenas Ayaipoma, Mario. "El Colegio de Caciques y el sometimiento ideológico de los residuos de la nobleza aborigen." *Revista del Archivo General de la Nación* 4, no. 5 (1975–76): 5–24.

Carrera Panchón, Antonio. *El problema del niño expósito en la España ilustrada*. Salamanca: Universidad de Salamanca, 1977.

Carton, Benedict. *Blood from Your Children: The Colonial Origins of Generational Conflict in South Africa*. Charlottesville: University of Virginia Press, 2000.

Casalino Sens, Carlota. "Higiene pública y piedad ilustrada: La cultura de muerte bajo los borbones." In *El Perú en el siglo XVIII: La era borbónica*, edited by Scarlett O'Phelan Godoy, 325–44. Lima: Pontificia Universidad Católica del Perú/Instituto Riva Agüero, 1999.

Castañeda, Carmen. "La memoria y las niñas violadas." In *La memoria y el olvido:*

Segundo Simposio de Historia de las Mentalidades, 107–15. Mexico City: Universidad Nacional Autónoma de México, 1983.

——. *Violación, estupro y sexualidad: Nueva Galicia, 1790–1821.* Guadalajara: Editorial Hexágono, 1989.

Chambers, Sarah C. *From Subjects to Citizens: Honor, Gender, and Politics in Arequipa, Peru, 1780–1854.* University Park: Pennsylvania State University Press, 1999.

Chandler, David. "Family Bonds and the Bondsman: The Slave Family in Colonial Columbia." *Latin American Research Review* 16, no. 2 (1981): 107–31.

Charney, Paul. "El indio urbano: Un análisis económico y social de la población india de Lima en 1613." *Revista Histórica* 12, no. 1 (1988): 5–33.

——. "Negotiating Roots: Indian Migrants in the Lima Valley during the Colonial Period." *Colonial Latin American Historical Review* 5, no. 1 (Winter 1995): 1–20.

Chatam, Josiah G. *Force and Fear as Invalidating Marriage: The Element of Injustice.* Catholic University Canon Law Series, no. 310. Washington, D.C.: Catholic University of America, 1950.

Chaves, María Eugenia. "Slave Women's Strategies for Freedom." In *Hidden Histories of Gender and the State in Latin America,* edited by Elizabeth Dore and Maxine Molyneux, 108–26. Durham: Duke University Press, 2000.

Cicerchia, Hector Ricardo. "Minors, Gender, and the Family: The Discourses in the Court System of Traditional Buenos Aires." *History of the Family: An International Quarterly* 2, no. 3 (1997): 331–47.

——. "*La vida maridable*: Ordinary Family, Buenos Aires, 1776–1850." Ph.D. diss., Columbia University, 1995.

Clément, Jean-Pierre. "Les enfants exposés de Lima á la fin du XVIIe siècle." In *L'enfant et l'adolescent dans les pays andins,* 167–97. Grenoble: CERPA, 1983.

——. *El Mercurio Peruano, 1790–1795.* 2 vols. Madrid: Iberoamericano, 1997.

Clendinnen, Inga. "Disciplining the Indians: Franciscan Ideology and Missionary Violence in Sixteenth-Century Yucatán." *Past and Present* 94 (February 1982): 27–48.

Coatsworth, John. "The Limits of Colonial Absolutism: The State in Eighteenth-Century Mexico." In *Essays in the Political, Economic, and Social History of Latin America,* edited by Karen Spalding. Newark: University of Delaware Latin American Studies Program, 1983.

Cope, R. Douglas. *The Limits of Racial Domination: Plebeian Society in Colonial Mexico City, 1660–1720.* Madison: University of Wisconsin Press, 1994.

Courturier, Edith. "Women and the Family in Eighteenth-Century Mexico: Law and Practice." *Journal of Family History* 10, no. 3 (1985): 293–304.

Cox, Pamela, and Heather Shore, eds. *Becoming Delinquent: British and European Youth, 1650–1950.* Burlington, Vt.: Ashgate, 2002.

Cox, Roger. *Shaping Childhood: Themes of Uncertainty in the History of Adult-Child Relationships.* New York: Routledge, 1996.

Cramaussel, Chantal. "Ilegítimos y abandonados en la frontera norte de la Nueva España: Parral y San Bartolomé en el siglo XVII." *Colonial Latin American Historical Review* 4, no. 4 (Fall 1995): 405–38.

Crevea y Altamira, Rafael. *Diccionario castellano de palabras jurídicas y técnicas tomadas de la legislación Indiana.* Mexico City: Instituto Panamericano de Geografía e Historia, 1951.

Cunningham, Hugh. *Children and Childhood in Western Society since 1550.* New York: Longman, 1995.

———. "Histories of Childhood." *American Historical Review* 103, no. 4 (October 1998): 1195–1208.

Curtin, Philip D., and Paul E. Lovejoy, eds. *Africans in Bondage: Studies in Slavery and the Slave Trade. Essays in Honor of Philip D. Curtin on the Occasion of the Twenty-Fifth Anniversary of African Studies at the University of Wisconsin.* Madison: African Studies Program, University of Wisconsin-Madison, 1986.

Cutter, Charles. *The Legal Culture of Northern New Spain, 1700–1810.* Albuquerque: University of New Mexico Press, 1995.

———. "The Legal System as a Touchstone of Identity in Colonial New Mexico." In *The Collective and the Public in Latin America: Cultural Identities and Political Order,* edited by Luis Roniger and Tamar Herzog, 57–70. Brighton: Sussex Academic Press, 2000.

———. *The Protector de Indios in Colonial New Mexico, 1651–1821.* Albuquerque: University of New Mexico Press, 1986.

Davis, David Brion. *The Problem of Slavery in the Age of Revolution, 1770–1823.* 1975. Reprint, New York: Oxford University Press, 1999.

Dean, Carolyn. "Sketches of Childhood: Children in Colonial Andean Art and Society." In *Minor Omissions: Children in Latin American History and Society,* edited by Tobias Hecht, 21–51. Madison: University of Wisconsin Press, 2002.

Deans-Smith, Susan. "The Working Poor and the Eighteenth-Century Colonial State: Gender, Public Order, and Work Discipline." In *Rituals of Rule, Rituals of Resistance: Public Celebrations and Popular Culture in Mexico,* edited by William Beezley and Cheryl English Martin, 47–75. Wilmington, Del.: Scholarly Resources, 1994.

De Mause, Lloyd. *The History of Childhood.* New York: Harper and Row, 1974.

Desan, Suzanne. *The Family on Trial in Revolutionary France.* Berkeley: University of California Press, 2004.

———. "What's after Political Culture? Recent French Revolutionary Historiography." *French Historical Studies* 23, no. 1 (Winter 2000): 163–96.

Díaz, Arlene Julia. *Female Citizens, Patriarchs, and the Law in Venezuela, 1786–1904.* Lincoln: University of Nebraska Press, 2004.

Díaz, María Elena. *The Virgin, the King, and the Royal Slaves of El Cobre: Negotiating Freedom in Colonial Cuba, 1670–1780.* Stanford: Stanford University Press, 2000.

Domínguez Ortiz, Antonio. *Carlos III y la España de la ilustración.* Madrid: Alianza Editorial, 1988.

———. *Sociedad y Estado en el siglo XVIII español.* 1978. Reprint, Barcelona: Editorial Ariel, 1990.

Dore, Elizabeth. "One Step Forward, Two Steps Back: Gender and the State in the Long Nineteenth Century." In *Hidden Histories of Gender and the State in Latin*

America, edited by Elizabeth Dore and Maxine Molyneux, 3–32. Durham: Duke University Press, 2000.

Dore, Elizabeth, and Maxine Molyneux, eds. *Hidden Histories of Gender and the State in Latin America*. Durham: Duke University Press, 2000.

Dougnac Rodríguez, Antonio. "Estatuto del huérfano en el derecho indiano." *Anuario Histórico Jurídico Ecuatoriano* 6 (1980): 16–56.

Dubois, Laurent. *A Colony of Citizens: Revolution and Slave Emancipation in the French Caribbean, 1787–1804*. Chapel Hill: University of North Carolina Press, 2004.

Dueñas Vargas, Guiomar. *Los hijos del pecado: Ilegitimidad y vida familiar en la Santafé de Bogotá colonial*. Bogotá: Universidad Nacional de Colombia, 1997.

Durán Montero, María Antonia. *Lima en el siglo XVII: Arquitectura, urbanismo y vida cotidiana*. Sevilla: Diputación Provincial de Sevilla, 1994.

Earle, Rebecca. "Rape and the Anxious Republic: Revolutionary Columbia, 1810–15." In *Hidden Histories of Gender and the State in Latin America*, edited by Elizabeth Dore and Maxine Molyneux, 127–46. Durham: Duke University Press, 2000.

Eley, Geoff, and Ronald Grigor Suny, eds. *Becoming National: A Reader*. New York: Oxford University Press, 1996.

Elias, Norbert. *The Civilizing Process: The History of Manners*. Translated by Edmund Jephcott. 1939. Reprint, New York: Urizen Books, 1978.

Elliot, J. H. *Spain and Its World, 1500–1700*. New Haven: Yale University, 1989.

Equipo Madrid de Estudios Históricos, ed. *Carlos III, Madrid y la ilustración*. Madrid: Siglo XXI, 1988.

Estensorro Fuchs, Carlos. "La plebe ilustrada: El pueblo en las fronteras de la razón." In *Entre la retórica y la insurgencia: Las ideas y los movimientos en los Andes, Siglo XVIII*, edited by Charles Walker, 33–66. Cuzco: CERA Bartolomé de las Casas, 1996.

Etienne, Mona, and Eleanor Leacock. *Women and Colonization: Anthropological Perspectives*. New York: Praeger, 1980.

Eugía Ruiz, Constancio. "A Staggering Blow to Education." In *The Expulsion of the Jesuits*, edited by Magnus Mörner, 175–180. New York: Knopf, 1965.

Eze, Emmanuel Chaukwudi. *Race and the Enlightenment: A Reader*. Cambridge: Blackwell, 1997.

Fildes, Valerie. *Wet Nursing: A History from Antiquity to the Present*. New York: Basil Blackwell, 1988.

Fischer, Sybille. *Modernity Disavowed: Haiti and the Cultures of Slavery in the Age of Revolution*. Durham: Duke University Press, 2004.

Fisher, John. *Government and Society in Colonial Peru: The Intendant System, 1782–1810*. London: University of London Press, 1958.

———. *Bourbon Peru, 1750–1824*. Latin American Studies 4. Liverpool: University of Liverpool Press, 2003.

Fisher, John R., Allan J. Kuethe, and Anthony McFarlane, eds. *Reform and Insurrection in Bourbon New Grenada and Peru*. Baton Rouge: Louisiana State University Press, 1990.

Fliegelman, Jay. *Prodigals and Pilgrims: The American Revolution against Patriarchal Authority, 1750–1800*. New York: Cambridge University Press, 1982.

Flores Galindo, Alberto. *La ciudad sumergida: Aristocracia y plebe en Lima, 1760–1830*. 1988. Reprint, Lima: Ediciones Horizonte, 1991.

Flores Galindo, Alberto, and Magdalena Chocano. "Los cargos del sacramento." *Revista andina* 2, no. 2 (December 1984): 403–23.

Foucault, Michel. *Discipline and Punish: The Birth of the Prison*. New York: Vintage, 1979.

——. *The History of Sexuality*. Vol. 1, *An Introduction*. 1979. Reprint, New York: Vintage, 1990.

——. "What Is Enlightenment?" In *The Foucault Reader*, edited by Paul Rabinowitz, 32–50. New York: Pantheon, 1984.

Fox-Genovese, Elizabeth. *Within the Plantation Household: Black and White Women of the Old South*. Chapel Hill: University of North Carolina Press, 1988.

Fuchs, Rachel G. *Abandoned Children: Foundlings and Child Welfare in Nineteenth-Century France*. Albany: State University of New York Press, 1984.

——. *Poor and Pregnant in Paris: Strategies for Survival in the Nineteenth Century*. New Brunswick: Rutgers University Press, 1992.

Galdo Gutiérrez, Virgilio. *Educación de los curacas: Una forma de dominación colonial*. Ayacucho: Universidad Nacional de San Cristóbal de Huamanga, 1982.

Gauderman, Kimberly. *Women's Lives in Colonial Quito: Gender, Law, and Economy in Spanish America*. Austin: University of Texas Press, 2003.

Genovese, Eugene. *From Rebellion to Revolution: Afro-American Slave Revolts in the Making of the Modern World*. Baton Rouge: University of Louisiana Press, 1979.

——. *Roll, Jordan, Roll: The World the Slaves Made*. 1972. Reprint, New York: Vintage, 1974.

Gerbi, Antonello. *The Dispute of the New World: The History of a Polemic, 1750–1900*. Translated by Jeremy Moyle. 1955. Reprint, Pittsburgh: University of Pittsburgh Press, 1973.

Ghachem, Malick W. "Montesquieu in the Caribbean: The Colonial Enlightenment between Code Noir and Code Civil." In *Postmodernism and the Enlightenment: New Perspectives in Eighteenth-Century French Intellectual History*, edited by Daniel Gordon, 7–30. New York: Routledge, 2001.

Gibson, Charles. *The Aztecs under Spanish Rule: A History of Indians in the Valley of Mexico*. Stanford: University of California Press, 1964.

Goldwert, Marvin. "The Search for the Lost Father-Figure in Spanish American History: A Freudian View." *Americas* 34 (April 1978): 185–87.

Gonzablo Aizpuru, Pilar, and Cecilia Rabell, eds. *La familia en el mundo iberoaméricano*. Mexico City: Instituto de Investigaciones Sociales, Universidad Nacional Autónoma de México, 1994.

González, Ondina E. "Down and Out in Havana: Foundlings in Eighteenth-Century Cuba." In *Minor Omissions: Children in Latin American History and Society*, edited by Tobias Hecht, 102–13. Madison: University of Wisconsin Press, 2002.

González del Riego E., Delfina. "Fragmentos de la vida cotidiana a través de los procesos de divorcio: La sociedad colonial limeña en el siglo XVI." *Histórica* 14, no. 2 (1995): 197–217.

Goodman, Dena. *The Republic of Letters: A Cultural History of the French Enlightenment.* Ithaca: Cornell University Press, 1994.

Gordon, Daniel, ed. "Introduction: Postmodernism and the French Enlightenment." In *Postmodernism and the Enlightenment: New Perspectives in Eighteenth-Century French Intellectual History*, edited by Daniel Gordon, 1–6. New York: Routledge, 2001.

———. *Postmodernism and the Enlightenment: New Perspectives in Eighteenth-Century French Intellectual History.* New York: Routledge, 2001.

Gordon, Linda. *Heroes of Their Own Lives: The Politics and History of Family Violence, Boston, 1880–1960.* New York: Viking, 1988.

———, ed. *Women, the State, and Welfare.* Madison: University of Wisconsin Press, 1990.

Graham, Richard. *Independence in Latin America: A Comparative Approach.* New York: Knopf, 1972.

Greer Johnson, Julie. *Satire in Colonial Spanish America: Turning the New World Upside Down.* Austin: University of Texas Press, 1993.

Griffin, Charles C. "The Enlightenment and Latin American Independence." In *Latin America and the Enlightenment*, edited by Arthur P. Whitaker, 119–44. 1942. Reprint, Ithaca: Cornell University Press, 1961.

Grover, Antonio Espinoza, "La reforma de la educación superior: El caso del Real Convictorio de San Carlos." In *El Perú en el siglo XVIII: La era borbónica*, edited by Scarlett O'Phelan Godoy, 205–41. Lima: Pontificia Universidad Católica del Perú/Instituto de Riva Agüero, 1999.

Guerra, François-Xavier. "Forms of Communication, Political Spaces, and Cultural Identities in the Creation of Spanish American Nations." In *Beyond Imagined Communities: Reading and Writing the Nation in Nineteenth-Century Latin America*, edited by Sara Castro-Klarén and John Charles Chasteen, 3–32. Baltimore: Johns Hopkins University Press, 2003.

Gutiérrez, Ramón. "Honor, Ideology, Marriage Negotiation, and Class-Gender Domination in New Mexico, 1690–1846." *Latin American Perspectives* 12, no. 1 (1985): 81–104.

———. *When Jesus Came the Corn Mothers Went Away.* Albuquerque: University of New Mexico Press, 1991.

Guy, Donna J. "Future Directions in Latin American Gender History." *Americas* 51, no. 1 (July 1994): 1–9.

———. "Parents before the Tribunals: The Legal Construction of Patriarchy in Argentina." In *Hidden Histories of Gender and the State in Latin America*, edited by Elizabeth Dore and Maxine Molyneux, 172–93. Durham: Duke University Press, 2000.

Haitin, Marcel Manuel. "Late Colonial Lima: Economy and Society in an Era of Reform and Revolution." Ph.D. diss., University of California, Berkeley, 1980.

Hardwick, Julie. *The Practice of Patriarchy: Gender and the Politics of Household Governance in Early Modern France.* University Park: University of Pennsylvania Press, 1998.

Harth-Terré, Emilio, and Alberto Márquez Abanto. *Historia de la casa urbana virreinal de Lima.* Lima: Librería Gil, 1962.

Hecht, Tobias, ed. *Minor Omissions: Children in Latin American History and Society.* Madison: University of Wisconsin Press, 2002.

Herrup, Cynthia B. *A House in Gross Disorder: Sex, Law, and the Second Earl of Castlehaven.* New York: Oxford University Press, 1999.

Herzog, Tamar. *La administración como un fenómeno social: La justicia penal de la ciudad de Quito, 1650–1750.* Madrid: Centro de Estudios Constitucionales, 1995.

Hiner, N. Ray, and Joseph M. Hawes. "Standing on Common Ground: Reflections on the History of Children and Childhood." In *Children in Historical and Comparative Perspective: An International Handbook and Research Guide,* edited by N. Ray Hiner and Joseph M. Hawes, 1–9. New York: Greenwood Press, 1991.

——, eds. *Children in Historical and Comparative Perspective: An International Handbook and Research Guide.* New York: Greenwood Press, 1991.

Hoff, Joan. "Gender as a Postmodern Category of Paralysis." *Women's History Review* 3 (1994): 149–68.

Hünefeldt, Christine. *Liberalism in the Bedroom: Quarreling Spouses in Nineteenth-Century Lima.* University Park: Pennsylvania State University Press, 2000.

——. *Paying the Price of Freedom: Family and Labor among Lima's Slaves, 1800–1854.* Los Angeles: University of California Press, 1994.

Hunt, Lynn. *The Family Romance of the French Revolution.* Berkeley: University of California Press, 1992.

Ingersoll, Thomas. "Free Blacks in a Slave Society: New Orleans, 1718–1812." *William and Mary Quarterly* 48, no. 2 (1991): 173–200.

Johns, Alessa. "Reproducing Utopia: Jeanne-Marie Leprince de Beaumont's *The New Clarissa.*" In *Postmodernism and the Enlightenment: New Perspectives in Eighteenth-Century French Intellectual History,* edited by Daniel Gordon, 147–60. New York: Routledge, 2001.

Johnson, John J. *Latin America in Caricature.* Austin: University of Texas Press, 1980.

Johnson, Lyman. "Manumission in Colonial Buenos Aires." *Hispanic American Historical Review* 59, no. 2 (1979): 258–79.

——. "Dangerous Words, Provocative Gestures, and Violent Acts." In *The Faces of Honor: Sex, Shame, and Violence in Colonial Latin America,* edited by Lyman Johnson and Sonya Lipsett-Rivera, 127–51. Albuquerque: University of New Mexico Press, 1998.

Johnson, Lyman, and Sonya Lipsett-Rivera, eds. *The Faces of Honor: Sex, Shame, and Violence in Colonial Latin America.* Albuquerque: University of New Mexico Press, 1998.

Kagan, Richard L. *Lawsuits and Litigants in Castile, 1500–1700.* Chapel Hill: University of North Carolina Press, 1981.

Karasch, Mary. "Anastácia and the Slave Women of Rio de Janeiro." In *Africans in Bondage: Studies in Slavery and the Slave Trade. Essays in Honor of Philip D. Curtin on the Occasion of the Twenty-Fifth Anniversary of African Studies at the University of Wisconsin,* edited by Philip D. Curtin and Paul E. Lovejoy, 79–105. Madison: African Studies Program, University of Wisconsin-Madison, 1986.

Kerber, Linda K. *Women of the Republic: Intellect and Ideology in Revolutionary America.* New York: Norton, 1980.

Kiernan, V. G. *The Lords of Human Kind: European Attitudes towards the Outside World in the Imperial Age*. Harmondsworth: Penguin, 1972.

King, Peter. "The Rise of Juvenile Delinquency in England, 1780–1840: Changing Patterns of Perception and Prosecution." *Past and Present* 160 (August 1988): 116–67.

Klarén, Peter F. *Peru: Society and Nationhood in the Andes*. New York: Oxford University Press, 2000.

Klein, Herbert. *African Slavery in Latin America and the Caribbean*. New York: Oxford University Press, 1986.

Kobayashi, José María. *Educación como conquista: Empresa franciscana en México*. Mexico City: El Colegio de México, 1974.

Korthe, Eugene, and Della Flusche. "Dowry and Inheritance in Colonial Spanish America." *Americas* 43, no. 4 (April 1987): 395–410.

Kubler, George, and Martín Soria. *Art and Architecture of Spain and Portugal and the American Dominions, 1500–1800*. Pelican History of Art. Baltimore: Pelican, 1959.

Kuznesof, Elizabeth Anne. "The Puzzling Contradictions of Child Labor, Unemployment, and Education in Brazil." *Journal of Family History* 23, no. 3 (1998): 225–40.

——. "The Role of the Female-Headed Household in Brazilian Modernization: São Paulo, 1765–1836." *Journal of Social History* 13 (Summer 1980): 589–613.

——. "Sexual Politics and Bastard-Bearing in Nineteenth-Century Brazil: A Question of Culture or Power?" *Journal of Family History* 16, no. 3 (1991): 241–60.

Landes, Joan B. *Women and the Public Sphere in the Age of the French Revolution*. Ithaca: Cornell University Press, 1988.

Lane, Kris. "Captivity and Redemption: Aspects of Slave Life in Early Colonial Quito and Popayán." *Americas*, 57, no. 2 (October 2000): 225–46.

Lanning, John Tate. "The Reception of the Enlightenment in Latin America." In *Latin America and the Enlightenment*, edited by Arthur P. Whitaker, 71–94. 1942. Reprint, Ithaca: Cornell University Press, 1961.

Laslett, Peter. "Introduction." In *Household and Family in Past Time*, edited by Peter Laslett and Richard Wall, 1–89. London: Cambridge University Press, 1972.

Lauderdale Graham, Sandra. "Honor among Slaves." In *The Faces of Honor: Sex, Shame, and Violence in Colonial Latin America*, edited by Lyman Johnson and Sonya Lipsett-Rivera, 201–28. Albuquerque: University of New Mexico Press, 1998.

——. *House and Street: The Domestic World of Servants and Masters in Nineteenth-Century Rio de Janeiro*. Cambridge: Cambridge University Press, 1988.

Lavallé, Bernard. *Amor y opresión en los Andes coloniales*. Lima: Instituto de Estudios Peruanos, 1999.

——. "La population conventuelle de Lima (XVIè et XVIIè siecles): Approches et problemes." In *Actes de 2è Colleque: Centre d'etudes et de rechereches sur le Péroue et les pays andins*, 167–95. Grenoble: Université de Langues et Lettres de Grenoble, 1975.

——. *Las promesas ambiguas: Criolloismo colonial en los Andes*. Lima: Instituto Riva Agüero, 1983.

Lavrin, Asunción. "Ecclesiastical Reform of Nunneries in New Spain in the Eighteenth Century." *Americas* 22 (October 1965): 182–203.

———. "*Lo femenino*: Women in Colonial Historical Sources." In *Coded Encounters: Writing, Gender, and Ethnicity in Colonial Latin America*, edited by Francisco Javier Cevallos-Candau, Jeffrey A. Cole, Nina M. Scott, and Nicomedes Suarez-Arauz, 153–76. Amherst: University of Massachusetts Press, 1994.

———. "Mexico." In *Children in Historical and Comparative Perspective: An International Handbook and Research Guide*, edited by N. Ray Hiner and Joseph M. Hawes, 421–46. New York: Greenwood Press, 1991.

———. "Sexuality in Colonial Mexico." In *Sexuality and Marriage in Colonial Latin America*, edited by Asunción Lavrin, 47–94. Lincoln: University of Nebraska Press, 1989.

———, ed. *Sexuality and Marriage in Colonial Latin America*. Lincoln: University of Nebraska Press, 1989.

Lewin, Linda. *Surprise Heirs I: Illegitimacy, Patrimonial Right, and Legal Nationalism in Luso-Brazilian Inheritance, 1750–1821*. Stanford: Stanford University Press, 2003.

———. *Surprise Heirs II: Illegitimacy, Inheritance Rights, and Public Power in the Formation of Imperial Brazil, 1822–1889*. Stanford: Stanford University Press, 2003.

Lewis, Laura A. *Hall of Mirrors: Power, Witchcraft, and Caste in Colonial Mexico*. Durham: Duke University Press, 2004.

———. "The 'Weakness' of Women and the Feminization of the Indian in Colonial Mexico." *Colonial Latin American Review* 5, no. 1 (1996): 73–95.

Lipsett-Rivera, Sonya. "The Intersection of Rape and Marriage in Late-Colonial and Early-National Mexico." *Colonial Latin American Historical Review* 6, no. 4 (Fall 1997): 559–90.

———. "Marriage and Family Relations in Mexico during the Transition from Colony to Republic." In *State and Society in Spanish America during the Age of Revolution*, edited by Victor Uribe-Uran, 121–48. Wilmington, Del.: Scholarly Resources, 2001.

———. "A Slap in the Face of Honor: Social Transgressions and Women in Late-Colonial Mexico." In *The Faces of Honor: Sex, Shame, and Violence in Colonial Latin America*, edited by Lyman Johnson and Sonya Lipsett-Rivera, 167–200. Albuquerque: University of New Mexico Press, 1998.

Lockhart, James, and Stuart B. Schwartz. *Early Latin America: A History of Colonial Spanish America and Brazil*. New York: Cambridge University Press, 1983.

Lowry, Lyn Brandon. "Forging an Indian Nation: Urban Indians under Spanish Colonial Control (Lima, Peru, 1535–1765)." Ph.D. diss., University of California, Berkeley, 1991.

Lucena Samoral, Manuel. *Los códigos negros de la América Española*. Alcalá: UNESCO/Universidad de Alcalá, 1996.

Lynch, John. *Bourbon Spain, 1700–1808*. London: Basil Blackwell, 1989.

———. *The Spanish American Revolutions, 1808–1826*. New York: Norton, 1986.

MacCormack, Sabine. *Religion in the Andes: Vision and Imagination in Early Colonial Peru*. Princeton: Princeton University Press, 1991.

Macera D'Ossorio, Pablo. "Noticias sobre la enseñanza elemental en el Perú durante el siglo XVIII." In *Trabajos de Historia*. Vol. 2. Lima: Instituto Nacional de Cultura, 1977.

——. *Trabajos de Historia*. 4 vols. Lima: Instituto Nacional de Cultura, 1977.

Mackay, Ruth. *The Limits of Royal Authority: Resistance in Seventeenth-Century Castile*. Cambridge: Cambridge University Press, 1999.

MacLachlan, Colin M. *Criminal Justice in Eighteenth-Century Mexico: A Study of the Tribunal of the Acordada*. Berkeley: University of California Press, 1974.

——. *Spain's Empire in the New World*. Berkeley: University of California Press, 1988.

Mallon, Florencia. *Peasant and Nation: The Making of Postcolonial Mexico and Peru*. Los Angeles: University of California Press, 1995.

Malvido, Elsa. "El abandono de los hijos: Una forma de control del tamaño de la familia y del trabajo indígena. Tula (1683–1730)." *Historia Méxicana* 29, no. 4 (1980): 521–61.

Mannarelli, María Emma. *Pecados públicos: La ilegitimidad en Lima, siglo XVII*. Lima: Ediciones Flora Tristán, 1994.

Martín, Luis. *Daughters of the Conquistadores: Women of the Viceroyalty of Peru*. Albuquerque: University of New Mexico Press, 1983.

Martín, Luis, and JoAnn G. Pettus. *Scholars and Schools of Colonial Peru*. Dallas: Southern Methodist University School of Continuing Education, 1973.

Martínez, Maria Elena. "Space, Order, and Group Identity in a Spanish Colonial Town: Puebla de los Angeles." In *The Collective and the Public in Latin America: Cultural Identities and Political Order*, edited by Luis Roniger and Tamar Herzog, 13–36. Brighton: Sussex Academic Press, 2000.

Martínez-Alier (Stolcke), Verena. *Marriage, Class and Colour in Nineteenth-Century Cuba: A Study of Racial Attitudes and Sexual Values in a Slave Society*. Cambridge: Cambridge University Press, 1974.

Mascareñas, Carlos, ed. *Nueva enciclopedia jurídica*. Barcelona: Editorial Francisco Seix, 1975.

Masur, Gerhard. *Simón Bolívar*. Albuquerque: University of New Mexico Press, 1948.

McCaa, Robert. "Gustos de los padres, inclinaciones de los novios y reglas de una feria nupcial colonial: Parral, 1770–1814." *Historia Mexicana* 40, no. 4 (1991): 579–614.

McClintock, Anne. "'No Longer in a Future Heaven': Nationalism, Gender, and Race." In *Becoming National: A Reader*, edited by Geoff Eley and Ronald Grigor Suny, 260–83. New York: Oxford University Press, 1996.

Mehta, Uday S. *Liberalism and Empire: A Study in Nineteenth-Century Political Thought*. Chicago: University of Chicago Press, 1999.

Melzer, Sara E., and Leslie W. Rabine, eds. *Rebel Daughters: Women and the French Revolution*. New York: Oxford University Press, 1992.

Mendiburu, Manuel de. *Diccionario Histórico-Biográfico del Perú*. 8 vols. Lima: J. Francisco Solis, 1874–90.

Mendieta Ocampo, Ilder. *Hospitales de Lima Colonial, Siglos XVII–XIX*. Lima: Universidad Nacional Mayor de San Marcos, Seminario de Historia Rural Andina, 1990.

Merchán Alvarez, Antonio. *La tutela de los menores en Castilla hasta fines del siglo XV*. Seville: Universidad de Sevilla, 1976.

Merrick, Jeffrey. "Fathers and Kings: Patriarchalism and Absolutism in Eighteenth-Century French Politics." *Studies on Voltaire and the Eighteenth Century* 308 (1993): 281–303.

Metcalf, Alida. *Family and Frontier in Colonial Brazil: Santana de Parnaíba, 1580–1822.* Berkeley: University of California Press, 1992.

Migdal, Joel S., Atul Kohli, and Vivienne Shue, eds. *State Power and Social Forces: Domination and Transformation in the Third World.* New York: Cambridge University Press, 1994.

Milanich, Nara. "Historical Perspectives on Illegitimacy and Illegitimates." In *Minor Omissions: Children in Latin American History and Society*, edited by Tobias Hecht, 72–101. Madison: University of Wisconsin Press, 2002.

Miller, Francesca. *Latin American Women and the Search for Social Justice.* Hanover, N.H.: University Press of New England, 1991.

Miller, Pavla. *Transformations of Patriarchy in the West, 1500–1900.* Bloomington: Indiana University Press, 1998.

Mills, Kenneth. *Idolatry and Its Enemies: Colonial Andean Religion and Extirpation.* Princeton: Princeton University Press, 1997.

Mills, Kenneth, and William B. Taylor, eds. *Colonial Spanish America: A Documentary History.* Wilmington, Del.: Scholarly Resources, 1998.

Milton, Cynthia E. "The Many Meanings of Poverty: Colonial Compacts and Social Assistance in Eighteenth-Century Quito." Ph.D. diss., University of Wisconsin, 2002.

Mirow, M. C. *Latin American Law: A History of Private Law and Institutions in Spanish America.* Austin: University of Texas Press, 2004.

Montrose, Louis. "The Work of Gender in the Discourse of Discovery." In *New World Encounters*, edited by Stephen Greenblatt, 177–217. Amherst: University of Massachusetts Press, 1993.

Moreno, José Luis. "La Casa de Niños Expósitos de Buenos Aires, conflictos institucionales, condiciones de vida y mortalidad de los infantes, 1779–1823." In *La política social antes de la política social (Caridad, beneficenica y polítical social en Buenos Aires, siglos XVII a XX)*, edited by José Luis Moreno, 91–128. Buenos Aires: Trama Editorial, 2000.

———, ed. *La política social antes de la política social (Caridad, beneficenica y polítical social en Buenos Aires, siglos XVII a XX).* Buenos Aires: Trama Editorial, 2000.

Mörner, Magnus. *Estado, razas, y cambio social en la Hispanoamérica colonial.* Mexico City: Setentas, 1970.

———. *Race Mixture in the History of Latin America.* Boston: Little Brown, 1967.

———, ed. *The Expulsion of the Jesuits from Latin America.* New York: Knopf, 1965.

Nader, Helen. *Liberty in Absolutist Spain: The Habsburg Sale of Towns, 1516–1700.* Baltimore: Johns Hopkins University Press, 1990.

Nandy, Ashis. "The Intimate Enemy: Loss and Recovery of Self under Colonialism." In *Exiled at Home.* Delhi: Oxford University Press, 1998.

Nazarri, Muriel. "An Urgent Need to Conceal." In *The Faces of Honor: Sex, Shame, and*

Violence in Colonial Latin America, edited by Lyman Johnson and Sonya Lipsett-Rivera, 103–26. Albuquerque: University of New Mexico Press, 1998.

Nicholas, Barry. *An Introduction to Roman Law.* 1962. Reprint, New York: Oxford University Press, 1975.

Nizza da Silva, María Beatriz. "Divorce in Colonial Brazil: The Case of São Paulo." In *Sexuality and Marriage in Colonial Latin America*, edited by Asunción Lavrin, 313–40. Lincoln: University of Nebraska Press, 1989.

Oakes, James. *The Ruling Race: A History of American Slaveholders.* 1982. Reprint, New York: Norton, 1998.

O'Phelan Godoy, Scarlett. "Algunas reflexiones sobre las Reformas Borbónicas." In *Entre la retórica y la insurgencia: Las ideas y los movimientos en los Andes, Siglo XVIII*, edited by Charles Walker, 309–17. Cuzco: CERA Bartolomé de las Casas, 1996.

———. "Introducción." In *El Perú en el siglo XVIII: La era borbónica*, edited by Scarlett O'Phelan Godoy, 7–11. Lima: Pontificia Universidad Católica del Perú/Instituto Riva Agüero, 1999.

———. *Un siglo de rebeliones andinas anticolonials: Perú y Bolivia, 1700–1783.* Cuzco: Centro Bartolomé de las Casas, 1988.

———, ed. *El Perú en el siglo XVIII: La era borbónica.* Lima: Pontificia Universidad Católica del Perú/Instituto Riva Agüero, 1999.

Ordóñez, Dwight, and María del Pilar Mejía. *El trabajo infantil callejero en Lima: Aproximación descriptiva.* Lima: CEDRO, 1994.

Orloff, Ann. "Gender and the Welfare State." *Annual Review of Sociology* 22 (1996): 51–79.

Ots de Capdequí, José María. *El derecho de familia y el derecho de sucesión en nuestra legislación de Indias.* Madrid: Imprenta Helenica, 1921.

———. *Manual de historia del derecho Español en las Indias y del derecho propiamente Indiano.* Buenos Aires: Editorial Losada, 1945.

Pagden, Anthony. *The Fall of Natural Man: The American Indian and the Origins of Comparative Ethnography.* 1982. Reprint, Cambridge: Cambridge University Press, 1994.

———. *Spanish Imperialism and the Political Imagination.* New Haven: Yale University Press, 1991.

Palma, Ricardo. "El poeta de las adivinanzas." In *Tradiciones Peruanas Completas*, edited by Edith Palma, 711–24. Madrid: Aguilar, 1957.

Pateman, Carole. *The Sexual Contract.* Stanford: Stanford University Press, 1988.

Pérez Cantó, María. *Lima en el siglo XVIII: Estudio socioeconómico.* Madrid: Universidad Autónoma de Madrid, 1985.

Pérez Estévez, Rosa María. *La España de la ilustración.* Madrid: Actas Editoriales, 2002.

Perry, Mary Elizabeth. *Gender and Disorder in Early Modern Seville.* Princeton: Princeton University Press, 1990.

Phelan, John Leddy. *The Millennial Kingdom of the Franciscans in the New World.* 2nd ed., rev. Berkeley: University of California Press, 1970.

——. *The People and the King: The Comunero Revolution in Colombia, 1781.* Madison: University of Wisconsin Press, 1978.

Pitt-Rivers, Julian. "Race, Color, and Class in Central America and the Andes." *Daedalus* 96 (1967): 542–59.

Pollack, Linda. *Forgotten Children: Parent-Child Relationships from 1500–1900.* New York: Cambridge University Press, 1983.

Premo, Bianca. "'Children of the Father King': Youth, Authority, and Legal Minority in Colonial Lima." Ph.D. diss., University of North Carolina, Chapel Hill, 2001.

Proctor, Frank T. "Slavery, Identity, and Culture: An Afro-Mexican Counterpoint, 1640–1763." Ph.D. diss., Emory University, 2003.

Potthast-Jutkeit, Barbara. "The Ass of a Mare and Other Scandals: Marriage and Extramarital Relations in Nineteenth-Century Paraguay." *Journal of Family History* 16, no. 3 (1991): 215–39.

Quiroz, Francisco. *Gremios, raza y libertad de industria.* Lima: Universidad Mayor Nacional de San Marcos, 1995.

Rama, Angel. *The Lettered City.* Translated by John C. Chasteen. Durham: Duke University Press, 1996.

Ramón, Gabriel. "Urbe y orden: Evidencias del reformismo borbónico en el tejido de Lima." In *El Perú en el siglo XVIII: La era borbónica,* edited by Scarlett O'Phelan Godoy, 295–324. Lima: Pontificia Universidad Católica del Perú/Instituto de Riva Agüero, 1999.

Ramos, Donald. "Single and Married Women in Vila Rica, Brazil, 1754–1838." *Journal of Family History* 16, no. 3 (1991): 261–82.

Reyerson, Kathryn L. "The Adolescent Apprentice/Worker in Medieval Montepellier." *Journal of Family History* 17, no. 4 (1992): 353–70.

Reyes Leoz, José Luis de los. "Carlos III, padre de Vasallos." In *Carlos III, Madrid y la ilustración,* edited by Equipo Madrid, 355–77. Madrid: Siglo XXI, 1988.

Rich, Adrienne Cecile. *Of Woman Born: Motherhood as Experience and Institution.* London: Virago, 1977.

Rípodas Ardanaz, Daisy. *El matrimonio en Indias: Realidad social y regulación jurídical.* Buenos Aires: Fundación para la Educación, la Ciencia y la Cultura, 1977.

Rodríguez, O. Jaime. *The Emergence of Spanish America; Vicente Rocafuerte and Spanish Americanism, 1808–1832.* Berkeley: University of California Press, 1975.

——. *The Independence of Spanish America.* New York: Cambridge University Press, 1996.

Rodríguez Camilloni, H. "Utopia Realized in the New World." In *Settlements in the Americas: Cross Cultural Perspectives,* edited by Ralph Bennett, 28–52. Newark: University of Delaware Press, 1993.

Rodríguez González, José. *La nulidad de matrimonio por miedo en la Jurisprudencia Pontificia.* Vitoria: Editorial Este, 1962.

Röggenbuck, Stefan. "Historia social de la infancia callejera limeña." *Apuntes* 39 (1996): 89–112.

Roniger, Luis, and Tamar Herzog, eds. *The Collective and the Public in Latin America: Cultural Identities and Political Order.* Brighton: Sussex Academic Press, 2000.

Rosas Lauro, Claudia. "Educando al bello sexo: La mujer en el discurso ilustrado." In *El Perú en el siglo XVIII: La era borbónica*, edited by Scarlett O'Phelan Godoy, 369–413. Lima: Pontificia Universidad Católica del Perú/Instituto Riva Agüero, 1999.

——. "Jaque a la Dama: La imagen de la mujer en la prensa limeña de fines del siglo XVIII." In *Mujeres y género en la historia del Perú*, edited by Margarita Zegarra, 143–71. Lima: Centro de Documentación sobre la Mujer, 1999.

Roseberry, William. "Hegemony and the Language of Contention." In *Everyday Forms of State Formation: Revolution and the Negotiation of Rule in Modern Mexico*, edited by Gilbert M. Joseph and Daniel Nugent, 355–66. Durham: Duke University Press, 1994.

Ruíz, Gustavo Adolfo. *La educación de Bolívar*. Caracas: Fondo Editorial Tropykos, 1991.

Ryan, Michael T. "Assimilating New Worlds in the Sixteenth and Seventeenth Centuries." *Comparative Studies in Society and History* 23, no. 4 (1981): 519–38.

Saether, Steinar A. "Bourbon Absolutism and Marriage Reform in Late Colonial Spanish America." *Americas* 59, no. 4 (April 2003): 475–509.

Salinas Meza, René. "Orphans and Family Disintegration in Chile: The Mortality of Abandoned Children, 1750–1930." *Journal of Family History* 16, no. 3 (1991): 315–29.

Sánchez de Albornoz, Nicolás. *The Population of Latin America: A History*. Berkeley: University of California Press, 1974.

Sangmeister, Rev. Joseph V. *Force and Fear as Precluding Matrimonial Consent: An Historical Synopsis and Commentary*. Catholic University Canon Law Series, no. 80. Washington, D.C.: Catholic University of America, 1932.

Scardaville, Michael. "(Hapsburg) Law and (Bourbon) Order: State Authority, Popular Unrest, and the Criminal Justice System in Bourbon Mexico City." *Americas* 50, no. 4 (April 1994): 501–26.

Schepper-Hughes, Nancy. *Death without Weeping: The Violence of Everyday Life in Brazil*. Berkeley: University of California Press, 1992.

Schwartz, Stuart B. "The Manumission of Slaves in Colonial Brazil, Bahia, 1684–1745." *Hispanic American Historical Review* 54, no. 4 (1974): 603–35.

Scott, H. M., ed. *Enlightened Absolutism: Reform and Reformers in Later Eighteenth Century Europe*. Ann Arbor: University of Michigan Press, 1990.

Scott, Joan Wallach. *Gender and the Politics of History*. New York: Columbia University Press, 1988.

Seed, Patricia. *Ceremonies of Possession in Europe's Conquest of the New World, 1492–1640*. New York: Cambridge University Press, 1995.

——. "Marriage Promises and the Value of a Woman's Testimony in Colonial Mexico." *Signs* 13, no. 2 (1988): 253–76.

——. *To Love, Honor, and Obey: Conflicts over Marriage Choice, 1574–1821*. Stanford: Stanford University Press, 1988.

Sherwood, Joan. *Poverty in Eighteenth-Century Spain: The Women and Children of the Inclusa*. Toronto: University of Toronto Press, 1988.

Shammas, Carole. *A History of Household Government in America*. Charlottesville: University of Virginia Press, 2002.

Shumway, Jeffrey. "Between Revolution, Power, and Liberty: Continuity and Change in

Family, Gender, and Society in Buenos Aires, Argentina, 1776–1870." Ph.D. diss., University of Arizona, 1999.

Silva, Renán. "La Revolución Francesa en el Papel Periódico de Santa Fe de Bogotá." In *América Latina ante la Revolución Francesa*, edited by Leopoldo Zea. Mexico City: Universidad Nacional Autónoma de México, 1993.

Silverblatt, Irene. *Moon, Sun, and Witches: Gender Ideologies and Class in Inca and Colonial Peru*. Princeton: Princeton University Press, 1987.

——. "'The Universe Has Turned Inside Out . . . There Is No Justice For Us Here': Andean Women under Spanish Rule." In *Women and Colonization: Anthropological Perspectives*, edited by Mona Etienne and Eleanor Leacock, 149–60. New York: Praeger, 1980.

Sociedad de Beneficencia Pública de Lima. *Album Fotógrafico*. Lima: Casa Editorial Moral, 1913.

Socolow, Susan M. "Acceptable Partners: Marriage Choice in Argentina, 1778–1810." In *Sexuality and Marriage in Colonial Latin America*, edited by Asunción Lavrin, 209–46. Lincoln: University of Nebraska Press, 1989.

——. "Introduction." In *Cities and Society in Colonial Latin America*, edited by Louisa Schell Hoberman and Susan Migden Socolow, 3–18. Albuquerque: University of New Mexico Press, 1986.

——. "Marriage, Birth, and Inheritance: The Merchants of Eighteenth-Century Buenos Aires," *Hispanic American Historical Review* 60, no. 3 (1980): 387–406.

——. "Women and Crime: Buenos Aires, 1757–97." *Journal of Latin American Studies* 12, no. 1 (May 1980): 39–57.

——. *The Women of Colonial Latin America*. New York: Cambridge University Press, 2000.

Soulodre-La France, Reneé. "Socially Not So Dead! Slave Identities in Bourbon New Granada." *Colonial Latin American Review* 10, no. 1 (2001): 87–103.

Spalding, Karen. *Huarochirí: An Andean Society under Inca and Spanish Rule*. Stanford: Stanford University Press, 1984.

Stearns, Peter M. "Social History and History." *Journal of Social History* 19 (Winter 1985): 319–34.

Stein, Stanley J. "Bureaucracy and Business in the Spanish Empire, 1759–1804: Failure of a Bourbon Reform in Mexico and Peru." *Hispanic American Historical Review* 61, no. 1 (1981): 2–28.

Stein, Stanley J., and Barbara H. Stein. *Apogee of Empire: Spain and New Spain in the Age of Charles III, 1759–1789*. Baltimore: Johns Hopkins University Press, 2003.

Stein, Steve. "The Paths to Populism in Peru." In *Populism in Latin America*, edited by Michael Coniff, 96–116. Tuscaloosa: University of Alabama Press, 1999.

Stern, Steve J. *Peru's Indian Peoples and the Challenge of Spanish Conquest: Huamanga to 1650*. Madison: University of Wisconsin Press, 1982.

——. *The Secret History of Gender: Women, Men, and Power in Late Colonial Mexico*. Chapel Hill: University of North Carolina Press, 1995.

Stienbrügge, Lieselotte. *The Moral Sex: Woman's Nature in the French Enlightenment* New York: Oxford University Press, 1995.

Stoler, Ann Laura. *Carnal Knowledge: Race and the Intimate in Colonial Rule*. Berkeley: University of California Press, 2002.

——. "Tense and Tender Ties: The Politics of Comparison in North American History and (Post) Colonial Studies." *Journal of American History* 88, no. 3 (December 2001): 1–28.

——. *Race and the Education of Desire: Foucault's History of Sexuality and the Colonial Order of Things*. Durham: Duke University Press, 1997.

Stone, Lawrence. *The Family, Sex, and Marriage in England, 1500–1800*. New York: Harper and Row, 1979.

Sussman, George D. *Selling Mother's Milk: The Wet-Nursing Business in France, 1715–1914*. Urbana: University of Illinois Press, 1982.

Swann, Julian. *Provincial Power and Absolute Monarchy: The Estates General of Burgundy, 1661–1790*. Cambridge: Cambridge University Press, 2003.

Tanck de Estrada, Dorothy. *Pueblos de indios y educación en México colonial, 1750–1821*. Mexico City: Centro de Studios Históricos, 1999.

Taylor, William B. *Drinking, Homicide, and Rebellion in Colonial Mexican Villages*. Stanford: Stanford University Press, 1979.

——. *Magistrates of the Sacred: Priests and Parishioners in Eighteenth-Century Mexico*. Stanford: Stanford University Press, 1996.

Theiercelin, Raquel, ed. *Cultures et sociétés Andes et Méro-Amérique: Melinger en hommage á Pierre Duviols*. Provence: Université de Provence, 1991.

Tikoff, Valentina. "Before the Reformatory: A Correctional Orphanage in Old Regime Seville." In *Becoming Delinquent: British and European Youth, 1650–1950*, edited by Pamela Cox and Heather Shore, 59–76. Burlington, Vt.: Ashgate, 2002.

Tilly, Louise. "Gender, Women's History, and Social History." *Social Science History* 13 (1989): 439–62.

Tilly, Louise A., Rachel G. Fuchs, David I. Kertzer, and David L. Ransel. "Child Abandonment in European History: A Symposium." *Journal of Family History* 17, no. 1 (1992): 1–23.

Tomaselli, Sylvana. "The Enlightenment Debate on Women." *History Workshop Journal* 20 (Autumn 1985): 101–24.

Townsend, Camilla. " 'Half My Body Free, the Other Half Enslaved': The Politics of the Slaves of Guayaquil at the End of the Colonial Era." *Colonial Latin American Review* 7, no. 1 (1998): 105–28.

Trazegnies, Fernando de. *Ciraco de Urtecho: Litigante por amor*. Lima: Pontificia Universidad Católica, 1981.

Trexler, Richard. "From the Mouths of Babes: Chrisitianization by Children in Sixteenth Century New Spain." In *Church and Community, 1200–1600*, edited by Richard Trexler, 549–73. Rome: Edizioni di Storia e letteratura, 1987.

Tutino, John. "Power, Class, and Family in the Mexican Elite, 1750–1810." *Americas* 39, no. 3 (January 1983): 359–81.

Twinam, Ann. "Honor, Sexuality, and Illegitimacy in Colonial Latin America." In *Sexuality and Marriage in Colonial Latin America*, edited by Asunción Lavrin, 118–55. Lincoln: University of Nebraska Press, 1989.

——. *Public Lives, Private Secrets: Honor, Gender, Sexuality and Illegitimacy in Colonial Spanish America*. Stanford: Stanford University Press, 1999.

Uribe-Uran, Victor M. *Honorable Lives: Lawyers, Family, and Politics in Colombia, 1780–1850*. Pittsburgh: University of Pittsburgh Press, 2000.

——, ed. *State and Society in Spanish America during the Age of Revolution*. Wilmington, Del.: Scholarly Resources, 2001.

van Deusen, Nancy. *Between the Sacred and the Worldly: The Institutional and Cultural Practice of Recogimiento in Colonial Lima*. Stanford: Stanford University Press, 2001.

van Kleffens, E. N. *Hispanic Law until the End of the Middle Ages*. Chicago: Edinburgh University Press, 1968.

Van Young, Eric. "Conclusion: Was There an Age of Revolution in Spanish America?" In *State and Society in Spanish America during the Age of Revolution*, edited by Victor M. Uribe-Uran, 219–46. Wilmington, Del.: Scholarly Resources, 2001.

——. "Millennium on the Northern Marches: The Mad Messiah of Durango and Popular Rebellion in Mexico, 1800–1815." *Comparative Studies in Society and History* 28, no. 3 (1986): 385–413.

——. *The Other Rebellion: Popular Violence, Ideology, and the Mexican Struggle for Independence, 1810–1821*. Stanford: Stanford University Press, 2001.

Valcárcel, Daniel. *Historia de la educación colonial*. Lima: Editorial Universal, 1968.

Vidal Galache, Benicia, and Florencia Vidal Galache. *Bordes y bastardos: Una historia de la Inclusa de Madrid*. Madrid: Compañía Literaria, 1995.

Vieira Powers, Karen. "Conquering Discourses of Sexual Conquest: Of Women, Language, and Mestizaje." *Colonial Latin American Review* 11, no. 1 (2002): 7–32.

Villasmil, Gastón Montiel. *La parentela y las relaciones femeninas del Libertador*. Maracaibo: Comisión Ejecutiva del Bicentenario del Libertador, 1985.

Viqueira Albán, Juan Pedro. *Propriety and Permissiveness in Bourbon Mexico*. Translated by Sonia Lipsett-Rivera and Silvio Rivera Ayala. Wilmington, Del.: Scholarly Resources, 1999.

Voekel, Pamela. *Alone before God: The Religious Origins of Modernity in Mexico*. Durham: Duke University Press, 2002.

——. "Peeing on the Palace: Bodily Resistance to Bourbon Reforms in Mexico City." *Journal of Historical Sociology* 5, no. 2 (June 1992): 181–207.

von Pastor, Freiherr Ludwig. *The History of the Popes from the Close of the Middle Ages*. 33 vols. Translated by Dom Ernst Graf, OSB. London: Kean Paul, Threch, Trubner and Co., 1940.

Wagley, Charles. "On the Concept of Social Race in the Americas." *Actas del XXXIII Congreso Internacional de Americanistas*, 1, San José (1959): 403–7.

Walker, Charles. *Smoldering Ashes: Cuzco and the Creation of Republican Peru, 1780–1840*. Durham: Duke University Press, 1999.

——. "The Upper Classes and Their Upper Stories: Architecture and the Aftermath of the Lima Earthquake of 1746." *Hispanic American Historical Review* 83, no. 1 (2003): 53–82.

——, ed. *Entre la retórica y la insurgencia: Las ideas y los movimientos en los Andes, Siglo XVIII*. Cuzco: CERA Bartolomé de las Casas, 1996.

Walker, Charles, and Peter Guardino. "The State, Society, and Politics in Peru and Mexico in the Late Colonial and Early Republican Periods." *Latin American Perspectives* 19, no. 2 (1996): 10–43.

Watson, Alan. *Slave Law in the Americas*. Athens: University of Georgia Press, 1989.

Weber, Max. *The Theory of Social and Economic Organization*. Edited by Talcott Parsons. Translated by A. M. Henderson. New York: Oxford University Press, 1947.

Webre, Stephen. "The Wet Nurses of Jocotenango: Gender, Science, and Politics in Late-Colonial Guatemala." *Colonial Latin American Historical Review* 10, no. 2 (Spring 2001): 173–98.

Whitaker, Arthur P. "Changing and Unchanging Interpretations of the Enlightenment in Spanish America." In *The Ibero-American Enlightenment*, edited by A. Owen Aldrich, 21–27. Urbana: University of Illinois-Champaign, 1971.

——. "The Dual Role of Latin America in the Enlightenment." In *Latin America and the Enlightenment*, edited by Arthur P. Whitaker, 3–22. 1942. Reprint, Ithaca: Cornell University Press, 1961.

——, ed. *Latin America and the Enlightenment*. 1942. Reprint, Ithaca: Cornell University Press, 1961.

Wilson, Stephen. "The Myth of Motherhood a Myth: The Historical View of European Child-Rearing." *Social History* 9, no. 2 (1984): 181–90.

Yazawa, Melvin. *From Colonies to Commonwealth: Familial Ideology and the Beginnings of the American Republic*. Baltimore: Johns Hopkins University Press, 1985.

Zea, Leopoldo, ed. *América Latina ante la Revolución Francesa*. Mexico City: Universidad Nacional Autónoma de México, 1993.

Index

208–10, 220–23. *See also* Affection: as basis for authority; Mothers

New imperialism, 12, 44

New Orleans, 218

Notaries, 8, 54, 56, 259–61. *See also* Apprenticeship: contracts; Guardianship: patterns of in contracts

Nuevo Febrero, 251

Nulidades de votos. *See* Annulments

Numeración de 1700, 43–51, 257, 298 (n. 93); rationale for, 44–45; biases in, 45. *See also* Households

Olavarrieta, Juan Antonio de, 150, 169–71. *See also Semanario Crítico*

O'Phelan Godoy, Scarlett, 140

Ormaza y Coronel, Francisco, 160, 162–63, 255

Orphans, 28, 34, 35, 57–58, 70, 86, 99, 103, 248; as metaphor for subordination, 21, 40, 57–58; meaning "mestizo," 114

Padre de familia, 23, 27, 29, 33, 216, 247. *See also* Fathers; Patria potestad; Patriarchy

Padre de menores, 35, 57

Panaderías, 114, 229

Pastelerías, 229–30

Pateman, Carole, 251

Paternalism, 9–10, 253, 265 (n. 21), 307 (n. 2). *See also* Patriarchy; Royal paternalism

Patria potestad: definition of, 23–24, 63, 180, 268 (n. 16), 269 (n. 24); powers and limits of, 24, 26–27, 30, 110, 188, 205, 208–10; and women, 25, 27, 63–64, 183, 191, 251, 253; invoked by men, 183, 205–6, 208

Patriarchy: definition of, 9–10, 76, 180–81, 265 (n. 18); and slavery, 9–10, 212–14, 241; as legal practice, 44, 181, 209–10; women and, 91; "weakness" of in families appearing in court, 122–25, 135, 161, 195, 305 (n. 43); prerogatives of for colonial elites, 142, 247; as contest, 180–81, 209; fraternal, 251. *See also* Fathers; Patria potestad; Potestad dominica; Royal paternalism

Patronage, 17, 221, 251, 253

Patronato, 239

Paul V (pope, 1605–21), 97, 99

Pauw, Corneille de, 168

Pecador, Luis, 97, 99

Peculio adventicio, 24

Peninsulares, 13, 125, 141, 154, 169–70

Personería. *See* Juridical personality

Philip III (1598–1621), 36

Physiocrats, 178, 151, 152

Piarron de Chamousset, Claude, 164

Pitucos, 255

Piura, 36, 133

Pizarro, Francisco, 13

Poorhouses. *See* Hospicio de Pobres

Potestad dominica, 30, 211

Pouget, Francisco Amado, 147

Prado, Monasterio de, 81

Pragmatic Sanction on Unequal Marriages, 60, 156–58, 218, 296–97 (n. 75); and caste, 157–58, 166

Presidios, 114, 133

Press: circulates fears of disorder, 131; as guide for child rearing, 131, 149–51, 177; and creole patriotism, 150; and advice columns for youths, 158–59; royalist, 167; readership of, 185, 295 (n. 55); criticizing abusive husbands, 193. *See also Diario de Lima*; *Mercurio Peruano*; *Semanario Crítico*

Protector de indios, 34, 37, 94, 102

Protector de pobres, 40

Public, 11, 20, 151

Punishment: in schools, 95, 148; laws on, 111–12; extralegal, 113–15; Enlightenment ideas about; 130, 147, 148, 229. *See also* Apprenticeship: as punishment; Convents: as sites of punishment; Criminal Cases: preferential sentencing in; Monasteries: as sites of punishment;

Panaderías; Pastelerías; Patria potestad: powers and limits of; Sevicia